JOURNAL FOR THE STUDY OF THE NEW TESTAMENT
SUPPLEMENT SERIES

292

Editor
Mark Goodacre

To my parents,
Channing and Janet Blickenstaff,
with much love

'While the Bridegroom is with them'

Marriage, Family, Gender and Violence in the Gospel of Matthew

Marianne Blickenstaff

T & T CLARK INTERNATIONAL
A Continuum imprint
LONDON • NEW YORK

A Continuum imprint

Published by T&T Clark International
The Tower Building, 11 York Road, London SE1 7NX
15 East 26th Street, Suite 1703, New York, NY 10010

www.tandtclark.com

British Library Cataloguing-in-Publication Data
A catalogue record for this book is available from the British Library

ISBN 0567041123   (hardback)

Typeset by Data Standards Ltd, Frome, Somerset, BA11 1RE
Printed on acid-free paper in Great Britain

CONTENTS

ACKNOWLEDGEMENTS

My deepest gratitude is given to Amy-Jill Levine for her indefatigable enthusiasm and encouragement that pushed me to strive far beyond what I thought I was capable of doing. Her standard of excellence in scholarship has been a constant inspiration, and her many gifts to me as mentor are invaluable. I am grateful for the support and inspiration provided by Annalisa Azzoni, Daniel Patte, Stephen Moore, and Tina Pippin.

Without the encouragement of friends, I would not have been able to make the final effort to finish this project. I am grateful to Marian Berky, Emily Askew, Chris Dungan, Heidi Geib, Alice Hunt, Vicki Phillips, and the many loving people at Trinity Presbyterian Church for helping to see me through.

My children, Andrew and Elizabeth, have patiently shared my attention with the research and writing. Liz was my technical support through a myriad of computer difficulties, and she often reversed mother–daughter roles to care for me when I was especially discouraged. Andrew's music, sense of humor, and spontaneity have lifted my spirits many times, and he showed his solidarity by attending my dissertation defense. This book has been as much a part of their lives as mine, and I thank them for their support.

There are no adequate words to express my thanks for the love and support I have received from my parents. Their faith and personal integrity are the example that helps me through difficult times. Their sense of wonder and commitment to lifelong learning started me on the path toward a career in biblical studies. They never once doubted that I could achieve my goals, and in countless ways have made it possible for me to do so.

INTRODUCTION

That Jesus never married and was not a 'real' bridegroom is agreed by Church tradition and most scholars.[1] The saying about Jesus as 'bridegroom' (Mt. 9.15; cf. also Mk. 2.19–20; Lk. 5.34–35; Jn. 3.29; *G. Thom.* 104)[2] – 'The wedding guests cannot mourn as long as the bridegroom is with them, can they? The days will come when the bridegroom is taken away from them, and then they will fast' – is thus a metaphor. On the one hand, the Matthean bridegroom signifies joy, because the 'sons of the bridal chamber' are unable to mourn in his presence (9.15). But on the other hand, Jesus' statement that 'the days are coming when the bridegroom will be taken away' (9.15), the motif of the bridegroom in Jewish and Greco-Roman literature, and the distinct Matthean wedding parables (22.1–14; 25.1–13) all associate the

---

1. Among the few exceptions is William E. Phipps, *Was Jesus Married? The Distortion of Sexuality in the Christian Tradition* (New York: Harper and Row, 1970); Phipps, 'The Case for a Married Jesus', *Dialogue* 7 (1972), pp. 44–49. (See John P. Meier's sustained argument against Phipps's theory in *A Marginal Jew: Rethinking the Historical Jesus. I. The Roots of the Problem and the Person* [New York: Doubleday, 1991], pp. 332–45.) See also a one-page article by Stephen Twycross, 'Was Jesus Married?', *Expository Times* 107 (1996), p. 334. James H. Charlesworth's forthcoming 'Is it Conceivable that Jesus Married Mary Magdalene?' (in Amy-Jill Levine [ed.], *A Feminist Companion to the Jesus Movement* [London: T&T Clark]) concludes that Jesus could have been married, although Charlesworth doesn't go so far to say that he was. Fictional speculations on Jesus' marriage include Niko Kazantzakis's *The Last Temptation of Christ* (trans. Peter A. Bien; New York: Simon and Schuster, 1960), and Dan Brown's *The Da Vinci Code* (New York: Doubleday, 2003).

2. The bridegroom saying, in various forms, points to a shared source tradition (Mt. 9.15; Mk. 2.19–20; Lk. 5.34–35; Jn. 3.29; *G. Thom.* 104). The bridal motif also appears extensively in later Gnostic writings, e.g., *Exegesis of the Soul* 131.29ff; 132.13–14; *Authoritative Teaching* 22, 35.1–20, 31.34–32.8; *Gospel of Philip* 55.6–14; 64; 65.1–26; 67.1–68.16–26; 69.5–14; 69; 70.10–23; 72.17–23; 74.19–24; Chs 76, 81, 84, 85; *Dialogue with the Savior* 120; 138.17–20; *Teachings of Silvanus* 94.26–27; 105. The Jesus Seminar has awarded the saying with a rare 'pink' rating: Jesus probably said something very much like this. See Robert Funk (ed.), *The Five Gospels: The Search for the Authentic Words of Jesus* (San Francisco: HarperSanFrancisco, 1997), p. 164. W.D. Davies and Dale C. Allison agree that it is an 'authentic saying' of Jesus, *The Gospel According to Saint Matthew* (3 vols.; ICC; Edinburgh: T&T Clark, 1988, 1991, 1997), II, p. 107. I am not interested in the logion's authenticity but in its function within Matthew's gospel.

bridegroom with separation and violence. The gospel's various references to the bridegroom, coupled with teachings on marriage, divorce, family, gender, and sexuality, contribute to conflict even as they present a vision of *shalom*.

While the bridegroom in John has been the topic of recent discussion,[3] the bridegroom in Matthew has not received scholarly attention. Recent scholarship views the Matthean bridegroom saying (9.15) as an incidental remark attached to a teaching on fasting or as an illustration of the theme of 'old and new.'[4] Scholars do acknowledge the Christological value of Jesus as the bridegroom,[5] but they typically restrict their discussion to paraphrase: they emphasize the appropriate joyful response to Jesus' presence and contrast it to the mourning and fasting when the bridegroom is taken away (be that the arrest, the crucifixion, or *pace* 28.20, the delay

3. See Adeline Fehribach, *The Women in the Life of the Bridegroom: A Feminist Historical-literary Analysis of the Female Characters in the Fourth Gospel* (Collegeville, MN: Liturgical Press, 1998); Fehribach, 'The Birthing Bridegroom: The Portrayal of Jesus in the Fourth Gospel', in Amy-Jill Levine (ed.), *A Feminist Companion to John* (2 vols.; Sheffield: Sheffield Academic Press, 2003), II, pp. 104–29; Harold Attridge, 'Don't Be Touching Me: Recent Feminist Scholarship on Mary Magdalene', in Levine (ed.), *A Feminist Companion to John*, II, pp. 140–66; Charlesworth, 'Is it Conceivable that Jesus Married Mary Magdalene?'; Lyle Eslinger, 'The Wooing of the Woman at the Well: Jesus, the Reader, and Reader-response Criticism', in Mark Stibbe (ed.), *The Gospel of John as Literature: An Anthology of Twentieth-century Perspectives* (Leiden: E.J. Brill, 1993), pp. 165–82; Teresa Okure, 'The Significance Today of Jesus' Commission to Mary Magdalene (Jn 20.11–18)', *International Review of Mission* 81 (1992), pp. 177–88; Carolyn Grassi and Joseph Grassi, 'The Resurrection: The New Age Begins: Mary Magdalene as Mystical Spouse', in Grassi and Grassi, *Mary Magdalene and the Women in Jesus' Life* (Kansas City: Sheed and Ward, 1986), pp. 104–15; Calum Carmichael, 'Marriage and the Samaritan Woman', *NTS* 26 (1980), pp. 332–46; Jerome Neyrey, 'Jacob Traditions and the Interpretation of John 4.10–26', *CBQ* 41 (1979), pp. 419–37.

4. Davies and Allison, *The Gospel According to Saint Matthew*, II, pp. 107–12; Eduard Schweizer, *The Good News According to Matthew* (trans. David E. Green; Atlanta: John Knox Press, 1975), pp. 226–27; Douglas R.A. Hare, *Matthew* (Interpretation; Louisville: John Knox Press, 1993) pp. 103–104; Robert H. Gundry, *Matthew: A Commentary on His Handbook for a Mixed Church under Persecution* (Grand Rapids: Eerdmans, 2nd edn, 1994), pp. 169–70; Daniel Patte, *The Gospel According to Matthew: A Structural Commentary on Matthew's Faith* (Philadelphia: Fortress Press, 1987), pp. 130–31; Ulrich Luz, *Matthew 9–20* (trans. James E. Crouch; Hermeneia; Minneapolis: Fortress Press, 2001), pp. 36–37; Craig S. Keener, *A Commentary on the Gospel of Matthew* (Grand Rapids: Eerdmans, 1999), pp. 299–300; Francis Wright Beare, *The Gospel According to Matthew* (San Francisco: Harper & Row, 1981), pp. 228–31; Donald Senior, *Matthew* (Abingdon New Testament Commentaries; Nashville: Abingdon Press, 1998), pp. 107, 110; Daniel J. Harrington, *The Gospel of Matthew* (Sacra Pagina, 1; Collegeville, MN: Liturgical Press, 1991), pp. 128–29; W.F. Albright and C.S. Mann, *Matthew* (AB, 26; New York: Doubleday, 1971), p. 107.

5. For example, George A. Buttrick (*The Parables of Jesus* [New York: Harper and Brothers Publishers, 1928], p. 224) calls a wedding celebration the 'acme of delight' and claims that the bridegroom's wedding feast 'makes joy a dominant note in the kingdom-music.'

of the Parousia [9.15; 25.5]).[6] Some scholars note that the bridegroom saying is related to the parables of the Wedding Feast (Mt. 22.1–14) and the Ten Virgins (25.1–13),[7] but no one, to my knowledge, explores this relationship in terms of violence.

Matthean violence is a topic of current discussion, but not in relation to Jesus as a bridegroom. Warren Carter, for example, cautions that Matthew's language of God's kingdom echoes the rhetoric employed in the wider society for imperial Rome, and that the deity's 'violent destruction of those who resist' means that 'God's empire resembles, rather than offers an alternative to, Rome's power.'[8] Barbara Reid notes that while the Sermon on the Mount urges non-violent resistance (5.39; cf. also 13.24–30, 36–43) and commends prayer for enemies (5.44),[9] several of the Matthean parables stand in contrast to non-violence and forgiveness by portraying the violence done to evildoers.[10] This study builds on such concerns about Matthean violence and applies them specifically to Matthew's portrayal of Jesus as a bridegroom.

That Matthew has a thematic interest in the bridegroom is evident in his inclusion of a wedding parable unique to the first gospel, that of the Ten Virgins (Mt. 25.1–13), as well as in the detailed redaction of the Parable of the Wedding Feast (Mt. 22.1–14; cf. Lk. 14.15–24; *G. Thom.* 64), which in Matthew becomes specifically a *wedding* banquet, and to which Matthew adds scenes of violence.[11] Moreover, Matthew returns several times to topics related to the bridegroom and marriage: the Kingdom of Heaven is a wedding banquet (22.1–14; 25.1–13); the bridegroom illumines teachings on marriage and divorce (5.31–32; 19.3–12; 22.30); he creates a fictive family of brothers, sisters, and mothers (12.46–50; cf. 10.34–38); and he

---

6. Davies and Allison, *Matthew*, II, pp. 109–10, 112; Hare, *Matthew*; pp. 103–104; Gundry, *Matthew*, pp. 169–70; Patte, *Matthew*, pp. 130–31; Luz, *Matthew 9–20*, pp. 36–37; Keener, *Matthew*, pp. 299–300; Beare, *Matthew*, pp. 228–31; Senior, *Matthew*, pp. 107, 110; Harrington, *Matthew*, p. 129; Albright and Mann, *Matthew*, p. 107.

7. Davies and Allison, *Matthew*, II, p. 110; Luz, *Matthew 9–20*, p. 37; Keener, *Matthew*, p. 300. Hare, *Matthew*, p. 104; Keener, *Matthew*, p. 300; Senior, *Matthew*, p. 107. Davies and Allison mention only one parable in relation to the bridegroom (Mt. 25.1–13) and discuss the kingdom as wedding banquet (*Matthew*, II, p. 110). Senior and Keener note the importance of the eschatological wedding banquet theme but do not develop it (Senior, *Matthew*, p. 107; Keener, *Matthew*, p. 300).

8. Warren Carter, *Matthew and the Margins: A Sociopolitical and Religious Reading* (Maryknoll, NY: Orbis, 2000), p. 5.

9. Barbara Reid, 'Violent Endings in Matthew's Parables and Christian Nonviolence', *CBQ* 66 (2004), pp. 237–55.

10. Reid, 'Violent Endings'. Reid discusses the Parable of the Wedding Feast but does not connect the bridegroom to violence.

11. A king gives a wedding feast for his son (γάμους τῷ υἱῷ αὐτοῦ [Mt. 22.2]), while in Luke, a man gives a 'great feast' (δεῖπνον μέγα) with no specific purpose (Lk. 14.16). See Davies and Allison, *Matthew*, I, pp. 123–24.

calls his disciples 'sons of the bridal chamber' (οἱ υἱοὶ τοῦ νυμφῶνος [9.14]). In turn, these 'sons' are to 'become like children' (γένησθε ὡς τὰ παιδία [18.2–3; cf. 19.13–14]), are to regard God as their only Father (23.9), and are to celebrate the bridegroom's presence with them (9.14–15). Yet consistently, violence permeates these relationships.

The Bridegroom as Metaphor

Discussion of the un-betrothed and never-to-be-married Jesus as a 'bridegroom' necessarily involves metaphor, the juxtaposition and comparison of two dissimilar concepts.[12] Metaphoric language allows the reader to look at how Jesus is both like and also unlike a bridegroom and, therefore, how he both fulfills and disrupts this role.[13] The slippage between dissimilar concepts – 'bridegroom,' a role normally associated with marriage, sexuality, and procreation, and 'Jesus,' who is apparently not married, who discourages new marriages, and who is most likely celibate – disrupts the 'normal' roles and creates a new way of perceiving marriage, sexuality, and procreation. For Matthew, becoming a 'eunuch' for the Kingdom of Heaven is preferable to marriage, and though marriage is indissoluble, husband and wife may be separated and their celibacy is commended.

Interpretation of the bridegroom metaphor, within Matthew's own

12.   Metaphors use a word or expression normally associated with one thing, idea, or action and apply it to another thing, idea, or action in order to suggest resemblance between the two (Chris Baldick, *The Concise Oxford Dictionary of Literary Terms* [Oxford: Oxford University Press, 1990], p. 134) with the result of fresh new meaning (Richard A. Lanham, *A Handlist of Rhetorical Terms* [Berkeley: University of California Press, 2nd edn, 1991], pp. 100–101). I do not want to devote a great deal of space exploring issues of literary philosophy in general nor metaphor in particular, because, as Wayne Booth has observed in regard to the vast amount of literature published on these topics: 'Metaphor has by now been defined in so many ways that there is no human expression, whether in language or any other medium, that would not be metaphoric in *someone's* definition.' See his 'Metaphor as Rhetoric: The Problem of Evaluation', in S. Sacks (ed.), *On Metaphor* (Chicago: University of Chicago Press, 1979), pp. 47–70 (48).

13.   The metaphorical relationship between 'bridegroom' and 'Jesus' changes readers' perception of both, so that things we associate with 'bridegroom' shape a new understanding of 'Jesus,' and the way we perceive 'Jesus' influences our understanding of 'bridegroom.' Jacobus Liebenberg, *The Language and the Kingdom of Jesus: Parable, Aphorism, and Metaphor in the Sayings Material Common to the Synoptic Tradition and the Gospel of Thomas* (Berlin: Walter de Gruyter, 2001), pp. 89–91; Max Black, *Models and Metaphors: Studies in Language and Philosophy* (Ithaca: Cornell University Press, 1992), p. 47, n. 23; Paul Ricouer, *The Rule of Metaphor: Multi-disciplinary Studies of the Creation of Meaning in Language* (trans. R. Czerny; Toronto: University of Toronto Press, 1977), esp. pp. 212–15; I.A. Richards, 'The Philosophy of Rhetoric', in Mark Johnson (ed.), *Philosophical Perspectives on Metaphor* (Minneapolis: University of Minnesota, 1981), pp. 48–62 (53), a reprint from his book *The Philosophy of Rhetoric* (Oxford: Oxford University Press, 1936).

socio-historical context, depends on what the first-century audience knows and expects of a bridegroom. One helpful mechanism for determining this range of knowledge is to track the literary associations that inform the comparison. Even so, each listener or reader, then and now, necessarily brings different associations to both parts of the metaphor; thus, the meanings of both 'bridegroom' and 'Jesus' individually remain polyvalent, and so the metaphor too opens to a variety of meanings.[14] Social constructions of 'kings' and 'householders' as well as of the roles of bridegrooms, wedding guests, and family shape understanding of the metaphor.[15]

For example, in the Parable of the Wedding Feast, modern readers (who typically interpret the king allegorically as God) often express surprise when the 'king' burns the city and binds up the garmentless man. But a first-century reader, reading non-allegorically and/or having familiarity with life under imperial rule, might not find this surprising. While readers today frequently regard kings, landowners, and householders – masters of all types – as representing the deity, in a first-century context, earthly kings are more likely to be tyrants or weaklings than benevolent, gracious, or just. Thus, analysis of Matthew's gospel that considers both the text's cultural context and its literary figurations opens the possibility that the masters in the parables are *not* divine and so not necessarily good or just. Granting this possibility, we can then raise additional questions about the response of the guests in the parables and so of the readers of the gospel: should the guests welcome the invitation to the feast or fear it? Should the king be worshiped or resisted? Should we expect an alternative to violent governments instead of replacing one tyrant with another? Is the bridegroom a representative of

14. Paul Ricoeur, 'The Metaphorical Process', in Sacks (ed.), *On Metaphor*, pp. 141–57; Black, *Models and Metaphors*, p. 43; Booth, 'Metaphor as Rhetoric', pp. 51–56; Donald Davidson, 'What Metaphors Mean', in Sacks (ed.), *On Metaphor*, pp. 29–45 (29); George Lakoff and Mark Johnson, *More Than Cool Reason: A Field Guide to Poetic Metaphor* (Chicago: University of Chicago Press, 1989), pp. 60–61; Paul Avis, *God and the Creative Imagination: Metaphor, Symbol, and Myth in Religion and Theology* (London and New York: Routledge, 1999), p. 94.

15. William R. Herzog II, *Parables as Subversive Speech: Jesus as Pedagogue of the Oppressed* (Louisville: Westminster/John Knox, 1994), pp. 53–73; Barbara E. Reid, *Parables for Preachers: The Gospel of Matthew, Year A* (Collegeville: Liturgical Press, 2001), pp. 7–8; Bernard Brandon Scott, *Hear Then the Parable: A Commentary on the Parables of Jesus* (Minneapolis: Fortress Press, 1989), pp. 79–98; J.R. Donahue, *The Gospel in Parable: Metaphor, Narrative, and Theology in the Synoptic Gospels* (Minneapolis: Fortress Press, 1988), pp. 13–15; A.J. Hultgren, *The Parables of Jesus* (Grand Rapids: Eerdmans, 2000), p. 9; J. Jeremias, *Die Gleichnisse Jesu* (*The Parables of Jews*; Abhandlungen zur Theologie des Alten und Neuen Testaments, 11; Zürich: Zwingli-Verlag, 1947), pp. 11–12; cf. Kenneth E. Bailey, *Poet and Peasant and Through Peasant Eyes: A Literary-cultural Approach to the Parables in Luke* (Grand Rapids: Eerdmans, combined edn, 1983), pp. 27–43.

hospitality or alienation? Why would guests go to a wedding feast where many are expelled or shut out?

Renita Weems observes that 'what makes metaphorical speech especially effective as a form of social rhetoric is precisely its ability to reorganize our way of thinking ... deliberately rousing certain kinds of emotional responses in the audience.'[16] Paul Ricoeur describes how readers submit to metaphors, a process he describes as less of a choice and more of a seduction or 'dreaming,' as if a person, understanding the metaphor, cannot help but participate in it.[17] But different readers come to different understandings, so that the final result of Ricoeur's 'seduction' is not predictable. Paul de Man uses the term 'powerfully coercive' to describe the nature of metaphors that reassemble and reinvent reality.[18] According to de Man, a metaphor has 'disruptive power' to take on a life of its own and produce new realities.[19] Again, the way in which a metaphor 'disrupts' or produces 'new realities' depends on the social constructions and perceptions of reality with which the audience begins.

Indeed, de Man's expressions of (rhetorical) violence – 'coercion, disruption' – along with Ricoeur's language of 'seduction,' and even Weems' less overt appeal to sensuality (i.e., 'rousing') perfectly epitomize the Matthean strategies of metaphor: the bridegroom seduces and coerces, metaphorically speaking of course. The bridegroom saying (9.15), the wedding parables (22.1–14 and 25.1–13), and the Matthean teachings on family, marriage, divorce, gender, and sexuality (primarily 10.34–38; 12.46–50; 19.3–12; 22.30; 23.9) convey themes of violence and separation. Their metaphorical implications therefore must be interrogated for understanding the potential dangers of Matthean Christology.

A metaphor can either challenge listeners' constructions of reality,[20] or

16. Renita Weems, *Battered Love: Marriage, Sex, and Violence in the Hebrew Prophets* (Minneapolis: Fortress Press, 1995), p. 23. See also Avis, *God and the Creative Imagination*, pp. 96–97.

17. Ricoeur, 'The Metaphorical Process', pp. 144–48, and *The Rule of Metaphor*, pp. 212–15.

18. Paul de Man, 'The Epistemology of Metaphor', in S. Sacks (ed.), *On Metaphor* (Chicago: University of Chicago Press, 1979), pp. 17, 19.

19. de Man, 'Epistemology', pp. 11–28.

20. Wilder describes the experience as being 'invaded' by the parable's imagery (*Language of the Gospel*, p. 92). Scott calls parables 'world-shattering' (*Hear Then the Parable*, p. 39; cf. pp. 37–39), and John Dominic Crossan toys with reality as parable (*In Parables: The Challenge of the Historical Jesus* [New York: Harper and Row, 1973], pp. xiv–xv). See also B.H. Young, *The Parables: Jewish Tradition and Christian Interpretation* [Peabody, MA: Hendrickson, 1998], pp. 4–5; David Buttrick, *Speaking Parables: A Homiletic Guide* [Louisville: Westminster John Knox Press, 2000], pp. 37–38; Jeremias, *Parables*, pp. 21–22; Reid, *Parables for Preachers*, pp. 163–76; Scott, *Hear Then the Parable*, pp. 237–53; Hultgren, *Parables of Jesus*, pp. 370–74; Donahue, *Gospel in Parable*, pp. 89–92; Jeremias, *Parables of Jesus*, pp. 70–77; M. Eugene Boring, *The Gospel of Matthew* (NIB, 8; Nashville: Abingdon Press, 1995), pp. 413–15.

it can reinforce their understanding of the way things are. For Matthew, the metaphor of the bridegroom does both. The Matthean bridegroom challenges societal constructions of marriage and the family, even as he presents to early Christian readers justification for their possible states of estrangement from family. At the same time, the violence attached to the metaphor challenges views of God and justice.

Procedure

Chapter 1 explores both extra-biblical literature (primarily from the fifth century BCE to the second century CE) and biblical texts concerning bridegrooms and weddings. While the survey reveals that bridegrooms are associated with joy, union, and life, they also frequently figure in scenes of violence, separation, and death. Biblical figures explicitly identified as 'bridegrooms' are both victims and perpetrators of violence. The frequent comparison in Greek literature of weddings to funerals and the violent foundations of marriage in Roman mythology confirm the logic of what might seem counter-intuitive to many readers today: weddings and violence are paired; the bridegroom represents both joy and sorrow, unity and separation.

Chapters 2 and 3 examine how typical allegorical interpretations of the Parable of the Wedding Feast (22.1–14) and the Parable of the Ten Bridesmaids (25.1–13) not only tend to implicate the deity in acts of violent eschatological retribution (22.7) but also reveal how Jesus as a bridegroom exacerbates conflict between community members (25.1–13). I resist this allegorical construction of divine violence, because, like Barbara Reid, I find strong hints for alternative readings elsewhere in the gospel. There is no necessity for interpreting the parables allegorically in this manner. As a feminist, I want to challenge readings that portray the gospel message in terms of violence and retribution. Specifically, I propose that the parables can be read in the context of Matthew's present social and political situation instead of the context of eschatological judgment.[21] Although I cannot escape the violence of the texts, my readings locate the violence in the human realm: human kings rather than the divine promote violence.

Chapter 4 discusses how the Matthean bridegroom disrupts families of origin (10.34–38; 19.29) to create a fictive family (12.46–50; cf. 23.9) based on allegiance to him. The bridegroom undermines biological reproduction by never consummating a marriage and by reproducing not by sexual means but by adopting new members into the community where all are children of the heavenly Father. Moreover, he urges non-reproductive masculinity by urging men to forsake procreation by becoming 'eunuchs'

---

21. Herzog, *Parables as Subversive Speech*, pp. 53–73.

for the sake of the Kingdom of Heaven ('For there are eunuchs who have been so from birth, and there are eunuchs who have been made eunuchs by others, and there are eunuchs who have made themselves eunuchs for the sake of the Kingdom of Heaven' [19.10–12]). The example of Joseph and Mary illustrates the Matthean ideal of non-reproductive adoptive fatherhood and a family founded in obedience to the heavenly Father's will.

Nevertheless, the example of Joseph and Mary also demonstrates and foreshadows the relationship of the fictive family to violence. The family's formation occurs in the midst of separation and violence both potential (e.g., Joseph's resolve to divorce Mary, 1.19–20) and actual (e.g., the 'slaughter of the innocents,' 2.16–18). So, also, the members of Jesus' fictive family will face separation and be exposed to violence.

Much as I would like, I cannot fully exonerate the violent Matthean portrayal of God, for the infancy materials implicate the deity in violence. Because the deity orchestrates Mary's pregnancy, Joseph's decision not to divorce her, and the family's escape from danger, so also the deity bears responsibility for the deaths of those who did not receive divine warning. If the infant Jesus and the Magi could be protected, why weren't the children of Bethlehem? Joseph, as adoptive father, is provided with the opportunity to save his wife and adopted child, but biological parents are not. The message is consistent with Matthew's dismissal of the biological family, but it is also morally abhorrent. Matthew tries to exclude divine responsibility through use of passive constructions, fulfillment citations concerning Jesus' escape to Egypt and Rachel's weeping, and by highlighting Herod's evil, but the failure of angelic warnings to Joseph and the Magi to reach the parents of the other children begs the question of theodicy.

Chapter 5 explores the bridegroom's teachings on marriage and divorce in the Sermon on the Mount (5.31–32) and reiterated in 19.3–9. The bridegroom commands that current marriages should stay intact: 'It is also said, "Whoever divorces his wife let him give her a certificate of divorce." But I say to you that anyone who divorces his wife, except on the ground of πορνεία, causes her to commit adultery; and whoever marries a divorced woman commits adultery' (5.31–32); and 'Have you not read that the one who made them at the beginning made them male and female and said, "For this reason a man shall leave his father and mother and be joined to his wife and the two shall become one flesh?" So, they are no longer two, but one flesh. Therefore, what God has joined together, let no one separate' (19.4–6). Even so, marriage is restructured apart from society's concern for the household and heredity, as Matthew promotes adoptive fatherhood and fictive family.

The bridegroom's prohibition of divorce (based on the teaching 'the two become one flesh,' cf. Gen. 2.24) sets as the ideal for marriage the

Edenic existence of Adam and Eve. The bridegroom urges that current marriages be kept intact, but that sexual relations (and reproduction) be curtailed, so that married couples mirror the chastity of the first couple. Completing this idealized vision, followers of the bridegroom are to live in anticipation of their future existence in an unmarried 'angelic' state, or possibly in imitation of the primordial androgyne, the 'Adam' who is both male and female (or neither). Ultimately, there will be no marriage: 'For in the resurrection they neither marry nor are given in marriage, but are like the angels in heaven' (22.30). The eunuch saying and prediction that marriage will cease indicate Matthew's leanings toward celibacy, even within marriage.

The study concludes that for Matthew's gospel, the bridegroom's presence holds the potential for joy and celebration, but it is also fraught with danger. Conflict, violence, and separation mar the wedding feast and family relationships: five virgins are shut out of the wedding feast, the man lacking a wedding garment is 'bound hand and foot and thrown into the outer darkness where there is wailing and gnashing of teeth' (22.13), cities are burned, children are slaughtered, and families are broken. Jesus the bridegroom comes 'not to bring peace but a sword' for he has 'come to set a man against his father, a daughter against her mother, and a daughter-in-law against her mother-in-law, and one's foes will be members of one's own household' (10.34–36).

The bridegroom disrupts expectations of weddings, marriage, family, and sexuality by discouraging new weddings: he is to be the *only* bridegroom, and all references to weddings are marked by violence. He promotes a fictive family that reproduces not by sexual means and not by developing an extended family of slaves and retainers, but by voluntary, filial and maternal roles. Followers must redefine allegiances as they choose between biological and fictive family ties, between earthly masters and the heavenly kingdom, and between traditional marriage and divorce and Matthean constructions of marriage and celibacy.

Chapter 1

THE BRIDEGROOM AND VIOLENCE

καὶ εἶπεν αὐτοῖς ὁ Ἰησοῦς, Μὴ δύνανται οἱ υἱοὶ τοῦ νυμφῶνος πενθεῖν ἐφ' ὅσον μετ' αὐτῶν ἐστιν ὁ νυμφίος; ἐλεύσονται δὲ ἡμέραι ὅταν ἀπαρθῇ ἀπ' αὐτῶν ὁ νυμφίος, καὶ τότε νηστεύσουσιν.

And Jesus said to them, 'Are the sons of the bridal chamber able to mourn as long as the bridegroom is with them? But the days are coming when the bridegroom will be taken away from them, and then they will fast.' (Mt. 9.15)

The bridegroom saying, 'Are the sons of the bridal chamber able to mourn as long as the bridegroom is with them? But the days are coming when the bridegroom will be taken away from them, and then they will fast' (9.15), has prompted comparison with prophetic warnings of divine judgment, such as: 'the voice of the bridegroom and bride will be heard no more' (Jer. 7.34; 16.9; 25.10; Joel 2.16; Bar. 2.23). For example, F.G. Cremer argues that the Matthean bridegroom saying (9.15) is the form of introduction for such prophecies ('*Einleitungsformel für eine Unheilsweissagung*').[1] Davies and Allison agree that the time when the bridegroom is taken spells eschatological affliction,[2] and Daniel Patte notes that the taking of the bridegroom is a point of judgment.[3] But the

---

1. F.G. Cremer, 'Der Beitrag Augustins zur Auslegung des Fastenstreitgesprächs (Mk 2,18–22 parr) und die mittelalterliche Theologie', *Recherches augustiniennes* 8 (1972), pp. 301–373 (334).

2. Davies and Allison, *Matthew*, II, p. 111.

3. Patte, *Matthew*, p. 130, also Keener, *Matthew*, p. 300, and Senior, *Matthew*, p. 110. Martin Luther (*The Table Talk of Martin Luther* [ed. T.S. Kepler; Grand Rapids, MI: Baker Book House, 1979], 15) said that when God decides to bring an end to this wicked world, a voice will say, 'Behold the bridegroom cometh' (cf. Mt. 25.1–13). William R. Farmer (*The International Bible Commmentary: A Catholic and Ecumenical Commentary for the Twenty-first Century* [Collegeville, MN: Liturgical Press, 1998], p. 1286) thinks the bridegroom saying refers to Isa. 53.8 – 'By a perversion of justice he was taken away.' Others who discuss the bridegroom saying in terms of Old Testament prophecies of judgment and restoration include Claude Chavasse, *The Bride of Christ: An Enquiry into the Nuptial Element in Early Christianity* (London: Faber and Faber, 1940), pp. 19–48, and Clifford W. Edwards, 'Bridegroom-Bride Imagery for Christ and the Church in the New Testament against Its

bridegroom saying has not been explored specifically in terms of violence.

The juxtaposition of 'bridegrooms' with 'violence' would not have occurred to me had I not discovered during a study of the uses of νυμφίος and its synonym γαμβρός[4] in Hebrew that men who bear the designation חתן are often associated with violence (as perpetrators or victims), some with extreme violence. These men are an unlikely assortment: Lot's sons-in-law, betrothed to marry his daughters (בנתיו חתניו לקחי, Gen. 19.12, 14), Moses (חתן דמים, Exod. 4.25–26), Samson (חתן, Judg. 15.6), a Levite from Ephraim (חתן, Judg. 19.5), David (חתן, 1 Sam. 18.18; 22.14 [cf. 18.21, 22, 23, 26, 27]), Ahaziah of the house of Ahab

---

Biblical Background' (Dissertation; Northwestern University, 1964), pp. 174–75; William B. Huntley, 'Christ the Bridegroom: A Biblical Image' (Dissertation; Duke University, 1964), p. 86; E. Stauffer, 'γαμέω, γάμος', *TDNT* 1, pp. 648–57 (654–65).

4. The ambiguity of חתן (whether it means 'son-in-law' or 'bridegroom') can be seen in the variant Greek translations, as translators seem to use νυμφίος and γαμβρός interchangeably. Nevertheless, a pattern can be discerned: νυμφίος generally but not exclusively is used to refer to the relationship of bridegroom to bride and to the status of the young man before, during, and immediately after the wedding, while γαμβρός usually, but not always, refers to the relationship of the daughter's husband (son-in-law) to his father-in-law or to the young man after he is married. Generally, חתן defines a relationship formed by marriage (Kutsch calls it a 'relationship of affinity, in contrast to consanguinity' brought into being by marriage, in 'חתן', *TDOT* 5, pp. 270–77 [270]). The related Assyrian *hatanu* (or *hatnu*) means both 'son-in-law' (or sometimes 'brother-in-law') and 'bridegroom' (I. Gelb, T. Jacobsen, B. Landsberger, and A.L. Oppenheim [eds.], *The Assyrian Dictionary* [Chicago: Oriental Institute, 1956], p.148). The Assyrian *hatanu* adds the nuance of 'protector', perhaps because the bridegroom will come under the protection of his father-in-law (so, Kutsch, 'חתן', p. 272), but as Kutsch himself recognizes, this meaning is unlikely, because the bride normally becomes a member of her husband's family. Therefore, I think the nuance of 'protector' more likely means that the bridegroom becomes the protector of his bride. The nuance of *hatanu* as 'lover' occurs in a variant reading of *Gilgamesh*, tablet 6, line 7 (I. Gelb, *Assyrian Dictionary*, p. 148) when Ishtar looks covetously on the beauty of Gilgamesh and says, 'Come Gilgamesh, be my bridegroom! Grant me your fruits, I insist!' (A.R. George [ed.], *The Babylonian Gilgamesh Epic* [2 vols.; Oxford: Oxford University Press, 2003], pp. 618–19). The nuance of bridegroom as a lover occurs also in Codex Sinaiticus and Codex Alexandrinus, where the bridegroom-lover in Song of Songs is termed a νυμφίος (Sinaiticus: 1.3, 12, 16; 2.10; 3.6; 5.1; 6.3; 8.5; Alexandrinus.1.4, 7, 8, 12, 15, 16; 2.1, 3, 6, 8, 9, 15; 3.4, 6; 5.1, 2; 6.3, 10, 11, 12; 7.1; 8.5), even though the word חתן does not appear in the Hebrew, and other Greek versions do not specifically mention a 'bridegroom.' See Edwin Hatch and Henry A. Redpath, *A Concordance to the Septuagint and the Other Greek Versions of the Old Testament* (2 vols.; Grand Rapids, MI: Baker Book House, 1987), II, p. 951. Apparently the translators of these codices associated 'bridegroom' with a lover, enough so as to introduce the terminology. The Matthean bridegroom does not fulfill any of these roles, because he has no bride; instead, he disrupts the role of groom, son-in-law, protector, and lover.

(חתן, 2 Kgs 8.27),[5] Tobiah (חתן, Neh. 6.18),[6] and the son-in-law of Sanballat (חתן, Neh. 13.28).[7]

These men are hardly remarkable as model bridegrooms (or husbands). In each case (except Ahaziah, who seems to have the designation חתן only to explain his link to the house of Ahab, although this relationship in itself is an association with ongoing violence), the designated bridegroom is either the recipient of violence or inflicts violence. In some cases, he is separated from his bride; in others, he abandons her. Cheryl Exum observes a sub-theme in these violent stories: the husband or bridegroom's punishment of independent wives or brides, or manipulation of these women toward their own ends. The husband or bridegroom's control of the women results, at best, in their subordination and silence, and at worst, in their violent death.[8] Given that bridegrooms in these Hebrew Bible stories all have brides, one expects a bride for Matthew's bridegroom; but there is no bride in any of the Matthean bridegroom and wedding texts. The various and violent roles of 'bridegrooms' in the Old Testament foreshadow the uncertain status and violence associated with the Matthean bridegroom. Allison cautions that, though the first gospel embeds many allusions to earlier texts, we cannot know for certain if a text was designed to invoke a certain association.[9] I cannot prove that Matthew had in mind the various bridegroom texts when the gospel was composed. Rather, the cumulative weight of the evidence of violent bridegrooms, the explicit use of bridegroom terminology, and Matthew's extensive use of Old Testament allusions, all serve to justify the reading of

---

5.   The LXX does not literally translate חתן בית-אחאב ('son-in-law or bridegroom of the house of Ahab') but renders the phrase: ἐπορύθη ἐν ὁδῷ οἴκου Αχααβ (he went in the way of the house of the Ahab). Minor variants have: γαμβρὸς γὰρ οἴκου Αχαάβ (son-in-law of the house of Ahab). See F. Field (ed.), *Origenis Hexaplorum quae Supersunt* (2 vols; Hildesheim: Georg Olms Verlagsbuchhandlung, 1964), I, pp. 667–68; A. Rahlfs (ed.), *Septuaginta* (Stuttgart: Deutsche Bibelgesellschaft, 1979), p. 711.

6.   The LXX (2 Esd. 16.18) translates γαμβρός.

7.   The LXX (2 Esd. 23.28) translates νυμφίος. Ironically, men who are successful at the role of bridegroom are not so designated: a good example is Tobias, who has a bride (Tob. 7.12–17), enters the bridal chamber (Tob. 8.1), and consummates the marriage (we know this because they have children [Tob. 14.3]) yet is never called νυμφίος. (Other bridegrooms who contract marriages, consummate, and keep their brides but do not bear the title 'bridegroom' include the patriarchs Isaac, Jacob, and Joseph.) Tobias's marriage is so dangerous, however, that his future father-in-law dug a grave for him on the wedding night (8.9–12), so sure was he that Tobias would be dead, because seven previous men had been killed in the wedding chamber on their wedding night (3.7–8; 6.14–15; 7.11).

8.   J. Cheryl Exum, *Fragmented Women: Feminist (Sub)versions of Biblical Narratives* (Valley Forge, PA: Trinity Press International, 1993), pp. 42–60, 61–93, 176–84.

9.   Dale C. Allison, *The New Moses: A Matthean Typology* (Minneapolis: Fortress Press, 1993), pp. 139, 155.

Jesus the bridegroom in light of these texts.[10] A bridegroom associated with violence and loss or abandonment of a bride is an Old Testament motif that Matthew apparently recognizes and uses for his own purposes to portray Jesus as a bridegroom associated with violence and without a bride. In the way that Matthew compares Jesus to Moses as savior of his people and as lawgiver, the bridegrooms of the Old Testament set up Matthew's portrayal of Jesus as a bridegroom who is without a bride and who is associated with violence.

1.1 *The Bridegrooms of Lot's Daughters*

Lot's 'future' sons-in-law (חתניו)[11] are bridegrooms who become victims of violence. Whether the men are betrothed (inchoate marriage) or have

---

10. Justification for comparison of Matthew's bridegroom to Greek and Roman texts, later in this chapter, is based on the embeddedness of Matthew within Hellenistic culture.

11. The King James translation suggests they are already married: 'his sons-in-law, which married his daughters' (KJV); but other translations assume only betrothal: 'den Männern, die seine Töchter heiraten sollten' (the men who were supposed to marry his daughters) (Martin Luther); 'sons-in-law who were to marry his daughters' (RSV and NRSV); 'his future sons-in-law who were to marry his daughters' (Jerusalem Bible); 'his intended sons-in-law' (NEB); 'his sons-in-law who were pledged to marry his daughters' (NIV); 'los prometidos de sus hijas' (*La Santa Biblica*); 'den Verlobten seiner Töchter' (*Hoffnung für Alle*). חתן is translated by both νυμφίος and γάμβρος in the various Greek recensions. Lot's sons-in-law (Gen. 19.12, 14; Greek γάμβροι) and the king's son-in-law David (1 Sam. 18.18; Greek γαμβρός [LXX and Theodotion], νυμφίος [Aquila and Symmachus]). T.C. Mitchell interprets the term חתן more generally, as anyone related by marriage, i.e., an in-law ('The Meaning of the Noun חתן in the Old Testament', *Vetus Testamentum* 19 (1969), pp. 93–112). This usage indicates that the bride's family considered a bridegroom to be a 'son-in-law' even before the wedding, or that a married son-in-law remained in the status of 'bridegroom' for an undefined period of time (Josephus, *War* 1.499–500). A νυμφίος (Mt. 9.15) could refer to (1) a suitor or man betrothed but not yet married (Aristonicus, *A. Ar.* 179; Chariton, *De Chaerea et Callirhoe* 1.1.15.3, 5.5.6.1; Alciphron, *Letters of Fishermen*, 16.3); Apollodorus (*Library and Epitome*, 3.10.8) provides the synonym μνηστευόμενος; (2) a man celebrating his wedding feast (Aristonicus, *De signis Iliadis* 18.492.4; Arrian, *Anabasis of Alexander*, 7.4.7–8; Athenaeus Soph., *Deipn.* 1.9.29–31; Diodorus Siculus, *Bibliotheca Historica* 5.18.2; Lucian, *Dialogues of the Dead* 28.427–429). Cf. also Ps. 18 (19).5; Isa. 61.10; 62.5; Jer. 7.34; 16.9; 25.10; 40.11 (Hebrew חתן, Greek νυμφίος); or occasionally (3) a husband, already married and no longer celebrating the wedding feast (Apollonius, *Lexicon Homericum* 20.18; Immanuel Bekker (ed.), *Apolloni Sophistae Lexicon Homericum* (Hildesham: Georg Olms Verlagsbuchhandlung, 1967), p. 20; cf. Homer, *Odyssey* 7.64. See also J. Jeremias, 'νύμφη, νυμφίος', *TDNT* 4, p. 1099. Cf. Judg. 15.6; 19.5; Neh. 13.28 (Hebrew חתן, Greek νυμφίος, except for Aquila's use of γαμβρός in Judg. 15.6 and 19.5). The plural νυμφίους sometimes refers to the bridal pair (Aeschylus, *Septem Contra Thebas* 757; Philostratus, *Life of Apollonius*, 3.1). G.O. Hutchinson (ed.), *Aeschylus: Septem Contra Thebas* (Oxford: Clarendon, 1985), pp. 27, 168; F.C. Coneybeare (trans.), *Philostratus: The Life of Apollonius of Tyana* (LCL, 16; Cambridge, MA: Harvard University Press, 1912, repr. 2000), p. 232. Josephus distinguishes γαμβρός as 'son-in-law' (a relationship to the bride's

actually consummated the marriage and are newly married 'sons-in-law' is not clear. The LXX translates חתנים with γαμβροὶ, and there are no variations among other translators. The Hebrew (חתניו לקחי בנתיו, 19.14) has the sense of the sons-in-law currently taking the daughters (Qal. active participle of לקח, take in marriage), but the Greek εἰληφότας (perfect active participle from λαμβάνω) used with an aorist main verb suggests that the translators thought that the sons-in-law already 'had received,' or 'had taken' Lot's daughters: τοὺς γαμβροὺς αὐτοῦ τοὺς εἰληφότας τὰς θυγατέρας αὐτοῦ (19.14).

God sends a conflagration to destroy Sodom, and these betrothed men do not escape (Gen. 19.12, 14, 24–25). The story of Lot's future sons-in-law – his daughters' bridegrooms – is an example of the bridegroom as victim of violence and the violent separation of bride and bridegroom. While Lot's sons-in-law differ in their roles from the victims in the story of the burning city in Matthew's wedding feast parable (Mt. 22.1–14) – in the parable, it is not the bridegroom who is killed but the messengers and those who murdered the messengers – the stories both highlight the consequences of ignoring a royal invitation or the warning of messengers, and both stories include the king's or deity's violent destruction of a city by fire.[12] Moreover, Matthew twice links the fate of unworthy houses or towns to the destruction of Sodom (Mt. 10.15; 11.23–24).

The destruction of Lot's sons-in-law also leads to the disruption of the bridal pair's reproductive role and so leads to the subsequent incest committed by the widowed brides. When their bridegrooms die, Lot's daughters resort to becoming pregnant by their own father (Gen. 19.30–36).

---

father) and νυμφίος as bridegroom (a relationship to the bride) (*War* 1.500). Philo also makes a clear distinction between νυμφίος, the bridegroom, and γαμβρός, the son-in-law (*Spec. Leg.* 1.111). Aeschylus combines the terms γάμος and νύμφη with the phrase 'newly married bride' (νεογάμου νύμφης), perhaps as opposed to the not-yet-married bride (*Agamemnon* 1179). While four Greek translations (the LXX, Aquila, Theodotion, and Symmachus) sometimes agree on their translation of חתן (e.g., all four refer to the husbands of Lot's daughters as γαμβροὶ [Gen. 19.12, 14], and all agree that the bridegroom emerging from his chamber [חתן] is a νυμφίος [Isa. 61.10; 62.5]), sometimes the Greek sources use the words interchangeably. For example, in Judg. 15.6 the newly married Samson (חתן) is a νυμφίος in the LXX, Symmachus, and Theodotion, but not in Aquila, where he is a γαμβρός (see Hatch and Redpath, *Concordance to the Septuagint*, II, p. 951). David, the king's son-in-law (חתן), is a γαμβρός in the LXX (1 Sam. 18.18) and in Theodotion, but Aquila and Symmachus translate νυμφίος (F. Field, *Origenis Hexaplorum*, I, p. 527). For further commentary, see J. Jeremias, 'νύμφη, νυμφίος', p. 1099; H.G. Liddell, *An Intermediate Greek-English Lexicon Founded on the Seventh Edition of Liddell and Scott's Greek English Lexicon* (Oxford: Clarendon Press, 1889, 1995), p. 159; and E. Kutsch, 'חתן', in G.J. Botterweck and H. Ringgren [eds.], *TDOT* 5, pp. 270–77 (273). Various manuscripts also give evidence of the interchangability of these terms: e.g., the 'son-in-law' in Judg. 19.6 is a νυμφίος according to Alexandrinus (LXX), but he is a γαμβρός in LXX Vaticanus (Alfred Rahlfs [ed.], *Septuaginta*, p. 405).

12.   The Matthean wedding parables are discussed in Chapters 2 and 3.

If we read the dead bridegrooms as men who have not yet consummated their marriages (and not as newly married 'sons-in-law'), Lot becomes the de facto bridegroom of his daughters (through consummation); the drunken and completely unaware Lot, who would have thrown his own daughters to the mob to be raped (Gen. 19.8), is himself a victim of rape and incest at the hands of his daughters (Gen. 19.30–36).

The daughters' action upon the loss of their legitimate bridegrooms anticipates the women who are part of irregular unions in the Matthean Jesus' genealogy: Tamar, Rahab, Ruth, 'the wife of Uriah,' and Mary (Mt. 1.3, 5, 6, 18), all of whom are associated with sexual relationships outside the social norm: Judah takes Tamar for a prostitute; Rahab is a prostitute; Ruth obtains Levirate marriage by lying next to Boaz and uncovering his 'feet'; Bathsheba, 'the wife of Uriah,' commits adultery with David, and Mary is found to be pregnant before she lives with Joseph. The bridegrooms' death and the daughters' unconventional sexual union with their father in Gen. 19 prefigure the way in which the Matthean bridegroom disrupts conventional marriage and the association of the wedding feast with the burned city.[13]

The father–daughter incest in Lot's family undermines the integrity of the father and father's house,[14] just as Matthew will undermine the role of human fathers, and, with the formation of a fictive family, will replace fathers' houses with the household of God the Father (12.46–50; 23.9). Lot's daughters, like daughters in Matthew, are touched by violence or death: Herodias' daughter who bore John's head on a platter (14.6–11); the 'Canaanite' woman's demon-possessed daughter (15.21–28); and the synagogue leader's dead daughter (9.18–22). These examples set an anti-familial tone in Matthew, where reproductive roles and biological family relationships are undermined.[15]

1.2 *Moses, the Bridegroom of Blood*

Sometimes חתן refers to 'the one who circumcises' (in reference to an old cultural tradition of circumcision before marriage) or 'one who undergoes circumcision,' so that Moses as חתן דמים, 'bridegroom of blood' (Exod. 4.24–26), is connected to circumcision.[16] Dale Allison details the

---

13. Chapter 5 discusses Matthean attitudes toward marriage and sexuality.

14. 'Uncovering the nakedness' of the father (Gen. 9.21–27) or of close relatives was condemned (Lev. 18.16–18; cf. *B. San.* 76A).

15. The Matthean 'family' is discussed in Chapter 4.

16. The Brown–Driver–Briggs lexicon demonstrates that חתן is linked to an Arabic root meaning 'circumcision' or 'circumciser' in reference to the father-in-law who might perform circumcision on a young man before the marriage, but the term also means simply 'bridegroom' (*BDB*, p. 368). The LXX (Ex. 4.24–26) does not translate חתן but refers instead

connections between Moses and Jesus in Matthew (e.g., the similar infancy narratives, temptation stories, teaching on the mountain, law-giving, miracles, and transfiguration),[17] but these comparisons have not been extended to the bridegroom and to violence. The association of Moses to the bloody bridegroom and Jesus the bridegroom is strengthened by Jesus' representing a 'new Moses' in the gospel of Matthew.

Athough Allison does not treat the bloody bridegroom story (Exod. 4.25–26), nor mention Jesus or Moses as a bridegroom,[18] he concedes the possibility that Jesus as bridegroom resonates with Moses as the 'bloody bridegroom.' He cautions, however, that Matthew does not include any mention of circumcision and that the early Church found the issue of circumcision problematic.[19] Though an argument from silence, Matthew's lack of reference to circumcision is completely consistent with Matthew's afamilial ethos. Matthew is not interested in members of the new community having children at all, let alone circumcising the sons. As for the Gentiles who might affiliate with the new community, they would affiliate not as Jews but as Gentiles and would not necessarily undergo circumcision.

Moses is already married and has a son when he is given the title 'bridegroom of blood' (חתן־דמים). Before becoming a bridegroom, Moses was a perpetrator of violence (Exod. 2.12), and he becomes a potential victim of violence when the deity seeks to kill him (Exod. 4.25).[20]

---

to 'the blood of the circumcision of Moses and Zipporah's son: τὸ αἷμα τῆς περιτομῆς τοῦ παιδίου μου, but other Greek versions translate the Hebrew literally: νυμφίος αἱμάτων [Symmachus and Theodotion]; νυμφίον αἵματος [Aquila]). See John W. Wevers, *Notes on the Greek Text of Exodus* (Septuagint and Cognate Studies Series, 30; Atlanta: Society of Biblical Literature, 1990), p. 55; Field (ed.), *Origenis Hexaplorum*, I, pp. 87–88; and Kutsch, חתן', p. 277. Examples of חתן as 'father-in-law' can be found in Exod. 3.1; 4.18; 18.1, 2, 5, 6, 7, 8, 12, 15, 17, 24, 27; Num. 10.29; Greek γαμβρός). See *BDB*, p. 368; David J.A. Clines, *The Dictionary of Classical Hebrew* (4 vols.; Sheffield: Sheffield Academic Press, 1996), III, pp. 336–37; Ludwig Koehler and Walter Baumgartner, *The Hebrew and Aramaic Lexicon of the Old Testament* (2 vols.; trans. M.E.J. Richardson; Leiden: Brill, 2001), I, pp. 364–65; Jacob Levy, *Wörterbuch über die Talmudim und Midraschim* (4 vols.; ed. H.L. Fleischer and Lazarus Goldschmidt; Berlin: Benjamin Harz Verlag, 2nd edn, 1924), II, pp. 129–30; Michael Sokoloff, *A Dictionary of Jewish Palestinian Aramaic* (Ramat-Gan: Bar Ilan University, 1990), p. 218; Gustaf H. Dalman, *Aramäisch-Neuhebräisches Handwörterbuch zu Targum, Talmud and Midrasch* (Hildesheim: Georg Olms Verlagsbuchhandlung, 1967), p. 164.

17. Allison, *New Moses*, esp. pp. 137–267.

18. Allison, *The New Moses*, passim.

19. Personal correspondence, Fall, 1999.

20. *Targum Pseudo-Jonathan* records that an angel attacked Moses because his father-in-law prevented him from circumcising his son. *Targum Onkelos* also replaces the deity with an angel-attacker. *Jub.* 48.2–4 alludes to Moses' attack but changes the protagonist to Mastema, and in this account, God becomes not the attacker, but Moses' rescuer, and no mention is made of the bridegroom of blood. Targumic texts from J.W. Etheridge [trans.], *The Targums*

Moses' wife Zipporah saves his life by circumcising their son and touching the bloody foreskin to Moses' 'feet.' The incident is so strange (why does God try to kill the newly commissioned leader?) and seemingly out of place in the narrative that interpreters have come up with many creative explanations, almost all of which involve discussion of violence. William Propp concludes that Zipporah's statement 'you are a bridegroom of blood to me' was her realization that she had married a murderer with blood guilt on his head and that חתן־דמים referred to the right of blood vengeance of the murdered man's in-laws.[21] Pamela Tmarkin Reis interprets the threat against Moses' life as an identity crisis, while Zipporah's sarcastic epithet hurled at her husband reveals her disgust at her discovery that he is not an Egyptian, but a Hebrew associated with the rite of circumcision.[22] Howard Eilberg-Schwartz claims that circumcision is a sign of Moses' submitting his masculinity to God.[23] Because this incident takes place immediately after God tells Moses that he intends to kill Pharaoh's first-born son (Exod. 4.23, a threat actualized in Chs 11–12), G.W. Ashby reads the violence in this story as a blood sacrifice that prefigures the Passover.[24] Samuel Hooke argues that the deity, not Moses, is the 'bridegroom of blood' in reference to sacred marriage,[25] and Elias Auerbach agrees that the deity is jealously demanding right of first penetration of Moses' bride; the bloodied foreskin resembles the bloodied phallus of first penetration.[26] The right of first penetration interpretation is repeated by Jonathan Kirsch,[27] but is problematic because Zipporah is not a virgin – she has a son – and thus cannot be so claimed. Martin Noth

of Onkelos and Jonathan Ben Uzziel on the Pentateuch with the Fragments of the Jerusalem Targum from the Chaldee, at *http://www.tulane.edu/~ntcs/pj/psjon.htm*. O.S. Wintermute (trans.), '*Jubilees*', in J.H. Charlesworth (ed.), *The Old Testament Pseudepigrapha* (2 vols.; New York: Doubleday, 1985), I, pp. 35–142, here p. 139. Philo, Josephus, and the *The Testament of Moses* (first century) do not treat the story at all. For discussion on ancient interpretations, see Cornelis Houtman, *Exodus* (trans. J. Rebel and S. Woudstra; Historical Commentary on the Old Testament; Kampen: Kok Publishing House, 1993), pp. 440–47, and Brevard Childs, *The Book of Exodus* (OTL; Philadelphia: Westminster Press, 1974), pp. 96–104.

21. W. Propp ('That Bloody Bridegroom [Exodus 4.24–6]', *VT* 43 [1993], pp. 495–518, esp. pp. 504–505, 509).

22. P. Tmarkin Reis ('The Bridegroom of Blood: A New Reading', *Judaism* 40 [1991], pp. 324–31).

23. H. Eilberg-Schwartz, *God's Phallus and Other Problems for Men and Monotheism* (Boston: Beacon Press, 1994), pp. 158–61.

24. G.W. Ashby, 'The Bloody Bridegroom: The Interpretation of Exodus 4.24–26', *ExTim* 106 (Ap. 1995), pp. 203–205.

25. S.H. Hooke, *The Origins of Early Semitic Ritual* (London: Oxford University Press, 1938), p. 62.

26. E. Auerbach, *Moses* (Detroit: Wayne State University Press, 1975), p. 49.

27. J. Kirsch, *Moses: A Life* (New York: Ballantine Books, 1998), pp. 136–38.

connects circumcision to the wedding night and interprets it as 'an apotropaic act which keeps away a nocturnal threat.'[28] Brevard Childs,[29] George W. Coats,[30] and Seth Kunin[31] think the story is an etiology that explains the importance of circumcision. Some scholars are so baffled by the pericope that they do not attempt to explain it: John Van Seters suggests it is a Midrashic tradition inserted later,[32] and Kirsch concludes that the story simply depicts God and Moses as capable of random and impulsive acts of violence.[33]

Ilana Pardes suggests that the 'bridegroom of blood' is a vestige of the Isis and Osiris myth, in which Isis rescues her dismembered husband and restores his cut-off penis, just as Zipporah rescues Moses from death through the cutting of a penis.[34] There is no bride to rescue the Matthean bridegroom; in Matthew, the violence is not averted, and the brideless bridegroom becomes actual victim. Moses as endangered bloody bridegroom, both chosen and attacked by God, prefigures Jesus the bridegroom, whose arrest and crucifixion, while not an attack, are described as part of the divine plan.[35]

That Moses sent his wife away (שׁלח, ἄφεσιν) (Exod. 18.2) in order to follow his calling as leader of the Hebrew people demonstrates the pattern of the bridegroom who has no bride. Ἄφεσιν means to release, free, pardon, or cancel, so that it would seem Moses released her from their marriage or divorced her. Later her father returns her to him (18.5). Moses and Jesus, as saviors of their people, are bridegrooms unencumbered with brides and whose roles disrupt marriage.

The similarities between the two 'bridegrooms' are strong: Jesus, like Moses, escapes from death as an infant (Exod. 2.1–10; Mt. 2.13–18), mediates the Law (Exod. 20.1–21; Mt. 5.17–48), and by tradition is

28. M. Noth, *Exodus: A Commentary* (OTL; Philadelphia: Westminster Press, 1962), pp. 49–50.

29. Childs, *Book of Exodus*, p. 104.

30. G.W. Coats, *Exodus 1–18* (2 vols.; Forms of the Old Testament Literature; Grand Rapids: Eerdmans, 1999), I, pp. 45–46.

31. S. Kunin, 'The Bridegroom of Blood: A Structural Analysis', *JSOT* 70 (1996), pp. 3–16.

32. J. Van Seters, *The Life of Moses: The Yahwist as Historian in Exodus–Numbers* (Louisville: Westminster/John Knox, 1994), p. 68.

33. Kirsch, *Moses*, p. 138.

34. I. Pardes, 'Zipporah and the Struggle for Deliverance', in Pardes, *Contratraditions in the Bible: A Feminist Approach* (Cambridge, MA: Harvard University Press, 1992), pp. 79–97 (esp. 89–93).

35. The Matthean bridegroom submits to God's will that he go through with being arrested: 'My Father, if it is possible, let this cup pass from me; yet not what I want but what you want' (26.39–44).

celibate.[36] Both men lead the formation of a new community, and both warn of divine punishment for recalcitrance. Both are associated with violence (e.g., Exod. 3.11–15; 12.29–30; 14.21–31; 32.27–29; Mt. 10.16–23, 34–39; 21.33–41; 22.1–14; 24.6–31; 25.31–46; 27.27–51). Each, then, in his own way, is a bridegroom of blood.

1.3 *Samson*

The bridegroom Samson (וחח, Judg. 15.6)[37] and the bridegroom Jesus also have similarities: both have their births announced by angels and have no apparent male contact when they are conceived,[38] both are called Nazoreans,[39] and both grow up to save their people.[40] Both suffer defeat, shame and death at the hands of foreigners occupying their land. Just as Samson's parents exhort Samson to marry endogamously, so only in Matthew Jesus exhorts his disciples, 'go nowhere among the Gentiles and enter no town of the Samaritans; go only to the lost sheep of the house of Israel' (10.5b–6 cf. 15.24). And yet, both Jesus and Samson see the end of their mission not among the Jews, but among the Gentiles: it is among the Philistines that Samson ends his life; it is 'to all the nations' or 'all the Gentiles' (28.19, πάντα τὰ ἔθνη) that the resurrected Jesus sends his disciples.

Both Samson and Jesus are betrayed in intimate settings by people close to them: Jesus, with a kiss, by one of his inner circle of disciples (Mt. 26.47–49), and Samson, by a woman he loved, while he slept in her lap (Judg. 16.4, 19). Both betrayers were paid for their treachery (Judg. 16.18; Mt. 26.14–16). Both Samson and Jesus seem to invite (or at least leave themselves open to) betrayal: Samson does not quit Delilah's bed after her repeated attempts to trick and disarm him (Judg. 16.8–9, 12, 14); Jesus predicts his betrayal ('One of you will betray me' [Mt. 26.20]) and

---

36. The tradition that Moses separated from his wife and was celibate is recorded in *b Yeb.* 62a. The chastity of Moses and Zipporah is mentioned by Philo (*On the Cherubim* 41, 47). Daniel Boyarin (*Carnal Israel: Reading Sex in Talmudic Culture* [Berkeley: University of California Press, 1993], pp. 159–65) discusses evidence that some scholars, using Moses' celibacy as an example, were opting to leave their wives for years at a time to devote themselves to study of Torah.

37. LXX Vaticanus translates ὁ νυμφίος. LXX Alexandrinus translates ὁ γαμβρὸς. See Field, *Origenis Hexaplorum*, I, p. 450; Rahlfs (ed.), *Septuaginta*, p. 467.

38. M. Bal, *Death and Dissymmetry* (Chicago: University of Chicago Press, 1988), pp. 74–76.

39. Richard G. Bowman and Richard W. Swanson, 'Samson and the Son of God or Dead Heroes and Dead Goats: Ethical Readings of Narrative Violence in Judges and Matthew', *Semeia* 77 (1997), pp. 59–73, esp. p. 63.

40. Bowman and Swanson observe that 'Samson is to begin to deliver Israel,' and that Jesus 'will save his people from their sins' ('Samson and the Son of God', p. 63).

passively waits for and announces Judas' arrival in the garden ('See, my
betrayer is at hand' [Mt. 26.46]). Both Samson and Jesus are mocked and
tortured before they die (the Philistines gouge out Samson's eyes, shackle
him, and make him entertain them [Judg. 16.21, 25]; Jesus is mocked [Mt.
26.67], flogged, mistreated, and crucified [27.26–31]). The death of both
men has a connection to the destruction of a temple (the house where the
Philistines worshipped Dagon [Judg. 16.26–30]; the Temple in Jerusalem
[Mt. 24.1–2; 26.61; 27.40]). Finally, both destroy others in final acts of
vengeance: Samson pulls down a building to crush thousands of his
tormentors (Judg. 16.4–31); Jesus consigns the 'accursed' to eternal
punishment (Mt. 25.31–46).

Samson is a violent bridegroom whose only actual wedding is a disaster:
he abandons his wife, then initiates a chain of violent acts when she is
given to his 'best man.' Samson burns her people's fields, and this action
results in the Philistines' retaliatory act of burning the woman and her
father (Judg. 14.19–20; 15.1–8; cf. Josephus, *Ant.* 5.295–96.). Mieke Bal
shows how this nameless bride becomes the victim of competition between
her bridegroom, her tribesmen, and her father in a no-win situation; no
matter what she does, she will suffer violent retribution at male hands.[41]
Because of both competition and the construction of the bride as male
property, Samson's wedding feast is ultimately not an occasion for joy as
much as for separation and violence.

The Matthean bridegroom's wedding feast is also an occasion for
threats of violence and burning (Mt. 22.6–13). That Samson's marriage
ends in death and destruction, that he never marries again, and that he is
betrayed by a woman he loves suggests to the reader (particularly male
readers) that marriage is not a good idea; that Jesus never marries in the
first place and affirms his disciples' observation that 'it is better not to
marry' (19.10–12) corroborates Samson's dubious portrayal of marriage.
Even the death of Samson's Timnite bride may be seen as foreshadowing
the fate of 'wedding guests' who are found unworthy in allegorical
interpretations of the parables. Leading to her death is the bridal bet of
'thirty linen garments and thirty festal garments' (Judg. 14.12–13 cf. v.19);
perhaps echoes of this bet can be heard in the Parable of the Wedding
Feast, where the guest without the right garment is expelled. Just as
Samson burns the fields, so the king in the wedding parable burns the
cities of those who refuse his invitation.

41.   Bal, *Death and Dissymmetry*, pp. 76–80 (also pp. 140–42).

1.4 *The Levite from Ephraim*

In one of the Bible's most gruesome stories, a Levite from Ephraim (חתן,
19.5) [42] abandons his concubine to a gang of rapists,[43] dismembers her
body, and sends the pieces to the tribes of Israel (Judg. 19.1–29).[44] The
text does not make clear that she is dead when he dismembers her.[45] The
story is reminiscent of the Parable of the Unfaithful Slave, where a master
cuts his slave to pieces (24.51) and throws him out with the hypocrites,
where there will be weeping and gnashing of teeth (Mt. 24.51). It also
resembles the Parable of the Wedding Feast, where someone who, as a
guest, was supposedly under the protection of the master of the house, is
instead violently cast outside (Mt. 22.11–13).

The Levite is a 'bridegroom' whose marital status is ambiguous, to a
certain degree. He is called a 'bridegroom' or 'son-in-law' but the woman
is called a 'concubine' (mistress or secondary wife) (פילגש or παλλακίς);
a secondary wife's main role is to provide sexual gratification;[46] she
apparently means little more than sex partner to the 'bridegroom,'
because he sacrifices her to the rapists outside. The concubine, even if she
has wifely status and no other wife is mentioned, does not apparently fall
within Matthew's ideal of marriage as the two becoming 'one flesh' (19.
3–9). As in the story of Lot's daughters, the father/daughter relationship is
disrupted, as the woman's father is unable or unwilling to protect his
daughter from the rapists or from her bridegroom. Therefore, in this
story, marital and biological family ties are marginalized.

In this intertextual resonance between Judg. 19 and Matthew, however,

---

42. LXX Vaticanus translates νυμφίος. Theodotion and LXX Alexandrinus translate
γαμβρός. See Field (ed.), *Origenis Hexaplorum*, I, p. 463; Rahlfs (ed.), *Septuaginta*, p. 481.
The Levite's story also illustrates that a man who had a 'concubine' (γυναῖκα παλλακὴν,
Judg. 19.1) or 'young girl' (νεᾶνις, Judg. 19.5), as opposed to a wife (γύνη), was considered a
bridegroom or son-in-law.

43. Gale A. Yee ('Ideological Criticism: Judges 17–21 and the Dismembered Body', in
Yee [ed.], *Judges and Method: New Approaches in Biblical Studies* [Minneapolis: Fortress
Press, 1995], pp. 146–70 [esp. p. 157]) explains that the woman is a wife of secondary rank,
often translated as 'concubine'. Yee notes the man's despicable character, in that he
'sacrifices his wife to save his own hide.'

44. Plutarch recounts a similar story, but without the gendered overtones, when a young
boy was pulled to pieces by a mob, and his father displayed the pieces of the body in the
marketplace to demand justice (Plutarch, *Moralia* 772F).

45. Yee, 'Ideological Criticism', p. 165; Dana Nolan Fewell and David M. Gunn, *Gender,
Power, and Promise: The Subject of the Bible's First Story* (Nashville: Abingdon Press, 1993),
p. 134.

46. While she might bear children, they would have lesser status than children of the first
wife. An exception would be women who bore children for barren wives, such as Hagar. See
Aline Rouselle, 'Body Politics', in Pauline Schmitt Pantel (ed.), *A History of Women: From
Ancient Goddesses to Christian Saints* (Cambridge, MA: Harvard University Press, 1992), pp.
296–337 (319–20).

Jesus does not resemble the bridegroom as much as he does the bride. Jesus the bridegroom is the battered bride, abandoned to tormentors and bearing the marks of torture and death on his own body. Moreover, his body is to be ritually dismembered and distributed (Mt. 26.26), just as the woman's body was distributed among the tribes (Judg. 19.29) in what Bal calls 'an attempt at communion.'[47] Both the concubine and Jesus are condemned by priests (the Levite is of the priestly class [Judg. 19.1; Mt. 26.27]).

The Levite and his concubine lived in a time when there was 'no king in Israel' (βασιλεὺς οὐκ ἦν ἐν Ἰσραηλ; Judg. 19.1), but according to Matthew, Jesus himself is the 'king of Israel' (βασιλεὺς Ἰσραήλ) (Mt. 2.2; 27.42). The Levite bridegroom's story anticipates the Davidic monarchy and even provides its justification; so too, the gospel anticipates the reign of David's heir.

1.5 David

Marriage, violence, abandonment and death are linked in the marital encounters of the bridegroom David (חתן, 1 Sam. 18.18, 22; cf. 22.14),[48] the explicitly named ancestor of Jesus the Matthean bridegroom (Mt. 1.1, 6). Baruch Halpern describes David as a 'serial killer' who was responsible for the deaths of Nabal, Saul and his sons, Ishbaal, Abner, Amnon, Absolom, Amasa, and Uriah, and whose military conquests claimed the lives of thousands of Philistines and other 'foreigners.'[49] David's life is marked by violence: he kills lions and bears (1 Sam. 17.34–37); he kills and beheads the Philistine Goliath (1 Sam. 17.48–51); he is a renowned military hero (1 Sam. 18.12–16, 30); and he survives several of Saul's attempts to murder him (1 Sam. 18.10–11; 19.2–3, 10–18; 20.1–42; 23. 24–29). David's heroics are reminiscent of Samson's: Samson kills a lion (Judg. 14.5–6), is a well-known killer of Philistines (Judg. 15.8, 15; 16.30), and he is the survivor of several attempts to murder him (Judg. 15.9–14; 16.2–3, 5–22). Both bridegrooms abandon their brides (who are subsequently given to others) and then demand them back (Judg. 15.1–2; 1 Sam. 3.14).

---

47. Bal, *Death and Dissymmetry*, p. 192.

48. Origen, Aquila, Theodotion, and Symmachus do not include 18.18; however, LXX Alexandrinus translates γαμβρός; LXX Sinaiticus translates νυμφίος. In 18.23, 26, the LXX uses a verbal form 'to become the son-in-law' (ἐπιγαμβρεῦσαι). In 22.14, the LXX translates חתן as γαμβρός, and Aquila and Symmachus render the word as νυμφίος. See Field (ed.), *Origenis Hexaplorum*, I, p. 519, 527; Rahlfs (ed.), *Septuaginta*, p. 538, 546.

49. Baruch Halpern, *David's Secret Demons: Messiah, Murderer, Traitor, King* (Grand Rapids: Eerdmans, 2001), esp. pp. 57–94, 133–98.

David is a bloody bridegroom whose status as Michal's husband and Saul's son-in-law was won by the bride price (מהר) of 200 Philistine foreskins (along with 200 Philistine lives) (1 Sam. 18.25–27; cf. 2 Sam. 3.14). Josephus says the price was 600 Philistine heads (*Ant.* 6.201). Saul set David to this task in the hope that David would be killed, but David does the killing (1 Sam. 18.21, 25).[50] David marries Michal, who loved him, and she, in turn, saves his life (1 Sam. 19.8–18). But David marries other wives and abandons Michal for such a lengthy time that she is given in marriage to another man (1 Sam. 25.43–44; 2 Sam. 3.15–16).[51] David demands her back (2 Sam. 3.13–16), but their mutual scorn and resentment eventually causes them to reject each other (2 Sam. 6.16–23).[52] Thus David is a bridegroom who is both victim and perpetrator of violence. He abandons his bride and is eventually separated from her permanently. As son of David, Jesus the bridegroom is a victim of violence, but Jesus never has a bride.

David continues his violent-bridegroom status in his encounter with Bathsheba, whose husband he effectively condemns to death in battle (2 Sam. 11.1–27). Baruch Halpern describes the 'cool professionalism' with which David orchestrates Uriah's murder and discusses David's willingness to sacrifice other lives in the plot.[53] The murder of Uriah was

50. Elna K. Solvang outlines the violence by which David achieves status as son-in-law to the king in *A Woman's Place Is in the House: Royal Women of Judah and Their Involvement in the House of David* (JSOTSupp, 349; Sheffield: Sheffield Academic Press, 2003), pp. 88–95. Steven L. McKenzie discusses the risks David took to make this politically advantageous marriage in *King David: A Biography* (Oxford: Oxford University Press, 2000), p. 87. Others who note the danger David faced and the violence with which David sought status in the royal house include Herbert Lockyer, 'Michal', in David J.A. Clines and T.C. Eskenazi (eds.), *Telling Queen Michal's Story: An Experiment in Comparative Interpretation* (JSOTSupp, 119; Sheffield: Sheffield Academic Press, 1991), pp. 227–33; Marti J. Steussy, *David: Biblical Portraits of Power* (Columbia, SC: University of South Carolina Press, 1999), pp. 49–82; and K.L. Noll, *The Faces of David* (JSOTSupp, 242; Sheffield: Sheffield Academic Press, 1997), pp. 54–56.

51. So, too, Samson's Timnite bride. Through careful study of law codes, Zafrira Ben-Barak shows that David was absent for a long enough time that Michal was free to marry again ('The Legal Background to the Restoration of Michal to David,' in Clines and Eskenazi (eds.), *Telling Queen Michal's Story*, pp. 74–90). Lockyer disagrees and deems Michal's second marriage illegal, because David is still alive, in 'Michal', p. 230.

52. Robert Alter and Cheryl Exum discuss how Michal is a political pawn throughout the narrative, and from this stems her scorn for David. See R. Alter, 'Characterization and the Art of Reticence', in Clines and Eskenazi (eds.), *Telling Queen Michal's Story*, pp. 64–73, and C. Exum, 'Murder They Wrote: Ideology and the Manipulation of Female Presence in Biblical Narrative', in Clines and Eskenazi (eds.), *Telling Queen Michal's Story*, pp. 176–98, esp. 181–86. Fewell and Gunn conjecture that David never loved anyone but used those who loved him (*Gender, Power and Promise*, esp. pp. 146–52).

53. Halpern, *David's Secret Demons*, pp. 93–94, 403–405. Solvang notes that the story of David and Bathsheba is not about sex but about the power to take what the king would take (*A Woman's Place*, p. 133).

preceded by the death of Abigail's husband Nabal (1 Sam. 25.36–39), and Abigail's subsequent marriage to David.[54]

Matthew connects Jesus to David by giving him the title 'son of David' (υἱοῦ Δαυὶδ) (e.g., Mt. 1.1) then invokes David's identity as adulterer and murderer by referring to Bathsheba as the 'wife of Uriah' (literally, 'she of Uriah'; τῆς τοῦ Οὐρίου) in Jesus' genealogy (Mt. 1.6) and identifies Bathsheba not by her own name, but by her relationship to the man David cuckolded and killed. Matthew shows that Jesus the bridegroom is not like David in regard to sexual exploits and marriage, but, rather, he defines these actions as adulterous (Mt. 5.30–32; 19.3–10). Jesus is a bridegroom who *never* marries (let alone marrying multiple times, like David); instead of killing others for their wives, he becomes the wifeless victim of murder. Both bridegrooms are thus associated with adultery, one as adulterer and one as a celibate (and descendant of adulterers) who strictly condemns adultery. In addition, both bridegrooms are associated with violence. Both are the objects of a king's jealous rage (David by Saul's in 1 Sam. 18.10–30 and Jesus by Herod's in Mt. 2.13–16). And, as David sends Uriah into battle, Jesus sends his followers into situations where they might be killed (10.28) and relegates the unrighteous to eternal fire (25.41).

David and Jesus are bridegrooms who are followed by numerous women, but neither is faithful to one bride: David takes women into his harem or abandons them. While Jesus heals or takes women into his fictive family (e.g., the hemorrhaging woman and revived girl [9.18–26], fictive 'mothers' [12.48–50], the 'Canaanite' woman and her daughter [15.21–28], the parabolic ten virgins [25.1–13], the anointing woman [26.6–13], and the women at the tomb [27.61; 28.1–10]), like David, Jesus hesitates to be in relationship (15.21–28) or threatens to abandon (25.11–13) those he deems unworthy.

Both Jesus and David have coercive power to keep people under their rule. God grants David a house and throne (θρόνος) forever through his son Solomon, whom God will claim as a 'son' (ἐγὼ ἔσομαι αὐτῷ εἰς πατέρα, καὶ αὐτὸς ἔσται μοι εἰς υἱόν [2 Sam. 7.11–17]), and David extended his kingdom by doing battle with many nations. Jesus, also claimed by God as 'son' (Οὗτός ἐστιν ὁ υἱός μου [Mt. 3.17]) sits on the

---

54. Halpern (*David's Secret Demons*, p. 77) speculates on David's guilt in this death, even though Abigail spared David from 'bloodguilt' when David intended to murder Nabal and all the males of his house [1 Sam. 25.32–34]). The storyteller further claims that it was the Lord who caused Nabal to die (1 Sam. 25. 36–38) because Nabal (who was surly and mean [1 Sam. 25.3]) insulted David ('Who is David? Who is the son of Jesse? There are many servants today who are breaking away from their masters ... shall I take my bread and water and meat ... and give it men who come from I do not know where?' [1 Sam. 25.10–11]) and refused to welcome him and his companions (1 Sam. 25.2–13). The story makes clear that it is David, not Nabal, who has murderous intentions (1 Sam. 25.32–34).

throne (θρόνος) of his glory to judge the nations (Mt. 25.31; cf. 28.18–20) and commands his followers to make disciples of all nations (28.19). Jesus' household, made up of fictive 'sons of the bridal chamber' (Mt. 9.15; cf. also 12.46–50), will last until the end of the age (cf. 28.20). Once people are part of Jesus' fictive family, they are liable to judgment and the hell of fire if they are found to be unworthy of the Kingdom of Heaven (25.31–46). Thus, both David and Jesus are bridegrooms that I find to be often more fearful than desirable.

1.6 *Tobiah and the Unnamed Son-in-law of Sanballat*

The interwoven tales of Tobiah (Neh. 6.18), a perpetrator of violence, and the son-in-law of Sanballat (Neh. 13.28), a victim of violence, illustrate how marriages create family alliances that either give the power to persecute others or that endanger the lives of family members. Tobiah is called son-in-law (חתן) of Shecaniah (Neh. 6.18),[55] and is an evidently wealthy person with a great deal of power in Judah due to his family and marriage connections: 'For many in Judah were bound by oath to him, because he was the son-in-law of Shecaniah, son of Arah, and his son Jehohanan had married the daughter of Meshullam son of Berechiah' (6.18). Moreover, he is a bridegroom who uses his power to bully others: Nehemiah claims that Tobiah (along with Sanballat) threatens to kill him (Neh. 6.10) and his workers (Neh. 4.7–12), and continually tries to intimidate him (Neh. 2.19; 6.12–13, 19). The intimidation tactics are effective: Nehemiah's workers are so afraid of an attack by Tobiah that they feel compelled to wear their swords at all times and to keep constant watch (Neh. 4.12–23).

The choice of bridegroom or bride has the potential to build up or tear down families. The bridegroom in Matthew creates power struggles and violence in the formation of his new family ('I have not come to bring peace, but a sword, for I have come to set a man against his father, a daughter against her mother, and a daughter-in-law against her mother-in-law; and one's foes will be the members of one's own household' [Mt. 10.34–36]), sometimes with the loss of biological family members (when Jesus' mother and brothers were waiting to speak to him, Jesus said, 'Who is my mother, and who are my brothers?' And pointing to his disciples he said, 'Here are my mother and my brothers! For whoever does the will of my Father in heaven is my brother and sister and mother' [Mt. 12. 46–50]). In a similar manner to Jesus' disruption of family ties and alliances with a new family, Tobiah and the unnamed son-in-law are involved in power struggles that result from choice of family alliances.

---

55. Tamara C. Eskenazi, 'Tobiah', *ABD* 6, pp. 584–85.

The son-in-law (חתן) of Sanballat is from the family of the high priest; he is a bridegroom who becomes a victim of violence when Nehemiah attacks Jews who are married to foreigners (Neh. 13.28). Nehemiah identifies this son-in-law/bridegroom both by his relationship to the high priest and his marriage alliance with Nehemiah's opponent Sanballat (who has a foreign name and is identified as a 'Horonite' [Neh. 2.10, 19; 13.28]); therefore, the son-in-law/bridegroom is both a descendant of a priestly family and married to the daughter of a foreigner. Nehemiah recounts his violent attack on those who are married to foreigners: 'I contended with them and cursed them and beat some of them and pulled out their hair; and I made them take an oath in the name of God saying, "You shall not give your daughters to their sons, or take their daughters for your sons or for yourselves" ' (Neh. 13.25). Nehemiah singles out the son-in-law of Sanballat as having committed a particularly egregious crime in his marriage to a Horonite woman, because he is from the family of the high priest. Nehemiah continues, 'And one of the sons of Jehoiada, son of the high priest Eliashib, was the son-in-law of Sanballat the Horonite; I chased him away from me. Remember them, O my God, because they have defiled the priesthood' (Neh. 13.28–29). Like Sanballat's son-in-law (whom Nehemiah castigates because he is a bridegroom with a foreign bride), Jesus the bridegroom is associated with violence and weddings that should not take place.

1.7 The Deity as Bridegroom or Husband

That God is portrayed as a metaphorical husband to a corporate group begs the question of what sort of husband the son of God might be to the Matthean community (Mt. 4.3, 6; 8.29; 14.33; 26.63; 27.40). Such a comparison is fraught with difficulty: Jesus is never a husband in Matthew. Therefore, Jesus' being a bridegroom to his community is not quite the same as God's metaphoric marriage to Israel. But because Matthew's gospel plays on the themes of marriage, I want to demonstrate how the divine husband's role informs the Matthean bridegroom's.

Isaiah (49.18; 54.5–6; 62.4–5), Jeremiah (2.32–33; 3.1–11, 20; 31.32), Ezekiel (16.8–52), and Hosea (2.1 – 3.5) describe the relationship of the people, the nation, or the city of Jerusalem[56] – as bride (νυμφή, Isa. 49.18;

---

56. For discussion of traditional metaphors for a city as woman, see Julie Galambush, *Jerusalem in the Book of Ezekiel* (SBLDS, 130; Atlanta, GA: Scholars Press, 1992); Elaine R. Follis, 'Daughter of Zion', *ABD* 6, p. 1103; Edith McEwan Humphrey, *The Ladies and the Cities: Transformation and Apocalyptic Identity in Joseph and Aseneth, 4 Ezra, The Apocalypse, and the Shepherd of Hermas* (JSPSup 17; Sheffield: Sheffield Academic Press, 1995), pp. 20–23; Peggy L. Day, 'The Personification of Cities as Female in the Hebrew Bible: The Thesis of Aloysius Fitzgerald, F.S.C.', in Fernando F. Segovia and Mary Ann Tolbert

62.5; Jer. 2.32); virgin (παρθενός, Isa. 62.4; Jer. 2.32); wife (γυναῖκα, Isa. 54.5 or γυνή, Jer. 3.20; Hos. 2.2 [LXX Hos. 2.4]); unfaithful wife (ἀσύνθετος, Jer. 3.11); adulterous wife (μοιχαλίδος, Ezek. 16.38; μοιχεία, Hos. 2.2 [LXX Hos. 2.4]); or like a whore (πόρνη, Jer. 3.1–3, 6; Ezek. 16.35; πορνεία, Ezek. 16.15–22; Hos. 2.2 [LXX Hos. 2.4]; γυναῖκα πορνείας, Hos. 1.2) [57] – to her divine husband.[58] Though the prophets rarely use the term חתן or νυμφίος (as in Isa. 62.5) to describe the deity (instead, they use κύριος, Isa. 49.18; 54.5, or ἀνήρ, Jer. 3.1; Hos. 2.2, 16 [LXX Hos. 2.4, 18]), the marriage metaphor resonates with Matthew's imagery of the bridegroom's relationship to a community of people (though they are not 'bride') and the theme of judgment.

Matthew does not call the deity 'husband' or the feminine-coded Church (ἐκκλησία) 'bride.' He does, however, portray the community as wedding guests: 'sons of the bridal chamber' who celebrate in the bridegroom's presence (9.15) and who are in attendance at the bridegroom's wedding feast (22.1–14; 25.1–13). He also uses marital image reminiscent of Ezek. 16.38 when he calls his generation 'adulterous' (μοιχαλίς, 12.39). First I will treat the marital imagery of an 'adulterous' generation and then the imagery of the Church as wedding guests.

(eds.), *Reading from This Place*. II. *Social Location and Biblical Interpretation in Global Perspective* (Minneapolis: Fortress Press, 1995), pp. 283–302; Barbara R. Rossing, *The Choice Between Two Cities: Whore, Bride, and Empire in the Apocalypse* (HTS, 48; Harrisburg: Trinity Press International, 1999), pp. 1–16; and Tikva Frymer-Kensky, who perceives Zion as an object not only of God's desire, but of male Israel's desire (*In the Wake of the Goddesses: Women, Culture and the Biblical Transformation of Pagan Myth* (New York: Fawcett Columbine, 1992), pp. 173–78.

57. The phrase 'wife of whoredom' in Hebrew does not necessarily mean 'prostitute,' but refers to a variety of sexual misbehavior, including adultery and inappropriate sexual relations with close relatives. Perhaps in Gomer's case, the 'whoredom' referred to cultic prostitution. See Gale Yee, 'Hosea', *NIB* 7, pp. 197–297 (216), and Phyllis Bird, 'To Play the Harlot: An Inquiry into an Old Testament Metaphor', in Peggy L. Day (ed.), *Gender and Difference* (Minneapolis: Fortress Press, 1989), pp. 75–94. William Doorly suggests that Hosea's wife might not be a prostitute, but an Israelite woman like any other. She is called a 'wife of whoredom' only because she is part of a whoring nation. See W.J. Doorly, *Prophet of Love: Understanding the Book of Hosea* (Mahwah, NJ: Paulist Press, 1991), p. 53.

58. Marriage imagery is not the exclusive means of expressing God's relationship to God's people. For example, the prophets also use parental imagery: God as father to a city or nation as mother, daughter, or son. Gary Hall suggests that the prophets borrowed the marriage metaphor from Canaanite Baalism, in which gods and goddesses were described in sexual terms. By adopting the marriage metaphor, the prophets could attack Baalism while transforming the sexual imagery into covenant imagery. Gary Hall, 'Origin of the Marriage Metaphor', *Hebrew Studies* 23 (1982), pp. 169–71 (169–70). See also Irene Kerasote Rallis, 'Nuptial Imagery in the Book of Hosea: Israel as the Bride of Yahweh', *St. Vladimir's Theological Quarterly* 34 (1990), pp. 197–219 (esp. pp. 198–200, 205, 207).

Matthew does not clarify if the adulterous generation is 'married' to God or to Jesus the bridegroom. If the adulterous generation is Israel (represented here by a group of religious leaders who ask Jesus for a sign [12.24–42]), the metaphor of being married to *God* fits the prophetic model, and Jesus then calls this generation 'adulterous' on behalf of God, the husband, not on behalf of himself as bridegroom. Jesus compares the generation (unfavorably) to Gentiles who were able to see and interpret signs (the people of Ninevah and the Queen of the South [12.41–42]), and thereby showed their righteousness. Like the Gentile women in the genealogy, these Gentiles have formed an irregular but legitimate bond with the God of Israel by their higher righteousness in listening to the word of God (through Jonah and through Solomon). The scribes and Pharisees, on the other hand, who were capable of a 'regular' union with God, are not listening to God's word through Jesus, so they are illegitimate and 'adulterous.' The 'household' is disrupted in favor of a voluntary community of faith, and marriage is portrayed negatively rather than positively.

That πορνεία – which includes but is not restricted to adultery – is grounds for divorce[59] in Mt. 5.32 and 19.9 suggests that the husband (or bridegroom) who accuses his bride of adultery is justified in divorcing her.[60] But Matthews does not say that God as husband (or Jesus as bridegroom) will divorce this 'adulterous generation.' Instead, he replaces the generation with a new fictive family made up of those who do the will of the Father in heaven (12.46–50). Yet Matthew sets up allegories in which some members of this new family will be found unfaithful (metaphorically guilty of πορνεία) (cf. Ezek. 16.15–22; Hos. 2.1–2) and will be violently expelled (e.g., the guest bound hand and foot and thrown into the outer darkness [Mt. 22.13]). The Matthean wedding parables (when interpreted allegorically) describe the host of the wedding feast (the 'king' in 22.1–14 and the 'bridegroom' in 25.1–13) meting out such judgment to unworthy members, who are cast in the role not of bride, but wedding guests.

Matthew's rhetoric about family is the same as the prophets': Hosea and Ezekiel's rhetoric about a wife's sexual misconduct, a mother's apparent abandonment of her children, and the punishments by a male God of a female people, cross over disturbingly into images of domestic

---

59. The meaning of πορνεία in the context of divorce is a topic for Ch. 5.

60. See Mary Rose D'Angelo, 'Remarriage and the Divorce Sayings Attributed to Jesus', in W. Roberts (ed.), *Divorce and Remarriage* (Kansas City: Sheed and Ward, 1990), pp. 78–106 (96–99) and Dale C. Allison, 'Divorce, Celibacy and Joseph (Matthew 1.18–25 and 19.1–12)', *JSNT* 49 (2003), pp. 3–10.

violence.[61] Male domination in Matthew also borders on domestic violence in scenes that take place in households: a man in power (allegorically interpreted as the deity) has a guest bound hand and foot and cast out (22.13), a servant expelled into the outer darkness (25.30), and a servant cut to pieces (24.51). The Matthean bridegroom shuts the door on the five foolish virgins and so severs his relationship with them (25.10–12).

However, when Matthew actually narrates a suspected case of πορνεία, the husband's actions are quite different. True to expectation, when Joseph discovers that his bride-to-be is pregnant, he assumes she is guilty of πορνεία and decides to divorce her (Mt. 1.18–19; cf. 5.32 and 19.9). Contrary to prophetic depiction of violent public exposure of an accused wife (she is given to a mob to be stripped and left naked, stoned and cut into pieces [Ezek. 16.38–42; cf. Hos. 2.3]), Joseph, a righteous man (δίκαιος, 1.19), resolves to dismiss Mary quietly and secretly, away from the public eye (λάθρᾳ ἀπολῦσαι), and without violent retribution. Further, Joseph learns that she is not guilty of πορνεία when he receives divine instruction *not* to divorce her (Mt. 1.18–24). Joseph, then, models a very different approach to marriage and divorce than does the divine husband (as portrayed by the prophets); like the women in the Matthean genealogy, Joseph makes an irregular union (with a woman pregnant with someone else's child), eschews divorce (going against the dictates of righteousness), and in so doing, demonstrates an even higher righteousness.

1.8 *The Bridegroom in Pauline Thought*

Paul does not call Jesus a 'bridegroom' but still imagines the Church's relationship to Christ as a metaphorical marriage. He uses marital language to express how he wants to 'present' (παρίστημι) the Church as a 'holy virgin to Christ' (παρθένον ἀγνὴν τῷ Χριστῷ) and that he has promised (ἡρμοσάμην)[62] the nascent Christian community to 'one

---

61. Naomi Graetz says Hosea's text 'details very explicitly a case of domestic abuse.' See her 'The Metaphoric Battering of Hosea's Wife', in Athalya Brenner (ed.), *A Feminist Companion to the Latter Prophets* (Sheffield: Sheffield Academic Press, 1995), pp. 126–45 (here p. 131). As Yee says, 'Hosea 2 pushes the marriage metaphor to dangerous limits, wherein Yahweh's legitimate punishment of Israel for breach of covenant is figuratively described as threats of physical violence against the wife' (Yee, 'Hosea', p. 224). See also Yee's discussion in 'Gomer', in Carol Meyers, Toni Craven, and Ross S. Kraemer (eds.), *Women in Scripture* (Grand Rapids: Eerdmans, 2000), pp. 84–86.

62. From ἁρμόζομαι, to promise or give in marriage.

husband' (ἑνὶ ἀνδρὶ) (2 Cor. 11.2).[63] If Matthew is read through Paul, the undesignated bride to the Matthean bridegroom is the Church. But Matthew deliberately leaves out the bride in all the bridegroom and wedding texts (9.15; 22.1–14; 25.1–13) and instead portrays community members as wedding guests or family members. Jesus remains the bridegroom, but the community's role is not bride; in fact, Matthew will build a picture of a community with no brides and no new marriages.[64] Matthew – with the invitation to become 'eunuchs' and like children (Mt. 18.3; 19.10–15), coupled with the statement that there is no marriage in the resurrection (22.30) – displays similarities to Paul, with his advice against marriage (if one could avoid sexual relations outside marriage), because virgins and celibates could better devote themselves to the Lord (1 Cor. 7.1–9; 29–31).

1.9 The Bridegroom in Revelation

The metaphor of the bridegroom ushering in a new heaven and earth is permeated with violence.[65] Like Matthew, John the Seer draws heavily on the prophets' wedding imagery (Ezek. 16.53, 62–63; 40.1- 48.35; Isa. 4.2–6; 6.1–3; 28.16; 33.20; 44.28; 54.11–12; 58.12; 65.17–25; Jer. 30.18–22; 31. 38–40; 33.10–13).[66] John portrays the 'New Jerusalem,' the idealized heavenly city, as the Bride[67] adorned for her bridegroom, the Lamb (19.7;

---

63. J. Paul Sampley, The Second Letter to the Corinthians NIB, II; (Nashville: Abingdon Press, 2000), pp. 1–180 (147–48). Later tradition would make similar claims that the Church is betrothed to Jesus the bridegroom (Odes of Solomon 3, 42; Tertullian, De Monog. V, De Fuga XIV; Origen, Commentary on St. Matthew, Bk. 14; Gregory of Nyssa, and Augustine; cf. Eph. 5.24–25); cf. also Shepherd of Hermas, Vision 3; 2 Clement 15; The Epitaph of Abercius. See Claude Chavasse, The Bride of Christ (London: Faber and Faber, 1940), pp. 196–97.

64. The absent bride and Matthew's portrayal of marriage and divorce are discussed in Chapter 5.

65. See Stephen D. Moore, 'Revolting Revelations', in Moore, God's Beauty Parlor and Other Queer Spaces in and around the Bible (Stanford: Stanford University Press, 2001), pp. 173–99, and in Ingrid Rosa Kitzberger (ed.), The Personal Voice in Biblical Interpretation (New York: Routledge, 1999), pp. 183–99; Tina Pippin, Apocalyptic Bodies: The Biblical End of the World in Text and Image (New York: Routledge, 1999), and T. Pippin, Death and Desire: The Rhetoric of Gender in the Apocalypse of John (Louisville: Westminster/John Knox Press, 1992); Greg Carey, 'Women, Men, and the Book of Revelation: Ethics and Exegesis', in Amy-Jill Levine (ed.), A Feminist Companion to Early Christian Apocalyptic Literature (London: Continuum/T&T Clark, forthcoming); Adela Yarbro Collins, 'Feminine Symbolism in the Book of Revelation', BibInt 1 (1993), pp. 20–33.

66. Lee Pilchan, The New Jerusalem in the Book of Revelation (WUNT; Reihe 2, 129; Tübingen: Mohr Siebeck, 2001) details Old Testament themes behind Revelation's New Jerusalem.

67. Pippin, Death and Desire, pp. 56–62, 72–86, 99.

21.2, 9–27; 22.1–5, 14, 17)[68] and contrasts her to Babylon, 'the great whore' (ἡ πόρνη μεγάλη, 17.1).

Sandwiched between the announcement of the triumphant wedding banquet and the arrival of the beautifully adorned Bride is a course of extreme and graphic violence: 'the wedding invitation merges with the vultures' feast.'[69] While the smoke of the burning city goes up forever (18.8–10, 15, 18, 21; 19.3), celebratory feasting begins with the consumption of enemies (19.17–21).[70] The Matthean Parable of the Wedding Feast contains the strikingly similar image of a burning city followed by a feast; the violence continues during the feast as a guest is forcibly expelled (Mt. 22.1–14).

The Lamb is a bridegroom who serves as military commander and instigator of atrocities. He is capable of extreme violence: just as the Lamb strikes the nations with his sword and rod of iron[71] (Rev. 19.15), the Matthean bridegroom says, 'I have come not to bring peace but a sword' (Mt. 10.34b). As the Lamb tortures his enemies without mercy (Rev. 14.10–11) and throws the beast and false prophet alive into the lake of fire (Rev. 19.20), so the Matthean bridegroom in his role as heavenly judge sends the accursed to eternal fire and punishment (Mt. 25.41, 46).

1.10 *Violence as a Literary Trope in Greco-Roman Contexts*

Greek literature from the fifth century BCE to second century CE contains numerous examples of death and violence associated with weddings. The frequent combination of marriage, death, and violence in fifth-century BCE tragedies becomes formulaic. The violent deaths of Iphigenia and Kassandra are portrayed as wedding rituals in Aeschylus' *Agamemnon*.[72]

---

68. See Humphrey, *Ladies and the Cities*, pp. 21–23, 115, 168–74.

69. Catherine Keller, *Apocalypse Now and Then: A Feminist Guide to the End of the World* (Boston: Beacon Press, 1996), p. 76. Keller notes the irony that in the gospels, Jesus ate *with* the whores, but in Revelation, the whore is dined *upon* (p. 76).

70. Pippin, *Death and Desire*, pp. 67–68. See Keller's treatment of the wedding feast as cannibalism of the Whore in *Apocalypse Now and Then*, pp. 76–77.

71. The Lamb's victory has as much to do with humiliating and emasculating the 'enemy' as it does with military strength. See Stephen Moore, 'Revolting Revelations', p. 188. When Matthew is read through Revelation, those who have become eunuchs for the Kingdom of Heaven (Mt. 19.10–12) are already (figuratively) emasculated. Even though the Matthean eunuchs' emasculation is metaphorical and by choice, reading through Revelation shows how this submission to a higher power (male-dominated Kingdom of Heaven) is a humiliation for men and informs the attitude with which they become like children (Mt. 18.3–4; cf. 19.13–14).

72. Especially lines 406–408, 686–749, 1107–116 (see Rush Rehm, *Marriage to Death: The Conflation of Wedding and Funeral Rituals and Greek Tragedy* (Princeton: Princeton University Press, 1994), pp. 43–58).

Antigone compares her wedding to a funeral in Sophocles' *Antigone*.[73] In Sophocles' *Trachiniae*, Deineira compares marriage to death and stabs herself in her bridal chamber.[74] Weddings resemble funeral rites in Euripides' *Alcestis* and *Medea*.[75] The juxtaposition of death and a wedding celebration was common, so that a bride or bridegroom could be associated with separation and sorrow as much as with gathering and joy. Wedding and funeral processions had many similarities that included torches,[76] food, ritual bathing, anointing, and carrying the person by cart from one place to another.[77] Funerary art from the fifth century BCE shows the god Hermes leading young women to the underworld by grasping their wrists, the same pose found in wedding illustrations.[78] An unmarried virgin was sometimes buried in wedding clothes, and the λουτροφόρος, the jar containing water for the nuptial bath, was placed at her grave.[79]

Marriage and death co-exist in the goddess-bride Kore/Persephone's marriage to Hades commemorated in the Eleusian mysteries and Roman *Thesmophoria*, celebrations contemporary with the early Church.[80] These festivals celebrated the changing seasons and the cycle of life and death associated with the goddess Ceres/Demeter. The abduction of Kore/Persephone inextricably links the themes of marriage, violence, and death, themes that recur in Matthew, as the bridegroom warns that the day will come when he will be taken away, die, and rise again.

The trope of the endangered bridegroom is common in ancient

---

73. Especially lines 519–25, 627–54, 760–61, 804–943, 1068–71, 1222–25 (see Rehm, *Marriage to Death*, pp. 59–71).

74. Especially lines 4–5, 913–42 (see Rehm, *Marriage and Death*, pp. 72–83).

75. Especially lines 159–95, 244–72, 851–957, 1049–118 (see Rehm, *Marriage and Death*, pp. 84–109).

76. In the context of a funeral or wedding, light is a symbol of birth (Plutarch, *Rom. Ques.* 2) and rebirth (Jn. 3.19–21; 8.12), and torchlight is associated not only with weddings, but with funeral rites (Zeus Chthonios, Hades). Oepke, 'λάμπω', *TDNT* 4, pp. 18–19. Oepke catalogs many more examples from mystery religions.

77. Donna C. Kurtz and John Boardman, *Greek Burial Customs* (Ithaca: Cornell University Press, 1971), pp. 154–55, plates 37 and 38. Rush Rehm details the similarities of wedding and burial customs in *Marriage to Death*; Larry K. Bennett and William Blake Tyrrell, 'What is Antigone Wearing?', *Classical World* 85 (1991), pp. 107–109.

78. Rehm, *Marriage to Death*, p. 37, figure 10, and p. 38, figure 11.

79. Bennett and Blake, 'What Is Antigone Wearing?', p. 108.

80. Cicero, *Balb.* 55; *Leg.* 2.21, 34–37; *Verr.* 2.4.99–102; see also Apollodorus, *Library*, I.4.5–I.5.1–3. Barbette Stanley Spaeth discusses the evolution of Ceres and Demeter in Roman cult practices (*The Roman Goddess Ceres* [Austin, TX: University of Texas Press, 1996], esp. pp. 21–23). The Greek counterpart is discussed by Allaire C. Brumfield, *The Attic Festivals of Demeter and Their Relation to the Agricultural Year* (Monographs in Classical Studies; Salem, NH: The Ayer Company, 1981), pp. 70–79.

biographies, historical accounts, and novels,[81] which lends support to my thesis that the bridegroom is as closely associated with violence as with joy. That the Matthean bridegroom dies before his wedding feast, although he is expected to return to celebrate it (Mt. 25.1–13), places him in good company with other tragic bridegrooms. For example, Xenophon (fifth to fourth centuries BCE) describes a bridegroom killed by a potential bride's father: καγὼ μὲν ὁ τάλας νεκρὸν ἀντὶ νυμφίου ἐκομισάμην (the young man's father laments, 'And I, a wretch, carried home a corpse instead of a bridegroom').[82] Achilles Tatius (second century CE) records a lament for the death of the bridegroom before his marriage.[83] A young man barely escapes being murdered and consumed by a bride who turned out to be a shape-shifting goblin (ἡ χρηστὴ νύμφη μία τῶν ἐμπουσῶν ἐστιν) in Flavius Philostratus' *Life of Apollonius* (second century CE).[84] Philostratus describes a hero who 'died unarmed and wreathed with a crown just like bridegrooms' (γυμνὸν ἀποθανεῖν ἐστεφανωμένον ὥσπερ οἱ νυμφίοι).[85] In some accounts the entire wedding party is disrupted by violence and death. Lucian (second century CE) presents a tale of a bridegroom's wedding feast turned to bitterness (πικρός) and he into a wretch (ἄθλιος) when violence breaks out during the festivities. The unlucky bridegroom and his guests are badly injured, and the bridegroom himself has to go home to recover rather than enjoy his wedding (*Carousal*, 47).[86] 1 Maccabees and Josephus record a horrific account of violence in which avenging brothers slaughter the entire wedding party of their enemy (1 Macc. 9.37–41; Josephus, *Ant.* 13.18–21). Josephus says that there were 400 people in the wedding party and all were slain.[87] Given

---

81. Adeline Fehribach, among others, demonstrates how ancient novels are a context for studying characterization in the New Testament in *The Women in the Life of the Bridegroom* (Collegeville, MN: Liturgical Press, 1998), pp. 9–20, and in 'The Birthing Bridegroom: The Portrayal of Jesus in the Fourth Gospel', in A.-J. Levine (ed.), *A Feminist Companion to John* (2 vols.; Sheffield: Sheffield Academic Press, 2003), II, pp.104–29.

82. Xenophon, *Cyropaedia* 4.6.5.

83. Achilles Tatius, *Clitophon and Leucippe*, 1.13.5–6.

84. Flavius Philostratus, *Life of Apollonius* 4.25.

85. Translated by J.K.B. Maclean and E.B. Aitkin, *Flavius Philostratus: Heroikos* (Atlanta: Society of Biblical Literature, 1977), pp. 140–43.

86. Lucian tells the tale as an amusing anecdote.

87. Brides suffer violence and death with some frequency, as well. Pausanias (1 BCE) records a description of a virgin who was seized and shamefully disfigured (ᾔσχυνεν) while being taken to her bridegroom (Pausanias, *Laconia* 6.7), in W.H.S. Jones and H.A. Ormerod (trans.), *Pausanias: Description of Greece* (4 vols.; LCL, 93; Cambridge, MA: Harvard University Press, 1992), II, pp. 348–49. Ἀισκυνω means to mar, disfigure, or make ugly, with a sense of shame (Liddell and Scott, *Greek–English Lexicon*, p. 24). Ross S. Kraemer ('Jewish Mothers and Daughters in the Greco-Roman World', in Shaye J.D. Cohen [ed.], *The Jewish Family in Antiquity* [BJD, 289; Atlanta: Scholars Press, 1993], pp. 89–112 [93]) describes an account of a mother's lament over her daughter's bridal preparations turned to funeral rites as Sheol becomes the young woman's wedding chamber. Philostratus describes how a

these literary examples, the bridegroom's violent death, or the appearance of violent death, is almost an expectation; therefore, the Matthean bridegroom can predict that he will be 'taken away' and that his disciples and will mourn and fast (9.15).

1.11 Violence as a Cultural Foundation for Marriage

Not only were violence and death fixtures in literary weddings, the very institution of Roman marriage was defined by an act of violence recounted in the often cited story of the rape of the Sabine women (Cicero, *Republic*, 2.12–14; Dionysius of Halicarnasis, *Antiquitates Romanae* 2.30–47; Livy, *History*, 1.9–1.13.8; Ovid, *Fasti* 3.167–258; Plutarch, *Roman Questions* 29, 31, 85, 105).[88] Gary Miles describes how first-century Roman historians Livy, Plutarch, and Cicero treated the rape of the Sabine women 'as a cornerstone of Roman society' and associated the event 'explicitly with the origins, and thus with the essence, of Roman marriage.'[89]

The first-century historian Livy (*History of Rome*, 1.9.1–16) recounts the tale of the rape of the Sabine women apologetically: he blames the fathers of the Sabine women for being selfish in refusing intermarriage (*conubium*) between the Romans and their people. Therefore, Roman men were obliged to resort to treachery. They arranged a festival, invited the

---

family's joy is cast into sorrow when a bride dies 'at the hour of the wedding' (ἐν ὥρᾳ γάμου), and her grieving bridegroom (νυμφίος) follows her funeral bier. Joy returns when Appolonius restores the bride to life (Philostratus, *Life of Apollonius*, 4.45) in Coneybeare, *The Life of Apollonius*, pp. 456–58. Plutarch (first to second centuries CE) writes a moral tale about a young virgin betrothed to Callisthenes who dies when Callisthenes and another jealous suitor try to pull her away from each other; when they see what they have done, the men kill themselves in anguish (Plutarch, *Moralia*, 772C; Harold N. Fowler [trans.], *Plutarch's Moralia* [LCL; Cambridge, MA: Harvard University Press, 1991]). In an ancient romantic novel by Achilles Tatius (third century CE), the couple's hopes for a happy wedding turn to grief as a prison replaces the bridal chamber, ropes become her necklaces and bracelets, and a funeral dirge replaces the wedding hymn (Achilles Tatius, *Clitophon and Leucippe*, 3.10.5; cf. 5.11.3). An undated epigram on a tomb describes how a bride named Baucis died before her wedding, and how the mourners 'lighted her funeral pyre with the torches they carried [for the wedding] while they sang to Hymenaeus, the marriage god: "And you, Hymenaeus, transformed the wedding dances into cries of lamentation"' (translated by M.R. Lefkowitz and M.B. Fant, *Women's Life in Greece and Rome: A Sourcebook in Translation* [Baltimore: John Hopkins University Press, 2nd edn, 1992], p. 6).

88. Plutarch (*Rom.* 271) alludes to 'the first wives [who were] carried away by force' (τὰς πρώτας γυναῖκας ἁρπάσαντες).

89. Gary B. Miles, 'The First Roman Marriage and the Theft of the Sabine Women', in Miles, *Livy: Constructing Early Rome* (Ithaca: Cornell University Press, 1995), pp. 179–219 (180). Miles repeats text from an earlier article by the same title in Ralph Hexter and Daniel Selden (eds.), *Innovations of Antiquity* (New York: Routledge, 1992), pp. 161–96.

Sabine people to come as families, and at a designated moment, stole numbers of young Sabine women for wives. Romulus, founder of Rome, consoled the abducted women by announcing what they would gain from these forced marriages: Roman citizenship and children. Therefore, they should 'give their hearts to the men who had already taken their bodies.' For their part, the Roman husbands would strive to make up for their wives' loss of parents and country.

Granting that the abduction of the Sabine women is an etiology that dramatizes the 'elements of a typical Roman marriage,' such as the potential rivalry between the bridegroom's and bride's families, the bride's trauma of separation from her family, the bridegroom's *machismo*, and the bride's eventual successful incorporation into the groom's family,[90] the story offers a striking insight into Roman understanding of marriage as right of domination, even as it exhorts the conquering husband to show regard for his wife's feelings (cf. Eph. 5.21–33). The story conveys the Romans' social, political, and economic reasons for marriage but also betrays the Roman attitude that they could take brides from other people simply because they were strong enough to do so.[91] Livy recounts how the Roman abductors won over their new wives by saying they were motivated by desire and love.[92]

Etiological and political interpretations aside, the story remains at its most basic a violent tale that reveals the Roman belief, whether merely symbolic or not, that the abduction, rape, and forced marriage of the Sabine women were appropriate means of creating families, society, and (counter-intuitive as it may seem) establishing alliances with neighbors.[93] The violent elements of the founding story were reinforced in Roman wedding celebrations: the parting of the bride's hair with a spear point is a reminder that the first Roman marriages were contracted through violence and war (Plutarch, *Rom. Ques.*, 87).[94] The cry '*Talasio!*' customarily raised in Roman weddings recalls the abduction: the servants of Talasius led a kidnapped Sabine woman of great beauty through the crowds to become his bride, and her abductors cried out 'for Talasius!' ('*Talasio!*') so that no one would try to take her for someone else (Plutarch, *Rom. Ques.*

90. Miles, 'First Roman Marriage', pp. 188–89, 192–93.

91. Miles, 'First Roman Marriage', pp. 179–86.

92. Translation by Aubrey de Selincourt in *Livy: The Early History of Rome* (New York: Penguin Books, 1982), p. 44.

93. Miles, 'First Roman Marriage', pp. 184–85.

94. H.J. Rose (trans.), *The Roman Questions of Plutarch* (Oxford: Clarendon Press, 1924), pp. 157–58. The Roman calendar included a celebration of *Consualia* (festival of Consus) on August 21 that commemorated the rape of the Sabine women.

31).[95] Wedding attendants or the bridegroom lifted the bride over the threshold of the bridegroom's house to re-enact the way in which the first Roman wives were brought into the house against their will (Plutarch, *Rom. Ques.* 29).

Matthew turns this paradigm over: the bridegroom, not the bride, is the one who is taken away (9.15; 26.50). The 'sons of the bridal chamber' who gather around the bridegroom do not bring him a bride and shout a cry of good luck, because he has no bride. Association with Jesus the bridegroom is voluntary (women eligible to be brides are not dragged into the house but are lined up at the bridegroom's door [25.1–13]) but difficult to maintain: his followers will be persecuted (10.16–23) and risk losing their families, homes, and perhaps even their lives (10.34–39; 19. 27–29). Moreover, none of these people associated with the bridegroom's wedding feast actually gets married: there is no wedding. The presence of the bridegroom creates a fictive family with no expectation of biological generation, and instead of forging alliances with neighbors, the wedding feast separates people into opposing groups: those who celebrate with the bridegroom and those who do not.

The tale of marriage by abduction exists across centuries and cultures to provide a context for the Matthean bridegroom and his association with violence, both as perpetrator and victim. The same story occurs in Judges 21.1–24, here as a direct consequence of the concubine's rape and murder in Judges 19. Violence breeds more violence: because of the violent death of the concubine in Benjaminite territory, the other Israelite tribes vowed not to marry their daughters to Benjaminites (Judg. 21.1, 7, 18). They did, however, slaughter the people of Jabesh-Gilead except for the young virgins, whom they abducted as brides for the Benjaminites (21.6–14). When there were still not enough brides, the Benjaminites went secretly to a festival at Shiloh, hid in the vineyards, and snatched brides from among the young women who came to dance (21.19–23). This tale of violence, abduction, and forced marriage does not serve as a foundational myth for the institution of marriage in Israelite culture, as it does in Roman culture: the Benjaminite abduction story ends with the refrain: 'In those days there was no king in Israel; all the people did what was right in their own eyes'

---

95. Rose (trans.), *Plutarch's Roman Questions*, p. 133. Plutarch explains that the marriage turned out to be a happy one, so that the cry '*Talasio!*' in subsequent weddings connoted good luck. Plutarch suggests that the cry may also derive from the Greek ταλασία (spinning) and Latin *talasus* (wool-basket) and is shouted when the bride brings in her spindle and distaff to her new home and wreaths the bridegroom's doorway with wool. Gary Miles explains that 'the cry "Thalassio/Talasio" at Roman marriage ceremonies perpetuates a view in which every Roman bride is a prize chosen for her beauty; every groom a distinguished young man whose good standing in the community is a shield of protection for his bride and promises a happy marriage' (G.B. Miles, *Livy: Reconstructing Early Rome* (Ithaca: Cornell University Press, 1995), pp. 188–89).

(21.25). In contrast, Matthew portrays Jesus as the 'son of David' (Mt. 1.1; 20.30; 21.15) and 'King of the Jews' (Mt. 2.2; 27.37) and exhorts his community to what is right in this particular king's eyes. Thus, the precedent that the Matthean Jesus sets for marriage is brideless bridegrooms, bridegrooms who become like brides, and virgins who come to the feast but do not themselves wed.

1.12 *Conclusion*

When the Matthean bridegroom is read in the context of Old Testament bridegrooms (חתנים, νυμφίοι, γάμβροι) a pattern becomes evident: as Old Testament bridegrooms are associated with violence as victims or as perpetrators, so Jesus the bridegroom is victim of violence and associated with the deity's perpetration of violence. As Old Testament bridegrooms lose or abandon their brides, Jesus the bridegroom has no bride. In the examples of Old Testament bridegrooms, marriage is not a secure institution, and reproductive roles are disrupted; this insecurity and disruption prefigure the way Matthew, while not overtly condemning marriage and reproduction, undermines the efficacy of weddings and production of children.

Violence associated with marriage is a common theme in ancient literature that prefigures violence associated with the Matthean bridegroom, especially in the two wedding parables. The Roman institution of marriage was founded on the rape and abduction of the Sabine women; the deity's role as retributive husband to Israel is tainted with domestic violence; and the bridegroom in Revelation captains bloody destruction. Nuptial and marital imagery in ancient literature reveals how death and separation of the couple is so common that it becomes a literary trope: Greek playwrights associated marriage with death; bridegrooms and brides frequently die before their weddings. Reading the Matthean bridegroom in the context of this trope suggests the bridegroom is something of a stock character who is *expected* to be brideless, and whose presence means joy turned to sorrow, destruction and death. Perhaps readers have resisted this connection because today our view of 'bridegrooms' and 'weddings' is one of joy and happiness. At weddings, we don't want to think of disruption and death, even while we retain some of the customs linking our ceremonies to ancient ones (breaking a glass at Jewish weddings; carrying the bride over the threshold; having a best man 'in case' something happens to the groom).

This survey of bridegroom material shows that the connections between the Matthean Jesus and the Old Testament go much deeper than fulfillment citations and allusions to Moses: they also extend to the use of bridegroom, nuptial, and marital imagery and therefore inform Matthean teachings on the efficacy of marriage and family.

When seen in the context of both Old Testament and Greek/Roman texts, the absence of the bride in Matthew becomes even starker. We first notice the absence of the bridegroom's bride (Jesus himself is not married; the metaphoric bridegroom has no bride), and then the absence of the use of bridal imagery for the covenant community. The closest Matthew comes to marital imagery for the community is when he says that 'this generation' is adulterous; there is no sense that the 'Church' is a 'bride' in Matthew. Indeed, Matthew resists comparing the Church to a bride in order to retain his negative view of weddings. Through a study of the bridegroom language, Matthew is establishing what becomes increasingly apparent in the gospel: marriages as normally construed have decreased value in the community; the means of creating family is not through marriage (for indeed 'marriage' leads only to destruction, death, separation, and adultery).

Finally, the connection of the deity in the role of bridegroom/husband to violence leads to my feminist suspicion that resistance to the Matthean wedding images and bridegroom metaphors is in order. The next two chapters demonstrate how, as the bridegroom approaches the passion and the time of the wedding feast draws closer, violence in Matthew escalates.

INTRODUCTION TO THE WEDDING PARABLES

In the wedding parables, the role of the wedding guests in relation to the bridegroom is ambiguous: the guests are expected to rejoice because the bridegroom's presence signals a period of joy, when mourning and fasting are inappropriate (9.15), but they will be expected to fast when he is taken away (9.15). The guests simultaneously participate in and anticipate the fulfillment of the Kingdom of Heaven at an undisclosed time (Mt. 22.1–14; 25.1–13). Thus the wedding parables depict how the bridegroom and the community remain in a state of liminality between the conventions of this world and the ideals of the next,[1] between the bridegroom's presence and the time he is taken away (9.15) The bridegroom is both present and absent; he is always with them (28.20) but also absent and imminently arriving (25.5). The community of wedding guests inhabits a liminal space between the promise and fulfillment of the kingdom. They never actually see the wedding take place, and they never return home and revert to non-guest status. The wedding parables express the liminal ambiguity of the bridegroom's relationship to the wedding feast and wedding guests.

The bridegroom is a liminal figure. He is in a transitional role as opposed to the permanent role of husband,[2] promised in marriage, but not yet married. Jesus remains bridegroom and never becomes husband, just as the Matthean community remains perpetually guests at a wedding that never takes place.

---

1. Recent treatments of the Matthean community as a counter-cultural or 'liminal' group include Warren Carter, *Matthew and the Margins: A Sociopolitical and Religious Reading* (Maryknoll, NY: Orbis, 2000), esp. pp. 1–49; Carter, *Households and Discipleship: A Study of Matthew 19–20* (Sheffield: JSOT Press, 1994), esp. pp. 46–55; Carolyn Osiek and David Balch, *Families in the New Testament: Households and House Churches* (Louisville: Westminster John Knox Press, 1997), esp. pp. 130–35; Stephen C. Barton, *Discipleship and Family Ties in Mark and Matthew* (New York: Cambridge University Press, 1994), pp. 125–219; J. Andrew Overman, *Matthew's Gospel and Formative Judaism: The Social World of the Matthean Community* (Minneapolis: Fortress Press, 1990), esp. pp. 106–113.

2. Amy-Jill Levine, 'Matthew,' in Carol A. Newsom and Sharon H. Ringe (eds.), *The Women's Bible Commentary* (Louisville: Westminster/John Knox Press, 1992), p. 256.

> The attributes of liminality or of liminal *personae* ('threshold people')
> are necessarily ambiguous, since this condition and these persons elude
> or slip through the network of classifications that normally locate states
> and positions in cultural space. Liminal entities are neither here nor
> there; they are betwixt and between the positions assigned and arrayed
> by law, custom, convention, and ceremonial. [3]

The Matthean community is in a '*permanently* liminal' state, that is, the
transition between the 'already' and 'not yet' has become a permanent
condition.[4] The Matthean community displays a quality that Turner calls
'*communitas*,' that is, the community exists in liminality, marginality, and
in a state of holiness, 'because it transgresses or dissolves the norms that
govern structured and institutionalized relationships.'[5] For example,
Matthew exhorts his community to display properties of liminality
common to millenarian movements, such as giving up status ('the first
shall be last and the last first' [19.30; 20.16]), wealth and property (19.27–
29), and family ties (10.21, 35–37; 12.46–50; 19.29), and by practicing
sexual continence (19.10–12), enduring suffering (10.38–39; 16.24–26),
and showing humility (18.2–5; 20.25–28).[6] The community has constructed a reality in which they are in 'radical social transition ... whether
the *terminus ad quem* is believed to be on earth or in heaven.'[7]

The wedding parables[8] illustrate the precarious state of perpetual

---

3. Victor Turner, *The Ritual Process* (Chicago: Aldine Press, 1969), p. 95. See also his
Dramas, Fields, and Metaphors: Symbolic Action in Human Society (Ithaca: Cornell
University Press, 1971), esp. pp. 231–71. Turner credits Arnold van Gennep with coining
the term 'liminality' in regard to transitional or marginal communities (p. 94). See Arnold
Van Gennep, *The Rites of Passage* (Chicago: University of Chicago Press, 1960), esp. pp.
116–45.

4. Turner, *Ritual Process*, p. 107.

5. Turner, *Ritual Process*, pp. 128–29. While the Matthean Church does display
institutional features, it still regards itself to be outside the dominant social structures.

6. See Turner, *Ritual Process*, pp. 106–107, 111–12.

7. Turner, *Ritual Process*, p. 133. In keeping with its permanent liminality, the Matthean
community displays what Turner calls 'normative' or lasting *communitas*, as opposed to the
more fleeting 'spontaneous' *communitas* (*Ritual Process*, p. 132).

8. Parables are a subgenre of metaphor, closely linked to allegory as 'extended
metaphors' (R. Lanham, *Handlist*, p. 4, 107). Παραβολή , a 'type' or 'figure' serving as 'a
model pointing beyond itself for later realization' (BDAG, p. 759), literally means 'to cast
beside' or 'to set beside,' as one sets two things side by side for comparison; the underlying
Hebrew is *mashal* (משל), 'to represent, to be like' (*BDB*, p. 605). C.H. Dodd classified
parables as 'similes or metaphors' (*The Parables of the Kingdom* [New York: Scribner's Sons,
rev. edn, 1961], p. 16); Amos Wilder and Robert Funk treat parables specifically as
metaphors (Amos Wilder, *The Language of the Gospel* [New York: Harper & Row, rev. edn,
1971] and R.W. Funk, *Language, Hermeneutic, and Word of God* [New York: Harper & Row,
1966], esp. pp. 137–38, 151–52). In Funk's view, because a parable does not merely compare
two things but represents a new reality in which listeners participate, a parable functions as
metaphor. Funk's understanding of parable as metaphor was answered by John Dominic

liminal tension between the 'already' and 'not yet,' because weddings themselves are transitional events: between the status of single and married, and between being part of one family and now part of another family. The bridegroom's anticipated wedding feast becomes a point of crossing from one status (being part of the world outside the wedding feast) to another (membership in the community that will enjoy the wedding feast). As those gathered around the bridegroom celebrate in his presence (9.15), they also anticipate the eventual boundary that will determine who is worthy to remain in the celebration.[9]

Choosing How to Read the Parables

The wedding parables are based on dualities such as 'in–out,' 'wise–foolish,' 'good–bad.'[10] Given these polarized choices, the audience has no middle ground and must choose one or the other. Readers face doubt when confronted with criteria for entry into the feast – such as not having enough oil or the right garment – and must ask themselves if they are prepared. Readers must evaluate their allegiances and the consequences of

---

Crossan (*In Parables: The Challenge of the Historical Jesus* [New York Harper & Row, 1973], esp. pp. 10–22; Crossan, *Cliffs of Fall: Paradox and Polyvalence in the Parables of Jesus* [New York: Seabury, 1980]); see also John R. Donahue, *The Gospel in Parable: Metaphor, Narrative, and Theology in the Synoptic Gospels* (Minneapolis: Fortress Press, 1988), pp. 4–13; Dieter Reinstorf and Andries van Aarde, 'Jesus' Kingdom Parables as Metaphorical Stories: A Challenge to a Conventional Worldview', *Hervormde Teologiese Studies* 54 (1998), pp. 603–22; Hans Weder, 'Verstehen durch Metaphern: Überlegungen zur Erkenntnistheorie und Methodik bildhafter religiöser Sprache im Anschluss an Adolf Jülicher', in Ulrich Mell (ed.), *Die Gleichnisreden Jesu 1899–1999: Beiträge zum Dialog mit Adolf Jülicher* (Berlin: Walter de Gruyter, 1999), pp. 97–112; Robert H. Stein, 'The Genre of Parables', in R.N. Longenecker (ed.), *The Challenge of Jesus' Parables* (Grand Rapids: Eerdmans, 2000), pp. 30–50; David Buttrick, *Speaking Parables: A Homiletic Guide* (Louisville: Westminster, 2000), pp. 18–19, 53–55; Kathleen Nash, 'The Language of Motherhood in the *Gospel of Thomas*: Keeping Momma Out of the Kingdom (*Gos. Thom.* 22)', in Mary Ann Beavis (ed.), *The Lost Coin: Parables of Women, Work, and Wisdom* (Sheffield: Sheffield Academic Press, 2002), pp. 174–95; Kathleen Rushton, 'The (Pro)creative Parables of Labour and Childbirth (Jn 3.1–10 and 16.21–22)', in M.A. Beavis (ed.), *The Lost Coin*, pp. 206–29; G. Haufe, 'παραβολή', *EDNT* 3, p. 16; Joachim Jeremias, *The Parables of Jesus* [New York: Scribner's Sons, 2nd edn, 1972), p. 16; Bernard Brandon Scott, *Hear Then the Parable: A Commentary on the Parables of Jesus* [Minneapolis: Fortress Press, 1989], pp. 19–20; Brad H. Young, *The Parables: Jewish Tradition and Christian Interpretation* [Peabody, MA: Hendrickson, 1998], pp. 3–4, 12–13.

9. Passages other than the wedding parables speak to the eventual judgment and separation: for example, the wheat and weeds (13.36–42); good and bad fish (13.47–50); sheep and goats (25.31–46).

10. G. Lakoff and M. Johnson, *Metaphors We Live By* (Chicago: University of Chicago Press, 1980), p. 118; Lakoff and Johnson, 'Conceptual Metaphor', *More Than Cool Reason* pp. 295–300.

allying with the 'wrong' side. Therefore, a great deal is at stake in
interpreting which is the 'right' and which the 'wrong' side, and thus, on
how to understand the Kingdom of Heaven through these parables.

Matthew invites a metaphorical reading[11] with his introductory phrases
'the Kingdom of Heaven is like ...' (22.2) or 'the Kingdom of Heaven will
be like ...' (25.1). Because Matthew sets these parables in the context of
conflict with the religious leaders (21.23–46) and states that the religious
leaders understood that he was talking about them (21.45), an allegorical
reading (a one-to-one association between characters in the parables and
specific persons or historical events)[12] becomes natural, even obvious. For
example, an allegorical interpretation of the Parable of the Wedding Feast
assumes that if the parable is about the Kingdom of Heaven, then the
'king' must be God, Jesus his 'son,' and the wedding feast a depiction of
the coming eschatological banquet. The allegory then suggests that the
first group of guests who killed the king's messengers (22.5–6) are the
religious leaders (who were identified in a similar manner in the previous
parable, as 'wicked tenants' [21.33–41]). The burned city then represents
the destruction of Jerusalem in 70 CE, and, frequently, the second group of
guests is equated with the mission to the Gentiles. Similarly, in an
allegorical reading of the Parable of the Ten Virgins, the 'bridegroom' is
Jesus, and his 'delay' is the expected but unknown hour of the Parousia.
The exclusion of the five foolish virgins is Jesus' judgment on those who
are unprepared for his return.

Even though Matthew seems to set up an allegorical interpretation
(granting that authorial intent cannot be proven), I want to resist[13] these
interpretations of God as retributive king, the bridegroom as, at best, an
indifferent host, and the dualities of wise/foolish and good/bad in the
wedding parables. I resist the allegorical interpretations of God as king
because of my feminist concern that the wedding feast/Kingdom of

---

11.   Scott (*Hear Then the Parable*, pp. 44–45) gives a brief history of interpretation of
parables as metaphor and allegory.

12.   A. Jülicher, *Die Gleichnisreden Jesu* (2 vols.; Freiburg: J.C.B. Mohr [Paul Siebeck],
1886), I, pp. 39–68.

13.   The 'resisting reader' is a term coined by Judith Fetterley (*The Resisting Reader: A
Feminist Approach to American Fiction* [Bloomington: Indiana University Press, 1978], pp.
xi-xxiv) to describe how women need to recognize how they assent to reading through a male
point of view. I use it here in a narrower sense to denote my resistance to traditional
interpretations of the deity as violent and coercive. Resisting readers who have been
especially helpful to me in formulating my own reading include Tina Pippin, *Death and
Desire: The Rhetoric of Gender in the Apocalypse of John* (Louisville: Westminster/John Knox
Press, 1992); Exum, *Fragmented Women*; Carter, *Matthew and the Margins*; Moore,
'Revolting Revelations'; John K. Roth, 'A Theodicy of Protest', in Stephen T. Davis (ed.),
Encountering Evil: Live Options in Theodicy (Atlanta: John Knox Press, 1981), pp. 7–22; and
Frederick Sontag, 'Anthropodicy and the Return of God', in S.T. Davis (ed.), *Encountering
Evil*, pp. 137–51. Others will be mentioned below, in context.

Heaven becomes a violent place and the host a vindictive father or judge, and because there is inherent danger in categorizing people by polarities, thus demonizing the non-privileged pole and disallowing any 'gray' areas that reflect the reality of the human condition: that all people have both 'good and wise' tendencies as well as 'bad and foolish' tendencies, and so cannot be so easily divided into two groups, as the parable would have.[14] I posit that if the parables are to be read as allegory, these problems arise: God as 'king' becomes a tyrant who owns slaves, murders his enemies, and casts out a garmentless man, while Jesus as 'bridegroom' becomes a cold and judgmental host who cuts off half his wedding attendants. Moreover, the parabolic king's and bridegroom's actions run counter to earlier teachings about loving enemies, forgiving, and sharing with those in need (e.g., 5.38–48). Possibly Matthew has constructed the parables to reflect his own theology of the end times in such a way that these parables are inconsistent with the teachings in the first part of his gospel. For this inconsistency alone the reader can find grounds to resist these wedding parables.

The apparent inconsistencies within the gospel offer another possibility: that of an intertext, a subversive reading hidden beneath the more obvious text. Brigitte Kahl describes how readers might look for a text embedded within a text, a method of resisting reading which she calls a 'hermeneutic of conspiracy.'[15] She describes telephone conversations in pre-1989 Eastern Europe, when both parties knew that the phone was tapped: they could still communicate, but some statements they uttered were meant for the hidden third party that was listening. 'Perhaps you even say something you do not mean,' writes Kahl, 'but ideally, the person to whom you speak will know that the statement was made for the third partner of your conversation, the well-known, unknown one.'[16] Because of the inconsistencies within the gospel, I wonder if the wedding parables are the 'cover story' told for the benefit of the listening third party, the

---

14.   Scott (*Hear Then the Parable*, pp. 44–47) argues that a sharp distinction between 'metaphor' and 'allegory' need not be made, because many parables can be treated as either metaphor or allegory, or a mixture of both. Scott recognizes that parables may be *posed* as allegory in reflection of an evangelist's ideology (a situation evident in the Matthean wedding parables). The reader need not interpret the parable rigidly with the one-to-one correspondence of specific referents to appreciate allegorical nuances but evaluate the parable as a continuum from metaphor to allegory and allow polyvalency of meaning.

15.   Brigitte Kahl, 'Reading Luke against Luke: Non-conformity of Text, Hermeneutics of Conspiracy, and the "Scriptural Principle" in Luke 1', in Amy-Jill Levine (ed.), *A Feminist Companion to Luke* (trans. B. and M. Rumscheidt; Sheffield: Sheffield Academic Press, 2002), pp. 70–88 (72–73). Kahl refers to J.C. Scott, *Domination and the Arts of Resistance: Hidden Transcripts* (New Haven: Yale University Press, 1990), and V.L. Wimbush (ed.) *Rhetorics of Resistance: A Colloquy on Early Christianity as Rhetorical Formation* (*Semeia* 79, 1997), pp. 1–118.

16.   Kahl, 'Reading Luke against Luke', p. 72.

'outsider.' Matthew may even say something he does not mean (as Kahl suggests), but the real message is embedded in the transcript. Only those 'insiders' who understand the clues to interpret it will understand the true meaning of the story. Of course, there is no way to prove that such a hidden intertext exists in the evangelist's parables; in fact, my study of Matthew leads me to believe that this is not the case. However, because a subversive reading can be supported by other texts in the gospel as a whole, my 'resisting reading' of the allegorical readings of the parable is possible.

Therefore, just as Kahl reads Luke against Luke, I want to read Matthew against Matthew. Following the example of William Herzog, I would like to offer alternative readings that portray the 'king' and 'bridegroom' in these parables as generic characters, who are not God and Jesus, but who are aligned with the powers of this world. In this alternative reading, the parable's action takes place in the evangelist's present social context rather than at the end of the world or in some other-worldly context.[17] This more literal way of reading allows a different understanding of the parable: if the king is like a human king (*not* God) – given the Matthean portrayal of kings as tyrants – then perhaps the guests *should* resist him. The subversive intertext made possible by reading the gospel's negative portrayal of kings makes possible the interpretation that it is one who resists the king (by standing garmentless and speechless before him [25.11–12]) and is bound and thrown out of the feast who ultimately is saved: 'You will be dragged before governors and kings ... but the one who endures to the end will be saved' (10.18, 22). Matthew tells us that those who endure against worldly powers will receive their reward in the Kingdom of Heaven (10.39, 42; 11.28–30; 16.24–27; 19.29). Similarly, in the Parable of the Ten Virgins, the 'wise' virgins carry real oil (not allegorical 'good deeds') and fail to honor earlier gospel teachings to share with those in need (5.42) and to come prepared with no extra commodities in the expectation of receiving what is needed (10.8–11). Moreover, the evangelist calls five of the virgins 'foolish' in violation of the warning that the one who calls someone else 'fool' is liable to the hell of fire (5.22). These contradictions complicate the readers' understanding of what is really the 'wise' thing to do.

A more literal reading of the social context of the Matthean community allows these parables to show the precariousness of a group of people who believe they must resist this world but know they will suffer consequent violence for their allegiance to the Kingdom of Heaven (e.g., 10.16–23). The community's choice to honor not the worldly 'king' (22.2) but the King of the Jews (2.2) means they will suffer violence and shame – not

17. William R. Herzog, *Parables as Subversive Speech: Jesus as Pedagogue of the Oppressed* (Louisville: Westminster/John Knox Press, 1994).

from God or Jesus as bridegroom – but at the hands of the worldly powers they resist (10.16–23).

The parables, as metaphors, have meaning on many levels. I will discuss various readings and judge the efficacy of these various interpretations by how well they comport with teachings of non-violent resistance in the gospel. While my reading can also be defined as 'allegorical,' because I too will correspond characters in the parables to people or events, my interpretation attempts to redefine these literary connections so that they resonate with the gospel's earlier teachings and so that they avoid blaming the deity for violence. I do not claim that the evangelist 'intends' one reading over another, because we cannot know what Matthew 'intended'; I offer these interpretations as possible alternatives as I read with Kahl's 'hermeneutic of conspiracy,' or at least a hermeneutic of suspicion.

Chapter 2

PARABLE OF THE WEDDING FEAST
(Mt. 22.1–14)

2 Ὡμοιώθη ἡ βασιλεία τῶν οὐρανῶν ἀνθρώπῳ βασιλεῖ ὅστις ἐποίησεν γάμους τῷ υἱῷ αὐτοῦ. 3 καὶ ἀπέστειλεν τοὺς δούλους αὐτοῦ καλέσαι τοὺς κεκλημένους εἰς τοὺς γάμους, και᾽ οὐκ ἤθελον ἐλθεῖν. 4 πάλιν ἀπέστειλεν ἄλλους δούλους λέγων, Εἴπατε τοῖς κεκλημένοις, Ἰδοὺ τὸ ἀριστόν μου ἡτοίμακα, οἱ ταῦροίμου καὶ τὰ σιτιστὰ τεθυμένα καὶ πάντα ἕτοιμα. δεῦτε εἰς τοὺς γάμους. 5 οἱ δὲ ἀμελήσαντες ἀπῆλθον, ὃς μὲν εἰς τὸν ἴδιον ἀγρόν, ὃς δὲ ἐπὶ τὴν ἐμπορίαν αὐτοῦ. 6 οἱ δὲ λοιποὶ κρατήσαντες τοὺς δούλους αὐτοῦ ὕβρισαν καὶ ἀπέκτειναν. 7 ὁ δὲ βασιλεὺς ὠργίσθη καὶ πέμψας τὰ στρατεύματα αὐτοῦ ἀπώλεσσεν τοὺς φονεῖς ἐκείνους καὶ τὴν πόλιν αὐτῶν ἐνέπρησεν. 8 τότε λέγει τοῖς δούλοις αὐτοῦ, Ὁ μὲν γάμος ἕτοιμός ἐστιν, οἱ δὲ κεκλημένοι οὐκ ἦσαν ἄξιοι. 9 πορεύεσθε οὖν ἐπὶ τὰς διεξόδους τῶν ὁδῶν καὶ ὅσους ἐὰν εὕρητε καλέσατε εἰς τοὺς γάμους. 10 καὶ ἐξελθόντες οἱ δοῦλοι ἐκεῖνοι εἰς τὰς ὁδοὺς συνήγαγον πάντας οὓς εὗρον, πονηρούς τε καὶ ἀγαθούς. Καὶ ἐπλήσθη ὁ γάμος ἀνακειμένων. 11 εἰσελθὼν δὲ ὁ βασιλεὺς θεάσασθαι τοὺς ἀνακειμένους εἶδεν ἐκεῖ ἄνθρωπον οὐκ ἐνδεδυμένον ἔνδυμα γάμου. 12 καὶ λέγει αὐτῷ Ἑταῖρε, πῶς εἰσῆθες ὧδε μὴ ἔχων ἔνδυμα γάμου; ὁ δὲ ἐφιμώθη. 13 τότε ὁ βασιλεὺς εἶπεν τοῖς διακόνοις, Δήσαντες αὐτοῦ πόδας καὶ χεῖρας ἐκβάλετε αὐτὸν εἰς τὸ σκότος τὸ ἐξώτερον. ἐκεῖ ἔσται ὁ κλαυθμὸς καὶ ὁ βρυγμὸς τῶν ὀδόντων. 14 πολλοὶ γάρ εἰσιν κλητοί, ὀλίγοι δὲ ἐκλεκτοί.

The kingdom of the heavens has become like a man – a king – who made a wedding banquet for his son. He sent his slaves to call those who had been invited to the wedding banquet, but they did not want to come. Again he sent other slaves, saying: 'Say to the ones who have been called: "Look, my dinner I have prepared, my oxen and my fat calves have been slaughtered, and everything is ready. Come into the wedding banquet." ' But making light of it, they went away, one to his farm, one to his business, and the rest seized his slaves, mistreated (them), and killed (them). The king was enraged, and sending his troops, he destroyed those murderers, and their city he burned. Then he said to his slaves: 'The wedding is ready, and those who were invited were not worthy. Go therefore to the crossing of the roads, and when you find as many as are there, call (them) to the wedding banquet.' Those slaves went out into the streets and gathered all whom they found, evil and also good; and the wedding was filled with those who were reclining (at the table). But when the king came in to the ones reclining, he saw there a man not dressed in a wedding robe. And he said to him: 'Friend, how did you get in here without having a wedding robe?' And he was speechless. Then the king said to the servants: 'Bind him feet and hands and throw him into the outer darkness: there will be weeping and gnashing of teeth. For many are called, but few are chosen.'[1]

2.1 *Introduction*

Matthew places this parable in the context of Jesus' entry into Jerusalem (21.1–23.39), when he engages in controversy with Jewish leaders. The parable follows immediately the Parable of the Wicked Tenants (21.33–41), which has the same message: that there is conflict between the Matthean community and other groups, and moreover, that Matthew thinks there are some in the community who will prove themselves to be unworthy of the Kingdom of Heaven.[2] My reading acknowledges these situations of conflict but questions allegorical readings that explain who the 'worthy' and 'unworthy' are in this parable.

Because Matthew describes the Kingdom of Heaven as being like (ὡμοιώθη [22.2]) a king who gave a wedding feast for his son, the most common allegorical interpretation is that the 'king' is God – because who but God is the king in the Kingdom of Heaven? – and because the Matthean audience knows the tradition of God as a king (e.g., Pss. 5.2; 24.7–10; 48.1–2). It follows that his 'son' is Jesus (cf. 3.17; 17.5), that Jesus is 'the bridegroom,' and that the wedding feast is the eschatological banquet (Mt. 8.11–12; cf. Isa. 25.6–9; 2 Esd. 2.37–41; Rev. 19.7, 9). Interpreters from the third century on are nearly unanimous in identifying the 'king' in this parable as God and his 'son' as Jesus.[3] But if we read the parable in other Matthean contexts (such as the negative Matthean portrayal of kings and

---

1. All translations are mine unless otherwise noted.
2. Davies and Allison, *Matthew*, III, p. 197; J. Drury, *The Parables in the Gospels: History and Allegory* (New York: Crossroad, 1985); M.D. Goulder, 'Characteristics of the Parables in the Several Gospels', *JTS* (1968), pp. 51–69; Albright and Mann, *Matthew*, p. 268.
3. For example, Origen, *Commentary on Matthew*, 17.20 ([*Origenes: Der Kommentar zum Evangelium nach Mattäus*; ed. Hermann J. Vogt; Bibliothek der Griechischen Literatur, 30; Stuttgart: Anton Hiersemann, 1990], II, p. 271); Hultgren, *Parables*, p. 343; Davies and Allison, *Matthew*, III, pp. 197–99; Hare, *Matthew*, p. 251; Beare, *Matthew*, p. 432. Bauckham, 'Parable of the Royal Wedding Feast', *JBL* 115/3 (1996), p. 483, n. 40; Iver K. Madsen, 'Zur Erklärung der evangelischen Parabeln', in Wolfgang Harisch, *Gleichnisse Jesus* (Darmstadt: Wissenschaftliche Buchgesellschaft, 1982), pp. 113–114.

the non-violence preached in the Sermon on the Mount) and read the 'king' as a generic oppressive king, the parable yields a startling glimpse of the Matthean community living in a dangerous place among *worldly* powers.[4] This reading is in keeping with the Matthean Jesus' warning that those who hope for the Kingdom of Heaven need to understand that it exists among dangerous worldly forces: 'The Kingdom of Heaven has suffered violence, and the violent take it by force,' the Matthean Jesus explains (11.12).

In my reading, the 'king' in the parable is not God, because Matthew codes 'kings' negatively, as being among the violent worldly powers: 'You know that the rulers (ἄρχοντες) of the people overpower them (κατακυριεύουσιν), and their great ones (οἱ μεγάλοι) exercise authority over them (κατεχουσιάζουσιν)' (20.25).[5] Matthew portrays rulers as powerful and cruel: Herod the Great murders the children of Bethlehem (2.16), and Joseph fears and avoids his successor Archelaus (2.22). Herodias demands John the Baptizer's head, and in a striking display of weakness that implicates her young daughter in the atrocity, Herod Antipas has John beheaded and be-plattered (14.3–11). Pilate executes an innocent man (27.15–26). Matthew mentions controversy over paying taxes to the Roman emperor (22.20–21), who is (although Matthew does not specifically name him as such) among rulers of the Gentiles who are tyrants that overpower the people (20.25). Moreover, the question about paying taxes to the emperor (22.15–17) immediately follows this wedding parable (22.1–14), so that when Matthew adds the detail that those who question Jesus about the tax include 'Herodians' (22.16), he suggests that the parable refers to an ordinary human king, like Herod and Caesar.[6] This interpretation bears the possibility that the king's banquet was paid for by the poor.

Matthew perceives that the kingdoms of earth and their rulers are oppressive; indeed, Mark Allan Powell demonstrates how Matthew equates the rulers of the world with the power of Satan when the tempter offers to give Jesus all the kingdoms of the world (4.8–9).[7] Thus, being

---

4. See Herzog, *The Parables as Subversive Speech*, pp. 6–52, and Barbara E. Reid, 'Violent Endings in Matthew's Parables and Christian Nonviolence', *CBQ* 66 (2004), pp. 237–55.

5. Translation mine. The NRSV nicely captures the nuance of κύριος in κατακυριεύουσιν with the translation 'lord it over.' I did not choose to follow this translation, because in my experience, the modern English phrase 'lord it over' implies people are acting as if they have power that they really don't have, that they are flaunting false authority. I think Matthew's intention is to show that these rulers really do have power, even if it is only on earth, so I translate κατακυριεύουσιν as true dominance, to 'overpower.'

6. We cannot know how the evangelist intended the parable to be read, but because of the polyvalent nature of metaphor, no single interpretation needs to be ascertained.

7. Mark Allan Powell, *Chasing the Eastern Star: Adventures in Biblical Reader-response Criticism* (Louisville: Westminster/John Knox Press, 2001), p. 143.

faithful to the Kingdom of Heaven (as was Jesus at his temptation) means ultimately incurring the wrath of earthly kings (as Jesus died on a Roman cross). Allegiance to the Kingdom of Heaven (in its liminal state between 'already' and 'not yet') is dangerous, but those who endure will receive reward (5.10–12; 10.39; 11.28–30; 16.24–27; 19.29). In the context of Matthean portrayal of oppressive worldly rulers, my reading of the Parable of the Wedding Feast attempts to avoid questions of theodicy (that pose God as oppressive king) while highlighting Matthean messages of endurance in the face of struggle and uncertainty.

Davies and Allison note that if the story is *not* read as an allegory, too many questions are left unanswered, e.g., why do the ungrateful guests kill the servants? Why is the city burned? Why does the king throw out the inappropriately garbed guest, a punishment that seems far harsher than his offense might warrant? Allegorical readings typically explain that the murdered servants represent the prophets, the burned city is the destruction of Jerusalem, and the guests in the wedding hall represent the Church containing both 'bad' and 'good'.[8] These readings further note that the story illustrates the post-70 CE world of the Matthean community that knows the murder of its servant, the destruction of Jerusalem, and the presence of both 'good and 'bad' members in the Church.[9] Davies and Allison (among many others) are correct in noting that Matthew apparently sets up such an allegorical interpretation and prompts associations with historical events. But the problem with these allegorical readings is that they disrupt the expectations of peacefulness, forgiveness, and compassion set forth in the Sermon on the Mount (e.g., 'Blessed are the merciful [5.7] ... blessed are the peacemakers [5.9] ... you shall not murder [or even be angry, [5.21–22] ... love your enemies [5.44]) and place the deity into the role of tyrant. In these readings, God becomes a ruthless 'king' who owns slaves, remorselessly sends these slaves to their deaths, kills his enemies and burns their city, then throws out the wedding guest who has improper clothing. Is the evangelist inconsistent with earlier teachings because the stakes have become higher and the situation more desperate, or could the parables be read differently to honor those earlier teachings?[10] Or, might there be a difference between what the people are exhorted to do and what the divine judge is permitted to do?[11]

Jan Lambrecht sums up my reaction to the violence in the parable when the 'king' is interpreted allegorically as a figure for God: 'We cannot but

---

8.   Hultgren (*Parables*, p. 331) counts this among parables that he deems 'decidedly allegorical through and through.' Also Scott, *Hear Then the Parable*, pp. 162, 169; H. Weder, *Die Gleichnisse Jesu als Metaphern* (Götting: Vandenhoeck & Ruprecht, 1978), p. 188–91; Donahue (*Gospel in Parable*, p. 95, n. 56).

9.   Davies and Allison, *Matthew*, III, p. 196, n. 18, and p. 201.

10.   Reid, 'Violent Endings', pp. 237–55.

11.   Reid, 'Violent Endings', pp. 254–5.

protest against these disturbing features. We revolt against an inhuman, cruel God. In the end, one is inclined simply to disregard such a parable.'[12] David Buttrick has done so, in part, as he advises those preaching on this text to avoid the violent portions.[13] But I think that the violence of this parable needs to be addressed and challenged.

If the 'king' is read as any human tyrant,[14] then the Kingdom of Heaven itself is not violent but exists in a violent place in the here and now, before it is fulfilled. The Matthean parables elsewhere depict the Kingdom of Heaven as something small but with great potential to take over, like a mustard seed (13.31–32) and leaven in bread (13.33). Just so, the seemingly powerless and insignificant garmentless guest and the apparently defeated city are things that have started inauspiciously but which will eventually take over. Only a few are able to discern the kingdom's presence in the mayhem and understand its potential.

As a ruthless king disposes of traitors or suspicious persons (in the same way that Jesus was eliminated as an enemy of the state), the parable's conclusion that 'many are called, but few are chosen' (22.14) no longer means that those who *stay* at the banquet are the ones chosen; rather, it is those who *resist* the king who are the chosen of the Kingdom of Heaven. In a reading where the king represents not God but a human tyrant, those who are 'chosen' (ἐκλεκτοί) *include* the garmentless man,[15] because he resisted a worldly ruler and so demonstrated his allegiance to the Kingdom of Heaven. In keeping with earlier teachings in the gospel, the man not only gives up his garment, but his coat as well (5.40); he does not worry about what he will wear (6.25); and he does not concern himself over what he will say before the king (10.19).

2.2 *Violence in the Matthean Redaction*

The Matthean Parable of the Wedding Feast is based on a well-known tradition,[16] as can be seen by the existence of two other gospel versions

12. J. Lambrecht, *Out of the Treasure: The Parables in the Gospel of Matthew* (Louvain Theological and Pastoral Monographs, 10; Louvain: Peeters Press, 1991), p. 128.

13. Buttrick, *Speaking Parables*, p. 161.

14. Scott, *Hear Then the Parable*, p. 49.

15. Scott, *Hear Then the Parable*, p. 174.

16. For discussion of sources and Matthean redaction of this parable, see Craig S. Keener, *A Commentary on the Gospel of Matthew* (Grand Rapids: Eerdmans, 1999), pp. 517–18; Ivor H. Jones, *The Matthean Parables: A Literary and Historical Commentary* (NovTSup, 80; Leiden: Brill, 1995), esp. pp. 400–404, 410–12; David C. Sim, 'Matthew 22.13a and 1 Enoch 10.4a: A Case of Literary Dependence?', *JSNT* 47 (1992), pp. 3–19; Lambrecht, *Out of the Treasure*, pp. 130–36; Davies and Allison, *Matthew*, III, pp. 194–95; Craig L. Blomberg, *Interpreting the Parables* (Downers Grove, IL: InverVarsity Press, 1990), pp. 233–40; Donahue, *Gospel in Parable*, pp. 93–94; Joachim Gnilka, *Das*

(Lk. 14.15–24; *G. Thom.* 64)[17] and numerous rabbinic parables that

---

Matthäusevangelium (2 vols; Herders Theologischer Kommentar zum Neuen Testament; Freiburg: Herder, 1988), II, pp. 234–36; Luise Schottroff, 'Das Gleichnis vom grossen Gastmahl in der Logienquelle', *EvT* 3 (1987), pp. 192–211; Eugene E. Lemcio, 'The Parables of the Great Supper and the Wedding Feast: History, Redaction, and Canon', *HBT* 8 (1986), pp. 1–26; Rudolph Schnackenburg, *The Gospel of Matthew* (trans. R.R. Barr; Grand Rapids: Eerdmans, 2002 [*Matthäusevangelium* [2 vols.]; Würzburg: Echter Verlag, 1985 and 1987]), p. 213; Weder, *Die Gleichnisse Jesu als Metaphern*, pp. 177–85; Thaddée Matura, 'Les Invites a la Noce Royale', *Assemblées du Seigneur* 58 (1974), pp. 16–27 (esp. pp. 16–20); E. Linnemann, *Parables of Jesus: Introduction and Exposition* (trans. J. Sturdy; London: SPCK, 3rd edn, 1966), pp. 93–95; Georg Eichholz, *Gleichnisse der Evangelien* (Neukirchen-Vluyn: Neukirchener Verlag, 1971), pp. 126–33; Klaus Haacker, 'Das hochzeitliche Kleid von Mt. 22.11–13 und ein palästinisches Märchen', *Zeitschrift des Deutschen Palästina-Vereins* 87 (1971), pp. 95–97; Dan O. Via, 'The Relationship of Form to Content in the Parables: The Wedding Feast', *Int* 25 (1971), pp. 171–84; Ferdinand Hahn, 'Das Gleichnis von der Einladung zum Festmahl', in Otto Böcher and Klaus Haacker (eds.), *Verborum Veritas: Festschrift für Gustav Stahlin zum 70. Geburtstag* (Wuppertal: Theologischer Verlag Rolf Brockhause, 1970), pp. 51–82; Ernst Haenchen, *Die Bibel und Wir: Gesammelte Aufsätze* (Tübingen: J.C.B. Mohr [Paul Siebeck], 1968), pp. 135–41; Robert Funk, *Language, Hermeneutic, and the Word of God* (New York: Harper and Row, 1966), pp. 163–87; Richard J. Dillon, 'Towards a Tradition-History of the Parables of the True Israel (Matthew 21.33–22.14)', *Bib* 47 (1966), pp. 1–42; Victor Hasler, 'Die königliche Hochzeit, Matth. 22.1–14', *TZ* 18 (1962), pp. 25–35 (esp. pp. 25–28); Otto Glombitza, 'Das Grosse Abendmahl: Luk. xiv.12–24', *NovT* 5 (1962), pp. 10–16; Eta Linnemann, 'Überlegungen zur Parabel vom grossen Abendmahl', *ZNW* 3–4 (1960), pp. 246–55; Francis W. Beare, 'The Parable of the Guests at the Banquet', in S.E. Johnson (ed.), *The Joy of Study: Papers on the New Testament and Related Subjects Presented to Honor Frederick Clifton Grant* (New York: MacMillan, 1951), pp. 1–14 (1–4); T.W. Manson, *The Sayings of Jesus* (London: SCM Press, 1949), pp. 224–28; Joachim Jeremias, *Die Gleichnisse Jesu* (Abhandlungen zur Theologie des Alten und Neuen Testaments, 11; Zürich: Zwingli-Verlag, 1947), pp. 44–48; B.T.D. Smith, *The Parables of the Synoptic Gospels* (Cambridge: Cambridge University Press, 1937), p. 202; B.W. Bacon, *Studies in Matthew* (New York: H. Holt, 1930), pp. 65–66; B.W. Bacon, 'Two Parables of Lost Opportunity', *Hibbert Journal* 21 (1922–23), pp. 337–2 (esp. pp. 341–46); Adolf Jülicher, *Die Gleichnisreden Jesu* (Freiburg: J.C.B. Mohr [Paul Siebeck], 1899), pp. 407–33. Among those who doubt that Matthew and Luke used the same source material are J.L. McKenzie, 'Matthew', *Jerome Biblical Commentary*, p. 100); Keener, *Matthew*, p. 517. Davies and Allison tentatively assign it to an oral tradition (*Matthew*, III, p. 194). Those who argue that the two versions are the same but told in different settings include John Cumming, *Foreshadows: Lectures on Our Lord's Parables* (Philadelphia: Lindsay and Blakiston, 1854), pp. 46–47; Capon, *The Parables of Judgment* (Grand Rapids, MI: Eerdmans, 1956–57), p. 118; and Humphrey Palmer, 'Just Married, Cannot Come', *NovT* 18 (1976), pp. 241–57 (255). Richard Bauckham prefers not to refer to a common source but a 'storytelling motif.' See R. Bauckham, 'The Parable of the Royal Wedding Feast (Matthew 22.1–14) and 'The Parable of the Lame Man and the Blind Man (*Apocryphon of Ezekiel*)', *JBL* 115/3 (1996), pp. 471–88 (480).

17. Keener warns that the parable in Matthew may not be the same one as Luke records, given the many versions that exist (Keener, *Matthew*, p. 517). Beare thinks the many versions show how much the parable has been altered, 'even mangled,' in transmission (Beare, *Matthew*, p. 432).

feature a king inviting guests to a banquet[18] or a king preparing wedding festivities for his son (or daughter).[19] A comparison of these versions reveals that Matthew has introduced the elements of violence and coercion that transform the benevolent host of other versions into a tyrant.

In Matthew, the host of the feast is specifically a king (βασιλεύς) (22.2), a role associated in Matthew with violence and tyranny. Even though the motif of a king inviting guests to a banquet is found in several rabbinic parables,[20] the kings in these versions do not resort to violence. Moreover, Matthew is unique in designating the banquet as specifically a *wedding feast* (γάμους) for the king's *son*[21] (a tie that also links it to the bridegroom saying [9.15] and to the Parable of the Ten Virgins [25. 1–13]).[22]

The Matthean parable does not merely include violence, a detail missing from the other versions, but *features* violence: the king's messengers are murdered, and the king becomes angry (ὡργίσθη) (22.7). He sends troops to destroy (ἀπώλεσεν) the murderers and burn their city (22.7) and binds a guest hand and foot and throws him into the outer darkness, where there will be weeping and gnashing of teeth (22.13). While the Lukan host becomes angry (ὀργισθείς) (Lk. 14.21; cf. Mt. 22.7) when his invited guests do not come, there is no violent retaliation, but only the somewhat miffed conclusion: 'None of those who were invited will taste my dinner.' In the *Gospel of Thomas* (logion 64), the host does not react at all to the snubbing of his invitation; he merely instructs the servants to bring other guests. In *y. San.* 6.23, the king does not dismiss the unworthy attendees: though he becomes angry with his unadorned guests, he does not attempt to replace them. Their punishment, that of having to stand and watch the others eat, is humiliating, but certainly not violent, nor a complete separation from the king's presence.

18.   *B. Sabb.* 153a; *b. Sukk.* 29a; *t. Sukk.* 2.6; *t. San.* 3.9; *Sem.* 8.10; *Sipre Deut.* 53; *Midr. Pss.* 4.11; 25.9; *Eccles. Rab.* 3.9.1; 9.8.1, discussed in Richard Bauckham, 'The Parable of the Royal Wedding Feast', pp. 480–81.

19.   Bauckham cites parables with similar themes: a king preparing for his son's or daughter's wedding. However, these do not involve a feast (*Gen. Rab.* 18.10; *Gen. Rab.* 28.6; *Qoh. Rab.* 4.11; *b. Sanh.* 108a; *Gen. Rab.* 9.4; *Pesiq. R.* 5.10; 20.1–2; and a parable recorded in Epiphanius, *Pan.* 64.70 from *The Apocryphon of Ezekiel* (which exists only in fragments). See Bauckham, 'The Parable of the Royal Wedding Feast', p. 481.

20.   *B. Sabb.* 153a; *b. Sukk.* 29a; *t. Sukk.* 2.6; *t. San.* 3.9; *Sem.* 8.10; *Sipre Deut.* 53; *Midr. Pss.* 4.11; 25.9; *Eccles. Rab.* 3.9.1; 9.8.1.

21.   *Gen. Rab.* 18.10; *Gen. Rab.* 28.6; *Qoh. Rab.* 4.11; *b. Sanh.* 108a; *Gen. Rab.* 9.4; *Pesiq. R.* 20.1; *Pesiq. R.* 5.10; 20.2; Epiphanius, *Pan.* 64.70 (*Apocryphon of Ezekiel*).

22.   Heinrich Schlier (*The Relevance of the New Testament* [New York: Herder and Herder, 1967], p. 254) supports this connection between Mt. 22.1–14 and 9.15, 'Can the wedding guests mourn as long as the bridegroom is with them?'

Matthew's version also includes more tension than the other versions: the suspense is heightened as the servants go out several times to gather in guests (in contrast, Luke and Thomas's servant go out twice; in *y. San.* 6.23, the servants are the guests themselves). Closure is not reached even after the guests come to the table: there is a final pass when the king finds the guest without a garment and throws him out. Matthew concludes: 'Many are called but few are chosen' (25.13) and thereby leaves readers in doubt as to whether they are 'in' or 'out.'

2.3 *The Wedding Banquet*

In allegorical treatments, the wedding banquet is the Kingdom of Heaven,[23] an allusion to the eschatological messianic banquet from Isaiah 25.6–10[24] (repeated in Rev. 19.7–9).[25] Whether or not this wedding feast is the eschatological banquet is not clear from the parable itself. Some interpreters suggest that the wedding feast has already begun; the celebration of the eucharist is interpreted by some as an enactment of this celebration.[26] That Jesus tells his disciples to 'take' and 'eat' but states that *he* will not drink of the fruit of the vine until he drinks it new with his disciples in the kingdom of his father (26.26–29) suggests to many interpreters that the wedding feast has not yet begun. The temporal ambiguity illustrates the liminal tension of 'already' and 'not yet' in which wedding guests are suspended.

Meals frequently figure as contexts for inclusion and exclusion in the gospel of Matthew. On the one hand, meals include a great number of people who enjoy the providential care of Jesus, who provides food (the Feeding of the 5000 and 4000; 14.13–21; 15.32–39) or who eat with him (9.10–13; 11.18–10). A meal is the setting at which the disciples are to remember Jesus (the Last Supper; 26.26–28). On the other hand, meals are

---

23. Ambrose, *De Fide* 4.2.15–16; Origen, *Commentary on Matthew*, 17.20–21; C. Keener, *Matthew*, p. 518.

24. Davies and Allison (*Matthew*, III, p. 199). Fulfillment of Old Testament expectation and the completion of salvation history (*Heilsgeschicht*) is a theme explored by V. Hasler, 'Die königliche Hochzeit', pp. 31–33.

25. Davies and Allison (*Matthew*, III, p. 199). Krister Stendahl observes that by making the feast into a wedding feast, Matthew has given the parable a distinct eschatological tone; see K. Stendahl, 'Matthew', *Peake's Commentary on the Bible* (London: Thomas Nelson and Sons, 1962), pp. 749–98 (791). Also P.H. Ballard, 'Reasons for Refusing the Great Supper', *JTS* 23 (1972), p. 347, and Schottroff, 'Das Gleichnis vom grossen Gastmahl', p. 202. Hilary of Poitiers (*On Matthew* 22) places the wedding feast in an eschatological context as the time when souls will be joined to their new heavenly bodies. Text from Hilaire de Poitiers, *Sur Matthieu* (ed. Jean Doignon; Paris: Les Éditions du Cerf, 1929), pp. 142–47.

26. Cyril of Alexandria, *Hom. Pasch.* 14. Matura notes the context of the eschatological wedding feast for Eucharistic celebration in the present ('Les Invites', p. 25).

the context for conflict and rejection when the religious leaders object to the types of people with whom Jesus eats (Mt. 9.10–13; 11.18–10) and at the supper when Judas is revealed as the betrayer (26.20–25, 47). Jesus uses food imagery to warn disciples about the teachings of the Pharisees (Mt. 16.5–12)[27] and argues with the Pharisees over plucking and eating grain on the Sabbath (12.1–8). Jesus the bridegroom disagrees with the disciples of John over the appropriateness of feasting or fasting while he is present (9.14–15).

If the wedding banquet in the parable is a place of acceptance or rejection, this acceptance and rejection can work both ways: the king accepts or rejects guests, but guests can also accept or reject the king. Reading with a hermeneutic of conspiracy, we need not necessarily regard the hosting 'king' as benevolent provider (like God or Jesus). The first set of guests rejects the king's invitation; their rebuff can be read as either moral resistance or the machinations of rich and powerful peoples (22.3). The second set of guests accepts the invitation, but the man without a wedding garment might be silently rejecting the invitation by his lack of festal garment. He knows that this earthly king does not offer what the Kingdom of Heaven offers.

2.4 The King's Slaves

The call to the wedding feast presents an ideological concern from the beginning of the parable: the king has slaves (a 'king' sends his 'slaves' [δοῦλοι] to call the guests to the feast [22.2]).[28] Slaves are regarded as property, part of a king's (or wealthy and powerful person's) possessions,[29] their lives are expendable (22.6), and it is not clear that they themselves are invited to the feast. Already in the parable, there is a gap into which falls the slaves' status in this kingdom: are they 'in' or 'out'? The parable suggests that slaves have gone to invite guests worthy of a king's feast, most likely those who are wealthy and powerful. If this is the case, then inclusion in the feast is based on social class: slaves are not welcome at the table. While social distinctions between rich and poor, powerful and lowly, are typical of *kings*, they do not honor characteristics of discipleship in the *Kingdom of Heaven* expressed earlier in the gospel, such as: do not worry about what to wear (6.25), the first shall be last

27. Carter, *Matthew and the Margins*, p. 434.
28. A δοῦλος is literally a slave, a person owned by another; Matthew also uses the term to describe how disciples are to relate to each other (20.27) (BDAG, p. 260).
29. Santiago Guijarro-Oporto discusses how the Matthean parables reflect the social stratification and economic dominance of rich landowners and kings ('The Family in First-century Galilee', in Halvor Moxnes [ed.], *Constructing Early Christian Families* [London: Routledge, 1997], pp. 42–65).

(19.30; 20.16), whoever wishes to be first must be a slave (20.25–28). If the 'king' is read as God, Matthew is deconstructing his own teachings about the Kingdom of Heaven. But if the king is just a king, then the slaves, along with the garmentless man, are the people that conform to the Kingdom of Heaven's ideals: slaves shall be first in the kingdom, and the garmentless man, who does not worry about what he wears, is among the 'last' to be invited who will then become 'first' in the Kingdom of Heaven.

Allegorical interpretations frequently identify the 'slaves' as the Old Testament prophets who have cajoled people to respond to God's invitation to relationship and whom Matthew indicates were killed (21.33–46; 23.29–39);[30] Matthew tells this parable and the one before it (21.33–41) against the religious leaders, whom he also accuses of being descendants of those who murdered the prophets (23.29–31; cf. 23.37).[31] Thus, the allegory blames religious leaders for the deaths of the prophets. Matthew indicates that Jesus' disciples are to be 'slaves' (20.27), so that the 'slaves' in the parable potentially represent would-be members of the Kingdom of Heaven. In typical allegorical interpretations, readers think that the king is the deity, but then when readers see the reaction to the slaves' death – the destruction of the murderers – they might begin to resist this interpretation: the deity shows no outrage at Jesus' death, nor

---

30. Hare, *Matthew*, p. 251; Senior, *Matthew*, p. 245; Carter, *Matthew and the Margins*, p. 435; Origen, *Commentary on Matthew* 17.22; Harrington, *The Gospel of Matthew*, p. 308; Hilary of Poitiers, *On Matthew*, 22; Honorius Augustodunensis, *Speculum ecclesiae*, 813–1108 (ed. J.-P. Migne; *Patrologiae cursus completes*, 172; [221 vols.; Paris: Garnier Frères, 1844–64]); Radulfus Ardens, *Homilies on the Gospels*, 43.2096 (ed. J.-P. Migne; *Patrologiae cursus completes*, 155 [221 vols.; Paris: Garnier Frères, 1844–64]; Albert the Great, *On Matthew* (Auguste Borgnet [ed.], *Opera Omnia* [38 vols.; Paris: Ludovicum Vivès, 1890–99], XX, pp. 34–44); Thomas Aquinas, *Commentary on Matthew* 542–46 (in Thomas Aquinas, *Opera Omnia* [ed. S.E. Fretté and Paul Maré; 34 vols; Paris: Ludovicum Vivès, 1871–80], XIX, pp. 226–668); Haimo of Auxerre, *Homilies on the Seasons*, 135.717–26 (ed. J.-P. Migne; *Patrologiae cursus completes*, 118 [221 vols.; Paris: Garnier Frères, 1844–64]); Paschasius Radbertus, *Expositio in evengelium Mattaei* 739–749 (in ed. J.-P. Migne; *Patrologiae cursus completus*, 120; [221 vols.; Paris: Garnier Frères, 1844–64]); Jerome (*On Matthew*, 22.4) discusses the possibility that the first servant (singular) was Moses and the subsequent servants the prophets and apostles (in E. Bonnard [ed.], *Saint Jerome: Commentarie sur S. Matthieu* [2 vols.; Sources Chrétiennes, 259; Paris: Les Éditions du Cerf, 1979], II, pp. 139–41. Notes in the Latin Vulgate of 1590 by Walahfrid Strabo (ninth century), Nicholas of Lyra (fourteenth century), Pablo de Santa Maria (fifteenth century), Mathias Döring (fifteenth century), and F. Feuardent (sixteenth century), *Biblia sacra, cum Glossa Ordinari* (Lyon, 1590), cited in Stephen L. Wailes, *Medieval Allegories of Jesus' Parables* (Berkeley: University of California Press, 1987), p. 156; Jones, *Matthean Parables*, p. 403; Gnilka, (*Matthäusevangelium*, pp. 238–39. Gnilka also sees a parallel with 2 Sam. 10.1–5 (David's envoys to the Ammonites are treated shamefully). Wainwright interprets the parable for today's church as a warning that refusal of God's invitation leads to violence against the poor and oppressed ('God Wills to Invite All to the Banquet,' *International Review of Mission* 77 (1988), p. 190).

31. Harrington, *Matthew*, p. 308.

does the deity destroy those that killed Jesus. Jesus has instructed disciples to forgive others and pray for enemies and persecutors; moreover, he has warned that such persecution comes from worldly powers.

2.5 The Call and Refusal

The 'call' is an invitation. Jesus and his mother are 'called' to a wedding (ἐκλήθη εἰς τὸν γάμον) in Jn. 2.2; servants 'call' a guest to Tobias's wedding feast (καλεῖ αὐτὸν εἰς τὸν γάμον) in Tob. 9.5;[32] Adonijah calls (ἐκάλεσσεν, from קרא) guests to a political feast (1 Kgs 1.9 [LXX 3 Kgs 1.9]). The choice of the word καλέω means more to Matthew than mere invitation, and the guests' acceptance or refusal is a grave decision:[33] the 'call' can also have salvific import,[34] because elsewhere in the gospel, Matthew uses καλέω to describe how God called (ἐκάλεσα) his son out of Egypt to save him from slavery (2.15; cf. Hos. 11.1, where the LXX reads μετεκάλεσα); Jesus called (ἐκάλεσεν) his disciples James and John (4.21) and came to call (καλέσαι) sinners (9.13). Matthew's term for the Jesus community is ἐκκλησία, the ones who are 'called out' (Mt. 16.18; 18.17).[35] The parable signals this interpretation when it ends: 'many are called (κλητοί), but few are chosen' (22.14). A non-allegorical reading suggests that the potential guests need to be able to distinguish between the 'call' of an earthly king and Jesus' 'call.'

In contrast to the specific excuses offered in Luke and Thomas ('I have bought a piece of land and must go out and see it; I have bought five yoke of oxen and am going to try them out; I have just been married and therefore cannot come' [Lk. 14.18–20]; and 'Some merchants owe me money and they are coming tonight; I have bought a house and have been called away for a day; my friend is to be married, and I am to arrange the banquet; I have bought an estate and am going to collect the rent' [G. Thom. 64]), Matthew does not list reasons why the guests do not come.

---

32. This wording is found in Codex Sinaiticus. Codex Vaticanus and Alexandrinus do not include καλέω (A. Rahlfs [ed.], Septuaginta [2 vols. in one; Stuttgart: Deutsche Bibelgesellschaft, 1979], I, p. 1025). For more examples of καλέω used for invitation, see K.L. Schmidt, 'καλέω', TDNT 3, pp. 487–536 (488).

33. This interpretation is also confirmed by the use of καλέω elsewhere: Wisdom sends her servants to 'call together' (ἀπέστειλε τοὺς ἑαυτῆς δούλους συγκαλοῦσα) guests to her banquet (Prov. 9.3–4; cf. Mt. 22.3, ἀπέστειλεν τοὺς δούλους αὐτοῦ καλέσαι ([Davies and Allison, Matthew, III, p. 199; Harrington, Matthew, p. 307]). Matthew (25.2) uses the same perfect participle (κεκλημένοι) as does John the Seer (Rev. 19.9) to claim that those who have been 'called' to the wedding banquet of the Lamb are blessed (Μακάριοι οἱ εἰς τὸ δεῖπνον τοῦ γάμου τοῦ ἀρνίου κεκλημένοι).

34. Schweizer, Matthew, p. 420.

35. For discussion of the use of this term in Matthew, see Schmidt, 'καλέω', pp. 518–26, and Davies and Allison, Matthew, II, pp. 629–30.

Thus Matthew focuses attention on the very fact that they refused,[36] and so highlights the disregard the guests show the king.[37] For Matthew's king, there is no acceptable excuse.[38] Unlike Luke, Matthew does not portray these guests putting on the pretense of being polite while expressing their regrets; Matthew states bluntly that they *do not want* to come (οὐκ ἤθελον ἐλθεῖν).[39] That the guests have not only no intention but no desire to come is frequently interpreted as apathy toward the Kingdom of Heaven; but their refusal could indicate that they are just as evil as the king. Because kings invite other people who have wealth and power to their banquets and not people off the streets, we see that the first set of guests are like the king, hence vindictive (they choose to snub his invitation) and murderous (they kill his slaves).

Perhaps *no* one wants to come, and the next batch of 'guests' must be dragged in off the streets. In the historical context of the Matthean portrayal of kings as tyrants (such as Herod the Great), such contempt and fear for the 'king' of the wedding parable is not a stretch of the imagination. In the context of this gospel, there is an expectation that the audience *should* resist kings, as the Magi resist honoring Herod's request that they return with news of the newborn Jesus (1.12), as Joseph took his family out of Herod's reach (1.13–14), and as John denounced Herod Antipas' marriage to Herodias (at the cost of his head [14.3]). It seems to me that this parable warns the reader *away* from this particular wedding feast.[40] This 'king' is a tyrant, and his feast is a dangerous place to be.

36. Senior remarks that the 'first call is simply rejected out of hand' (*Matthew*, p. 245).

37. See Bauckham, 'The Parable of the Royal Wedding Feast', p. 484; Schweizer, *Matthew*, p. 420. Patte explores how the refusal to come shows that the guests believe their own work to be better than anything the king might have to offer and so disvalue and even fear the king's invitation (Patte, *Matthew*, pp. 302–303). Funk explains that it does not matter why the guests did not want to come, as their refusal is a condition vital to the plot (*Language*, pp. 188–89).

38. Blomberg (*Interpreting Parables*, p. 238), in his allegorical interpretation, puts it bluntly that there is no excuse for refusing the invitation. To accept but come without proper attire is not much better, for it is to stand before God's judgment unprepared and 'expect to presume upon his grace.'

39. Patte, *Matthew*, p. 301; Carter, *Matthew and the Margins*, p. 435.

40. That there is something very wrong with this wedding feast is observed by Bailey, Linnemann, and Bauckham, who indicate how radical a breach of etiquette this refusal was and that it is odd that anyone would *not* want to enjoy such a lavish event. See Kenneth E. Bailey, *Through Peasant Eyes* (Grand Rapids: Eerdmans, 1983), pp. 94–95; Linnemann, *Parables of Jesus: Introduction and Exposition*, p. 89. Patte wonders why anyone would not want to be so honored (*Matthew*, p. 302). A wedding feast (γάμους; cf. Mt. 22.2; 25.10) was typically a large event to which an entire village or city might be invited (Keener, *Matthew*, pp. 518–19). An undated papyrus (*P. Oxy.* 33.2678) records an invitation to a wedding banquet: ἐρωτᾷ Διοσκοροῦς δειπνῆσαι εἰς γάμους τοῦ υἱοῦ ('Dioskorus asked [you] to dine at the wedding of [his] son'). An early (*c.* second century BCE) papyrus gives a reckoning of the preparations for a village celebration (κῶμος) of a wedding (*P. Giss.* 31) in *Greichische*

At the point the meal was ready, servants were sent to summon the guests who had agreed to come.[41] Bailey interprets the present imperative δεῦτε ('come,' 22.4) as a command to continue an action that had already begun. He summarizes: 'guests who accept the invitation are duty-bound to appear.'[42] But in this parable, not even a sense of duty overrides the guests' refusal to come; they feel no duty to honor this king. The king does not command the guests to attend, but his authority is in the invitation itself,[43] and by extension, in the messengers who bring it. To refuse such an invitation is to refuse the king's authority.[44] The invitees' snub is tantamount to political rebellion.[45] That the king's subjects refuse to come to such an important occasion as the marriage of a son who might become successor to the throne is an expression of extreme disloyalty: 'they are

Papyri im Museum des oberhessischen Geschichtsvereins zu Giessen, from *Perseus* website (www.perseus.tufts.edu). That weddings were traditionally lavish affairs can be seen from at least the fifth century BCE, when Aristotle refers to the public venue of a wedding (γάμος … εἰ περί ἡ πᾶσα πόλις σπουδάζει) and the magnitude of the wedding feast (*Nicomachean Ethics* 4.1123.a). Preparations could be lavish. Catullus describes guests packing the banquet hall to enjoy a beautiful feast of many courses (*Poem* 64.32–47, 303–304; cf. Mt. 22.10). Chariton tells of the sumptuous wedding banquet provided for all the residents of the city (*Callirhoe*, 3.2.7, 10–11). Tobit describes a wedding feast that includes many loaves of bread, two steers, and four rams (Tob. 8.19). Lucian (*Carousel* 38) gives a menu for a wedding feast at which each guest was served a bird, boar's and rabbit's meat, fish, sesame cakes, and sweetmeats, 'μία ὄρνις ἑκαστοῳ καὶ κρέας ὑὸς καὶ λαγῶα καὶ ἰχθὺς καὶ σησαμοῦντες καὶ ὅσα ἐντραγειν', A.M. Harmon (trans.), *Lucian* (Cambridge, MA: Harvard University Press, 2000), pp. 460–61. Other ancient sources that describe large wedding feasts include Chariton, *Chaer.* 3.2.10; Jos., *Ant.* 13.18–21; Diodorus Siculus, 16.91–92. The feasting and celebrating might last for several days (cf. Judg. 14.12; Tob. 8.19–20; *Jos. As.* 21.8; *b. Ket.* 4b).

41. Hilma Granqvist, an anthropologist who lived in a village south of Bethlehem in the 1920s, reports that she knew it was time to go to the house where the wedding was taking place when she heard the song of the women processing through the village. Thus, the 'summons' was the women's singing and processing, and the guests did not arrive until this point in the festivities (*Marriage Conditions in a Palestinian Village* [Helsingfors: Akademische Buchhandlung, 1935], p. 112.

42. Linnemann (*Parables of Jesus*, p. 89) agrees with Bailey that the invitation had already been accepted and that the servants were notifying the guests that it was time to come. Paul Ballard refutes Linnemann on the grounds that if this were typical behavior, the host would not be so angry ('Reasons for Refusing the Great Supper', *JTS* 23 [1972], pp. 341–350 [342]). The expectation that the guests will attend is consistent with Roman custom, where it was considered a duty to accept a wedding invitation and attend the wedding (Treggiari, *Roman Marriage: Iusti Coniuges from the Time of Cicero to the Time of Ulpian* (Oxford: Clarendon Press, 1991), p. 162, nn. 10, 11).

43. Patte, *Matthew*, p. 302.

44. Bauckham, 'Parable of the Royal Wedding Feast', p. 484; Patte, *Matthew*, p. 302.

45. Carter, *Matthew*, p. 435; Bauckham, 'Parable of the Royal Wedding Feast', p. 484; Boring, *Matthew*, p. 417.

deliberately treating the king's authority with contempt.'[46] If these guests snub the king out of loyalty to the Kingdom of Heaven, readers should honor them for their action, but I have read these first guests as people on a par with the king; their resistance is not noble. They are the first to show violence when they kill the king's messengers.

Matthew has portrayed kings and rulers as tyrants, so that an allegorical reading of this parable identifying the 'king' as God becomes extremely problematic, if not impossible: God as 'king' will fly into a rage and murder those who offend him and will violently expel a guest who is not appropriately garbed. Such an allegorical reading interprets God to be a 'king' no better than violent earthly kings.

2.6 *The Second Invitation: 'Come to the Feast'*

The king sends messengers a second time to call the first invitees (in contrast to Luke, *Gospel of Thomas* and other versions). The dual sending matches that of the previous parable (Mt. 21.34, 36),[47] where the landowner sends servants twice to the vineyard. For Wainwright, this second chance is merciful and recollects Matthew's Parable of the Two Sons: the son who initially says 'no' is given a chance to change his mind and do the will of the father (21.29), just as the guests who have refused to come receive another chance to change their minds.[48] But the second calling turns out to be a threat: 'come – or else.' The consequences of refusing to come are severe, and even responding to the imperative does not guarantee a place at the table.

The notification that the 'animals are slaughtered' (τεθυμένα) is a violent image that recalls the king's murdered slaves and foreshadows the slaughter of his subjects. The words 'all is ready' (πάντα ἕτοιμα) is also reminiscent of Wisdom's dinner (Prov. 9.2–3). Wisdom also has slaughtered her animals (θύματα), and she has made ready (ἡτοιμάσατο) her table.[49] Wisdom also sends out slaves (δοῦλοι) to call people to the

---

46. Bauckham, 'Parable of the Royal Wedding Feast', p. 484. Also Keener, *Matthew*, p. 520 and Patte, *Matthew*, p. 302. Thus, in an allegorical reading, the guests treat God with contempt and challenge God's honor. See Jerome Neyrey, *Honor and Shame in the Gospel of Matthew* (Louisville: Westminster John Knox Press, 1998), p. 60.

47. Davies and Allison, *Matthew*, III, p. 199; Schnackenburg, *Matthew*, p. 214.

48. Wainwright, 'God Wills to Invite All', p. 189.

49. Medieval interpreters found allegorical meaning in the food the king has prepared: Origen said that the meal represents nourishment from the divine mysteries (*Commentary on Matthew*, 17). Quite a few commentators followed Gregory the Great's interpretation that the bullocks represent the fathers of the Old Testament (who physically attacked their adversaries) and the fatlings represent the fathers of the New Testament (who receive the richness of inner grace and could elevate themselves in contemplation). See Gregory the Great (*Homilies*, 38), Haimo of Auxerre (*Homilies on the Seasons*, 719D) in Haimo of

banquet (Prov. 9.3). But while Wisdom's table offers life (Prov. 9.6) and refusal to come might lead to death eventually (9.18), her servants and guests do not die violently, nor does she cast out people from her feast.

The command δεῦτε (with the nuance of 'come now, come right away!') changes from ominous imperative to the joyful announcement of final inclusion among the elect in the Parable of the Last Judgment (25. 31–46).[50] In this parable, Jesus is a king (βασιλεύς) (25.34) who has the power to judge. The king tells those on his right, 'Come (δεῦτε), you that are blessed by my Father, inherit the kingdom prepared for you' (25.34). The 'son' acts in his role as 'king,' and the elect now 'inherit' the kingdom (they become like sons). They are no longer merely guests but heirs.[51] In this parable, those who are invited to come have *already* earned their place in the kingdom prepared for them. The invitation to 'come' is a welcome reward and can no longer be viewed as an obligation. The 'sheep' on Jesus' right would not want to refuse this invitation.

In a scene strikingly similar scene to Matthew's Parable of the Wedding Feast,[52] a heavenly messenger (ἄγγελος) says: 'Come' (Δεῦτε) to the 'great supper of God' (τὸ δεῖπνον τὸ μέγα τοῦ θεοῦ), at which will be eaten the flesh of kings, captains, the mighty, the horses and their riders, free and slave (Rev. 19.17–18). This violent scene is apparently the bridegroom Lamb's wedding feast, because it immediately follows an announcement of the 'marriage supper of the Lamb' (τὸ δεῖπνον τοῦ γάμου τοῦ ἀρνίου 19.9). Therefore, the violent military action taken against the bridegroom Lamb's enemies (Rev.19.17–18) is the beginning of his wedding feast, and the wedding guests actually feast on their enemies.[53]

If the parable is interpreted allegorically, the gracious invitation loses some of its grace; but if the parable is treated as a depiction of violent earthly oppression of kings, the resisting reader can find a subversive warning that urges faithfulness to the Kingdom of Heaven and resistance to the earthly king.

Auxerre, *Homiliae de tempore* (ed. J.-P. Migne, *Patrologiae cursus completus*, Latin series, 118; 221 vols.; Paris: Garnier Frères, 1844–64), columns 747–804. Paschasius Radbertus (*Expositio*, 1242C), *Expositio in evangelium Matthaei* (ed. Migne, *Patrologiae cursus completus*, 120), columns 31–994; Christian of Stablo (*Expositio*, 1439B), *Expositio in Matthaeum evangelistam* (ed. Migne, *Patrologiae cursus completus*, 106; col. 1261–1504); Ludolph of Saxony, *Vita Jesu Christi e quatuor Evangeliis et scriptoribus orthodoxies concinnata* (Paris: V. Palmé, 1865), pp. 515–18. Bruno of Segni interprets the bullocks as doctrine and the fatlings as inspiration (*On Matthew*, 250D–253C, cited in Wailes, *Medieval Allegories*), p. 160.

50.   This parable is clearer about its setting in the end times than is the Parable of the Wedding Feast, with its language about the Son of Man coming in his glory with the angels.

51.   While they inherit the kingdom (κληρονομήσατε τὴν βασιλείαν) (25.34), the parable does not call them 'sons.'

52.   The similarity may indicate a shared tradition of the heavenly banquet.

53.   Pippin, *Death and Desire*, p. 68.

2.7 *The Burned City*

Modern readers tend to see the king's burning the city as extreme: 'It is a straight punitive expedition,' writes Lambrecht, who wonders 'why vengeance should be extended to the city of the murderers.'[54] Given Matthew's portrayal of kings and rulers as tyrants, Matthew's audience would likely not be surprised to hear that a king went to destroy insurrectionists;[55] they would probably regard such a response as a matter of restoring the king's honor.[56] Not clear is whether or not they would regard the destruction of the entire city as typical or extreme (cf. Jdt. 1. 7–12). A similar story of a king's spurned invitation to a dinner (2 Chron. 30.1–12; Josephus, *Ant.* 9.263–65) depicts a king who did *not* retaliate or attempt to regain honor when his invitation was spurned, although this story is told as an example of this particular king's unusual piety; hence, he is not a typical king. King Hezekiah invites all Israel to celebrate the feast of the Passover in Jerusalem. Most of the people not only refuse to come, they mock and mistreat the king's messengers, in the same way, according to Josephus, they mocked and killed the prophets (*Ant.* 9.265), and the same way the people mock and mistreat the servants in the parable. However, a good many did come to Hezekiah's feast. Instead of retaliating against those who did not come, the king turned his attention to constructive tasks: he restored the sanctity of the priests; there was healing; and the people who came kept the festival for an extra seven days with great joy and feasting (2 Chron. 30.13–27). A city is not burned but its holiness restored (2 Chron. 31.5–21). Thus, while Matthew portrays a slighted king sending troops to burn offenders' cities, there is precedence for a king who does not respond with vindictiveness.

The burned city in the parable is almost unanimously interpreted as Jerusalem, which was destroyed by the Roman army in 70 CE.[57] A burned

---

54. Lambrecht, *Out of the Treasure*, pp. 132–33. This interpretation first occurs in Trilling, *The Gospel According to Matthew* (2 vols.; New York: Herder and Herder, 1969), p. 155. Funk (*Language*, p. 165) uses the same phrase 'punitive expedition' to describe the king's actions. Others who note the extreme reaction of the king include Carter, *Matthew and the Margins*, p. 435; Hare, *Matthew*, p. 251; Patte, *Matthew*, p. 303; and Bacon, 'Two Parables', p. 345.

55. Bauckham, 'Parable of the Royal Wedding Feast', p. 484; Keener, *Matthew*, pp. 520–21; Schweizer, *Matthew*, pp. 418–19.

56. Keener, *Matthew*, p. 521. Jones (*Matthean Parables*, p. 404) agrees that the burned city represents the 'repressive activities of kings.' Patte and Carter say that the ungrateful guests bring upon themselves the king's destructive anger (Patte, *Matthew*, p. 303; Carter, *Matthew and the Margins*, p. 435), an interpretation with which I disagree and will discuss below.

57. Davies and Allison, *Matthew*, I, pp. 131–32, and III, pp. 201–202; Keener, *Matthew*, p. 518; H. Hendrickx, *The Parables of Jesus* (San Francisco: Harper and Row, 1986), p. 125; Lambrecht, *Out of the Treasure*, p. 133; Harrington, *Matthew*, p. 308; J. Andrew Overman, 'Matthew's Parables and Roman Politics: The Imperial Setting of Matthew's Narrative with

city is a literary *topos* for human warfare established in such texts as Josh.
6.21–24; Judg. 1.8; 18.27; 20.48; 1 Macc. 5.28, 35; Josephus, *Ant.* 12.329,
336; *War* 3.132–4.[58] Burned cities sometimes refer to divine retribution
(as in the case of Sodom, onto which the Lord rained down fire [Gen.
19.24; cf. Mt. 10.15; 11.23–24]). Matthew frequently uses fire as a means
of dividing the bad from the good: trees that do not bear fruit are thrown
into the fire (3.10; 7.19); chaff and weeds are separated from the grain and
burned (3.12; 13.40); those who are angry (ὀργίζομαι, like the king in the
parable! [22.7]), give insult (εἴπῃ 'Ρακά)[59] or say 'you fool' (εἴπῃ Μωρέ)
are consigned to the fire (5.22); evildoers will be cast into the furnace of
fire where there will be weeping and gnashing of teeth (13.42, 50; cf.
22.13); it is better to cut off a hand or foot and throw it into the fire or
pluck out an eye than to be thrown whole-bodied into the fire (5.29–30;
18.8–9); the accursed on the king's left will be banished into the eternal
fire (25.41). Thus the burning city in 22.7 may be a reference to the
destruction of Jerusalem, but it is also a typical instance of Matthew's
separation of the unworthy from the worthy.

A resisting reading notes that the judgment by fire should, by
Matthew's definition, include the murderous wedding guests and the
'king' himself. As the Matthean Jesus earlier instructs: 'You have heard it
said that it was said to those in ancient times, "You shall not murder,"
and "whoever murders will be liable to judgment," but I say to you that if
you are angry with a brother, you will be liable to judgment.'[60] The king is
not only 'angry,' but enraged enough to murder (22.7), the very sin against
which the 'fence' of avoiding anger is designed to protect (5.21–22). If the

---

Special Reference to His Parables', *Society of Biblical Literature Seminar Papers* (SBLSP, 34;
Atlanta: Scholars Press, 1995), pp. 425–36 (434); Blomberg, *Interpreting Parables*, p. 237;
Drury, *Parables in the Gospels*, pp. 97–98; Viviano, 'Matthew', p. 665; Hare, *Matthew*, p. 251;
Schweizer, *Matthew*, pp. 418–19; Beare, *Matthew*, p. 432; Albright and Mann, *Matthew*, p.
269; Schnackenburg, *Matthew*, p. 215; Matura, 'Les Invites', p. 21; Funk, *Language*, p. 184;
McKenzie, 'Matthew', p. 100; Hasler, 'Die Königliche Hochzeit', p. 34; Weder, *Gleichnisse*,
p. 191; Trilling, *Matthew*, pp. 155–56; Bacon, 'Two Parables', p. 345; Jülicher suggests that
the troops are Vespasian's legions (*Gleichnisreden*, p. 421). Boring cautions that the
destruction of Jerusalem could just as easily be Matthew's reflection on Isa. 5.24–25 and thus
not necessarily a reference to the Roman sacking of Jerusalem (*Matthew*, p. 418).

58. Davies and Allison, *Matthew*, III, p. 202. Carter provides further examples of kings
destroying cities in order to subjugate defiant people: 1 Macc. 1.19, 29–32; 5.5, 27–28, 35,
50–51, 65; Josephus, *War* 2.504–505 (Carter, *Matthew and the Margins*, p. 435).

59. 'Ρακά is a term of abuse that has something to do with 'empty-headedness,' from
Aramaic רֵיקָא or רֵיקָה, 'empty one' (BDAG, p. 903). Therefore, it reinforces the
'foolishness' of calling someone 'moron' (Μωρέ) (also in 5.22).

60. An American Lutheran pastor, Edward Mitchell, stated that 'It is not the Lord that
destroys men, but the fire is in themselves' (Edward C. Mitchell, *The Parables of the New
Testament Spiritually Unfolded* [Philadelphia: William H. Alden, 2nd edn, 1900], p. 234).
Carter discusses instances of divine justice by fire (*Matthew and the Margins*, p. 436).

king gets away with murder because he is 'king,' so much the more tyrannical is the portrait of the parable's monarch, and the more untenable is the allegorical interpretation of God as the 'king.'

Luke's transition from the king's anger to the command to go find other guests is smooth (Lk. 14.21), while in Matthew's version, there is a gap in the story: the dinner is apparently abandoned so the king can send troops to destroy the offending city. Only after the destruction does he send servants out to invite others to the feast.[61] Hendrickx follows the verisimilitude of the story to the conclusion that the wedding feast (which was 'ready' [ἕτοιμα, 22.4]) must have sat waiting on the table the whole time the king was at war,[62] an observation that suggests that for Matthew, punishment is more important than celebration in this parable. The punishment could have waited until after the festivities, but instead, everything else waits until the slaughter and destruction are complete.

The violence fits a pattern established in the Parable of the Tenants (21.33–41) and developed in the Parable of the Great Judgment (25. 31–46). 'Seize' (κρατήσαντες), used to describe the unworthy invitees' treatment of the king's slaves (22.6), is the same word used to describe how the tenants overpower and kill the servants and the heir (21.35–39).[63] Matthew uses κρατέω to describe the arrest and murder of John (14.3) and the attempts to seize and kill Jesus (21.46; 26.4), as well as his arrest (26.48, 50, 55, 57).[64] Therefore, the use of κρατέω to describe what happened to John and Jesus subversively suggests that the slaves and the garmentless man – all of whom were seized – are the characters in the story aligned with the Kingdom of Heaven.

The wedding feast is a scene of greater violence than the vineyard.[65] The occasion is no longer the collection of rent, but a feast in honor of the king's son's wedding. Thus the consequences for showing contempt for the son and his father are now higher: the wicked guests are not only killed, their entire city is burned. The burning signals utter annihilation, the complete removal of the unworthy guests and an attempt to erase everything that holds any memory of them. Who, then, are the unworthy guests? Most allegorical readings interpret the unworthy guests as Israel, because Israel killed the prophets and rejected Jesus as

61. Hendrickx, *Parables*, p.125.
62. Hendrickx, *Parables*, p. 125. This concern is voiced also by John A.T. Robinson (*Redating the New Testament* [Philadelphia: Westminster Press, 1976], p. 19), Keener, *Matthew*, p. 521; Hare, *Matthew*, p. 251; and Beare, *Matthew*, p. 433.
63. Matura ('Les Invites', p. 21) details the similarities between the two parables.
64. Keener, *Matthew*, p. 521; Carter, *Matthew and the Margins*, p. 435.
65. Jones, *Matthean Parables*, p. 403.

the Messiah;[66] others interpret the unworthy not as Israel in general, but only those who oppose Matthew's theology.[67] But other characters also fit the roles in the parable: the 'son' for whom the feast was held could represent Israel, because the Matthean audience knows the tradition that Israel is a 'son' (Exod. 4.22; Ps. 2.7; Hos. 11.1–3), and Matthew specifically refers to this tradition in the birth narrative: 'out of Egypt I have called my son' (Mt. 2.15).[68] Jesus fits the allegorical role of 'king' ('king of the Jews' [2.2; 27.29, 37], 'king of Israel' [27.42], and the 'king' who judges the nations [25.34]).[69] The text does not require that Israel is rejected – on the contrary, Israel is the 'son' for whom the feast is given, and the final judgment is not upon Israel but upon 'all the nations' (πάντα τὰ ἔθνη) (25.32).

2.8 *The Next Group of Guests*

After the city has been burned, the king sends his slaves to find people at the crossroads and bring them to the feast. The διεξόδους is the crossing of main streets, or the roads in and out of town, so that one would expect to find a number of people there.[70] 'When you find' (ἐὰν εὕρητε) is a subordinate clause that expects a positive outcome: the king indicates that there *will* be people to invite.[71] Matthew does not tell us what sorts of people the slaves can expect to find (in contrast to Luke, who specifies the

66.   Trilling, *Matthew*, p. 156; Beare, *Matthew*, p. 432. Trilling compares the burning of Jerusalem by Rome to the sack of Jerusalem by Babylon and the resulting conversion of a 'remnant' of the people. Jülicher (*Gleichnisreden*, p. 421) says that Vespasian's legions were sent by God to bring Israel to justice for the deaths of Stephen, and James. V. Hasler ('Die königliche Hochzeit', p. 33–34) goes so far as to say the destruction of Jerusalem is God's outraged revenge ('*die zornige Vergeltung Gottes*') on the entire Jewish people ('*das ganze Volk*') for the murder of the prophets and the Messiah, based on Mt. 27.24 ('his blood be upon us and our children').

67.   Overman, 'Matthew's Parables and Roman Politics', p. 434; Davies and Allison, *Matthew*, p. 202. Amy-Jill Levine argues that the focus of the parable is on the fate of the leaders, not on historical context (*Social and Ethnic Dimensions of Matthean Salvation History* [Studies in the Bible and Early Christianity, 14; Lewiston: Edwin Meller Press, 1988], p. 214). The Matthean Jesus targets the chief priests, elders (21.23), Pharisees (21.45; 22.15; 23.31), Sadducees (22.23), and scribes (23.1) but saves his greatest criticism for the scribes and Pharisees who lead others astray (23.1–15), as he does Church members who lead others astray in 18.6–14.

68.   From Hos. 11.1, 'When Israel was a child, I loved him, and out of Egypt I called my son.'

69.   This interpretation becomes problematic, because Jesus is not 'father' (so, the king in the parable) and remains a 'son' even while he is in the role of 'king' (25.34).

70.   BDAG, p. 194. Harrington (*Parables*, p. 306) disagrees, because he views these 'thoroughfares' as the way out of town, so that the servants would have to make an effort to find people.

71.   BDAG, p. 211.

poor, crippled, blind, and lame [Lk. 14.21]). However, given the setting, it is likely they are the working poor or beggars. The king invited people closer to his own social status the first time around; now he is bringing in the poor, who were not deemed worthy of an invitation earlier, off the streets.

Matthew does not say the slaves are to 'lead' (εἰσάγαγε, Lk. 14.21) the people to the banquet, which implies compulsion, but simply to 'call,' as with the first guests. While this 'call' could be seen an act of graciousness and a lessening of violent intent, it might also indicate that there is no chance that this group, in their less powerful condition, will not obey him, for two reasons: if the second group does represent mostly poor people, they will come to the feast because they do not want to pass by a chance to eat a free meal, and second, they may be afraid *not* to come, because they know what happened to the first group.

A common allegorical interpretation of the command to invite other guests is that the mission among the Jews has run its course; now the focus broadens to include the Gentiles, or the universal mission of the Church.[72]

---

72. For example, medieval commentators allegorized the 'main roads' or 'crossroads' to mean the various heathen teachings from which the Gentiles are rescued (Geoffrey Babion, *On Matthew*, 1437A), idolatry and sin (Radalfus Ardens, *Homilies on the Gospels*, 2096B), failures of earthly activity (Gregory the Great, *Homily* 38) (all cited in Wailes, *Medieval Allegories*, pp. 157–58), or errors of the Gentiles (Thomas Aquinas, *Catena Aurea* 22.1–14 in Aquinas, *Catena Aurea: Commentary on the Four Gospels Collected Out of the Works of the Fathers* [trans. John Henry Cardinal Newman; London: Saint Austin Press, 1997], p. 745). Robert Funk discusses the implications of this interpretation in terms of city and country, but does not think 'city' necessarily means Israel and 'country' the Gentiles (*Language*, pp. 171, 184–85). Others who discuss the parable in terms of the Gentile mission include Davies and Allison, *Matthew*, III, p. 202; Hendrickx, *Parables*, pp. 126, 132; Drury, *Parables*, pp. 97–98; Weder, *Gleichnisse*, pp. 191–92; Gnilka, *Matthäusevangelium*, pp. 239–40; Winterhalter and Fisk, *Jesus' Parables: Finding Our God Within* (Mahwah, NJ: Paulist Press, 1993), p. 77; Jeremias, *Die Gleichnisse Jesu*, pp. 20–25, and Jeremias, 'Von der Urkirche zu Jesus Zurück', in Harnisch (ed.), *Gleichnisse Jesu* (Darmstadt: Wissenschaftliche Buchgesellschaft, 1982), pp. 180–237 (esp. 190–91); Madeleine Boucher, *The Parables* (New Testament Message, 7; Dublin: Veritas, 1981), p. 103; Paul H. Ballard, 'Reasons for Refusing the Great Supper', *JTS* 23 (1972), pp. 341–50 (349); John P. Meier, *Matthew* (New Testament Message, 3; Dublin: Veritas, 1980), p. 247; Linnemann, *Parables of Jesus*, p. 95; Wilhelm Michaelis, *Das hochzeitliche Kleid* (Berlin: Furche Verlag, 1939), pp. 57–58. R. Swaeles, 'L'Orientation ecclésiastique de la parabole du festin nuptial en Mt 22.1–14', *ETL* 36 (1960), pp. 655–84 (673); Hasler, 'Die königliche Hochzeit', pp. 25–35; J. McKenzie, 'Matthew', p. 100; Beare, 'Guests', p. 5; Willoughby C. Allen, *A Critical and Exegetical Commentary on the Gospel According to Matthew* (ICC; New York: Charles Scribner's Sons, 1907), p. 235. Heinrich Schlier emphasizes that the parable speaks to 'Christians from among Gentiles' (H. Schlier, *The Relevance of the New Testament* [New York: Herder and Herder, 1967], pp. 249–50, 253); Andries van Aarde concludes that the unworthy guests symbolize the Jewish leaders, while the newly invited guests represent members of the Matthean community (A. van Aarde, *God-with-Us: The Dominant Perspective in Matthew's Story* (Hervormde Teologiese Studies, 5; Pretoria: University of Pretoria, 1994), p. 247. Dodd (*Parables*, p. 94) disagrees while citing the anti-Gentile sentiments in Matthew (10.5–6). Dodd thinks

However, the second group does not need to be so narrowly defined as Gentiles to the exclusion of Jews, because as we have seen, the parable can be read in exactly the opposite way, with Israel as honored son. Moreover, Matthew ultimately divides not between Jews and Gentiles (28.18–20), but between those who follow his theology and those who do not.

A resisting reading of Matthew's version brings class issues into play (in a similar way to Luke's parable). A king would normally invite wealthy and influential guests to a feast. Only when these elites refuse to come does he invite a new crowd of guests that represents the poor.[73] A rabbinic parable illustrates a wealthy and politically well-connected man choosing between the powerful and the marginal in exactly the same way as the king in the parable: 'Once a tax collector gave a breakfast for the leading men of town, and they had not come. So he gave orders that the poor were to be invited to eat it, lest it should go to waste' (*y. San.* 6.23c).[74] The second invitation to the poor seems generous until one considers that these people were left out of the first invitation because they lacked social status, and that the only reason they are invited is to avoid wasting the food.

In the Matthean parable, members of the second group are still liable to rejection when the king comes to make sure his new guests have the proper 'wedding garment.' Another selection is to come, because the

---

this parable guards against the Church letting in the Gentiles too easily. Lemcio ('Parables of the Great Supper', pp. 14–15) cites Matthean emphasis on the Davidic genealogy of Jesus that precludes such a division and argues that the exclusion of the first group of guests, even if they do represent the Jews, is only an historical reprisal, while the consequences for the second set of guests is eschatological.

73.   Amy-Jill Levine points out that there is no need to apply ethnic categories, because the two groups are divided along lines of status: the privileged and well-settled elite refuse the first invitation, while the marginalized and mobile non-elites accept the second (A.-J. Levine, *Social and Ethnic Dimensions*, pp. 212–13). Benedict Viviano ('Matthew', p. 665) notes that the streets would be filled with people from all walks of life and professions. George Buttrick (*Parables*, pp. 227–28) colorfully describes how rejection by the 'classes' brings on the 'masses,' an odd mixture of people who crowd the banquet hall: 'cripples, ne'er-do-wells, lame, blind, and dumb beggars, vermin-eaten saints with mouldy breath, drabs and vixens, weasel heads, sages, sibyls, athletes clean, rulers of empires.' Lemcio ('Parables of the Great Supper', p. 10) compares the inclusion and exclusion of certain types of people from the Dead Sea Scrolls communities, particularly 1QM 7.4–6 and 1QSa 2.5–22. Against James A. Sanders ('The Ethic of Election in Luke's Great Banquet Parable', in J. Crenshaw and J. Willis [eds.], *Essays in Old Testament Ethics* [New York: KTAV, 1974], pp. 245–71), Lemcio argues that the Qumran community did not exclude anyone, but merely relegated those deemed less worthy to lower ranking positions at the messianic banquet.

74.   The moral of this particular parable is more about the worthiness of the host than the guests: even one good deed such as this does not outweigh a lifetime of sin.

wedding feast is filled with both 'evil and good' people (πονηρούς καὶ ἀγαθούς).[75] That Matthew lists the evil (πονηρούς) first places emphasis on this group. But for now, they are all together, and the final sorting will occur later, as another Matthean parable (13.47–50) makes clear: 'The Kingdom of Heaven is like a net that was thrown into the sea and all were drawn out together (συναγαγούσῃ). When it was full (ἐπληρώθη), they drew it ashore, sat down, and put the good (καλά) into baskets but threw out the bad (σαπρά). So it will be at the end of the age. The angels will come out and separate the evil (πονηρούς) from the righteous (δικαίων) and throw them into the furnace of fire where there will be weeping and gnashing of teeth' (ἐκεῖ ἔσται ὁ καλυθμὸς καὶ ὁ βρυγμὸς τῶν ὀδόντων). 'Weeping and gnashing of teeth' is the same fate that awaits the garmentless guest in the Parable of the Wedding Feast.[76] The Parable of the Great Judgment (or Sheep and Goats) (25.31–46) contains similar language: all people are gathered together (συναχθήσονται) and later judged.[77]

But in a more literal reading, there is much less graciousness than manipulation in the second invitation that includes both bad and good, because even after two sets of invitations, the king is still being selective about who comes to his feast. He is toying with his guests. Moreover, a reading of the 'king' as a human tyrant disrupts our assumptions of who the 'good' and 'bad' guests represent: perhaps in the eyes of the Kingdom of Heaven, the man without a wedding garment is among the 'good.'

2.9 *The Guest without a Wedding Garment*

The second group has come to wedding feast, but acceptance of the invitation does not mean that everyone will be worthy to stay. Patte voices the audience's surprise that the story is not yet over: 'one of the *new* guests

---

75. Trilling, *Matthew*, p. 158; Lambrecht, *Out of the Treasure*, pp. 135–36 (Lambrecht very closely follows Trilling but does not refer to his work); Davies and Allison, *Matthew*, III, pp. 202–203 ; Donahue, *Gospel in Parable*, p. 94; Jeremias, *Die Gleichnisse Jesu*, pp. 20–25, and 'Von der Urkirche zu Jesus Zurück', pp. 190–91; Hasler, 'Die königliche Hochzeit', p. 29; Hahn, 'Das Gleichnis', p. 82; Weder, *Gleichnisse*, pp. 188–91; Günther Baumbach, *Das Verständnis des Bösen in den synoptischen Evangelien* (Berlin: Evangelische Verlagsanstalt, 1963), pp. 74–75; Alberto Vaccari, 'La Parabole du Festin de Noces', *RSR* 39 (1951), pp. 138–45 (esp. pp. 141–42); Jülicher, *Gleichnisreden*, p. 423.

76. The Parable of the Weeds (13.24–30) is another example of the good and bad sown together that will be separated at a later time.

77. I am not as inclined to resist this parable, because Matthew provides reasons for the division of the 'sheep and goats' based on their deeds of righteousness that comport with teachings elsewhere in the gospel.

is also excluded.'[78] Cripps allegorizes that the garmentless man is *not* new, but a long-standing member of the community, even one of the inner circle: Judas.[79] I think the element of surprise is the more powerful reading.

The logistics of attending the feast are strained. Many interpreters note the difficulty of the expectation that a person on the streets, who had no prior invitation, should have a proper garment, especially if that person has not had time to change clothes before coming or is too poor to have a festal robe (like people gathered from the crossroads).[80] Interpreters who view the 'king' allegorically as God attempt to soften the situation by suggesting that appropriate garments merely need to be clean and not soiled, thus even a poor person could come with freshly washed garments.[81] I do not see how this is a viable possibility, given that the narrative shows the people coming directly from the street, and they would not have time to wash their clothing, either.

Therefore, if we do not read allegorically but literally, it appears that the king judges this man based on his clothing, and that the king makes no attempt to help him obtain the appropriate garment. The king's judgment of the garmentless man comports with wealthy persons' attitudes toward the working poor in Matthew's time.[82] The king's judgment of the

---

78. Patte, *Matthew*, p. 301. Italics mine. In the past, those who have been thrown out of the community were already members and not new converts (8.11–12). However, previous parables have stages of judgment, as the weeds among the wheat that are not separated until later (e.g., 13.24–30).

79. K. Cripps, 'A Note on Matthew xxii.12', *ExpTim* 69 (1957–58), p. 30.

80. Keener, *Matthew*, p. 522; Hare, *Matthew*, p. 252; Harrington, *Matthew*, p. 306; Patte, *Matthew*, p. 301. Schnackenburg (*Matthew*, p. 215) calls it 'surprising and unsettling.' Dan Via sees evidence of two parables, one about a wedding feast and another about a wedding garment. Via posits that the original parable of the wedding garment had a beginning that Matthew replaced with the parable of the wedding feast, so that the circumstances of the man's not having the proper garment are not made clear (Dan O. Via, *The Parables: Their Literary and Existential Dimension* [Philadelphia: Fortress Press, 1967], p. 129). Others who posit the joining of two separate parables include Donahue, *The Gospel in Parable*, p. 92; Winterhalter and Fisk, *Jesus' Parables*, p. 61; Buttrick, *Parables*, p. 228, n. 17; Schweizer, *Matthew*, p. 417; Hahn, 'Das Gleichnis', p. 75; Weder, *Gleichnisse*, p. 183; Dillon, 'Towards a Tradition-History', esp. pp. 10–11; Linnemann, 'Überlegungen zur Parabel', p. 253; Funk, *Language*, pp. 169–70; Dodd, *Parables*, p. 94; Herbert A. Musurillo, 'Many Are Called, but Few Are Chosen', *TS* 7 (1946), pp. 583–89 (583).

81. E.g., Jeremias, *Parables*, pp. 187–88; Davies and Allison, *Matthew*, III, p. 204; Schnackenburg, *Matthew*, p. 215; U. Luz, *Das Evangelium nach Matthäus* (EICICNT, 476; Zurich: Benziger Verlag, 1990), III, p. 244. Keener cites *Damascus Document* rules (CD 11.22) for wearing clean clothing into the house of worship (Keener, *Matthew*, p. 522, n. 189).

82. Paul Veyne demonstrates how the rich regarded the poor as lesser human beings and how they both idealized and scorned the poor with bucolic poetry and grotesque statuary. See Veyne, 'Work and Leisure', in Veyne (ed.), *A History of Private Life: From Pagan Rome to Byzantium* (trans. A. Goldhammer; Cambridge, MA: Harvard University Press, 1987), pp. 117–37.

garmentless man is often interpreted allegorically as the final judgment;[83] however, if a non-allegorical interpretation is followed, the king's actions simply reveal the typical attitude of the wealthy and powerful toward the poor. That the gospel earlier tells us not to worry about what to wear (6.25–31) is a clue that the 'king' is not God but a human tyrant, and further, that the man without a proper garment is following the advice given in the Sermon on the Mount not to be concerned with clothing.

Osiek and Balch suggest that the host's receiving this stranger as a guest, 'especially the invitation of a meal, creates a bond within the patronage system whereby the stranger is welcomed as fictive kin.' That the guest dishonors the host by not wearing the proper garment causes the host to dishonor and harm the guest.[84] If this is so, then the 'king' also violates the rules of hospitality: he fails to protect and welcome this guest as fictive kin. The king's reaction to the garmentless guest runs counter to the cultural obligations of the patron to protect fictive kin and shows the king's pitiless judgment of a poor man.

That the king addresses the unworthy guest as 'friend' (ἑταῖρε) indicates that he has already picked out this man from the crowd.[85] In two other instances, Matthew identifies a person thought to be a friend or companion as worthy of reproach: one of the complaining workers in the vineyard (Mt. 20.13) is addressed as 'friend' (ἑταῖρε), and Jesus asks, 'Friend (ἑταῖρε), why are you here?' (Mt. 26.50) of Judas when he kisses Jesus to betray him to those who would arrest him.[86] Ἑταῖρε refers to a comrade, a member of one's group or to one's pupil; Danker specifies that this relationship is 'not necessarily at the level of a φίλος or φίλη.'[87] Indeed, there is a nuance of underhandedness associated with a ἑταῖρος. For example, one of Samson's ἑταῖροι (his thirty companions at his wedding) is given Samson's bride (Judg. 14.11–20). Amnon's ἑταῖρος Jonadab (2 Sam. 13.3) persuades Amnon to trick Tamar into his bed chamber so that he can rape her (2 Sam. 13.1–14). David's ἑταῖρος Hushai traitorously switches his allegiance to Absalom (2 Sam. 16.17; cf.

---

83. Davies and Allison, *Matthew*, III, pp. 203–204; Beare, *Matthew*, p. 436. Drury interprets the parable as an allegory of the Church's coming judgment: once established, churches 'need to be kept in order by the prospect of doomsday and the fear of hell. The man without the wedding garment is an improper and fraudulent Christian ... God will judge him in the end' (Drury, *Parables*, p. 99). Origen, noting that both bad and good were called, remarks: 'The outcome was not to be that the bad should remain bad, but that they should change their habits' (*Commentary on Matthew*, 17).

84. Osiek and Balch, *Families in the New Testament World*, p. 39.

85. Just as Matthew designates five of the ten virgins as 'foolish' in Mt. 25.1–13.

86. Via, *The Parables*, p. 129; D. Harrington, *Matthew*, p. 306. When used of Judas, the phrase is even sarcastic.

87. Socrates referred to his pupils as ἑταῖροι (BDAG, p. 388). The term is not used elsewhere in the New Testament.

15.37). Thus, while ἑταῖρος is usually translated 'friend' or 'companion,' in these instances it does not refer to someone who has one's best interests in mind.[88]

Matthew uses *familial* language to describe true disciples (e.g., 'brothers' [ἀδελφοί] and 'mother' [μήτηρ, 12.48–50]). The distinction between 'friend' and 'brother' or 'mother' as intimate comports with the theme of fictive family Matthew develops: those who do the will of Jesus' Father in heaven are his brothers and mother (12.48–50). Those who are merely ἑταῖροι (companions) do not do the will of Jesus' Father and have not truly joined the fictive family. The absence of familial language, in an allegorical interpretation, would indicate that God as king does not recognize this man as being part of his fictive family and so expels him. However, if the king is not God, the absence of familial language does not necessarily mean that the garmentless man is unworthy of the fictive family, but could indicate instead that this particular wedding feast does *not* represent the fictive family. The man's expulsion from the king's feast does not exclude him from the fictive family but on the contrary might indicate that he is worthy of the fictive family, because he has resisted the evil king.

Readers are left with a certain amount of anxiety over exactly what the 'garment' is, whether one *should* obtain it, and if so, how one obtains it. Allegorically, the 'garment' has been interpreted as a sign of the messianic kingdom, good deeds, holiness or consecration, the spiritual or resurrected body,[89] or as the flesh that must be stripped

---

88. 'Friend' is the simplest English translation for the vocative. Other words that are more appropriate for the degree of intimacy do not work well as terms of address: companion, associate, fellow, member.

89. Augustine (*Sermon* 90), follows 1 Tim. 1.5 in saying that the garment is charity (*caritas*), a pure heart, good conscience, and true faith. Augustine's interpretation is followed by Gregory the Great (*Homily on Evang.* 38), Jerome (*Commentary on Matthew* 22.11–12); Haimo of Auxerre (*Homilies on the Seasons* 724A), Radulfus (*Homilies* 2097A), Zacharias Chrysopolitanus (*In Unum ex Quatuor*), and Ludolph of Saxony. According to Origen (*Commentary on Matthew* 17), the garment represents mercy, kindness, humility, gentleness, and long-suffering. Chrysostom (*Homily on Matthew* 50) compares the garment to life and conduct (βίος καὶ πρᾶξις). A fourth-century Syriac Christian named Ephrem claims that the human body of Jesus and the bodies of Christians are the wedding garment that clothes the immortal bridegroom, and Aphrahat, also a fourth-century Syriac Christian, summarizes salvation history in terms of the 'garment of glory' (see discussion of the garment theme by Kuriakose A. Valavanolickal, *The Use of the Gospel Parables in the Writings of Aphrahat and Ephrem* [Studies in the Religion and History of Early Christianity, 2; Frankfurt am Main: Peter Lang, 1995], pp. 157–64). A fifth-century anonymous commentary titled *Opus Imperfectum in Matthaeum* and Hugh of Saint-Cher (*Postils on the Gospels*) identify the garment as true faith and justice (cited in Wailes, *Medieval Allegories*, p. 157; J. van Banning [ed.], *Opus Imperfectum in Matthaeum* [Corpus Christianorum, Latin Series 87B; Turnholt: Brepols, 1988]). For Isaac the Syrian (*Homily* 76), the garment represents pure thoughts. For

off.[90] The faithful will be clothed (ἐνέδυσεν) as a bridegroom (ὡς νυμφίω) and bride (ὡς νύμφην) with a garment of salvation and robe of righteousness (ἱμάτιον σωτηρίου καὶ κιτῶνα εὐφροσύνης) (Isa. 61.10). The interpretation of the garment as 'good deeds' or 'righteousness' comports with Matthew's exhortations to do good deeds and to strive for righteousness (e.g., Mt. 5.17–7.12) and is supported by other citations: those who pursue justice will attain and wear (ἐνδύσῃ) it like a glorious robe (ποδήρη δόξης)[91] (Sir. 27.8). Revelation 3.2–5 refers to those who have continued to do good works as not having soiled their clothes (ἱμάτια); the victorious will be clothed in white robes (ἱματίοις λευκοῖς; see also Rev. 6.11; 7.9, 14; 19.8; 22.14).[92] An allegorical reading concludes

---

Christian of Stablo, the garment represents baptism (Christian of Stablo, *Expositio in Matthaeum evangelistam* [ed. Migne, *Patrologie cursus completus*, 106, columns 1261–1504]). Thomas Aquinas (*Commentary on Matthew*) and Martin Luther state that the garment is Christ himself, put on by faith (*Luther's Church Postil: Gospels, Vol. 5* [trans. J.N. Lenker; Minneapolis: Fortress Press, 1905], pp. 227–51). For Hermas, the garment is the spiritual aspect of a person that belongs to God (*Shepherd of Hermas*, Similitudes 9.32.1–4). Bede says the garment is virtue (Bede, *Tabern.* 3.6). For John Calvin the garment is sanctification (*Institutes* 3.24.8). John Locke likened the garment to repentance, amendment of life, sincere obedience to Jesus' law (John Locke, *The Reasonableness of Christianity as Delivered in the Scriptures* [ed. J.C. Higgins-Biddle; Oxford: Clarendon Press, 1999], p. 128. A.-J. Levine (*Social and Ethnic Dimensions*, p. 214), says the garment represents faith and obedience to God. J. Massingberd Ford suggests the wedding garment is a scholar's cloak, as the wedding feast itself is completion of the study of Torah (J.M. Ford, 'The Parable of the Foolish Scholars', *NovT* 9 [1967], pp. 107–23 [114]). See also Keener, *Matthew*, p. 522; Jan Fekkes, *Isaiah and Prophetic Traditions in the Book of Revelation* (JSNTSup, 93; Sheffield: JSOT Press, 1994), pp. 236–37; Luz, *Matthäus*, p. 245; Matura, 'Les Invites', p. 24; Viviano, 'Matthew', p. 665; Gnilka, *Mattäusevangelium*, p. 241; Buttrick, *Parables*, p. 230; Trilling, *Matthew*, p. 158; Michaelis, *Das hochzeitlich Kleid*, pp. 65–67.

90.   The garments as metaphor for 'flesh' is found in *G. Thom.* 22 and 37: 'When you strip without being ashamed and you take off your garments and put them under your feet like little children and trample them, then you will see the child of the living one and not be afraid.' Meeks discusses the ritual implications of disrobing and putting on new clothing as a sign of rebirth. He cites Gal. 3.28, Col. 3.8–10, Eph. 4.17–24, and the spiritual garments in the 'Hymn of the Pearl' (*Acts of Thomas* 76–99) as examples of becoming a new person by removing the old and putting on new garments ('Image of the Androgyne: Some Uses of a Symbol in Early Christianity', *HR* 13, [1974], pp. 183–84). The children in *Thomas*' gospel, however, do not put on anything new.

91.   A ποδήρη is a robe reaching to the feet.

92.   Tertullian interprets the unsoiled clothes in Rev. 3.4–5 as the beauty of unwedded flesh (*On the Resurrection of the Flesh* 27). On Christ's own unspotted robe and the robes washed in his blood, see Augustine, *Exposition on Psalms* 45.20). Other examples of the symbolic value of the garment include association with holiness: the deity is majestically clothed (εὐπρέπειαν ἐνεδύσω), and wears garments of light (φῶς ὡς ἱμάτιον) (LXX Ps. 105.1–2; Ps. 104.1–2). The seven angels carrying seven golden bowls full of the wrath of God (Rev. 15.6) wear pure shining linen (ἐνδεδυμένοι λίνον καθαρὸν λαμπρόν). The armies of heaven are clad in fine, pure, and shining linen (ἐνδεδυμένοι βύσσινον λευκὸν καθαρόν) (Rev.

that the man with no wedding garment did not do good deeds nor has a right relationship to God. His being clothed in the wrong type of garment represents his dishonor before God (cf. Pss. 35.26; 109.29; 132.18; 1 Macc. 1.28).

On a literal level, we can see that clothing is not always used metaphorically. Matthew uses ἔνδυμα elsewhere to describe actual clothing, such as John's camel hair garment (3.4), a necessity of life (6.25–29), Jesus' own clothes (27.31), the snow-white clothing of the angel at Jesus' tomb (28.3). Matthew is heir to a biblical tradition in which certain garments are given by fathers to sons, by kings to subjects, or by the people to their leaders to show favor or higher status. For example, Joseph received a special garment (κιτῶνα) from Jacob (Gen. 37.3); Pharaoh dressed (ἐνέδυσεν) Joseph in fine linen (Gen. 41.42); Aaron and his sons were clothed (ἐνδύσεις) in priestly garments to set them apart for their service to the Lord (Exod. 29. 5, 8, 30; 40.13–14; Lev. 6.10, 11; 8.7; 16.4, 23, 24, 32; 21.10; Num. 20.26, 28; 2 Chron. 5.12; Ezek. 42.14; 44.17–19; cf. also 1 Esd. 5.40; Sir. 45.8, 13); King Ahasuerus orders that Mordecai be clothed in kingly robes (στολὴν βυσσίνην) (Est. 6.8; cf. 6.1–11).[93] Joseph, as a high Egyptian official, gives garments to his brothers (Gen. 45.22), and Samson promises to give thirty linen garments and thirty robes (τριάκοντα σινδόνας καὶ τριάκοντα στολάς)

19.14), as are the saints (Rev. 3.4–5; 4.4; 6.11; 7.13–14). The Son of Man himself is clothed in a long white robe (Rev. 1.12–13).The angels at Jesus' tomb wear white garments (Mt. 28.3; Mk 16.5; Lk. 24.4; Jn 20.12). In the transfiguration, Jesus' garments become dazzling white (Mk 9.3//Mt. 17.2//Lk. 9.29). In a vision, Zephaniah sees himself putting on the garments of angels, praying and conversing in their language (*Apoc. Zeph.* 8.3–4). Hermas sees a vision of the Church as a woman clad in shining white garments (*Shepherd of Hermas*, Vision 1.2.2), as twelve virgins clothed in glorious garments (*Shepherd*, Similitude 4.2.4), and as a bride 'proceeding from the bridal chamber, clothed entirely in white, and with white sandals' (*Vision* 4.2.1). Being overcome by the spirit of the Lord is likened to being clothed (with forms of ἐνδύειν): the spirit of the Lord clothed Gideon (Judg. 6.34); the spirit of God clothed Zechariah (2 Chron. 24.20; cf. 1 Chron. 12.18). The garments may also represent truth, with which the mind is clothed (Mitchell, *Parables*, p. 238), or inner holiness and capacity to love given by God (W. Selwyn Dawson, 'The Gate Crasher', *ExpTim* 85 [1974], pp. 304–306). Garments represent salvation and divine favor: 'I will greatly rejoice in the Lord ... for he has clothed me (ἐνέδυσεν) with a garment of salvation (ἱμάτιον σωτηρίου) (cf. also Ps. 132.16; 2 Chron. 6.41) and with a robe of righteousness (κιτῶνα εὐφροσύνης) (cf. also Ps. 132.9; Wis. 5.18), like a bridegroom (ὡς νυμφίῳ) with a garland or victor's crown, and like a bride (ὡς νύμφην) with ornaments' (Isa. 61.10; cf. 62.1–5). The Lord clothed (ἐνέδυσά) Israel in fine linen to show favor to her (Ezek. 16.10, 13), and Isaiah exhorts Jerusalem to awake and put on her strength and glory (ἔνδυσαι τὴν ἰσχύν καὶ τὴν δόξαν) to celebrate release from captivity (Isa. 52.1). Hippolytus describes putting off the filth of sin to be made white and to put on the heavenly, pure Holy Spirit (*On Daniel*, 3.9).

93. Cf. Lk. 15.22, where a father welcomes home his wayward son by having him clothed in the best robe (στολὴν τὴν πρώτην καὶ ἐνδύσατε αὐτόν).

to his 'companions' (ἐταίροι) during the week of the wedding feast if they can solve his riddle.

A literal interpretation therefore suggests that the 'king' (the one in a position of authority like Jacob, Pharaoh, Moses, or King Ahasuerus), did not give the guest an appropriate garment and thus shows his disfavor.[94] It is not the man's lack of appropriate garments *per se*, but his failure to receive the king's honor that puts him in the position of being without a robe at the wedding feast.[95] The king's singling the man out and questioning him only calls attention to his disfavor. Like Samson, who will give the garments to his guests on the condition they guess his riddle, the parabolic king's question is posed like a riddle or problem to be solved: 'How did you get in here without a wedding garment?' ('If you can tell me, perhaps I will give you one.')

Unlike Samson's guests, the Matthean wedding guest has no answer ('he was speechless' [22.12]). The passive voice (ἐπιμώθη) (literally, 'he was muzzled' or 'he was silenced')[96] indicates that the garmentless man's 'silence' could have been imposed on him by force or by denial of the privilege of speaking to the king. His inability to answer is perceived as guilt, just as Jesus' speechlessness is perceived as culpability as he stands before the high priest (26.63). Jesus and the garmentless man are alike in their silence before their interrogators, and both suffer condemnation. Readers are inclined to accept Jesus' silence as a sign of integrity, but we are not so generous in the case of the garmentless man, because we are used to hearing allegorical interpretations of his guilt before God, and probably also because we are not inclined to like people from the streets. But if we grant that Jesus' silence indicates his resistance and innocence in the face of false testimony against him, perhaps we should afford the speechless man the same reading. Given the reputation of kings and rulers in Matthew to be unjust, the man without a wedding garment is speechless because he, like Jesus before his interrogators, is innocent.

---

94. Some interpreters appeal to a custom that the king might provide robes. For example Gundry, *Matthew*, p. 182, and Klaus Haacker, 'Das hochzetliche Kleid von Mt. 22. 11–13 und ein palästinisches Märchen', *Zeitschrift des Deutschen Palästina-Vereins* 87 (1971), pp. 95–97. Others note that Matthew's parable, unlike Luke's, does not mention that the guests are poor; therefore, the man could have been wearing an appropriate robe (e.g., G.R. Beasley-Murray, *Jesus and the Kingdom of God* [Grand Rapids: Eerdmans, 1986], p. 121).

95. Haacker ('Das hochzeitliche Kleid', p. 96) suggests that the giving of garments to unattired guests was customary; he draws on similarities between this parable and a Palestinian parable about three poor maidens who ask the king for appropriate garments to wear to the palace.

96. BDAG, p. 1060. The lexicon renders the usage in Mt. 22.12 as 'he was silent' or 'could say nothing.'

Perhaps he has been 'dragged before governors and kings' like Jesus' disciples (10.18).[97]

The guest, like Jesus, is bound and dismissed in disgrace. Their shared debasement echoes a familiar pattern that dishonor and grief are expressed through the condition of one's clothing. The soldiers dishonor Jesus when they strip (ἐκδύσαντες) him, dress him in a mock royal robe, then strip (ἐξέδυσαν) him again and dress (ἐνέδυσαν) him in his own clothes (Mt. 25.28–31).[98] Luz, among others, comments that the man is tied up like the worst sort of criminal (22.13).[99] David Sim details similarities to the angel Raphael binding the evil angel Azazel hand and foot to cast him into the darkness (1 *Enoch* 10.4–5) and notes that Azazel has also lost his heavenly garment (*Apoc. Abr.* 13.14).[100] These

97.   Or, perhaps the man is speechless because he is waiting for divine inspiration when the king questions him: 'When they hand you over, do not worry about how you are to speak or what you are to say; for what you are to say will be given to you at that time; for it is not you who speak, but the spirit of the Father speaking through you' (10.19–20). Instead, he remains speechless, as did Jesus.

98.   Rossing provides examples of stripping used to designate demotion, reversal, loss of status, resources, power and prestige (B.R. Rossing, *The Choice Between Two Cities* [HTS, 48; Harrisburg: Trinity Press International, 1999], pp. 93–97). Many more examples of stripping or rending garments, or putting on sackcloth, show that garments can indicate grieving, just as they can indicate joy. For example, Israel is exhorted to mourn like a virgin (νύμφη) who laments in sackcloth for her husband (Joel 1.8); Job tears his robe (διέρρηξεν τὰ ἱμάτια αὐτοῦ) upon learning his children are all dead and his property destroyed (Job 1.20), and each of Job's friends tears his own garment (ῥήξαντες ἕκαστος τὴν ἑαυτοῦ στολὴν) when he sees Job's great suffering (Job 2.12). The Ninevites repent by wearing sackcloth (ἐνεδύσαντο σάκκους) instead of garments (Jon. 3.5–6). Joseph's brothers, conspiring to kill him, strip him of his special robe (Gen. 37.23). Reuben tears his clothes (Gen. 37.29) and Jacob tears his garments and puts on sackcloth when they think Joseph has been killed (Gen. 37.34). See also LXX Gen. 42.25, 35; Lev. 11.32; Josh. 9.4; Judg. 4.10, 11, 14; 8.5, 31; 9.1; 10.3; 2 Kgs 3.31; 21.10; 3 Kgs 20 or 21.16, 27, 31, 32; 4 Kgs 19.1, 2; 1 Chron. 21.16; Neh. 9.1; Esth. 4.1, 2,3, 4; Job 16.16; Pss. 29.11; 34.13; 68.11; Sir. 25.17; Amos 8.10; Joel 1.13; Isa. 3.24; 15.3; 20.2; 22.12; 32.11; 37.1, 2; 45.1; 50.3; 58.5; Jer. 4.8; 6.26, 30.3; 31.37; Bar. 4.20; Lam. 2.10; Ezek. 7.18; 27.31; Dan. 9.3; 1 Macc. 2.14; 3.47; 2 Macc. 3.19; 10.25.

99.   The outer darkness is, for Luz, hell (*Matthäus*, III, p. 244). Jerome, *On Matthew*; Haimo, *Homilies on the Seasons*, 135. Thomas Aquinas saw the weeping as the punishment of the soul and the gnashing of teeth as punishment of the body. Ludolph of Saxony enumerates the number of times the phrase 'weeping and gnashing of teeth' appears in the New Testament (he finds seven) and likens these to the seven main failures of Church leadership. The outer darkness is separation from the bridegroom. Allegorically, the outer darkness is damnation; so, Gregory the Great, *Homily* 38; Jülicher, *Gleichnisreden*, p. 425; Funk, *Language*, p. 171.

100.   Sim, 'Matthew 22.13 and 1 Enoch 10.4a', pp. 3–19; also Davies and Allison, *Matthew*, III, p. 206. Davies and Allison note that while the garmentless man in Mt. 22.13 is not a fallen angel, he nonetheless suffers the same fate. I find a parallel also with the story of Haman, who attends the royal banquet expecting to be honored but is revealed as the man who would destroy the Jews, so he is taken outside and hanged (Est. 7.1–10); earlier, the royal garments he expected to wear were given instead to Mordechai (Est. 6.10–11).

interpretations provide a context for the gravity of the garmentless man's situation. The bound angel is so treated as a result of his rebellion against God; so, allegorically, the man without a wedding garment is rebelling against God the king. But if we do not interpret the parable allegorically, his rebellion – not against God, but against a king like Herod or Caesar – is *appropriate*. As Jesus was silent before his accusers and was considered a rebel worthy of crucifixion, so the garmentless man is a silent rebel who is bound up and disposed of, to borrow Luz's phrase, like the 'worst sort of criminal.'[101] In a non-allegorical reading, the guest, like Jesus, is treated as a criminal, but the audience can hope that, like Jesus, he will receive consolation and reward for remaining non-violent (as the Sermon on the Mount exhorts) and for enduring against the tyrannical powers that be.

2.10 *Many Are Called but Few Are Chosen*

Allegorical treatments of the parable's final statement, 'many are called but few are chosen,' suggest that one must be prepared for judgment and that no one can assume that salvation is guaranteed.[102] The saying resonates with warnings of judgment in 4 *Ezra* 9.16 ('there are more who perish than those who will be saved') and 2 *Bar.* 44.15, where the merciful and righteous will be given the coming world, but many others will be damned. [103] The *Epistle of Barnabas* expresses dread: 'Let us pray so that we never might be found [in the situation], as it is written, "many are called but few are chosen"' (Προσέχωομεν, μήποτε, ὡς γέγραπται, πολλοὶ κλητοί, ὀλίγοι δὲ ἐκκλεκτοὶ εὑρεθῶμεν) (*Epistula Barnabae*, 4.14).[104] Augustine, in his usual predestinarian style, argues that 'few

---

101. Luz, *Matthäus*, III, p. 244. There is an example of binding that does not result in expulsion, death, or consignment to hell. Abraham bound Isaac (συμποδίσας) (Gen. 22.9), literally tied his feet together, and Isaac remained silent like the speechless man whom they bound 'feet and hands' (δήσαντες πόδας καὶ κεῖρας); Isaac was rescued by the angel of the Lord (Gen. 22.1–14), but the garmentless man is not rescued in the narrative.

102. So Schweizer, *Matthew*, p. 421; Schnackenburg, *Matthew*, p. 215.

103. Harrington, *Matthew*, p. 306. Harrington adds 4 *Ezra* 8.3 ('many have been created but few will be saved'), but this does not fit the parable's context as well. Lemcio supports this interpretation that while all are invited to the table, there is no 'blanket endorsement' for those who accept the invitation: they must come prepared. Thus, the covenant is breached only by action or inaction of those who respond (Lemcio, 'Parables of the Great Supper', pp. 21–22).

104. Kraszewski translates: 'Let us pray, so that we never find ourselves among those who, as it is written "are called" but "not chosen"' (*The Gospel of Matthew with Patristic Commentaries* (Studies in Bible and Early Christianity, 40; Lewiston, NY: Edwin Mellen Press, 1999), p. 342). εὑρεθῶμεν is an aorist passive subjunctive that Kraszewski chooses to translate as a reflexive. Other early commentators discuss Matthew's balance of human responsibility and God's choice, but with the same result that they undermine the point of the

are chosen' means only some are *granted* the ability to accept the call: 'If God does call many, He has mercy on those whom He calls in such a way that they are able to follow the call' (*De diversis quaestionibus ad Simplicianum* 1, 2, 13).[105] If it is God who gives a person the ability to follow the call (so, Augustine), but God did not give it to this man, so his damnation is sealed. The point of the parable as an allegory of the final judgment – to warn or to shock the listener into obtaining the 'wedding garment' before it is too late – is lost to a predetermined outcome.

A resisting reading suggests that many are called, but there was only one who remained true: the one who did not concern himself with what to wear to the wedding, and who stood speechless and innocent before the king as Jesus did, is the one who best fulfills the role of Jesus' disciple.

2.11 *Conclusion*

The Parable of the Wedding Feast reinforces Matthew's tendency to disrupt weddings and to portray the separation of bride and bridegroom: the wedding feast in the parable lacks both bride *and* groom (the king's son is mentioned in the first line, but never appears again). Instead of focusing on a bridal pair (as one might expect of a story that begins with a wedding feast), this wedding parable features the actions of a tyrant. The wedding never happens, and the feast itself is marred by insurrection, murder, a burning city, and the violent expulsion of wedding guests.

While I grant that the evangelist seems to set up the parables to be read allegorically, I have chosen to resist allegorical readings that view the king as the deity, because Matthew portrays kings as tyrants. My feminist concern is that reading the 'king' in the parable as God suggests that God is no better than earthly kings who fly into a rage, kill, and burn those

---

parable. Basil interprets the final statement of the parable to mean: 'Never let the multitude of the crowd daunt you, for they are swayed by the winds as is the water of the sea. For if even but one is saved, as was Lot at Sodom, he ought to abide by his right judgment ... because the Lord will not abandon his holy ones' (Basil, *Letter* 258). Translation by R.J. Deferrari and M.R.P. McGuire, *Saint Basil: The Letters* (4 vols.; LCL; Cambridge, MA: Harvard University Press, 1950), IV, p. 35. Calvin (*Commentary on a Harmony of the Evangelists*) also reminds the reader that personal responsibility is important, but it is ultimately God's choice: for Calvin, the external profession of faith is not sufficient proof that God will acknowledge all his people.

105. Translation by Kraszewski, *Gospel of Matthew*, pp. 347–48. McKenzie links this passage to the doctrine of predestination ('Matthew', p. 100). In a similar interpretation, Edmond Boissard appeals to humanity's freedom of choice and the resulting condition that abuses this independence. The result is simply a statement of fact: many are called, but necessarily few are chosen, because they have not willed it so (E. Boissard, 'Note sur l'interpretation du texte "Multi sunt vocati, pauci vero electi"', *Revue Thomiste* 60 [1952], pp. 569–85 [esp. 584–85]).

deemed unworthy, when elsewhere in the gospel the deity is portrayed as a loving and providential father (6.25–33; 7.7–11).

I also want to resist allegorical readings that identify the first batch of guests as 'the Jews' or Jewish leaders, because these readings often lead to 'anti-Jewish' interpretations. A resisting reading identifies the 'king' as an unjust ruler and his first invited guests as elite members of society who are just as murderous as he is (they abuse and kill the slaves sent to fetch them). The second group of wedding guests, when portrayed allegorically as the Gentiles, also leads to anti-Jewish interpretations. I have suggested that the second group of guests represents the poor or those whose social status was deemed too low to warrant an invitation the first time around – these people are gathered at the last minute. A subversive reading, based on Matthean portrayals of disciples being dragged before kings, suggests that these 'guests' were brought against their will before the tyrant.

The man without a wedding garment is typically interpreted as a guest who was not prepared for the last judgment, and his speechlessness is regarded as a sign of his guilt before the deity. However, a resisting reading of the garmentless man suggests his innocence as he stands speechless, like Jesus, before the human tyrant. His lack of a garment may be a sign of his poverty but also represents his compliance with the teaching not to be concerned about clothing (6.25–32). A subversive reading of the garmentless man also reveals that calling someone 'friend' in this gospel is not necessarily a good thing; what is desired in Matthew is familial language instead.

This reading concludes that the king and wedding feast in the parable do not necessarily represent the Kingdom of Heaven. Rather, the parable shows that royal trappings are signals of danger; that kings are evil, and that, in Jesus' kingdom, the one who is expelled from the king's presence may be the one who is actually in a right relationship to Jesus' community.

Chapter 3

THE PARABLE OF THE TEN VIRGINS
(Mt. 25.1–13)

1 Τότε ὁμοιωθήσεται ἡ βασιλεία τῶν οὐρανῶν δέκα παρθένοις, αἵτινες λαβοῦσαι τὰς λαμπάδας ἑυατῶν ἐξῆλθον εἰς ὑπάντησιν τοῦ νυμφίου. 2 πέντε δὲ ἐξ αὐτῶν ἦσαν μωραὶ καὶ πέντε φρόνιμοι. 3 Αἱ γὰρ μωραὶ λαβοῦσαι τὰς λαμπάδας αὐτῶν οὐκ ἔλαβον μεθ' ἑαυτῶν ἔλαιον 4 Αἱ δὲ φρόνιμοι ἔλαβον ἔλαιον ἐν τοῖς ἀγγείοις μετὰ τῶν λαμπάδων ἑαυτῶν. 5 Χρονίζοντος δὲ τοῦ νυμφίου ἐνύσταξαν πᾶσαι καὶ ἐκάθευδον 6 Μέσης δὲ νυκτὸς κραυγὴ γέγονεν, Ἰδοὺ ὁ νυμφίος, ἐξέρχεσθε εἰς ἀπάντησιν 7 τότε ἠγέρθησαν πᾶσαι αἱ παρθένοι ἐκεῖναι καὶ ἐκόσμησαν τὰς λαμπάδας ἑαυτῶν. 8 αἱ δὲ μωραὶ ταῖς φρονίμοις εἶπαν, Δότε ἡμῖν ἐκ τοῦ ἐλαίου ὑμῶν, ὅτι αἱ λαμπάδες ἡμῶν σβέννυνται. 9 ἀπεκρίθησαν δὲ αἱ φρόνιμοι λέγουσαι, Μήποτε οὐ μὴ ἀρκέσῃ ἡμῖν καὶ ὑμῖν. πορεύεσθε μᾶλλον πρὸς τοὺς πωλοῦντας καὶ ἀγοράσατε ἑαυταῖς. 10 ἀπερχομένων δὲ αὐτῶν ἀγοράσαι ἦλθεν ὁ νυμφίος, καὶ αἱ ἕτοιμοι ἐσῆλθον μετ αὐτοῦ εἰς τοὺς γάμους καὶ ἐκλείσθη ἡ θύρα. 11 ὕστερον δὲ ἔρχονται καὶ αἱ λοιπαι παρθένοι λέγουσαι, Κύριε κύριε, ἄνοιχον ἡμῖν. 12 ὁ δὲ ἀποκριθεὶς εἶπεν, Ἀμὴν λέγω ὑμῖν, οὐκ οἶδα ὑμᾶς. 13 γρηγορεῖτε οὖν, ὅτι οὐκ οἴδατε τὴν ἡμέραν οὐδὲ τὴν ὥραν.

Then the kingdom of the heavens will be like ten virgins who, taking their lamps, went out to meet the bridegroom. Now, five of them were foolish, and five were wise. For the foolish, while bringing their own lamps, did not bring with them oil. But the wise brought oil in containers with their lamps. When the bridegroom was delayed, all of them became drowsy, and they all fell asleep. In the middle of the night, there came a cry: 'Behold the bridegroom! Come out to meet [him]!' Then they rose up, all those virgins, and trimmed their own lamps. And the foolish said to the wise, 'Give to us some of your oil, because our lamps are going out.' The wise answered, saying, 'No, or else there will not be enough for us and for you. You go instead to the merchants and buy [some] for yourselves.' And after they went to buy, the bridegroom came, and the ones who were prepared went with him into the wedding feast, and the door was shut. Later the other virgins came, saying, 'Lord, Lord! Open to us!' But answering, he said, 'Amen, I say to you, I never knew you.' Therefore, keep awake! For you do not know the day or the hour.

3.1 *Introduction*

The Parable of the Ten Virgins (22.1–14), Matthew's second wedding parable, shares similar messages to the first: those who accept an invitation are not guaranteed a place at the table; certain preparations must be made before the feast begins. Like the first parable, allegorical interpretations of the Ten Virgins that place the story in the context of the last judgment portray a less than satisfactory portrait of Jesus as a bridegroom who is late to his own wedding and displays rudeness to the point of violence in closing the door and denying relationship to those who await him. The five 'wise' virgins, in allegorical interpretations, come across as self-righteous, cold, and unwilling to help others in need. If we resist this image of Jesus and this portrayal of how 'wise' members of the community act, we have a very different reading. If we read this parable as the story of a generic bridegroom and some young women who await his arrival, we can recognize the bridegroom's tardiness, seeming indifference, and exclusion of some of his guests for what it is: rudeness. A resisting reading of the 'wise' virgins reveals that their actions are contrary to what Jesus has earlier advised his disciples: don't bring extra; rely on your friends; share with those in need; be innocent. This interpretation leads to a different understanding of whom the 'foolish' virgins may represent: the innocent in the kingdom, the ones who should be cared for. Without the allegory, we have instead, Matthean morality.

Matthew introduces the parable with the formula 'the Kingdom of Heaven will be like ...' The future ὁμοιωθήσεται (the kingdom *will be* like) and τότε (then, at that time) signals an event yet to come and invites an allegorical treatment. But the parable is also descriptive of a real social situation, in this case, a wedding.[1] Moreover, the parable can represent the community's life after the 'turn of the age' (28.16–20) and thus the setting need not be the eschaton, but rather the ongoing, albeit liminal, setting of the Matthean community.

The parable revolves around the drama of the ten women's interactions with each other and with the bridegroom, interactions that can, at best, be described as strained. The bridegroom is unaccountably late for his own wedding (the parable could be called 'The Parable of the Rude Bridegroom') and keeps ten women waiting for so long that they fall asleep, and their lamps begin to go out. When the bridegroom's arrival is

---

1. See William R. Herzog, *Parables as Subversive Speech: Jesus as Pedagogue of the Oppressed* (Louisville: Westminster/John Knox Press, 1994), esp. pp. 80–84 and 130–35. Herzog calls the interpretative blurring 'theology' (p. 80).

announced at last, five of the virgins (called 'foolish') realize that they do not have enough oil for their lamps and ask the others to share. The five who have extra oil (called 'wise') refuse to share and coldly dismiss the five 'foolish' to go buy their own oil. While the five foolish are gone to the market, the apparently unapologetic bridegroom finally arrives, allows the five 'wise' virgins in, and closes the door. His chilling statement to the five 'foolish' virgins, 'I do not know you,' or 'I never knew you', erases any prior relationship, as well as any future relationship, with five of the women who waited so long for him to arrive (cf. also 7.21–23). There is no happy ending to this wedding story. The scene is marred by the ten virgins' separation into opposing groups and by the bridegroom's banishment of the five 'foolish' virgins.

While this parable contains no overt violence, the five wise virgins' refusal to help their companions and the bridegroom's utter rejection qualify as emotional violence, and the five foolish virgins are in a place parallel to that of the inappropriately garbed guest of the previous wedding parable: 'although the evangelist does not add a reference to outer darkness and grief, the reader can supply these from the night-time imagery of the parable.'[2] But the resisting reader recognizes that, as in the previous parable, the one who is expelled is potentially the only one who is truly faithful or innocent. If the garmentless man is innocent, why not the foolish virgins? Moreover, if we have read the 'king' in the previous parable not as God, but as a human tyrant, then the 'bridegroom' of this parable, whose role as host of the wedding feast is the same as the 'king's,' can also be read not as Jesus but as simply a rude and judging bridegroom. Those who attend this bridegroom's wedding feast and are complicit in his shutting others out, are just as rude and judging as he is.

When one is with Jesus the bridegroom, matters should be different. The fear that Matthew seeks to instill in his community – that they may be shut out of the eschatological kingdom/wedding feast – remains in other parables, such as the Weeds and Wheat and the Sheep and Goats, and to be sure, the parables of the Wedding Feast and Ten Virgins do echo those themes. But more is going on in these two wedding parables than community maintenance. Parables are polyvalent in meaning, and this parable of the Ten Virgins offers more than one message. On the one hand, if we read the 'bridegroom' as Jesus (which Matthew does imply with his bridegroom saying in 9.15), we get a 'sheep and goats' type of message: 'I never knew you.' On the other hand, if we read the

---

2.   Vicky Balabanski, 'Opening the Closed Door: A Feminist Rereading of the "Wise and Foolish Virgins" (Mt. 25.1–13)', in Mary Ann Beavis (ed.), *The Lost Coin: Parables of Women, Work and Wisdom* (London: Sheffield Academic Press, 2002), pp. 71–97 (93). Balabanski adds that the narrative context is another clue to the eschatological judgment inherent in the parable (cf. Mt. 24.51).

'bridegroom' in the Matthean context that portrays weddings as places not of celebration but of separation, then the a-familial ethos of the gospel is enhanced. The five virgins' exclusion from the wedding feast is not eternal damnation but a predictable casualty of the formation of the Matthean fictive family: traditional family ties enhanced by weddings are disrupted. The resisting reader does not expect the wedding to be joyful and inclusive, but an occasion for separation and violence.

Matthew is the only gospel to recount the story of the ten virgins waiting for the bridegroom. While some interpreters categorize the parable as a purely Matthean invention,[3] they do notice similarities between this parable and a Lukan parable about servants waiting for a midnight arrival *from* a wedding banquet (Lk. 12.35–38).[4]

> Be dressed for action and have your lamps lit; be like those who are waiting for their master to return from the wedding banquet, so that they may open the door for him as soon as he comes and knocks. Blessed are those slaves whom the master finds alert when he comes; truly I tell you, he will fasten his belt and have them sit down to eat, and he will come and serve them. If he comes during the middle of the night, or near dawn, and finds them so, blessed are those slaves.

3. That the parable is entirely a Matthean composition written to explain the delayed Parousia is emphatically stated by Rudolf Bultmann, 'This is a Church formation completely overgrown by allegory,' from which it was not possible to ascertain the original 'similitude,' if there was one (*The History of the Synoptic Tradition* [Peabody: Hendrickson, 5th edn, 1963], pp. 119, 176, cf. p. 205). David Buttrick writes that the parable is 'a product of eager early Christianity' (*Speaking Parables*, p. 167). Others who think this parable is an allegory invented by the Church include J.C. O'Neill, 'The Source of the Parables of the Bridegroom and the Wicked Husbandmen', *JTS* 39 (1988), pp. 485–89; K.P. Donfried, 'The Allegory of the Ten Virgins (Matt 25.1–13) as a Summary of Matthean Theology', *JBL* 93 (1974), pp. 415–28; Linnemann, *Gleichnisse*, pp. 132–33; Manson, *Sayings*, pp. 243–45; Boring, *Matthew*, 7, p. 450.

4. Among scholars who discuss the Matthean redaction of the parable are: Davies and Allison, *Matthew*, III, p. 393; Buttrick, *Speaking Parables*, pp. 167–68; Elizabeth Waller, 'The Parable of the Ten Virgins', *Proceedings: Eastern Great Lakes Biblical Society* 1 (1981), pp. 85–109 (86); Arthur Baird, *The Justice of God in the Teaching of Jesus* (Philadelphia: Westminster Press, 1963), esp. pp. 105–106, 129–31; W. Michaelis, *Es ging ein sämann aus, zu säen: eine Einführung in die Gleichnisse Jesu über das Reich Gottes und die Kirche* (Berlin: Furche-Verlag, 1938), pp. 92–94. W.O.E. Oesterley, *The Gospel Parables in the Light of Their Jewish Background* (New York: Macmillan, 1936), p. 136. Dan O. Via, *The Parables: Their Literary and Existential Dimension* (Philadelphia: Fortress Press, 1967); W.G. Kümmel, *Promise and Fulfillment: The Eschatological Message of Jesus* (Studies in Biblical Theology, 23; London: SCM, 1957), pp. 56–58; Schnackenburg, *Gospel of Matthew*, p. 250; Schweizer, *Matthew*, p. 466; Thomas G. Long, *Westminster Bible Companion: Matthew* (Louisville: Westminster/John Knox Press, 1997), p. 280; W. Carter, *Matthew and the Margins*, p. 484; Beare, *Matthew*, p. 483; Hultgren, *The Parables of Jesus*, p. 175; Donahue, *Gospel in Parable*, p. 103; Viviano, 'Matthew', p. 668. Joseph A. Fitzmyer deems the Lukan parable to be 'L' material (*The Gospel According to Luke* [AB, 28A; New York: Doubleday, 1985], p. 984).

The Lukan parable contains similar features: lamps, a wedding feast, a door, waiting servants, and the master's arrival in the middle of the night. In the Lukan version, the master is not himself a bridegroom, though he is returning from a wedding, and the servants are not numbered and qualified as virgins, but the settings are remarkably similar.[5] The similarities between the Matthean and Lukan parables point to a shared memory of something Jesus said; if not a written source, then a common oral tradition both authors know.[6]

The resulting messages, however, differ: Luke offers *blessing* to those who are prepared and teaches that the master is their faithful servant, while Matthew threatens punishment to the unprepared and teaches that the bridegroom is an exacting judge. Luke's parable focuses on inclusion and reward; Matthew focuses on separation and punishment. Luke does not attempt to group the servants. While those who are unprepared for the master's arrival do not receive a blessing, they are never punished nor banished from the master's presence. For the servants who *are* ready at his return, the Lukan master puts on an apron, makes them recline at the table, and serves them himself (Lk. 12.37)! Matthew initially divides the virgins into two opposing groups (Mt. 25.2) and focuses not on blessing the five prepared (they are allowed to enter the feast), but on the failure and punishment of the five unprepared. While Luke does not say that unprepared servants will be banished, Matthew's five virgins are excluded forever from the bridegroom's presence.

The Matthean parable portrays a wedding disrupted by the bridegroom's delay, the separation of bride and bridegroom (there is *no* bride), and conflict between the wedding guests. The bridegroom's arrival is not a scene of joy but of conflict and judgment. Matthew turns from earlier messages about sharing and service to messages that seem to promote greed and self-promotion.

3.2 *Ten Virgins Go to Meet the Bridegroom*

The setting of the parable is a wedding procession, but, from the outset, there are peculiarities that signal that this is a very odd wedding: no one is escorting or going out to meet a bride; instead, there are ten virgins going out to meet the bridegroom (25.1). We do not have very much information

5. Those who remark on similarities include Luke Timothy Johnson, *The Gospel of Luke* (Sacra Pagina, 3; Collegeville, MN: Liturgical Press, 1991), p. 203; Keener, *Matthew*, p. 595; Gundry, *Matthew*, p. 498; Dodd, *Parables*, p. 128, 137. Tatian recognized the similarities by conflating Lk. 12.37–41 with this parable (*The Diatessaron of Tatian*, section 43).

6. Richard Bauckham argues that similar themes in parables need not be attributed to written sources but could result from a common pool of story telling themes, in R. Bauckham, 'The Parable of the Royal Wedding Feast (Matthew 22.1–14) and The Parable of the Lame Man and the Blind Man (*Apocryphon of Ezekiel*)', *JBL* 115/3 (1996), pp. 471–88.

about first-century weddings, but sources indicate that the bridegroom typically processed through the streets with his relatives and friends to meet the bride and her wedding party,[7] or waited at a designated place to receive the bride and take her to his home.[8] Matthew does not portray the bridegroom doing any of these things. He is arriving, but he is not portrayed as processing through the streets. Instead, the Matthean bridegroom arrives without a bride,[9] in the middle of the night.

7.   The wedding procession was a public event: the streets were decorated with garlands, and people came out of their houses to see the bride pass and admire her beauty (Chariton, *Callirhoe*, 3.2.17; Lucan, 2.370; cf. Josephus, *Ant.* 13.18; cf. *Jos. Asen.* 21.4). While the bride is most commonly described as beautiful, Alciphron provides an unflattering description of an ugly bride (Aliciphron, *Letters of Courtesans*, 13) in Allen Rogers Benner and Francis H. Fobes (trans.), *The Letters of Alciphron, Aelian, and Philostratus* (LCL, 383; Cambridge, MA: Harvard University Press, 1949, repr. 1990), pp. 280–82. A wedding procession could draw a crowd; everyone abandoned fields and work to join the happy throng (Catullus, *Poem* 64.32–47; cf. Mt. 22.1–10) (trans. Thomas Banks, *Diotima*, 1997). See also Aristides, 78.10.
8.   Chariton names the temple of Concord as a place where bridegrooms waited to receive their brides (*Callirhoe*, 3.2.16) and describes the bridegroom's desire to bring home his bride (νυμφαγωγεῖν; *Callirhoe*, 2.1.2; cf. 3.10.8). Chariton also describes the bride's mother and father conducting her to the house of the bridegroom (προπεμπομένην αὐτὴν ὑπὸ πατρὸς καὶ μητρὸς εἰς τὴν οἰκίαν τοῦ νυμφίου) (*Callirhoe* 5.5.5). Lucian mentions the bridegroom's plan to take home the bride in a carriage or chariot drawn by a pair of oxen or horses after the wedding banquet (*Carousal*, 47).
9.   The striking omission of a bride was so disturbing to some ancient copyists that they felt compelled to add a bride to the text at 25.1: τοῦ νυμφίου καὶ τῆς νύμφης (D Θ Σ, various texts in the Old Latin tradition, the Vulgate, Syriac, and a version of Origen and Tyconius Jerome). The Vulgate, which influences interpretations by some of the later Church fathers, reads: 'tunc simile erit regnum caelorum decem virginibus quae accipientes lampadas suas exierunt obviam sponso *et sponsae.*' The stronger manuscript witnesses include only the bridegroom (א B C L W Z Δ, several other uncials and miniscules, variants in Byzantine, Palestinian Syriac, Coptic [Sahidic and Boheric], and Ethiopic texts, Basil Hyperechius, Chrysostom, Theodoret, and Augustine). Willoughby C. Allen (*A Critical and Exegetical Commentary on the Gospel According to Matthew* [New York: Charles Scribner's Sons, 1907], p. 262, and p. 263, n. 1) describes the addition of the bride as a 'natural but thoughtless interpolation.' Alfred Plummer sums up the majority opinion that the words 'and the bride' (καὶ τῆς νύμφης) in some texts are an 'insertion made by copyists who knew that a bridegroom implied a bride but did not see that the mention of a bride would disturb the parable' (*An Exegetical Commentary on the Gospel According to St. Matthew* (Grand Rapids: Baker Book House, 1982), p. 343). Representing the minority opinion, Albright and Mann argue that manuscripts containing 'and the bride' (καὶ τῆς νύμφης) *are* the original text. They further claim that the bride is Israel (*Matthew* [AB, 26; New York: Doubleday, 1971], p. 302). For example, see Günther Bornkamm, 'Die Verzögerung der Parusie', in W. Schmauch (ed.), *In Memoriam Ernst Lohmeyer* (Stuttgart: Evanglisches Verlagswerk, 1951), pp. 116–26 (esp. p. 121). Some interpreters want to privilege the manuscripts that include the bride because, they argue, the parable makes more sense if one considers the custom of the bridegroom going to fetch the bride: e.g., Julius Schniewind, *Das Evangelium nach Matthäus* (Göttingen: Vandenhoeck and Ruprecht, 1954), p. 250; A.H. McNeile, *The Gospel According to St. Matthew* (London: Macmillan, 1949), p. 361; F.C. Burkitt, 'The Parable of the Ten Virgins', *JTS* 30 (1929), pp. 267–70.

The Parable of the Ten Virgins leaves other gaps: why do the virgins go to meet the bridegroom and do not attend the bride?[10] Where is the bride? Why is the groom late? Why does Matthew specify that these women are 'virgins' (παρθένοι) and what is their role in the wedding? These questions are typically answered by allegorical interpretation: the virgins are Christians who are awaiting judgment; the delayed bridegroom is Jesus before his return at the eschaton, the women's role is to be prepared with requisite good deeds to merit heavenly reward. But if the parable is read as an ordinary wedding in ordinary time, the wedding is so very strange that it signals 'something is wrong with this picture' and invites a subversive reading.

I think the ten virgins represent ordinary people attending an event, some of whom have plentiful commodities and some of whom do not. The ten virgins' role and their relationship to the bridegroom are not clearly defined: the virgins could be servants,[11] family members, or wedding guests.[12] The text merely says that they went out to meet the bridegroom with their lamps (25.1). The bridegroom does not necessarily have to be Jesus; he could the sort of bridegroom that Jesus the bridegroom does *not* represent.

Rosenblatt notes that the absence of the bride, coupled with the disenfranchisement of half of the virgins, serves to highlight the women's passive role, their lack of organization, solidarity, and purpose in the parable.[13] But the women *are* active: they wait, they talk about the oil, they attend, they question and give advice, and five go to the market to buy oil. Their designation as παρθένοι recalls the Virgin Mary

---

10. In ancient accounts of weddings, there is little mention of a gender division between those who attend the bride and groom, so that we do not know if such a division was assumed and needed no comment, or if it made no difference. Women attend the soon-to-be-bride Asenath (*Jos. Asen.* 10.4–8; 17.4–5), but also are available to attend the groom (*Jos. Asen.* 20.2–3). Aristophanes mentions a person who sits with the bridegroom in his carriage or chariot (πάραχος γάμοων), who is likely a groomsman (Aristophanes, *Birds*, line 1738). Josephus describes a large wedding party of several hundred people escorting *both* the bride and the bridegroom (*Ant.* 13.18–21). Michael Sokoloff cites an Aramaic example of a man having a female close friend (שׁושׁביני נא), a term also used to describe a close male friend or best man (*A Dictionary of Jewish Babylonian Aramaic of the Talmudic and Geonic Periods* [Ramat-Gan, Israel: Bar Ilan University Press; Baltimore: Johns Hopkins University Press, 2002], p. 1125. Sources simply say that bridegrooms were accompanied by relatives and friends, and it stands to reason that these would include both genders (Lucan 2.370; Chariton, *Callirhoe*, 3.1.3).

11. So Levine, 'Matthew', p. 261, because of the servants in the previous parable (24.45–51); also Pheme Perkins, *Hearing the Parables of Jesus* (New York: Paulist Press, 1981), p. 106.

12. Luz, *Matthäus*, p. 472; Balabanski, 'Opening the Closed Door', p. 83.

13. M.E. Rosenblatt, 'Got into the Party After All: Women's Issues and The Five Foolish Virgins', in Levine (ed.), *A Feminist Companion to Matthew* (Sheffield: Sheffield Academic Press, 2001), p. 184.

(παρθένος), who, after a very bearing a son, seems to fade into the background while her bridegroom Joseph does everything else (1.20–25).[14] However, Mary is not passive: she shows up later in the text, at a door, trying to get in to see Jesus, and she is all but dismissed as he gives her role as 'mother' to his disciples. We never hear if she actually comes in the door (12.46–50). In a like manner, the ten virgins wait while a bridegroom orchestrates the action. They all seek to enter the door, but some are rebuffed. The door of the wedding hall represents a barrier between those who are 'inside' or 'outside' Jesus' fictive family and may show that it is not being unprepared but being unrelated (or related in the wrong way) that excludes the five 'foolish' virgins.

Some interpreters think 'virgins' is not a significant term and that it merely indicates that they are young women. Philip Culbertson identifies them as 'young women of the town,'[15] and Robert Capon envisions them as 'giggly teenagers.'[16] While these descriptions of the 'virgins' – as simply women – befit a non-allegorical and resisting reading (in which the 'bridegroom' is simply a man), there are clues in Matthew that suggest that 'virginity' *does* have significance for Matthew's portrayal of the place of weddings and the role of childlike innocence in community life. The evangelist's designation of the ten women specifically as 'virgins' (παρθένοι) draws attention, on the one hand, to their unmarried status,

---

14. In the Matthean text, we do not even see Mary actively taking care of Jesus (a topic that will be discussed in detail in Chapter 4). Davies and Allison give a detailed explanation of the use of παρθένος in the LXX and its interpretation by the early Church (Davies and Allison, *Matthew*, I, pp. 214–16). Waller suggests that 'virgin' designates marital status rather than sexual purity ('Parable of the 10 Virgins', pp. 95–97). For a brief history of the place of virginity in antiquity and the context for early Christian attitudes toward virginity and sexuality, see Uta Ranke-Heinemann, *Eunuchs for the Kingdom of Heaven* (New York: Doubleday, 1990), esp. pp. 9–109; Leif E. Vaage and Vincent L. Wimbush (eds.), *Asceticism in the New Testament* (New York: Routledge, 1999); Peter Brown, *The Body and Society: Men, Women, and Sexual Renunciatin in Early Christianity* (New York: Columbia University Press, 1988); Michel Foucault, *The Use of Pleasure: The History of Sexuality Volume 2* (3 vols.; New York: Vintage Books, 1985), II, esp. pp. 63–77; and Aline Rousselle, *Porneia: On Desire and the Body in Antiquity* (Cambridge, MA: Blackwell, 1988). Marvin Meyer (*The Gospel of Thomas: The Hidden Sayings of Jesus* [San Francisco: Harper SanFrancisco, 1992], p. 97) and Pheme Perkins ('The Gospel of Thomas', in E. Schüssler Fiorenza [ed.], *Searching the Scriptures: A Feminist Commentary* [2 vols.; New York: Crossroad, 1994], II, pp. 534–60 [553]) note a link between 'many standing at the door' and the ten virgins waiting at the door in Mt. 25.1–13.

15. Philip L. Culbertson, *A Word Fitly Spoken: Context, Transmission, and Adoption of the Parables of Jesus* (SUNY Series in Religious Studies; New York: SUNY Press, 1995), p. 136.

16. Robert F. Capon, *The Parables of Judgment* (Grand Rapids: Eerdmans, 1989), p. 160.

their sexuality, and their marriageability,[17] and on the other hand, to their innocence. They are potential brides, but they are *not* brides, as befits the Matthean message that while already contracted marriages should stay intact, new marriages should not take place.[18] The ten virgins also represent the youthful innocence of children that the Matthean Jesus lauds and even tells his disciples to imitate (18.1–5; 19.13–15). That the Matthean Jesus welcomes the 'children' and blesses them is another indication that the 'bridegroom' in this parable is *not* Jesus. Moreover, Jesus warned his disciples not to despise or put a stumbling block before any of the 'little ones' (18.6–14) – actions that describe what the parable's 'bridegroom' does when he discounts five of the childlike 'virgins' and blocks their entrance into the feast.

Some interpreters, reading allegorically, think that the ten virgins represent the Church as virgin bride to the Jesus the bridegroom: Matthew's choice of παρθένοι comports with the Pauline Church described as a virgin (παρθένος) to be given to Christ as her husband (2 Cor. 11.2).[19] However, in Matthew, the virgins are not to be seen as brides.[20] And, although it is the case that the only people we see waiting for the 'bridegroom' are virgins, Matthew makes clear that virginity itself is not a qualification for entrance into the feast: all the women are 'virgins,' but only half get into the feast.

Allegorical readings explain that the virgins' status derives from *how* they wait for the coming of the bridegroom: the 'foolish' (μωραί) are caught unprepared, while the 'wise' (φρόνιμοι) (25.2) have enough oil for their lamps.[21] Thus, just as coming to the wedding feast did not guarantee

---

17.   Balabanski, 'Opening the Closed Door', p. 84.

18.   The efficacy of contracting new marriages will be discussed in Chs 4 and 5.

19.   Hare, *Matthew*, p. 284. Beare (*Matthew*, p. 481) also notes the similarity to 2 Cor. 11.2 and remarks, without citing examples, that 'certain religious rites and duties pertain to virgins.' The virgin bride interpretation is shared by Alfred Plummer, *Matthew*, p. 343; Gundry, *Matthew*, p. 498, as well as ancient exegetes Bruno of Segni (*Homilies*, 278B), Augustine (*Sermon* 93), Gregory the Great (*Homilies on the Gospels*, 12), Pseudo-Bede (*In Matthaei evangelium expositio* 106–107), in Migne (ed.), *Patrologiae cursus completus*, 92, columns 9–132 (here col. 106–107); Christian of Stablo (*Expositio in Matthaeum evangelistam* 1463C), in Migne (ed.), *Patrologiae cursus completus* 106, columns 1261–1504.

20.   Cf. 1 Cor. 7.25–31; Donahue, *Gospel in Parables*, p. 103; Levine, 'Matthew', p. 261. Nicholas of Lyra explains that chastity helps elevate the mind to contemplation of the truth (cited in S.L. Wailes, *Medieval Allegories*, p. 183). The implications for family ties, marriage, and sexuality will be explored in Chs 4 and 5.

21.   Robert F. Capon, *Kingdom, Grace, and Judgment: Paradox, Outrage, and Vindication in the Parables of Jews* (Grand Rapids: Eerdmans, 2002), p. 356; M.E. Rosenblatt, 'Got into the Party', pp. 186–87; Jeremias, *Parables*, p. 52; Dodd, *Parables*, p. 137.

the garmentless man's stay (22.11–14), so waiting for the bridegroom is not a guarantee that all the virgins will enter the feast.[22] But a resisting reading asks if the virgins *should* want to enter this wedding feast, and if so, why? Perhaps, like the parable of the garmentless man, entrance into the wedding feast is a dangerous thing. Rather than joining the judgmental and boorish bridegroom at his exclusive wedding feast, the ten virgins might aspire to belonging to Jesus the bridegroom's fictive family, where those who do the will of the Father in heaven (7.21–23) know to share when someone asks and to open the door when someone knocks (7.7–11).

3.3 *Wise and Foolish*

This parable exemplifies how the Matthean portrayal of bridegrooms (both Jesus and the figure in the parable) cause division: between family members (10.35–39; 12.46–50); between disciples and worldly powers (10.16–33); between the bridegroom's disciples and the religious leaders and disciples of others (9.14–15; 23.1–36); between the bridegroom and his own disciples (26.14–25; 56); and between nations (24.7–14). The beginning of the parable (25.2) informs the audience that the ten virgins are divided and thereby sets up the wedding feast as an occasion for conflict and separation.[23] Ulrich Luz writes that the division of the women into two groups, five φρόνιμοι (wise) and five μωραί (foolish; literally 'morons'), alerts the reader immediately that no sympathy should be given to the 'dumm Frauen,' but it also causes uncertainty as the reader wonders if he or she might also miss the bridegroom's coming: 'Kann man

---

22. Even early champions of virginity, such as Clement of Rome, explain that merely being a virgin does not suffice for gaining entrance to the feast, because one must have oil for light in order not to be shut out from the joy of the bridegroom (Clement, *First Epistle on Virginity*, 3). Thomas Johnston (1630) thought that honesty and having a 'carriage modest and shamefast' are necessary, and that a virgin is holy in both mind and body (T. Johnston, *Christ's Watchword: Being The Parable of The Virgins Expounded* [London: printed by W. Jones for John Barlet, 1630], p. 11); Jerome (*Letter to Eustochium* 6; *Letter to Chromatius, Jovianus, and Eusebius*, 6) and Chrysostom (*Homily* 28.16) distinguish between virgins in spirit (the wise) and virgins of the flesh (the foolish) who have no oil (although Chrysostom also thinks the lamps symbolize physical virginity). Augustine (*Sermon* 43, 4) granted that even married couples could be considered 'virgins of faith.' Methodius (late third, early fourth centuries CE) interprets the ten maidens' virginity as righteousness (Methodius, *Concerning Chastity*, 6.2). Thomas Aquinas (*Commentarium super Matthaeum*) thought that the women's physical virginity was important to the meaning of the parable, for 'if these are damned, how much the more will others be.'

23. Marie Eloise Rosenblatt notes that, unlike other Matthean parables, in which the outcome unfolds gradually, the narrator makes the judgment on the five foolish virgins clear from the beginning ('Got into the Party', p. 183).

den Bräutigam auch verpassen?'[24] This is the reaction I have as a reader: 'surely *I* am not foolish – but what if I am?'[25] But given my retrospective reading of the gospel, in which I question the 'wisdom' of the five who do not share their oil, I also must ask if I really *want* to be 'wise' (φρόνιμος). Given the previous parable's revelation that the one who is *dishonored* is actually the one we should emulate (an interpretation in keeping with 'many who are first shall be last and the last shall be first' [19.30]), and in the context of Matthew's teachings on how to treat others, the better role actually might be 'foolishness.'

The distinction set up at the beginning of the parable puts readers in a position of having to choose sides. Philosophical sayings[26] and wisdom[27] are often constructed as moral tales (similar to this parable) in which there are two distinct ways from which to chose: for example, 'There are two ways: one of life and one of death' (*Didache* 1.1). These sayings offer opposing choices, such as good or evil, life or death, wise or foolish, from which the reader is expected to choose the better part.[28] Because Matthew expected that there will be a final judgment, and in part because there was conflict between Matthew's community and other communities over how to interpret what righteousness entailed, Matthew wanted members of his community to choose *his* interpretation of what was right over the interpretations of others. Matthew's cautionary sayings and parables (such as the 'Two Sons' [21.28–33]; the Parable of the Vineyard [21.33–41]; the Parable of the Wedding Feast [22.1–14]; the Parable of the Talents [25.14–30], and the Parable of the Sheep and Goats [25.31–46]), like this parable of the Ten Virgins, exhort the community to follow his lead. A resisting reading notes that Matthew classifies those who reject his lead as 'foolish,' unworthy of his community, and even damned.

Other dualities present themselves: the parable can be read not only as the opposition between 'wise and foolish.' That the parable features ten *women* poses a question about the audience: would male readers in the community identify with the ten virgins? Because I am a female reader, I

---

24. Luz, *Matthäus*, III, p. 474. Viviano calls the labeling 'premature' ('Matthew', p. 668). Also Elaine Wainwright, 'Matthew', in Elisabeth Schüssler Fiorenza (ed.), *Searching the Scriptures: A Feminist Commentary* (2 vols.; New York: Crossroad, 1994), II, pp. 635–77 (657).

25. A question asked at the Last Supper when Jesus says that one of the disciples will betray him: 'Surely not I?' (26.22, 25).

26. Davies and Allison note that the grouping of people into 'wise' and 'foolish' categories was a Cynic and Stoic convention of teaching (Davies and Allison, *Matthew*, III, p. 396).

27. Balabanski, 'Opening the Closed Door', p. 79. She offers Deut. 30.15–20 and Prov. 12.28 as examples.

28. See discussion of the 'two ways' in Davies and Allison, *Matthew*, I, pp. 695–99; Harrington, *Matthew*, pp. 109–10; Balabanski, 'Opening the Closed Door', p. 79. Culbertson offers Talmudic examples (*A Word Fitly Spoken*, pp. 126–28).

am often expected to identify with male characters, but male readers, in turn, are usually not socialized to identify with female characters.[29] Vicky Balabanski suggests a reading in which men do not identify with the female characters, regardless of whether they are wise or foolish; in her reading, they instead identify with the bridegroom. Balabanski proposes that the parable does not offer male readers the choice between 'wise and foolish' as much as it forces the male readers to 're-vision' their world-view when the bridegroom – with whom they have identified – behaves counter to the expectations of a gracious host in rejecting five of the guests. Male readers sense that 'the lines of identification and sympathy have been destabilized,'[30] and they can no longer assume that they are 'safely in the banquet,' nor regard the ten women as 'other.'[31] I have come across only a few readings by male writers that confirm her thesis[32] – rather, those men who treat the parable interpret the wise and foolish virgins as examples of who will enter and who will be barred from entering the wedding feast. While it is not clear to what extent these authors 'identify' with the female characters, they do discuss the women's decisions and actions, and so have 'read' these characters.[33] The fact that some male authors do not treat this particular parable in their monographs on parables (though an argument from silence) may be indicative that they do not, in fact, 'identify' with the ten virgins and thus do not devote time to discussing them.[34] Reading the

29. See Fetterley, *The Resisting Reader*, pp. xi–xxvi.

30. Balabanski, 'Opening the Closed Door', p. 86.

31. Balabanski does not say the male readers eventually identify with the women, simply that they no longer feel as comfortable identifying with the bridegroom ('Opening the Closed Door', p. 86). 'Re-visioning' is a term used by Fetterley in resistant reading (*Resisting Reader*, p. xxii), so that Balabanski suggests men become resisting readers when confronted with this parable.

32. Dodd (*Parables of the Kingdom*, pp. 136–38) avoids talking directly about the virgins by referring to 'the folly of unpreparedness and the wisdom of preparedness.' Capon (*Kingdom, Grace, Judgment*, pp. 490–501) distances himself by identifying the virgins as 'silly little girls' and 'giggly,' but ultimately he does discuss their choices as illustrative of how disciples will be judged.

33. For example, Armand Puig i Tàrrech devotes an entire monograph to the parable and discusses the virgins' roles throughout (*La Parabole des dix vierges* [Rome: Biblical Institute Press, 1983]). Other male writers who do interpretations of the ten virgins include Hultgren, *Parables of Jesus*, pp. 169–78; Culbertson, *A Word Fitly Spoken*, pp. 135–36; Donfried, 'Allegory of the Ten Virgins', pp. 415–28; Lambrecht, *Out of the Treasure*, pp. 199–215; D.J. Harrington, 'Polemical Parables in Matthew 24–25', *Union Seminary Quarterly Review* 44.3-4 (1991), 287–98 (294–96); Hare, *Matthew*, pp. 284–86; Buttrick, *Speaking Parables*, pp. 166–71; Jeremias, *Parables of Jesus*, pp. 51–52; Strobel, 'Zum Verständnis von Mt xxv 1–13', *NovT* 2 (1958) pp. 199–227; F.H. Borsch, *Many Things in Parables* (Philadelphia: Fortress Press, 1988), pp. 82–89; Weder, *Die Gleichnisse Jesus*, pp. 239–49; Gnilka, *Matthäusevangelium*, II, pp. 346–54; Trilling, *Matthew*, pp. 209–11.

34. For example, Herzog (*Parables as Subversive Speech*) and Crossan (*In Parables*) do not treat the Parable of the Ten Virgins.

bridegroom as a rude, indifferent, and unjust host is not necessarily a male point of view. Indeed, a feminist who comes to the text with suspicion about dominant male characters might more quickly come to the conclusion that the groom is not to be trusted. Thus, it is likely that Balabanski's own feminist reading has provided this insight into the bridegroom's character, not a conjectured male point of view.

Balabanski is correct that the parable becomes an example of how the bridegroom should *not* act: the 'bridegroom' for whom others have come to wait should not be late; and he should invite all ten virgins into the wedding feast. Unresolved is whether or not, in this resisting reading, the 'foolish' virgins bear responsibility for their lack of oil; perhaps they have done what they could. The lingering ambiguity fits the genre of parable, designed to discomfort.

Marie Eloise Rosenblatt tacitly agrees that male readers would not identify with the ten virgins when she examines the parable as an address aimed at women in the Matthean community. For Rosenblatt, the parable exhorts women to choose the side of the 'wise' by conforming to certain behaviors prescribed by those in power (whom Rosenblatt identifies as primarily the men in the community). Thus, 'wisdom' becomes merely the 'proper' behavior that men wish to impose on women. Rosenblatt notes that Matthew's labeling the virgins as 'wise' or 'foolish' from the outset sets up the five foolish virgins for failure, and it encourages the five wise virgins (and so the readers who are supposed to identify with them) to shun the foolish. The choice between 'wise and foolish' serves not only to keep the women in line, but to divide the women against each other, and thus reduce any power they might have had as a group.[35] Rosenblatt's feminist concern, a concern I share, is that the parable alienates the two groups of women and encourages strife between them.[36] More, it alienates women readers and forces them to choose among the female characters.

Dan Via (a male reader who *does* identify with the women characters) works with the distinction of 'wise and foolish' and suggests that some readers (presumably both male and female) feel sympathy for the five foolish virgins and are sympathetic to their problem.[37] I am one of those sympathetic readers. In my first readings of this parable, I felt frustration and regret on behalf of the five foolish, as I wondered why they were not let in, even after they have gone to get the necessary oil. Now that I have done a resisting reading of the Parable of the Wedding Feast and have

35. Rosenblatt, 'Got into the Party After All: Women's Issues and the Five Foolish Virgins', in Amy-Jill Levine (ed.), *A Feminist Companion to Matthew* (Sheffield: Sheffield Academic Press, 2001), pp. 171–95, here pp. 182–83; reprinted from *Continuum* 3 (1993), pp. 107–37.

36. Rosenblatt, 'Got into the Party', pp. 186–87. Balabanski, 'Opening the Closed Door', p. 79.

37. Via, *Parables*, p. 126.

studied Matthew's view of weddings and bridegrooms, I have discovered that I need not feel sorry for the five 'foolish,' because this wedding is *not* the place they should want to be.

Therefore, I want to complicate the sharp distinction between the wise and foolish that Matthew presents.[38] For me, the wise and foolish are not so starkly distinguished from each other, and the interaction between the two groups has the potential to soften the boundary between them. For example, Matthew uses the same terms (φρόνιμος; μωρός) to identify the wise man and foolish man: the wise man built his house on rock, so his house stayed standing, but the foolish man built his on sand, and it washed away (7.24–27).[39] But I do not feel the same sympathy for the foolish man (ἄνδρι μωρῷ) who built his house on sand as I do for the foolish virgins, because the foolish man never *interacts* with the wise man. If the five foolish virgins were just fools, like the foolish man, I might not care about them, but because I see how the wise deny aid to them, I feel sympathy for them. Therefore, it is the *relationship* between the wise and foolish virgins that draws me into the story and blurs the distinction between the two groups. If I were one of the five 'wise' virgins who sent the foolish off to get their own oil and then went into the feast without them, I suspect I would feel regret over their loss, because I knew them, even if the bridegroom says he never did (25.12).

Another complication that blurs the distinction between 'wise' and 'foolish' in this parable (and so invites a resisting reading) is an inconsistency in how Matthew uses 'fool.' The Matthean Jesus says, 'The one who says "Fool!" (Μωρέ) – that one will be in the Gehenna of fire' (5.22),[40] but he himself calls the scribes and Pharisees 'fools' (μωροί) (23.17) and 'sons of Gehenna' (23.15) (υἱὸν γεέννης). Not only does the Matthean Jesus apparently contradict his own advice, he later says that the Pharisees are both fools (μωροί, 23.17) *and* 'serpents' (ὄφεις, 23.33), which is odd, because serpents are 'wise' (φρόνιμοι ὡς οἱ ὄφεις, 10.16). A resisting reading suggests that the distinction between 'wise' and 'foolish' is muddy, and that perhaps readers ought not to emulate the 'wise' virgins.

That the wise (φρόνιμοι) virgins (25.2) share the same type of wisdom as the serpents (φρόνιμοι ὡς οἱ ὄφεις, 10.16) means that their wisdom has a dubious reputation in this gospel, because of the Pharisee's condemnation

---

38. The division of the ten virgins between 'wise' and 'foolish' follows a Matthean pattern of separating people into groups (e.g., 24.40–41; 25.14–30).

39. For discussion of the similarities between the two parables, see Luz, *Matthäus*, III, p. 474; and Trilling, *Matthew*, II, p. 210.

40. Μωρός means foolish or 'stupid.' The term is juxtaposed in 5.22 with 'Ρακά , a term of abuse that has something to do with 'empty-headedness,' from Aramaic ריקא or ריקה, 'empty one' (BDAG, p. 903). Therefore, it reinforces the 'foolishness' of calling someone 'moron' (Μωρέ).

as the spawn of serpents (ὄφεις, 23.33).[41] Balabanski demonstrates that φρόνιμος is the word that describes 'practicality': the 'wise' man is he who builds on a rock foundation (Mt. 7.24) and the prudent and trustworthy slave who manages the master's household (Mt. 24.45). Luke uses the word φρόνιμος to describe the 'unjust' (Lk. 16.8), an unsavory character whose shrewdness saves him from harm.[42] Thus, Balabanski concludes that the type of 'wisdom' (φρόνιμος) demonstrated by the five 'wise' virgins is not *relational* in nature, but self-serving; the five φρόνιμοι are not compassionate and do not look out for the good of the whole group but simply to do what they need to do to fulfill their own duties.[43]

The snake-shrewd type of wisdom is not congruent with teachings in the gospel as a whole,[44] and the resisting reader questions the efficacy of trying to get into the same wedding feast with these people. The snake-shrewd virgins' refusal to share contradicts the Matthean injunction to give to anyone who begs from you (Mt. 5.42). If the parable is not read allegorically, then the oil is a commodity that *can* be shared. If these women are as shrewd as serpents, they are lying to preserve what they have in order to preserve their own interests. I am not convinced that they don't have enough to go around (as they claim). Their example does not befit the Kingdom of Heaven, because their lack of compassion is not up to the Matthean standard of righteousness (25.31–46). They could give away all their possessions (their oil to the 'fools') and receive treasure in heaven (19.21), but they do not. Thus, φρόνιμος does not to fit the Kingdom of Heaven.[45]

41. Capon (*Kingdom, Grace and Judgment*, pp. 496–97) uses Pauline definitions of wise and foolish to suggest that the foolish virgins live by the readily visible wisdom of the world (σοφία τοῦ κόσμου), a wisdom that God made foolish (ἐμώρανεν) (1 Cor. 1.20). Capon concludes that the 'wise' virgins represent the wisdom of trusting in the foolishness of God in Christ crucified, while the 'foolish' live by the wisdom of the world. In Capon's reading, the so-called 'foolish' virgins (Mt. 25.1) are the ones who seem wise (by the world's standards) in the beginning: they do not take any more oil than they think they will need. The maidens labeled 'wise' are, in the eyes of their companions, overprepared: they are 'fussbudgets preoccupied with what might possibly go wrong.' For Capon, their wisdom is apparently folly until the bridegroom is delayed. Capon's argument works quite well if the ten virgins were in Corinth, but it is not particularly Matthean.

42. Balabanski, 'Opening the Closed Door', pp. 80–81. For discussion of Matthew's identification of Jesus with σοφία, see Frances Taylor Gench, *Wisdom in the Christology of Matthew* (Lanham, MA: University Press of America, 1997); Celia Deutsch, *Lady Wisdom, Jesus, and the Sages* (Valley Forge, PA: Trinity Press International, 1996); Elisabeth Schüssler Fiorenza, *Jesus: Miriam's Child and Sophia's Prophet* (New York: Continuum, 1995); Ben Witherington, *Jesus the Sage: the Pilgrimage of Wisdom* (Minneapolis: Fortress Press, 1994); M. Jack Suggs, *Wisdom, Christology, and Law in Matthew's Gospel* (Cambridge, MA: Harvard University Press, 1970).

43. Balabanski, 'Opening the Closed Door', pp. 80–82.

44. Balabanski, 'Opening the Closed Door', pp. 81–82. See also Rosenblatt, 'Got into the Party', pp. 186–87.

45. I cannot offer σοφία as an alternative type of wisdom, because the kingdom is hidden from these sorts of 'wise' people (11.25).

The resisting reader does not care to be 'foolish' nor 'wise like the serpents,' but sees the parable as a subversive message: this wedding feast is not the real Kingdom of Heaven.

3.4 *Ten Virgins: The Full Measure*

Even though Matthew presents only five virgins entering the feast, Rosenblatt suggests that all ten virgins are supposed to enter, because the number ten is a figure of wholeness.[46] Whether the virgins enter the 'wedding feast,' are left out (in an allegorical reading), or avoid it (in a resisting reading), five go one way and five another. The 'whole' is divided, because the parable directs that the women remain in groups of five. I resist this division, because elsewhere in the gospel, when even *one* is left out of the whole, there is no longer cause for celebration (the appropriate attitude at the wedding feast [9.15]). There is rejoicing in heaven when the

46.   Rosenblatt, 'Got into the Party', pp. 171–95. Plummer (*Matthew*, p. 343) write that ten represents a full measure. Carter (*Matthew and the Margins*, p. 485) notes that ten was a 'perfect' number, and Philo corroborates this when he says that the number ten represents perfection or completion (τέλειος) (*Vita Moses*, 1.96; *Spec. Leg.* 2.201; 4.105). Davies and Allison (*Matthew*, III, pp. 394–95) cite the importance of the number ten with Old Testament examples: the Ten Commandments, the ten plagues, the ten per cent tithe, and that ten forms a congregation. John Donahue sees the number of attendants as evidence of a wedding on a grand scale, although there is no information to back up this claim (Donahue, *Parables*, p. 63). Beare (*Matthew*, p. 481) claims there is no significance to the number ten in this parable. In the Roman period, monetary and measuring units were divided by tens, so that a full measure always would be a multiple of ten, as evidenced in Matthew: one hundred sheep (18.12–14), a debt of ten thousand talents and one hundred *denarii* (18.24, 28), five talents increased to ten (25.15–16) (Rosenblatt, 'Got into the Party', p. 173, n. 4). Ten is the number of men required for a circle of study, for example, the ten judges in the *Damascus Document* (CD 10.4). See Ford, 'The Parable of the Foolish Scholars', p. 116. Plummer also suggests that ten is the minimum number for a congregation (*Matthew*, p. 343). Culbertson cites Ruth 4.2 as an example of just such an assembly of ten gathered to say the benediction over the bridegroom (*b Ket* 7b). Culbertson, *A Word Fitly Spoken*, p. 135, n. 24. Also Davies and Allison, *Matthew*, III, p. 395. Davies and Allison also include Zech. 8.23, where ten men from every nation will take hold of a Jew and say 'Let us go with you, for we have heard that God is with you.' To point out that a quorum was ten men, not virgins, takes the symbol too literally; the ten virgins represent a complete number that come to celebrate the bridegroom's wedding feast, and therefore the complete number are intended to get into the feast. Augustine (*Sermon* 43) recognizes ten as a representation of the whole Church. Those who follow Augustine's interpretation include Bruno of Segni (*Commentary on Matthew*, 278B) and Nicholas of Lyra. Moschner thinks that ten suggests a 'great multitude, without limiting it more exactly' (perhaps in reference to the Church?). See F.M. Moschner, *The Kingdom of Heaven in Parables* (trans. D. Heimann; London: Herder, 1960), p. 200. Adrian Leske agrees that all ten of the virgins belong in the kingdom, but five were unprepared to enter it (A. Leske, 'Matthew', in W.R. Farmer (ed.), *The International Bible Commentary: A Catholic and Ecumenical for the Twenty-first Century* [Collegeville, MN: Liturgical Press, 1998], pp. 1253–1330 [p. 1320]).

shepherd leaves 99 to go rescue the one lost (18.12–14).[47] If celebration does not occur in heaven when only one per cent of the hundred is lost, the virgins should not be able to celebrate when fifty per cent of their number is lost. (In my resisting reading, the wedding feast is not the Kingdom of Heaven, so it is the five who enter the 'feast' that are 'lost.') With Rosenblatt, I resist the division of the women and suggest that all ten could leave the rude bridegroom to his wedding feast; they could then all enter the Kingdom of Heaven together.

3.5 *Lamps and Oil*

References to lights borne by wedding attendants are numerous in ancient sources (λαμπάδας,[48] δᾳδας,[49] *faces nuptiales*,[50] *cerei*[51]) and thus support a literal reading of the parable, that the 'lamps' and 'oil' are tangible. The five virgins with extra oil possess a real commodity that can be shared.

However, metaphorical readings of the parable insist that the 'lamps' represent good deeds. While Matthew does not use the word λαμπάς

---

47. Rosenblatt, 'Got into the Party', p. 173.

48. The Greek–English lexicon lists both 'torch' and 'lamps' BDAG (2nd edn), p. 465; BDAG (3rd edn), p. 585. λαμπάς can refer to either clay lamps fueled with oil or to torches made of a resinous pine, dry wood coated with pitch, or a long pole with oil-soaked rags bundled at the top (Oepke, 'λάμπω, ἐκλάμπω, περιλάμπω, λαμπάς, λαμπρός', TDNT 4, pp. 16–28 [16]). The gospels often use the term to refer to household oil lamps (Mk. 4.21; Mt. 5.15; 7.2; 10.26; 13.12; 25.29; Lk. 6.38; 8.16–18; 11.33; 12.2; 19.26). Davies and Allison wonder if the reference to 'trimming' shows that 'lamps' (with wicks) is the correct translation in Davies and Allison (*Matthew*, III, p. 396, 398). See also Moschner, *Kingdom of Heaven in Parables*, p. 201; Hultgren, *Parables*, pp. 171–72; Donfried, 'Allegory', p. 417; Schweizer, *Matthew*, pp. 465–66; Jülicher, *Gleichnisreden*, II, p. 448; Weder, *Gleichnisse*, p. 241, n. 149. Hultgren also prefers 'lamps,' not only because of the 'trimming,' but because the parable seems to indicate they burned throughout the evening (25.8), something a torch would not do (*Parables*, p. 173). In John 18.3, λαμπάδας (torches) are distinguished from lamps (φανῶν) (lanterns or lamps). Thomas Johnston suggests that the virgins carried both lamps and torches (*Christ's Watchword*, p. 9). Joachim Jeremias argues that 'torches' is the preferred translation, not only because oil lamps would be impractical for outside use (they give off dim light and are easily extinguished), they do not fit the situation in the parable because lamps burn a long time, so that extra oil is not a necessity (J. Jeremias, 'ΛΑΜΠΑΔΕΣ Mt 25.1,3,7', *ZNW* 56 [1965], pp. 196–201). Jeremias claims that torches were used in festive processions in Palestine. These were long sticks wrapped with rags soaked in olive oil that burned for only a short time before needing to be replenished with oil. The rag torches were carried by young women in a procession to the house where the wedding was taking place, and the girls performed dances with them until the flames went out (Jeremias, 'ΛΑΜΠΑΔΕΣ', pp. 197–98). Ulrich Luz and Robert Gundry agree that the oil lamps would be impractical for outdoor use, and that the more likely translation is 'torch' (*Fackel*). See Luz, *Matthäus*, III, pp. 469–70, and Gundry, *Matthew*, p. 498. That Jeremias bases his findings on the reminiscences of a nineteenth-century Lutheran minister who grew up in Jerusalem is problematic for making a sound case that such customs were in place centuries before,

anywhere but in the parable, the gospel does support a metaphorical reading, because Matthew describes Jesus' followers as the light of the world (τὸ φῶς τοῦ κόσμου) and reminds readers that they should let a lamp (λύχνον) shine from the lampstand (λυχνίαν) so that it will illuminate all things in the house (λάμπε; here the verbal form; Mt. 5.15). Matthew also uses the verbal form of λαμπάς to exhort readers: 'let your light shine before people' (λαμψάτω τὸ φῶς ὑμῶν) (5.16) and 'the righteous shine like the sun (ἐκλάμψουσιν ὡς ὁ ἥλιος) in the kingdom of the Father' (13.43). Metaphorical interpretations of the oil and the lamps as good deeds or charity[52] resonate with Matthew's insistence on charity

---

but he does offer a plausible option for what the λαμπάδες might have looked like and the nature of their use. Lövestam suggests that the lights consisted of copper bowls affixed to poles; the bowls contained oil-soaked rags (*Spiritual Wakefulness in The New Testament* [Gleerup: Lund, 1963], p. 114, n. 4). Greek and Roman weddings also involved carrying torches (Festus [2 CE], *Sexti Pompei Festi* 245a; Varro [2 BCE], *Nonius*, 112).

49. Chariton, *Callirhoe* 1.1.13; 1.3.2; Lucian, *Herodotus* 5; Aeschylus, *Agamemnon* 1180; Achille Tatius, *Leucippe et Clitophon* 1.13.6.

50. Lucan 2.356; Tacitus, *Annals* 15.37.

51. Plutarch (*Roman Questions* 2).

52. Methodius, *On Chastity*, 6.4; Chrysostom, *Homily* 23; *Homily* 60; *Commentary on Galatians*, 6.10; Augustine, *Sermon* 43.5; *Opus Imperfectum* 930; Boring, *Matthew*, p. 450; Donfried, 'Allegory', pp. 422–23; D.O. Wenham, *The Parables of Jesus* (Downess Grove, IL: InterVarsity Press, 1989), p. 82; Lambrecht, *Out of the Treasure*, p. 211. Other allegorical interpretations include: the fruit of good works (Hilary of Poitiers, *Sur Matthieu* 25.4), righteousness (Senior, *Matthew*, p. 277); blessing or repentance (Albright and Mann, *Matthew*, p. 302); patience, hope, and truth (Davies and Allison, *Matthew*, p. 992); 'the outward marks of a Christian life (Plummer, *Matthew*, p. 344); Torah study (cf. Ps. 109.105 (Ford, 'Foolish Scholars', p. 116.); spiritual grace (Arnobius Iunior, *Expositio Matthaei* 27; trans. Kraszewski, *Gospel of Matthew*, p. 356); God's spirit (Johnston, *Christ's Watchword*, p. 28). That good works and charity may be too simplistic an allegorical interpretation of the lamps and oil is suggested by Chrysostom (*Homily 50*), who warns that doing good works is not enough; the spiritual fire can be quenched by evil desires, inhumanity, and cruelty, even if the oil does not run out. Hare (*Matthew*, p. 285) and Davies and Allison (*Matthew*, p. 397) agree that the evangelist lists many obligations above and beyond good works: for example, abstaining from bad behavior (15.19), loving enemies and each other (5.44; 24.12); forgiving (18.21–35), faith (21.21), loyalty to Jesus (10.32), and love for God (22.37). Plummer says the lamps are useless in and of themselves unless they give light to others (*Matthew*, p. 344). Lövestam likens the burning lamps to 'life and salvation' that do not expire (*Spiritual Wakefulness*, p. 117). Emily Cheney interprets 'oil' as a necessity for preparation for the Parousia: the Parable of the Virgins occurs between two trips to the Mount of Olives (24.3 and 26.30) during which Jesus talks about the necessity for watchfulness (24.36) and includes the woman anointing Jesus with oil at Bethany (26.6–13). Cheney concludes that just as anointing Jesus for his burial is important, so is having oil in preparation for his return. This interpretation is intriguing, but the perfumed oil for anointing (μύρον) and the oil for lamps or torches (ἐλαίον) are not the same and are used in entirely different ways (a problematic distinction Cheney grants) (Emily Cheney, 'Ten Maidens Awaiting the Bridegroom', paper given at the Society of Biblical Literature annual meeting in Denver, Colorado, November 18, 2001).

(e.g., 25.31–46).[53] These interpretations suggest that the five foolish virgins' light goes out because they did not show their good works to the world, did not light the way for others, and failed to glorify the Father.[54] A non-metaphorical reading takes note that the virgins are not *supposed* to be lighting the way for others: their job is to light the way only for the bridegroom (25.1). Nor are they showing any 'good works' or glorifying the Father. They are simply acting as wedding attendants. The five foolish virgins' lack of oil is simply that: they didn't have enough oil, a situation easily rectified by a trip to the market or by the generosity of others who might share.

Lamps (λαμπάδας) are part of wedding feasts, but they also frequently illuminate scenes of violence and separation: Demeter sought her kidnapped daughter Persephone by torchlight (μετὰ λαμπάδων νυκτός) in Apollodorus (1 CE), *Bibliotheca* 1.5. Gideon's men hide torches (λαμπάδας) in jars for a surprise attack on a city (Judg. 7.16–20); Samson burns fields of grain with torches (λαμπάδας) tied between foxes' tails (Judg. 15.4–5); the men who arrest Jesus come with torches (λαμπάδας) (Jn. 18.3); torches (λαμπάδας) illuminate the room while Paul preaches into the night, and a young man falls asleep (like the ten virgins) and then plummets from a window to his death (Acts 20.8–9).[55] Thus λαμπάδας are ambiguous features in the parable: they can be associated with joyful celebrations, but also with danger and violence.

A resisting reading notes a gap in the narrative: it is not clear how *any* of the ten virgins could have known to bring extra oil.[56] Why did the *'wise'* bring extra oil, when the gospel has presented the opposite expectation, that they should *not* be so prepared? The evangelist previously has given 'wise' disciples (10.16) advice not to bring extra things, because what they need will be provided: 'Take no gold, or silver, or copper in your belts, no bag for your journey, or two tunics, or sandals, or a staff, for laborers deserve their food' (10.9–10). If the ten virgins are disciples, servants, laborers, or even 'daughters' of the bridal chamber (cf. 9.15), then their need for extra oil should have been provided by the host.

That their needs are not met suggests that they have come to an unwelcoming house (10.12–13), a house that is not part of the Kingdom of Heaven. People in this house are having a wedding feast, a sure sign

53. Moschner (*Kingdom of Heaven in Parables*, p. 200) interprets the lamp light as the joy of the ten virgins as they celebrate the good fortune of the bridegroom, which suggests that they cannot mourn in the bridegroom's presence, but share the joy of the 'sons of the bridal chamber' (9.15), although Matthew does not say anything about the ten virgins' joy.

54. Donfried, 'Allegory of the Ten Virgins', p. 423; Leske, 'Matthew', p. 1320. Matthew refers to lamps and light that illuminate good works and glorify the Father in heaven (5.15; Origen, *Contra Celsum* 6.5).

55. Paul revives the young man (20.10).

56. Rosenblatt, 'Got Into the Party', pp. 186–87.

of impending doom, for as in the days of Noah, they were marrying and giving in marriage until the flood swept them away (24.38–39), and weddings are frequently associated with doom, as we saw in Chapter 1. Indeed, according to Matthew, if the virgins are not welcomed to the house where the wedding takes place, they should shake the dust from their feet (10.14; cf. 10.40–41). A resisting reader should do the same.

3.6 *The Bridegroom's Delay*

The bridegroom's delay (χρονίζω) creates the conflict in the narrative; had he not been delayed, perhaps all the virgins would have had enough oil and got into the feast. There is an element of blame in the bridegroom's tardiness. Readers are not privy to the reason for his tardiness; we only know that he is late to his own wedding, so late, in fact, that the wedding attendants fall asleep. At this wedding, no one behaves well; the bridegroom is late, and the wedding attendants, wise and foolish alike, sleep. While readers want to find a 'good' example among the characters, no one is exemplary. Perhaps the point of the parable is that waiting for a bridegroom is a waste of time. For Matthew, 'real' weddings are no longer important.

The bridegroom's delay compels explanations from many interpreters. Some say the bridegroom is late as a result of the long distance he had to travel[57] or because he had to spend extra time negotiating the bride price with the bride's parents.[58] These explanations presume too much that the parable does not tell us. Some argue that the bridegroom's delay is merely an element of the plot that serves to heighten tension about the coming end times.[59] But 'elements of the plot' include every detail in this spare story, so that by that argument, we should dismiss the whole parable as mere story.

A majority of interpreters argue that the parable is an allegory of the

---

57. Smith, *Parables*, p. 100.

58. Jeremias, *Parables*, pp. 172–74 (cf. Jeremias, 'ΛΑΜΠΑΔΕΣ,' p. 198), and Gundry, *Matthew*, pp. 499–500.

59. Hultgren, *Parables*, p. 174; Harrington (*Matthew*, p. 350) and Senior (*Matthew*, p. 275) suggest that Jesus referred to God and not himself as the bridegroom (based on Isa. 54.5; Jer. 31.32; Hos. 2.1–20). Eduard Schweizer also thinks Jesus meant that the bridegroom is God. But Schweizer concedes that Matthew identifies Jesus with the bridegroom in 25. 11–12 (Schweizer, *Matthew*, p. 465). Albright and Mann (*Matthew*, p. 302) are definite in their identification of God as the bridegroom and Israel the bride in this parable. The parable illustrates how 'Israel, God's bride, has been badly served by some of her custodians.'

Parousia.[60] The evangelist places the parable of the Ten Virgins between two other parables about servants waiting for their master's return (24. 45–51; 25.14–30); interpreters suggest that these three parables together illustrate the delayed Parousia. Given the circumstances that Matthew's community is positioned between the Kingdom of Heaven and the world, that is, simultaneously waiting for the return of Jesus but at the same time settling down as a Church, this allegorical reading warns members of the community to be prepared for the bridegroom's sudden return.

Interpreters have seen the virgins' sleep as death; i.e., the virgins have died, and the cry at midnight is the resurrection moment when Christ returns.[61] Certainly, sleep and death can be synonymous. Καθεύδειν often refers to the act of lying down to rest or sleep (e.g., LXX 1 Kgs 3.2–9; also 2 Kgs 4.5–7; Prov. 3.24; 6.22; Ezek. 4.9; Tob. 8.13) but also describes those who sleep among the dead, like the slain that lie in the grave (LXX Ps.

---

60. Discussion of the delay as Parousia and the parable as allegory is found in: Bultmann, *History of the Synoptic Tradition*, p. 176. Donfried, 'Allegory' article; Crossan, 'Parable as Religious and Poetic Experience', *JR* 53 (1973), and *In Parables*; R.E. Brown, 'Parable and Allegory Reconsidered' in *New Testament Essays* (Milwaukee: Bruce, 1965), pp. 254–64; Dodd, *Parables*, p. 23; Via, *Parables*, p. 5; Harrington, 'Polemical Parables', p. 295; Drury, *Parables in the Gospels*, pp. 97–103; Luz, *Matthäus*, III, p. 469–75; Armand Puig i Tàrrech, *La Parabole des dix vierges,* pp. 232–37; Davies and Allison, *Matthew*, III, p. 392; Senior, *Matthew*, p. 274; Buttrick, *Speaking Parables*, p. 167; Dale C. Allison, 'Matthew', *The Oxford Bible Commentary* (Oxford: Oxford University Press, 2000), pp. 844–86 (878); Lambrecht, *Out of the Treasure*, pp. 211–14; Perkins, *Hearing the Parables of Jesus*, p. 104; Gnilka, *Das Matthäusevangelium*, II, pp. 346–47; Weder, *Die Gleichnisse Jesu als Metaphern*, pp. 242–43; J.M. Sheriff, 'Matthew 25.1–13: A Summary of Matthean Eschatology?', in E.A. Livingstone (ed.), *Studia Biblica 1978: Sixth International Congress on Biblical Studies* (JSNTSup, 2; Sheffield: Sheffield Academic Press, 1980), pp. 301–305; Lövestam, *Spiritual Wakefulness*, pp. 108–10; Bornkamm, 'Die Verzögerung der Parusie,' pp. 122–23; Michaelis, *Es ging ein Sämman aus, zu säen*, pp. 162–63; McKenzie, 'Matthew', p. 101.

61. Wailes (*Medieval Allegories*, p. 183) reports that all early authorities except the *Opus imperfectum* interpret the virgins' sleep as death. Also Aphrahat, 401.7–10, 23–25, cited in Kuriakose A. Valavanolickal, *The Use of the Gospel Parables in the Writings of Aphrahat and Ephrem* (Studies in the Religion and History of Early Christianity, 2; Franfurt am Main: Peter Lang, 1995), pp. 184–85. Methodius writes that the virgins' rising to the cry means that 'the dead shall be raised after the voice comes from heaven' (*On Chastity*, 6.4. Methodius here conflates imagery from 1 Thess. 4 to describe the shout of the Lord and the sound of the trumpet as the dead are raised to life first. He says those who are truly alive shall meet him in the clouds bearing their lamps trimmed (cf. Mt. 25.7). Augustine, likewise, refers to the virgins' 'sleep of death,' and the bridegroom's cry of resurrection (*Sermon 43*, 6–9). Johnston notes that the parable warns that the reader must be prepared, because no one can know the day of one's death (*Christ's Watchword*, pp. 61 and 70). Among modern scholars, Donfried, 'Allegory', p. 421; Wenham, *Parables*, p. 83. But others disagree that 'sleep' refers to death, including W. Carter and J.P. Heil (*Matthew's Parables: Audience-oriented Perspectives* [CBQMS, 30; Washington, DC: The Catholic Biblical Association of America, 1998], pp. 194–96) and Gundry (*Matthew*, p. 500). Davies and Allison think that the sleep may refer to death, but they think it is going too far to see the awakening as resurrection (*Matthew*, III, p. 398, n. 170).

88.5).[62] Matthew uses κοιμᾶν to speak of the dead (Mt. 27.52; as does Paul in 1 Thess. 4.13–14 and 1 Cor. 15.20) and distinguishes between death and sleep: 'The girl did not die (ἀπέθανεν) but sleeps (καθεύδει) (9.24).' Therefore, καθεύδειν describes the virgins' slumber, not death, just as the disciples merely sleep (καθεύδοντας, 26.40) – and are not dead – in Gethsemane.

The occasion of the virgins' sleep reveals yet another contrast between Jesus, the true Bridegroom, and the 'bridegroom' in the parable: their means of waking someone from sleep. In a story that occurs immediately after Jesus identifies himself as the Bridegroom (9.15), he goes to a man's house to heal the man's daughter; he takes the sleeping girl by the hand, and she gets up (9.18, 23–24). The parabolic bridegroom has the ten girls come to *his* house rather than going to theirs; and instead of taking them by the hand to waken them, someone shouts them awake. Therefore, readers would do well to heed the subversive message: resist falling asleep outside the 'bridegroom's' door.

If remaining awake is the parable's exhortation, none of the virgins passes the test. All ten fall asleep (ἐκάθευδον, 25.5).[63] That even the 'wise' fall asleep echoes a Matthean theme that disciples do not always stay awake and ready; they do not always perform well. Jesus beseeches his disciples to stay awake with him in Gethsemane (26.38, γρηγορεῖτε; cf. 25.13), but they all fall asleep (καθεύδοντας, 26.40, 43, 45). The disciples awaken only at the moment when he is arrested and taken away (26.46; cf. 9.15); the virgins awaken only when they hear the cry that he is coming at last. A reading that resists identifying Jesus as the bridegroom in the parable shows that the difference between Gethsemane and the wedding feast is not found with the sleepers, who all alike slumber, but between the two 'bridegrooms.' The bridegroom in the parable is late, but the true bridegroom at Gesthemane is ready for the entourage that comes for him.

The sleepers at Gesthemane also suggest a new reading for the ten sleepers in the parable. The sleeping disciples deserted Jesus and fled but

---

62. Though the verb for death as sleep is usually κοιμᾶν. Death is lying or sleeping (κοιμᾶν) with one's ancestors (κοιμᾶν, incidentally, also refers to sexual intercourse [e.g., LXX Gen. 19.32–35; 26.10; 30.15]). The Lord promises Moses the he will lie with his ancestors (LXX Deut. 31.16); David sleeps with his ancestors (LXX 3 Kgs 11.21). More examples include LXX 3 Kgs 43; 14.20, 31; 15.8, 24; 16.6, 28; 22.40, 50; 4 Kgs 8.24; 10.35; 13.9, 13; 14.16, 22, 29; 15.7, 22, 38; 16.20; 20.21; 21.18; 24.6; 2 Chron. 9.31; 12.16; 14.1; 16.13; 21.1; 26.2, 23; 27.9; 28.27; 32.33; 33.20). New Testament examples include the saints that 'slept' arose and walked about (Mt. 27.52); and those who 'sleep' will be the first fruits of the resurrection (1 Cor. 15.20).

63. In an interpretation that ignores the actual wording in 25.5 ('they *all* grew weary and slept' [ἐνύσταξαν πᾶσαι καὶ ἐκάθευδον]), the *Epistula Apostolorum* (second century CE) says (in both its Ethiopic and Coptic versions) that only the five *foolish* virgins slept (*Epis. Ap.* 43–44), probably in an attempt to make a more complete distinction between the wise and foolish.

are deemed faithful enough to receive the Great Commission (28.16–20) (Ironically, one who *stayed awake* – Judas – is the one who ultimately failed to remain with Jesus). Perhaps all ten of the virgins, who all slept, will also be rehabilitated by the true bridegroom.

3.7 *The Cry at Midnight*

The cry is the moment for which the virgins should be prepared: 'Behold, the bridegroom is coming!'[64] Matthew does not inform the reader *who* cries: we are simply told 'there was a cry' (κραυγὴ γέγονεν). Moschner says that this omission adds to the 'mysterious, distant, unnatural tone that covers the whole parable'[65] The cry is reminiscent of other disembodied voices crying out, like the voice crying (φωνὴ βοῶντος) in the wilderness to prepare the way of the Lord at the beginning of Jesus' ministry (Mt. 3.3),[66] the voice (φωνή) from heaven at Jesus' baptism that identifies him as the beloved son of God (Mt. 3.17), and the trumpet call that announces the Lord's return (Mt. 24.31; 1 Thess. 4.16).[67]

The cry at midnight that signals the bridegroom's arrival is a portent of fear, conflict, desperation, and violence. Richard Batey confirms that the arrival of the bridegroom is not joyful 'because his coming results in judgment and separation ...'[68] Matthew uses the verbal form of κραυγή several times. Many of these cries take place in situations of fear: the demons cry out (ἔκραξαν) in alarm before Jesus exorcises them (8.29); the disciples cry out from terror (ἀπὸ φόβου ἔκραξαν) because they think Jesus is a ghost (14.26), and Peter, fearing for his life (ἐφοβήθη), cries out

64. A fifth-century BCE poem includes a similar cry to Hymen or Hymenaios, a god of weddings: 'Hymenaios! The bridegroom is coming!', in D.A. Campbell (trans.), *Greek Lyric* (5 vols.; LCL, 143; Cambridge, MA: Harvard University Press, 1982), I, p. 111.

65. Moschner, *Kingdom in Parables*, p. 202.

66. Unfortunately for my comparison, the Greek is not the same: φωνὴ βοῶντος; however, the sense of a cry coming out of nowhere resonates. (The voice of Rachel crying [2.18] will be covered in Ch. 4.)

67. Augustine, *Sermon* 93; Johnston, *Christ's Watchword*, pp. 84–85. For Martin Luther (*Table Talk*, 15), the cry at midnight is the moment at which the evilness of the world will be judged by God, and for John Calvin (*Commentary on Matthew, Mark, and Luke*, Mt. 25.6), the cry announces the sudden arrival of the bridegroom when the dead will be raised and those who are asleep will be wakened. J. Massingberd Ford sets this parable in the context of Torah study, based on rabbinic stories that the Law should be studied both day and night. That midnight was the hour of revelation when scholars should be studying is, for Ford, the key to why the bridegroom's cry comes at midnight. Only those scholars who are studying the Law are ready to respond. Ford, 'Foolish Scholars', p. 116, nn. 1, 2. Ford cites *Lev. R.* 2.18–19; 9.1–2; *Cant. R.* 5.11. I find this interpretation plausible, given Matthew's interest in keeping the Law, but I do not think it fits with the virgins' falling asleep, if they must be awakened for the hour of revelation.

68. Richard A. Batey, *New Testament Nuptial Imagery* (Leiden: Brill, 1971), p. 61.

(ἔκραζεν) when he begins to sink (14.30). Some cries occur in situations of conflict and desperation: the Canaanite woman cries out to Jesus (ἔκραζεν), and when he does not answer, she continues to cry out (κράζει) (15.22–23) and argues with him until he responds favorably. The crowd tells the two blind men crying out (κράζοντες) to shut up, but they cry out more loudly until Jesus responds (20.30–31). Finally, cries occur in situations of violence: the crowds cry out (ἔκραζον) that Jesus be crucified (27.23). Jesus himself, as victim of violence, cries out (κράξας) from the cross as he dies (27.50).[69] Such a cry does not belong at a wedding; the cry signals that something is very wrong with this wedding.

The sudden appearance in a night-time setting corresponds to the Matthean portrayal of the Son of Man as a 'thief in the night' (Mt. 24.43), when 'one will be taken' and 'one will be left' (24.40–41). The bridegroom, like the thief, comes upon the ten virgins suddenly, at an unexpected time. Like a thief, he catches them unaware. Only the cry (25.6) gives him away. This picture of the thief-like bridegroom reinforces his association with violence. Matthew has combined images of a 'bridegroom' with that of 'thief' – a jarring juxtaposition that echoes the rape of the Sabines and the capture of the women by the Benjaminites in Judges. A bridegroom who comes unexpectedly in the middle of the night is associated with harm, fear, and division, as 'one is taken and one left' (24.40–41). In a similar way, five virgins are allowed into the feast and five are not (25.10–12).

A cry at midnight resonates with other instances of divine intervention in human affairs that involve judgment and violence: the angel slew the first-born of Egypt at midnight (μεσούσης τῆς νυκτός) (Exod. 11.4; 12.29), and there was a great cry (ἐγενήθη κραυγὴ μεγάλη) (Exod. 12.29–30). Paul and Silas are freed from prison by a violent earthquake at midnight (μεσονύκτιον) causing a guard to draw his sword to kill himself, and Paul shouts in a loud voice (ἐφώνησεν δὲ μεγάλη φωνῇ) for him to stop (Acts 16.25–28).[70] The 'cry' (κραυγή) coupled with the lighting of the virgins' lamps is reminiscent of the angel of fire crying out (κράζων) (Rev. 14.18) that the hour has come for reaping the harvest of the earth,[71] an horrifically violent scene where blood will flow like wine from the wine press (Rev. 14.15–20). Midnight is the time of the bridegroom's arrival,

---

69. The only time in this gospel when a cry is not in a situation of conflict or violence is when the crowds and children cry (ἔκραζον, κράζοντας) 'Hosanna!' (21.9, 15) as Jesus enters Jerusalem. However, their cries portend his final conflict with the authorities and his crucifixion.

70. While other interpreters note the similarities between the parable and these other 'cries at midnight,' they do not discuss violence; e.g., Barbara Reid, *Parables for Preachers: The Gospel of Matthew: Year A* (3 vols.; Collegeville, MN: Liturgical Press, 2001), I, p. 196; Strobel discusses the cry at midnight (Mt. 25.6) and the great cry (κραυγὴ μεγάλη) in Exod. 12.30 (*Untersuchungen*, p. 240).

71. Reid, *Parables*, p. 196.

but his coming is not a joyful event, given these associations with dead children, earthquakes, and the bloody reaping of the angels. Readers might conclude that it would be better if the bridegroom stayed away, or at least hope that they never need confront him (e.g., 'do not lead us into the time of trial' [6.13]). The bridegroom's presence is no longer joyful (9.15) but dreadful.

3.8 Go Buy for Yourselves

A central question is why the five 'wise' women did not share their oil. Certainly sharing the oil would have been in keeping with admonitions to share with those in need (e.g., 'Give to everyone who begs from you, and do not refuse anyone who wants to borrow from you' [Mt. 5.42] and the command to 'love your neighbor as yourself' [19.19]).[72] Their refusal confounds the metaphorical reading that wants to equate the 'wise' virgins with good deeds. These 'wise' are revealed to be shrewd like a snake: their refusal to share strikes many readers, including myself, as unnecessarily harsh and selfish. Daniel Patte notes that the refusal sounds 'rude and insensitive.'[73] Margaret Atwood calls them 'bloodless paragons' and notes that 'we suspect them of having mean hearts.'[74] Capon says, 'They were simply snotty.'[75] Rosenblatt comments, 'If this is wisdom, it is unattractive.'[76]

Some interpreters point out that the five wise virgins' refusal to share is given by the wise themselves: they protest that if they share, there will not be enough oil for anyone.[77] Ulrich Luz thinks that the refusal to share is a literary necessity in presenting the story as a tragedy,[78] but such a dismissal neglects important features of the parable: the relationship of the five wise and five foolish virgins, their comportment as would-be disciples, and their ultimate fate at the door of the wedding feast. Balabanski suggests that the five wise virgins do not want to forfeit the honor of being in the procession (as have the five foolish virgins), by

---

72. Lambrecht, *Out of the Treasure*, p. 202.

73. Patte, *Matthew*, p. 344.

74. Margaret Atwood, *Good Bones and Simple Murders* (New York: Doubleday, 1994), p. 60.

75. Capon, *Parables of Judgment*, p. 164.

76. Rosenblatt, 'Got into the Party', p. 182.

77. Levine, 'Matthew', p. 261.

78. Luz, *Matthäus*, III, p. 476. Nor, argues Luz, is there any reason to speculate on why there was no extra oil at the bride's house, because this tale is allegorical. Garland agrees that the reader need not be concerned about sharing the oil, because the parable is not about the Golden Rule but about being prepared spiritually (David E. Garland, *Reading Matthew: A Literary and Theological Commentary on the First Gospel* [New York: Crossroad, 1993], p. 240).

risking they won't have enough oil,[79] but in this parable, we see no procession ever take place.[80] Thus, there is no viable excuse for not sharing.

Still, interpreters are compelled to offer a solution. The most popular reason interpreters give for the wise virgins' refusal to share is allegorical: the oil for the lamps represents faith, good deeds, or merit that cannot be transferred,[81] much as the *Acts of Philip* intones, 'Who gives up his own lamp to another and himself sits in darkness?'[82] and as Thomas Johnston asserts, 'one cannot borrow grace of another, it being incommunicable, as the foolish would borrow oyle of the wise virgins.'[83] In an allegorical reading, the five foolish virgins show they are irresponsible and thoughtless, lack faith, and have done no good deeds. Thus, no amount of generosity on the part of the their five companions can suffice for the foolish virgins' lack of character.[84]

But this interpretation is problematic if we read the parable literally, so that the oil is a commodity that *can* be shared. The five wise refuse to share something that can be shared; they simply don't want to share it. Their refusal resonates with the hostility and self-righteous indignation of the vineyard workers who worked all day and complained about the injustice that the one-hour workers received the same wage (Mt. 20.1–16). In Herzog's reading of the Parable of the Vineyard, the landowner is not God but a rich and exploitive landowner: he is *not* generous in giving equal payment to all the workers[85] but rather takes advantage of the workers' desperation for employment and their lack of bargaining power. He shames them all into submission by devaluing the work of those who

---

79.   Balabanski, 'Opening the Closed Door', p. 84.

80.   Jerome Neyrey agrees that the lack of oil is a loss of honor (*Honor and Shame in the Gospel of Matthew* [Louisville: Westminster/John Knox Press, 1998], p. 60). Neyrey's point is to show how ostentatious wedding celebrations could be in contrast to Jesus' lack of wealth.

81.   So John Calvin, *Commentary on Matthew, Mark, and Luke*, Mt. 25.9; Plummer, *Matthew*, p. 345; Batey, *Nuptial Imagery*, p. 47; Ford, 'Foolish Scholars', p. 117; Donfried, 'Allegory', p. 427; Leske, 'Matthew', p. 1320; Viviano, 'Matthew', p. 668.

82.   A. Cleveland Cox (trans.), 'The Acts of Philip', in A. Roberts and J. Donaldson (eds.), *The Ante-Nicene Fathers* (10 vols.; Peabody, MA: Hendrickson Publishers, 1994), VIII, p. 501. (This translation contains no chapter or line numbers.)

83.   Johnston, *Christ's Watchword*, p. 20; Donfried, 'Allegory', p. 427, n. 55. Tertullian (*On Modesty*, 22) says that no one has sufficient oil of their own to be able to share: 'If you have no sin, you can redeem others through your witness and death,' he wrote, 'but if you are a sinner, how will the oil of your small torch be able to suffice for you and me?'

84.   Via, *Parables*, p. 126; Nancy J. Duff, 'Wise and Foolish Maidens (Matthew 25.1–13)', *USQR* 40 (1985), pp. 55–58 (56); Patte, *Matthew*, p. 344; Johnston, *Christ's Watchword*, pp. 110–15.

85.   Rosenblatt ('Got into the Party', p. 188) notes that the ending of the Parable of the Ten Virgins 'has no relation to the "eleventh hour" generosity of the master of the vineyard who pays the same wage to those who worked one hour as to those who worked all day.'

labored all day and by setting up the latecomers to receive the resentment of the all-day workers. The landowner exploits the workers' lack of cohesion and is able 'to conquer them by dividing them.'[86] By reading the Parable of the Ten Virgins through Herzog's interpretation of the Vineyard, we can see that the five wise virgins share the day-long laborers' sense of injustice: they begrudge sharing their reward with those who did not work as hard (or who had not come prepared) and think that those who come late should not be given full payment (or access to the feast). In the case of the Parable of the Ten Virgins, the bridegroom is an absentee lord, and the ten must adjudicate the situation on their own, but the result is the same: their lack of cohesion divides them. This reading also demonstrates that the 'bridegroom' in the parable cannot be Jesus, because the bridegroom confirms the 'divide and conquer' system that the snake-shrewd virgins have set up.

Aside from Matthew's assignation of the labels 'wise and foolish,' there is no difference between the two groups of virgins except that one group has a commodity and the other group doesn't.[87] Because the parable has set them up as opposites (wise and foolish), they act as rivals rather than as comrades. The parable implies that 'wise' people should not share what they have with those in need, and that they should use their 'wisdom' as shrewdness competitively to gain advantage over others. As noted earlier, this 'wisdom' goes against other Matthean teachings, not only about wealth and charity, but that the first shall be last and the last first (20.16), and that disciples must be servants to others (20.24–28).

The five *foolish* virgins are in good company with the parabolic servant who did not invest well (25.14–30). Like him, they find themselves in a situation that reflects the wealthy person's exploitation of the poor, where 'to the ones who have, more is given, and to those who have nothing, even what they have is taken away' (25.29). Like that unfortunate servant, the five foolish virgins remain in the outer darkness (25.30). In a literal reading (following Herzog),[88] the servant is representative of a weak person who is exploited by a powerful person. I feel sympathy for the servant who hid the talent, as I do for the five foolish virgins, because he

---

86.   Herzog, *Parables as Subversive Speech*, pp. 86–95. Mary Kay Dobrovolny offers a reading of the parable's economic injustice by reading from the viewpoint of the landowner in 'Who Controls the Resources? Economics and Justice in Mt. 20.15', (Seminar Paper, SBL, San Antonio, TX, November 22, 2004).

87.   Rosenblatt ('Got into the Party', p. 186) writes, 'If an ordinary community member had looked only at the deeds of the wise and foolish, the women's differences would have been indistinguishable … they had all been invited, all gone forth to meet the bridegroom, they all took lamps, they all slumbered and slept, they all awoke and trimmed their lamps … if all the women appeared to be so much alike, how can half prove to be so radically different from the others?'

88.   See Herzog, *Parables as Subversive Speech*, pp. 9–29.

made a choice based on fear: he knew that his master was a harsh and powerful man (25.25). His motive for burying the talent was not laziness, stupidity, or lack of ambition, but quite the contrary: he acted wisely in seeking to avoid punishment, because of his terror of what the master might do to him if he lost the money. His ultimate misunderstanding of the master's expectations is his undoing. The five foolish virgins also have acted in a conservative way: they do not bring extra oil, as the servant began with only one talent and did not earn any extra money (25.14–30).

3.9 *The Door*

The closed door is the ultimate sign of the separation between the two groups. A door represents the point between 'inside' and 'outside,' as the word 'liminal' literally means threshold.[89] Doors figure in other scenes of separation and yearning for entrance: the bridegroom[90] knocks at the door (θύρα) of his beloved: 'Open to me, my sister, my love' (Song 5.2). The Lamb says, 'Behold, I stand at the door and knock; if you hear my voice and open the door, I will come in to you and eat with you, and you with me' (Rev. 3.20). The five foolish virgins stand on the outside and call out 'Open to us!' because they yearn for union with the bridegroom. But they are left on the outside, a place associated with the 'outer darkness' and 'weeping and gnashing of teeth.'[91] But if we resist this interpretation,

89. Ancient sources describe the door of a bridegroom's house as a significant boundary over which the newly married couple crossed into a new status (Pliny, *NH* 28.142; Chariton, *Callirhoe*, 1.3.1–2; Lucan 2.354–55); that the bridegroom does not actually marry anyone in this parable means it is not the couple who crosses the threshold, but those who are worthy to be at the wedding feast.

90. The LXX records that it is her 'brother' (ἀδελφιδοῦ) who knocks at the door (an echo of 'my sister'), but Symachus has bridegroom (νυμφίος).

91. Numerous examples show that doors separate those within from danger without: the door of the ark (θύρα τῆς κιβωτόν) (Gen. 6.16) is closed against the chaos of the flood; the door of Lot's house (θύρα) at Sodom (Gen. 19. 6, 9, 10, 11) is closed against violent intruders; a door (θύρα) is closed against the rapists (and the concubine remains in the danger outside the door) (Judg. 19.22, 26, 27); the door (θύρα) marked with blood kept Moses' people safe from the punishment of the Egyptians (Exod. 12.22–23; cf. Isa. 26.20). The restored wall with doors or gates (θύρα) around Jerusalem keep the people safe from their enemies (Neh. 7.1–4; cf. Ezek. 38.11). Queen Esther risks execution if the king will not welcome her beyond the door (θύρα) of the court (Est. 5.1; cf. 4.11). See Strobel, 'Zum Verständnis vom Mt XXV 1–13', pp. 199–27 (204), and *Untersuchungen zum Eschatologischen Vergzögerungsproblem*, pp. 238–40. Doors can also represent safety on the *outside* and danger on the *inside*, as does the door (θύρα) to the bridal chamber (Tob. 8.4) in which a murderous demon lurks. Thus being on the wrong side of the door signifies not only separation from Jesus the bridegroom, but the threat of danger for the five foolish virgins. Doors also figure in metaphors of inclusion in the community; for example, in Johannine tradition, Jesus himself is the door (θύρα) that offers the only means of entrance into the community and that keeps intruders out (Jn. 10.1–10). The wise wait by Wisdom's gates and beside her doors (θύραις, εἰσόδων,

we see that 'outside' is not necessarily a bad thing in the context of Matthew. Good things happen outside: baptism (3.13–17), miraculous feedings (14.13–21; 15.32–39), healing (8.1–17; 9.18–38), and learning (5.1–7.29). Given the dubious nature of weddings in Matthew, perhaps the virgins (and readers) are better off staying outside the feast.

3.10 *'I Never Knew You'*

At the conclusion of the parable, the bridegroom acts as a judge by deciding who will enter his feast and who will not.[92] Allegorical readings state that Jesus the bridegroom makes the final separation between 'wise' and 'foolish,' based on their preparedness at his return. But if we read non-allegorically, the bridegroom's harshness is unexpected, because the true bridegroom assured disciples that if they ask, they will receive, and if they knock, the door will be opened to them (7.7–8).[93]

However, the five foolish virgins' failure to enter the feast fulfills Matthew's 'narrow door' saying (7.13–14): 'Enter through the narrow door; for the door is wide and the road is easy that leads to destruction, and there are many who take it. For the door is narrow and the road is hard that leads to life, and there are few who find it.'[94] Davies and Allison comment that the unidentified 'many' who take the door to destruction

---

Prov. 8.34), just as do the five wise virgins in the parable. The Johannine Jesus is the gate or door (ἐγω ἐιμι ἡ θύρα) (Jn. 10.9, cf. Jn. 10.1, 2, 7) and guards the entrance to the sheepfold and the sheep know his voice (cf. the bridegroom's statement to the five foolish virgins: 'I do not know you'). Ignatius (*Ep. Philadelphians* 9.2.10) writes of the 'door of knowledge' (ἡ θύρα τῆς γνώσεως), through which enters the bride of Christ (ἡ νύμφη τοῦ Χριστοῦ). God opens a door of faith (θύραν πίστεως) for the Gentiles (Acts 14.27; cf. 1 Cor. 16.9) or a door (θύρα) for the word (Col. 4.3). But a closed door (κλείσουσιν θύρας) signifies the end of life (Eccl. 12.4).

92. Beare, *Matthew*, p. 485. Also Scott, *Hear Then the Parable*, p. 285. Balabanski points out that the bridegroom steps out of his cultural role as host (celebrant) and becomes judge, because he seems to prioritize punctuality over welcoming all to the feast (Balabinski, 'Opening the Closed Door', p. 76). However, I would argue that it is not the bridegroom but his father the 'king' that is the host, that is really not punctuality *per se* but preparedness beforehand that matters to bridegroom. We cannot be sure what would have been expected of a bridegroom and wedding attendants in ancient Mediterranean culture.

93. Reid (*Parables*, p. 197) says that the time for knocking is over and judgment is at hand. Elsewhere, the door seems to remain open: 'I have set before you an open door which no one is able to shut' (Rev. 3.8). Donfried ('Allegory', p. 427, n. 55) thinks that the bridegroom is willing to give the five foolish virgins audience (he comes to the door), and it is when he finds them still without oil that he rejects them (the text does not make clear if the five foolish succeeded in buying oil).

94. Matthew does not use the same term (θύρα) to describe the narrow way that leads to life (Mt. 7.13–14). Luke 13.23–24 uses θύρα, but Matthew has πύλη (cf. Mt. 16.18, πύλαι ἅδου, the gates of Hades).

leaves open 'the frightening possibility that the reader may end up among them.'[95] The narrow door saying is soon followed by the warning that 'Not everyone who says to me "Lord, Lord!" will enter the Kingdom of Heaven, but only the one who does the will of my Father in heaven. On that day many will say to me, "Lord, Lord, did we not prophesy in your name, and cast out demons in your name, and do many deeds of power in your name?" Then I will declare to them, "I never knew you; go away from me, you evildoers!" ' (Mt. 7.21–23; cf. Lk. 13.22–27).[96] The five foolish virgins address the bridegroom in this exact manner: 'Lord, Lord!' (25.11). Davies and Allison, while commenting on the first use of this double vocative (7.21–23), suggest that those who cry 'Lord, Lord' are false prophets who do great things but do not have true faith.[97] They have prophesied in Jesus' name, cast out demons in his name, and have done many deeds of power in his name but are still 'unknown' to him (7.22–23).

The abrupt coldness of the bridegroom's words conveys the stark finality in the parable's warning,[98] but they also seem incongruously harsh in the context of the joyful wedding feast and the joy expected of those in the bridegroom's presence (9.15). Moreover, my concern as a feminist is that the five 'wise' still do nothing to help the five 'foolish.' An early reader noted gaps in this ending to the story and offers a resisting reading (at least in part): the author of the *Epistula Apostolorum* wonders about the fate of the five virgins who were shut out: 'did not the five who went into the feast open the door for them or grieve for them, or try to persuade the bridegroom to open the door for them?' In the Coptic version, the Lord answers that the five wise virgins were not yet able to find grace on their behalf. Finally, in both the Ethiopic and Coptic versions, the *Epistula Apostolorum* sadly concludes that the five wise virgins will never be able to do anything for their foolish sisters: 'Whoever is shut out is shut out' (*Epis. Ap.* 43).

Whether it is read literally or allegorically, the perfect tense οἶδα means not only 'I do not know you,' but 'I *never* knew you,' a damning statement

95. Davies and Allison, *Matthew*, I, p. 698.

96. Luke's version contains a group of people knocking at the door and being left out of a feast, elements included in Matthew's Parable of the Ten Virgins: 'when the owner of the house has got up and *shut the door*, and you begin to stand outside and to *knock on the door*, saying "Lord, open to us," then in reply he will say to you, "I do not know where you came from. Go away from me, all you evildoers!" There will be weeping and gnashing of teeth when you see Abraham and Isaac and Jacob and all the prophets in the Kingdom of God, and you yourselves thrown out. Then people will come from the east and west, from north and south, and will eat in the Kingdom of God" ' (Lk. 13.22–29). See discussion by Ivor H. Jones, *The Matthean Parables* (Leiden: E.J. Brill, 1995), p. 443. Further discussion on the similarities of the Matthean and Lucan parables and their relation to the Q source can be found in Batey, *Nuptial Imagery*, p. 45.

97. Davies and Allison, *Matthew*, I, pp. 711–17.

98. Via, *Parables*, pp. 125–26.

that implies the five foolish virgins never had a chance to be part of the wedding festivities. Davies and Allison explain that this statement cannot be taken literally (that is, that the bridegroom has never met them) but is a 'formula of renunciation' that means 'I never recognized you as one of my own.'[99] Even so, there is definite sense that the bridegroom knows all along that these people, ignorant of their fate, are among those who will be excluded from his feast.[100] And thus the character of the 'bridegroom' merges with Jesus as the narrator, who begins the parable by establishing a division between the women. The parable consequently resists the subversive reading and reverts to an allegorical reading. But then again, that's how good parables function: they disrupt, unsettle, and ultimately leave us with no definite answers.

3.11 Conclusion

The parable of the Ten Virgins follows upon the Parable of the Wedding Feast by contradicting earlier gospel teachings and so encouraging a resisting reading, especially one that resists the tendency to allegorize the rich, powerful, male characters as divine. Just as I resisted reading the 'king' as divine, so I resist seeing this parable's 'bridegroom' as Jesus, the one who in the Sermon on the Mount proclaimed an ethic of sharing and solidarity that is apparently ignored by the five 'wise' virgins. If the bridegroom is not Jesus in this parable, then there is no reason to see any of the virgins as 'disciples'. Rather, they may be read as antitypes, since the 'wise' (who are not marked by compassion but by snakiness) act in ways contrary to what Jesus intends.

The parable reinforces the gospel's negative portrayal of weddings and so of traditional family units. Indeed, given the behavior of the host and his guests at this entirely irregular wedding, the reader wonders why anyone would want to get into this wedding feast. The resisting reader wonders if there is another wedding feast, and another bridegroom, where one can find joy.

Yet, the genius of the parable is that at the same time the resisting reading holds, the parable still evokes allegorical associations.

---

99.   Davies and Allison, *Matthew*, I, p. 717.

100.   Augustine appeals to the combined omniscience and inscrutability of God: it is not for humans to question what (or who?) God knows and does not know (*De diversis quaestionibus* 83.60). Elsewhere Augustine claims that because the bridegroom himself knows no sin, he cannot know anyone who does not repent of their sin in time (*Sermon 43*, 16). Albright and Mann (*Matthew*, p. 302) claim that the bridegroom is simply saying 'I will have nothing to do with you.' Craig Keener theorizes that the five foolish virgins' lateness was an insult, so that the bridegroom's 'I don't know you' is a sarcastic remark that renders them strangers (Keener, *Matthew*, p. 598).

Connections between the 'bridegroom' and Jesus can be resisted, but not completely avoided. The parable simultaneously warns the reader that this 'wedding feast may not be the Kingdom of Heaven, while it also warns of the final judgment when not all who cry 'Lord Lord' will get in. These ambiguities serve to keep the reader from complacency, and so meet Matthew's interest in keeping his community and his readers disciplined, always wondering, evaluating, and unsure if they will be 'in' or 'out' of the feast.

Chapter 4

THE BRIDEGROOM'S FICTIVE FAMILY

Μὴ δύνανται οἱ υἱοὶ τοῦ νυμφῶνος πενθεῖν ἐφ' ὅσαν μετ' αὐτῶν ἐστιν ὁ νυμφίος; ἐλεύσονται δὲ ἡμέραι ὅταν ἀπαρθῇ ἀπ' αὐτῶν ὁ νυμφίος, καὶ τότε νηστεύσουσιν.

'Can the sons of the bridal chamber mourn while the bridegroom is with them? The days will come when the bridegroom is taken away from them, and then they will fast.' (Mt. 9.15)

Ἔτι αὐτοῦ λαλοῦντος τοῖς ὄχλοις ἰδοὺ ἡ μήτηρ καὶ οἱ ἀδελφοὶ αὐτοῦ εἱστήκεισαν ἔξω ζητοῦντης αὐτῷ λαλῆσαι. Εἶπεν δέ τις αὐτῷ, Ἰδοὺ ἡ μήτηρ σου καὶ οἱ ἀδελφοί σου ἔξω ἑστήκασιν ζητοῦντές σοι λαλῆσαι. ὁ δὲ ἀποκριθεὶς εἶπεν τῷ λέγοντι αὐτῷ, Τίς ἐστιν ἡ μήτηρ μου καὶ τίνες εἰσιν οἱ ἀδελφοί μου; καὶ ἐκτείνας τὴν χεῖρα αὐτοῦ ἐπὶ τοὺς μαθητὰς αὐτοῦ εἶπεν, Ἰδοὺ ἡ μήτηρ μου καὶ οἱ ἀδελφοί μου. ὅστις γὰρ ἂν ποιήσῃ τὸ θέλημα τοῦ πατρός μου τοῦ ἐν οὐρανοῖς αὐτός μου ἀδελφὸς καὶ ἀδελφὴ καὶ μήτηρ ἐστίν.

While he [Jesus] was still speaking to the crowds, look: his mother and brothers stood outside, seeking to speak to him. Someone said to him, 'Look, your mother and your brothers stand outside seeking to speak to you.' But answering he said to the one who spoke to him: 'Who is my mother, and who are my brothers?' And while extending his hand over his disciples, he said, 'See my mother and my brothers! For whoever does the will of my father, the one in the heavens, he is my brother and sister and mother'. (Mt. 12.46–50)

εἰσὶν γὰρ εὐνοῦχοι οἵτινες ἐκ κοιλίας μητρὸς ἐγεννήθησαν οὕτως, καὶ εἰσὶν εὐνοῦχοι ὅτινες εὐνουχίσθησαν ὑπὸ τῶν ἀνθρώπων, καὶ εἰσὶν εὐνοῦχοι οἵτινες εὐνούχισαν ἑαυτοὺς διὰ τὴν βασιλείαν τῶν οὐρανῶν. ὁ δυνάμενος χωρεῖν χωρείτω. Τότε προσηνέχθησαν αὐτῷ παιδία ἵνα τὰς χεῖρας ἐπιθῇ αὐτοῖς καὶ προσεύξηται. οἱ δὲ μαθηταὶ ἐπετίμασαν αὐτοῖς. ὁ δὲ Ἰησοῦς εἶπεν, Ἄφετε τὰ παιδία καὶ μὴ κωλύετε αυτὰ ἐλθεῖν πρός με, τῶν γὰρ τοιούτων ἐστὶν ἡ βασιλεία τῶν οὐρανων. καὶ ἐπιθεὶς τὰς χεῖρας αὐτοῖς ἐπορεύθη ἐκεῖθεν.

For there are eunuchs who out of the mother's womb are born thus, and there are eunuchs that are made eunuchs by humans, and there are eunuchs that made themselves eunuchs for the sake of the kingdom of the heavens. The one who is able to hear, let him hear!

Then children were brought to him in order that he might lay his hands upon them and bless them. The disciples rebuked them. But Jesus said, 'Allow the children and do not forbid them to come to me, for of such as these is the kingdom of the heavens.' And while laying hands on them he blessed them and went from there. (Mt. 19.12–15)

4.1 *Introduction*

Recent studies have demonstrated that the gospel of Matthew reflects the ideals of a millenarian community. It redefines first-century Hellenistic and Roman concepts of 'family' by replacing traditional domestic structures (consisting of blood relatives, marital relations, slaves, and clients) with a theologically based household consisting of the children of God the Father (23.9, 12.46–50). Matthew's alternative group has been called a 'fictive family,' 'spiritual family,' or 'theological family' (10.34–39; 12.46–50; 18.2–3; 19.14, 29–30; 23.9).[1] In anticipation of the coming end

---

1. The 'household' is metaphorical for the family of God the Father and also refers to a house church or to members' households where the community met for instruction and worship. Recent studies of the early Church as fictive family include Santiago Guijarro-Oporto, 'Kingdom and Family in Conflict: A Contribution to the Study of the Historical Jesus', in John J. Pilch (ed.), *Social Scientific Models for Interpreting the Bible* (Biblical Interpretation Series, 53; Leiden: Brill, 2001), pp. 210–38; Joseph H. Hellerman, *The Ancient Church as Family* (Minneapolis: Fortress Press, 2001), pp. 27–80; and W. Carter, *Matthew and the Margins: A Sociopolitical and Religious Reading* (Maryknoll, NY: Orbis, 2000), esp. pp. 278–79, 385–86; Dennis Duling, 'The Jesus Movement and Social Network Analysis: Part II. The Social Network', *BTB* 30 (2000), pp. 3–14; Amy-Jill Levine, 'Women in the Q Communit(ies) and Traditions', in Ross Shepard Kraemer and Mary Rose D'Angelo (eds.), *Women and Christian Origins* (Oxford: Oxford University Press, 1999), pp. 150–70; Jerome H. Neyrey, *Honor and Shame in the Gospel of Matthew* (Louisville: Westminster/John Knox Press, 1998), pp. 52–55; Carolyn Osiek, 'Jesus and Cultural Values: Family Life as an Example,' *Hervormde Teologiese Studies* 53 (1997), pp. 800–11; Halvor Moxnes (ed.), *Constructing Early Christian Families: Family as Social Reality and Metaphor* (New York: Routledge, 1997); Anthony Saldarini, *Matthew's Christian Jewish Community* (Chicago: University of Chicago Press, 1994), pp. 90–102, esp. 90–94; Stephen C. Barton, *Discipleship and Family Ties in Matthew and Mark* (Cambridge: Cambridge University Press, 1994); Warren Carter, *Households and Discipleship: A Study of Matthew 19–20* (Sheffield: Sheffield Academic Press, 1994), pp. 90–114; Michael H. Crosby, *House of Disciples: Church, Economics, and Justice in Matthew* (Maryknoll, NY: Orbis, 1988), pp. 106–11; Dennis Duling, 'Matthew's Plurisignificant "Son of David" in Social Science Perspective: Kinship, Kingship, Magic, and Miracle', *BTB* 22 (1992), pp. 99–116 (esp. 111). For a helpful reconstructions of Greco-Roman kinship patterns and households, see Suzanne Dixon, *The Roman Family* (Baltimore: The Johns Hopkins University Press, 1992), pp. 1–18, and K.C.

times and fulfillment of the kingdom, the Matthean bridegroom overturns traditional social structures.[2] He displaces earthly fathers with the heavenly Father (23.9) and defines his mother and brothers as 'those who do the will of the Father in heaven' (12.46–50).[3] He warns that he has come to disrupt existing family relationships: he sets a man against his father, a daughter against her mother, and a daughter-in-law against her mother-in-law (10.34–37; cf. Mic. 7.6). Jesus promises rewards to those who have left their family of origin and their property to follow him (19.29–30), and he disapproves of a potential disciple who wants first to bury his father (8.22).[4] He encourages his disciples to be like children of the heavenly Father (18.1–5; 23.9; cf. 5.45; 7.9–11; 19.14). Though Jesus does reiterate the commandment to honor one's father and mother (Mt. 15.4; 19.19; cf. Exod. 20.12; Deut. 5.16), he discourages the community from producing their own children (19.10–12). Julian Sheffield has argued convincingly that by 'father and mother' (15.4; 19.19), Jesus means the heavenly Father and the 'mothers' represented by the new theological family.[5] And, as we have seen in the two parables, when Matthew does talk about weddings, the occasions are sites of disruption and violence rather than unity and joy.

Building on this research, I propose that the Matthean Jesus community should be defined not only as a new family composed of children of God the Father, but also as 'the sons of the bridal chamber' (οἱ υἱοὶ τοῦ νυμφῶνος) who anticipate the eschatological wedding banquet, even as they celebrate Jesus' presence as a bridegroom among them (9.15). These children are the product of a new family created by the

---

Hanson, 'Kinship', in Richard L. Rohrbaugh (ed.), *The Social Sciences and New Testament Interpretation* (Peabody, MA: Hendrickson, 1996), pp. 62–79; Shaye J.D. Cohen, *The Jewish Family in Antiquity* (BJS, 289; Atlanta: Scholars Press, 1993); Carolyn Osiek and David L. Balch, *Families in the New Testament World: Households and House Churches* (Louisville: Westminster/John Knox Press, 1997).

2.   Levine, 'Women in the Q Communit(ies)', pp. 159–60.

3.   While the early Church sometimes regarded Peter as a father of the Church because he is the foundation stone of the Church, and to him are given the keys to the kingdom and authority on earth (Mt. 16.17–19), the evangelist does not indicate that this status is a type of fatherhood. In fact, Peter is identified as a 'son' rather than a father: 'Blessed are you Simon son of Jonah' (16.17), who receives revelation from the Father in heaven (16.17). Moreover, the Church is instructed to call no one on earth 'father,' only the one Father in heaven (23.9).

4.   See John M.G. Barclay, 'The Family as the Bearer of Religion in Judaism and Early Christianity', in H. Moxnes (ed.), *Constructing Early Christian Families*, pp. 66–80, esp. p.74; Levine, 'Women in the Q Communit(ies)', pp. 157–59.

5.   Julian Sheffield, 'The Father in the Gospel of Matthew', in Amy-Jill Levine (ed.), *A Feminist Companion to Matthew* (Sheffield: Sheffield Academic Press, 2001), pp. 52–69. For a thorough study of Jesus' 'real' family, see Richard Bauckham, *Jude and the Relatives of Jesus in the Early Church* (Edinburgh: T&T Clark, 1990).

bridegroom's presence as celebrant and the anticipation of the fulfillment of the eschatological wedding feast: as weddings unite people into families, so those who celebrate with the bridegroom are united as children of the Father into one family of brothers and sisters.[6] This new construction of Jesus – the brideless bridegroom – along with 'the sons of the bridal chamber,' replaces the traditional wedding, with its conjugal connotations.

Moreover, the new fictive family is not based on inheritance rights to wealth and status. The new family does not reproduce by biological means but by incorporation of new members as all disciples become 'children' of God the Father (18.1–5; 23.9; cf. 5.45; 7.9–11; 19.14). A test case is the story of Joseph who adopted Jesus into his family and thus became a father without biological reproduction. Later, when we meet the individuals identified as Jesus' actual 'brothers and sisters,' Joseph 'the father' is absent; thus his actual role in the narrative is restricted to that of adoptive father (12.46–50). Confirming this as the case is the bridegroom's teaching on the efficacy of not marrying and becoming 'eunuchs,' which is congruent with adoptive rather than biological fatherhood.

4.2 *Households in the First Century*

Matthew redefines his 'new' family paradoxically both on the basis of and against the model of first-century households (οἰκία; *domus*; בית).[7] The fictive household of God resembles first-century households at the same time as it overturns and replaces them.[8]

---

6. Cf. Crosby, *House of Disciples*, p. 71. The status of children is 'liminal,' like that of the wedding guests betwixt and between the world and the Kingdom of Heaven (Carter, *Households*, p. 91).

7. The 'house' or 'household' (οἶκος, οἰκία [Mt. 10.6; 12.25; 15.24]) and בית [cf. Gen. 7.1; 24.2; Num. 16.32; 18.31; Deut. 6.22; Josh. 24.15]) was the basic social unit (Hanson, 'Kinship', p. 66). For discussion of households as the basis for the house church, see Osiek and Balch, *Families in the New Testament World*, pp. 32–35; Saldarini, *Matthew's Christian-Jewish Community*, pp. 90–94; Crosby, *House of Disciples*, pp. 44–75.

8. Don S. Browning and Ian S. Evison, 'Series Forward', in Osiek and Balch, *Families in the New Testament World*, p. viii; Stephen C. Barton, 'The Relativisation of Family Ties in the Jewish and Graeco-Roman Traditions', in Moxnes (ed.), *Constructing Early Christian Families*, pp. 81–99; Eva Marie Lassen, 'The Roman Family: Ideal and Metaphor', in Moxnes (ed.), *Constructing Early Christian Families*, pp. 103–20 (esp. 114–15).

As a social construct, the definition of 'family'[9] varies across geographical, class, and economic lines[10] but not (at least in the first century) across 'ethnic' lines. Differences between Jewish and Gentile families of similar class apparently did not exist: Shaye Cohen concludes that the 'Jewish family in antiquity seems not to have been distinctive by the power of its Jewishness; rather, its structure, ideals, and dynamics seem to have been virtually identical with those of its ambient culture(s).'[11]

No Greek or Latin term exists in the first century corresponding to modern Western concepts of 'family.'[12] The Latin *familia*, from which the modern 'family' derives, has to do with hierarchy and subordination – the word comes from *famulus*, meaning 'household slave' or 'servant.' An ancient *familia* is not, then, our Western ideal of a nuclear family (that is,

9.   By 'family,' I refer to the broader first-century concept of 'household' or '*familia*.' Miriam Peskowitz discusses the plurality of the concept of 'family' in Greco-Roman antiquity in ' "Family/ies" in Antiquity: Evidence from Tannaitic Literature and Roman Galilean Architecture,' in Cohen (ed.), *The Jewish Family in Antiquity*, pp. 9–36. Halvor Moxnes discusses the difficulty of reconstructing the many types of household and kinship configurations in the first century in his 'Introduction' and 'What Is Family: Problems in Constructing Early Christian Families', in Moxnes (ed.), *Constructing Early Christian Families*, pp. 13–41. Also Robert Parkin, *Kinship: An Introduction to the Basic Concepts* (Oxford: Blackwell, 1997), p. 28.

10.   Osiek and Balch, *Families*, pp. 36–40.

11.   Shaye Cohen, in his 'Introduction', in Cohen (ed.), *The Jewish Family in Antiquity*, p. 2. Cohen draws on work published in the same volume: O. Larry Yarbrough, 'Parents and Children in the Jewish Family of Antiquity', pp. 39–60; Adele Reinhartz, 'Parents and Children: A Philonic Perspective', pp. 61–88; Ross S. Kraemer, 'Jewish Mothers and Daughters in the Greco-Roman World', pp. 89–112; Dale B. Martin, 'Slavery and the Ancient Jewish Family', pp. 113–29. Dixon offers the caveat that, in the first century, most of the extant information about families was written by or about the upper class, so that relatively little is known about the majority of the population (Dixon, *Roman Family*, p. 17).

12.   *Webster's New World Dictionary* defines 'nuclear family' as a 'basic social unit consisting of parents and their dependent children living in one household,' and states that this concept is an 'Americanism' (p. 929). The dictionary's primary definition of 'family' is not much different: 'a social unit consisting of parents and the children they rear; the children of the same parents; one's husband (or wife) and children … .' Cf. *Webster's New World Dictionary*, ed. Victoria Neufeldt, *et al.*, (New York: MacMillan, 3rd edn, 1994), p. 489. See Parkin, *Kinship*, pp. 28–29; Andrew Wallace-Hadrill, 'Houses and Households: Sampling Pompeii and Herculaneum', in Beryl Rawson (ed.), *Marriage, Divorce, and Children in Ancient Rome* (Oxford: Clarendon Press, 1991), pp. 191–227 (p. 225); Sarah B. Pomeroy, 'Some Greek Families: Production and Reproduction', in Cohen (ed.), *The Jewish Family in Antiquity*, pp. 155–57 (155). See also Dixon, *Roman Family*, pp. 16–18; Halvor Moxnes, 'What is Family?', in H. Moxnes (ed.), *Constructing Early Christian Families*, pp. 13–41. A given social construction of 'family' does not necessarily reflect statistical reality; e.g., recent census data for the United States (1990–2000) shows that the American definition of 'nuclear family' given above does not represent the vast majority of American households (granted that the census data itself is a social construct). See United States Commerce Department, Census Bureau, Public Information Office, at *http://www.census.gov/population/socdemo*.

a married couple and their children residing in a single dwelling), but represents all persons and property (including biological relations and slaves) subjected to the *paterfamilias* (head of the household, typically male, though examples of female heads of household exist, e.g., Lydia [Acts 16.14–15]),[13] even if they did not live in the same dwelling.[14] The ancient family's function was mutual protection and production of the necessities of life.[15] Because of this economic and hierarchical basis of household structure, apprentices and clients who had no blood relation to the *paterfamilias* were regarded as extended family,[16] and *familia* sometimes referred broadly to the family's means of living or business, such as the family farm, shop, craft, or trade.[17] Matthew demonstrates this household hierarchy in parables where male characters in the role of *paterfamilias* oversee the economic functions of the household: a man commands his sons (τέκνα) to work (21.28–31), a lord (κύριος) leaves the household in charge of slaves (δοῦλοι) while he is absent (24.45–51; 25. 14–30), a landowner (οἰκοδεσπότης) hires laborers (μισθωτοί, γεωργοῖς)

13. Margaret Y. MacDonald, 'Rereading Paul: Early Interpretations of Paul on Women and Gender', in R.S. Kraemer and M.R. D'Angelo (eds.), *Women and Christian Origins*, pp. 236–53 (239–40); Clarice J. Martin, 'Acts of the Apostles', in E.Schüssler Fiorenza (ed.), *Searching the Scriptures*, II, pp. 763–99 (784–85); Gail R. O'Day, 'Acts', in Carol A. Newsom and Sharon H. Ringe (eds.), *The Women's Bible Commentary* (Louisville: Westminster/John Knox Press, 1992), pp. 305–12 (310); F. Scott Spencer, 'Women of "the Cloth" in Acts: Sewing the Word', in Amy-Jill Levine (ed.), *A Feminist Companion to Acts* (Sheffield: Sheffield Academic Press, 2004) pp. 134–54. Examples of women's community and household leadership are discussed in Karen Jo Torjesen and Virginia Burrus, 'Household Management and Women's Authority', in K.J. Torjesen, *When Women Were Priests* (San Francisco: HarperSanFrancisco, 1993), pp. 53–87. Burrus and Torjesen revisit their article and examine ways in which these women's leadership is compromised by Lucan stereotypes of women in 'Afterword to Household Management and Women's Authority', in in Amy-Jill Levine (ed.), *A Feminist Companion to Acts of the Apostles*, forthcoming.

14. Ulpian, *Digest* 50, 16.195. Santiago Guijarro-Oporto, 'The Family in First-century Galilee', in Moxnes (ed.), *Early Christian Families*, pp. 42–65; Guijarro-Oporto, 'Kingdom and Family in Conflict', pp. 224–28; Lassen, 'The Roman Family: Ideal and Metaphor', pp. 103–20; Moxnes, 'What is Family?', pp. 13–41; John C. Traupman (ed.), *The New College Latin and English Dictionary* (New York: Bantam Books, 1995); Osiek and Balch, *Families in the New Testament World*, p. 6. See also Susan Treggiari, *Roman Marriage: Iusti Coniuges from the Time of Cicero to the Time of Ulpian* (Oxford: Clarendon Press, 1991), pp. 15–16; Crosby, *House of Disciples*, p. 27.

15. Moxnes summarizes that a household is a social structure that makes a living together (Moxnes, 'What is Family', p. 23); also Osiek and Balch, *Families*, pp. 42–43. According to Michael Crosby, ancient households can best be understood as economic units, as microcosms of a hierarchical society (Crosby, *House of Disciples*, pp. 23–29).

16. Dixon, *Roman Family*, pp. 1–3, 26; Crosby, pp. 31, 38–39.

17. Dixon, *Roman Family*, p. 2; Osiek and Balch, *Families*, p. 37.

(20.1–16; 21.33–41), and a king (βασιλειύς) who has slaves (δούλοι) gives a wedding banquet for his son (22.1–14).

Matthew describes the nascent Church in terms of a household. Thus, Matthew models the community on the household: the Matthean Jesus replaces his biological family with new 'brothers, sisters, and mother' who do the will of the Father (12.46–50); disciples are to become like children (18.1–5; 19.13–15), and Church members are to keep discipline within the community (18.15–20). Jesus implies that disciples might have to leave their families to join this new household (12.47–50; 19.29). Because disciples must give up the economic resources represented by family association (19.21, 27–29) and rely on the community,[18] Matthew's alternative family replaces households headed by a human *paterfamilias* with the deity as *paterfamilias*.

Matthew inherits a tradition in which a 'household' also referred to a nation or ethnic group that consisted of people from a range of social classes[19] (e.g., Abraham goes from his father's house [ἐκ τοῦ οἴκου τοῦ πατρός σου, Gen. 12.1] to found a nation; the tribes are 'houses' of ancestral fathers [κατ᾽ οἴκους πατριῶν; בית־אבת; Num. 1.4, 44; 3.24, 30, 35; 17.2–3, and the nation the 'house of Israel' [οἶκος τοῦ Ἰσραηλ; בית ישראל; e.g., Ezek. 3.4, 7; or οἶκος Ἰσραηλ, e.g. Hos. 5.1; Amos 5.1, 4, 25]). The fatherhood of God is a common theme (Exod. 4.22; Deut. 32.6; Ps. 2.7; Isa. 63.16; Jer. 31.9; Hos. 11.1).[20] Matthew envisions the household of God the Father as a large group, inclusive of many people.

The concept of Matthean inclusivity is further illustrated by the permeability and public nature of households in antiquity.[21] Matthean house churches could easily have been accommodated in larger homes. The entrance hall, courtyard, and porticoes were public rooms where

18.   Guijarro-Oporto, 'The Family in First-century Galilee', pp. 48–49.

19.   Osiek and Balch, *Families,* p. 6; Moxnes, 'What is Family?', p. 29.

20.   James Nohrnberg, *Like Unto Moses: The Constituting of an Interruption* (Bloomington, IN: Indiana University Press, 1995), p. 126.

21.   Wallace-Hadrill, 'Houses and Households', pp. 206ff, and Carter, *Matthew and the Margins,* pp. 28–29. The public nature of the first-century house is a foreign concept to modern Western interpreters (Miriam Peskowitz, ' "Family/ies" in Antiquity', esp. pp. 30–31). The Greco-Roman household included a much higher ratio of persons-per-room than would be comfortable by modern American standards. For comparison, Americans prefer to live in households that allow each person in the household a room to him or herself, and they perceive that a person-to-room ratio of more than 1.1 is crowded; see Wallace-Hadrill, 'Houses and Households', p. 207. In the U.S. from 1960–99, the median number of rooms per housing unit was five, with an average of three persons per housing unit, giving a ratio lower than 1.1 (cf. U.S. Census Bureau, note 12 above).

people could enter uninvited.[22] Business and commerce were conducted from the house, so that the door was open to all who passed by.[23]

4.3 *Voluntary Associations as Fictive Family*

Because people joined the Matthean fictive family by choice rather than birth, the fictive family also resembles voluntary organizations that were popular in the first century. Voluntary societies resembled family structures and were a type of fictive kin group.[24] Matthew describes his community as an ἐκκλησία,[25] a word that came to stand for the Christian Church (Acts 5.11; 8.3; Rom. 16.5; 1 Cor. 16.19) but originally stood for a voluntary assembly. The term ἐκκλησία was used almost interchangeably

---

22. Vitruvius, a first-century Roman architect, indicates that while some areas of a house were reserved for privacy (i.e., bedrooms and bath), much of the house was public space. In some busy households, there was so much traffic that it was necessary to assign a doorkeeper. According to Vitruvius, the house of a wealthy merchant had a room in which to keep livestock, and the entrance hall featured a display of produce. A money-lender, orator, or politician needed an impressive entrance hall, wide courtyards, libraries, and other visible signs of their wealth and importance (*On Architecture*, 6, 5.1–2). See Osiek and Balch, *New Testament Families*, pp. 43–45 and Guijarro-Oporto, 'The Family in First-Century Galilee,' pp. 52–53.

23. Wallace-Hadrill, 'Houses and Households,' pp. 226–27; Osiek and Balch, *Families*, pp. 6–12, 17, 24–25. Activities that modern Westerners would consider to be private become social occasions in a first-century Greco-Roman household. Osiek and Balch (*Families*, p. 10) remark that 'ideas of private space are culturally relative' as they contrast modern Western and ancient Middle Eastern houses. Even a wealthy family's 'private' bath was staffed with attendants who assisted in the bathing. Archaeological evidence shows that outside the household, people shared public latrines and baths (Osiek and Balch, *Families*, p. 12). For a description of the social importance of public baths, see Paul Veyne (ed.), *A History of the Private Life: From Pagan Rome to Byzantium* (trans. A. Goldhammer; Cambridge, MA: Harvard University Press, 1987), pp. 198–99; 380–81, and John R. Clarke, *Looking at Lovemaking: Constructions of Sexuality in Roman Art 100 BC–AD 250* (Berkeley: University of Califorinia Press, 1998), pp. 129ff. Numerous people stayed to keep vigil around the bed of the gravely ill or dying, and even giving birth could become a crowded affair when besides a midwife or two and the people summoned to witness the birth, 'not more than ten free women and six slave women' were allowed in the delivery room' (Beryl Rawson, 'Adult–Child Relationships in Roman Society', in B. Rawson [ed.], *Marriage, Divorce, and Children in Ancient Rome*, p. 11).

24. Dennis Duling, 'Matthew 18.15–17: Conflict, Confrontation, and Conflict Resolution in a "Fictive Kin" Association', *BTB* 29 (1999), pp. 4–22, esp. 6–8; Joseph H. Hellerman, *Ancient Church as Family*, pp. 4–7.

25. Stephen G. Wilson, 'Voluntary Associations: An Overview', in John S. Kloppenborg and S.G. Wilson (eds.), *Voluntary Associations in the Graeco-Roman World* (London and New York: Routledge, 1996), pp. 1–15 (1–2). Kloppenborg also discusses the inconsistency of authors in use and definition of the terms ('*Collegia* and *Thiasoi*: Issues in Function, Taxonomy and Membership', in Kloppenborg and Wilson [eds.], *Voluntary Associations*, pp. 16–30.

with other names for voluntary societies in ancient literature (e.g., κοινωνία,[26] συναγωγή,[27] φράτρα,[28] *societas*[29]).

These societies provided a communal life separate from the city or state or family and had a variety of purposes not easily grouped under the same heading.[30] Some were religious, social, political, and philosophical, and some a combination of several elements. Membership in some groups served as a sort of insurance to provide funerals for members who died or loans to help a business or food to feed the hungry. Many voluntary societies were local organizations exclusive in nature (e.g., one had to be of a certain social status, a practitioner of a certain trade, undergo initiation, be able to contribute to the membership, or adhere to a certain lifestyle) but welcomed traveling members of sister organizations, such as a troupe of musicians or actors who sought out the Dionysos mystery cult in whatever locale they were serving.[31] The apostle Paul traveled from town to town preaching the gospel (1 Cor. 1.16; 1 Thess. 1.7–9; Acts 14.21–25; 16.1, 6) and sought synagogues (Acts 14.1; 17.1, 10, 16; 18.19; 19.8) or house churches (1 Cor. 16.5–8; Acts 14.27–28; 15.30, 41; 28.14). The Matthean household is based on inclusivity ('go make disciples of all nations', 28.19) but membership in the household did require adherence to a certain (Matthean) interpretation of the Law, and members might have undergone baptism as an 'initiatory' rite.[32] Voluntary societies often met in the house of a wealthy member who served as patron. 'The overlap

26. An association or fellowship; Paul used this term to describe nascent Christian communities (1 Cor. 1.9; Phil. 2.1).

27. Generally, 'a gathering,' but also referred specifically as a place of assembly for Jews (Mt. 4.23; 6.2, 5; 9.35; 12.9; 13.54; Philo *Omn. Prob. Lib.* 81). Peter Richardson, 'Early Synagogues as Collegia in the Diaspora and Palestine', in Kloppenborg and Wilson (eds.), *Voluntary Associations*, pp. 90–109. On the other hand, Wayne McCready argues (less convincingly than Richardson) that there is relatively little evidence for synagogues in the first century ('*Ekklesia* and Voluntary Associations', in Kloppenborg and Wilson [eds.], *Voluntary Associations*, pp. 59–73 [62–63]).

28. A 'brotherhood' that describes itself using familial language like the Matthean community of 'brothers and sisters' and the basis of the word 'fraternity' used in modern times for a voluntary society. E.g., Plutarch, *Publ.*7 and in an inscription (*Tenos*, ii BCE): φυλῆς καὶ δήμου καὶ φρατρίας ὧν ἄν βούληται ἀπογραψάμενον (*IG*12.110.16).

29. Cicero, *Leg.* 1.10.28; *Rep.* 1.32.49. Other terms for voluntary associations included *collegium, secta, factio, curia,* θίασος, ἐρανός, φιλοσοφία, ἀγωγή, ὁδός, ἄσκησις or *disciplina*, and βίος.

30. Wilson, 'Voluntary Associations', p. 1; McCready, '*Ekklesia* and Voluntary Associations', p. 61.

31. Wilson, 'Voluntary Associations', pp. 2–3. McCready discusses boundary issues in voluntary groups: the desire to distinguish insiders from outsiders coupled with willingness to accept new members (McCready, '*Ekklesia* and Voluntary Associations', pp. 66–67.

32. Baptism of members is not explicitly described in Matthew, but the evangelist states that Jesus was baptized at the beginning of his ministry (3.13–17), and that the risen Jesus directs his disciples to baptize new converts (28.19).

between associations and households is thus considerable,' writes Wilson.[33] Voluntary associations provided fictive kinship for members.[34]

That membership in a voluntary association could involve risks, such as expulsion from a city or persecution, is evident from restrictions placed upon them. For example, Suetonius reports that Tiberius (14–37 CE) abolished many voluntary and ethnic groups from Rome, including the Jewish population (*Tiberius*, 36; cf. Josephus, *Ant.* 16). During the reign of Nero (54–68 CE), Suetonius classified early Christian groups as '*genus hominum superstitionis novae ac maleficae*,' that is, a group of people who belonged to a new and harmful superstition (*Nero*, 16), an indication that Christian practices had attracted attention and suspicion, perhaps the grounds for persecution.[35] Such evidence of suspicion or even persecution of voluntary associations in the Roman Empire gives a context for understanding conflict between the Matthean fictive family and the governors, kings, and councils before whom they might be dragged (10.17–20).

Conflict or disruption of normal life was not, however, typical of membership in a voluntary society. Nor did membership in voluntary associations usually involve separation from biological family ties; the 'fictive family' was *supplemental* to biological family. However, some religious or philosophical societies did expect members to renounce family ties for the sake of a higher calling, a situation we see demonstrated in the Matthean community (10.35–37; 19.27–29).[36] Greek and Roman philosophers (e.g., Cynics and Stoics) set themselves apart from family and possessions in order to pursue wisdom through the practice of self-control. Epictetus describes the Cynics' freedom from distractions (such as home and family) that allows full attention and service to God (*Diss.* III.xxii.45–48, 69–72).[37] Like Matthew, the Cynics portrayed humankind as a family with God (Zeus) as their father (*Diss.* III.xxii.81–82).[38] The Stoics also subordinated family ties to the higher good of studying

33. Wilson, 'Voluntary Associations', p. 13.

34. Sandra Walker-Ramisch, 'Graeco-Roman Voluntary Associations and the Damascus Document: A Sociological Analysis', in Kloppenborg and Wilson (eds.), *Voluntary Associations*, pp. 128–45 (132–34).

35. Steve Mason, '*Philosophai*: Graeco-Roman, Judean and Christian', in Kloppenborg and Wilson [eds.], *Voluntary Associations*, pp. 31–58 (33); Wendy Cotter, 'The Collegia and Roman Law: State Restrictions on Voluntary Associations, 64 BCE–200 CE', in Kloppenborg and Wilson (eds.), *Voluntary Associations*, pp. 74–89.

36. Stephen C. Barton discusses this situation in 'The Relativisation of Family Ties in the Jewish and Graeco-Roman Traditions', in Moxnes (ed.), *Constructing Early Christian Families*, pp. 81–100.

37. Barton, 'Relativisation of Family Ties', pp. 94–96.

38. Cited in Barton, 'Relativisation of Family Ties', pp. 94–95. Barton describes the differences between Cynic 'freedom' and Christian commitment, pp. 95–96. See also Barton, *Discipleship and Family Ties*, pp. 47–52.

philosophy. The Stoics did promote marriage and family, but only as a duty for the good of the state (Musonius Rufus 14).[39]

Barton cites Philo's exhortation, based on Deut. 13.1–11, that kinship as 'sons of God' is a higher commitment than human kinship (*Spec. Leg.* 1.316–318)[40] and Philo's description of the proselyte leaving family and homeland to become part of a new family (*Spec. Leg.*1.51–53).[41] Philo gives special attention to Abraham's departure from his homeland at God's command as an illustration of how one should put relationship to God before blood kinship ties (*De Abr.* 67).[42] These descriptions resonate with the disruption of biological family ties in 10.21, 34–37 ('Whoever loves father or mother more than me is not worthy of me, and whoever loves son or daughter more than me is not worthy of me'), and the formation of the Matthean fictive family described in 12.46–50 ('Here are my mother and my brothers! For whoever does the will my Father in heaven is my brother and sister and mother!'). Matthew describes the disciples leaving their homes, families, and possessions to follow Jesus in 19.27 ('Then Peter said, "Look, we have left everything and followed you"').

Evidence of familial groups at Qumran, Josephus and Philo's descriptions of a sect they call 'Essenes,' along with Philo's 'Therapeutae' and 'Therapeutrides' indicate that some people separated from biological kin to form groups that provided the economic and social support of families.[43] Philo writes about ideal communities that abandoned family and property to live communally while using family or household language to describe their relationships as a sort of spiritual kinship (*De Vita Cont.* 13, 18).[44] For example, the Therapeutae called their community an οἶκος (household) (*De Vita Cont.* 72).[45] The Essenes, according to Philo, identified themselves as brothers in a fictive family that shares all economic resources (*Omn. Prob. Lib.* 79, 85–86).

Another feature of these fictive family communities – singleness – is important to the study of the bridegroom in Matthew's community. Josephus indicates that some of the 'Essenes' did not marry, in order to

---

39.   Barton, *Discipleship and Family Ties*, pp. 52–54,

40.   Cited in Barton, 'Relativisation of Family Ties', p. 82.

41.   Cited in Barton, 'Relativisation of Family Ties', p. 83.

42.   Cited in Barton, 'Relativisation of Family Ties', pp. 86–87.

43.   Moxnes, 'Introduction', p. 4; Hellerman, *Ancient Church as Family*, pp. 73–80; David W. Chapman, 'Marriage and Family in Second Temple Judaism', in Ken M. Campbell (ed.), *Marriage and Family in the Biblical World* (Downers Grove, IL: InterVarsity Press, 2003), pp. 183–239 (211–15).

44.   We do not know if these groups actually existed, but the point is that Philo describes qualities of ideal communities he admires, whether actual or fictive.

45.   Barton treats Philo's descriptions of fictive family in *Discipleship and Family Ties*, pp. 23–35.

concentrate full attention on religious matters (*War* 2.119–20).[46] The Matthean fictive family resembles these communities' subordination of family and household as a 'summons from a lesser piety to a greater piety.'[47] Themes in Matthew also resonate with the beliefs of millenarian groups: the expectation that the present or near future is a time of suffering (10.16–39); the fervent hope for righting of wrongs and divine deliverance (11.20–30); a tendency to divide world into 'good' and 'bad' (22.1–14; 25.1–13; 31–46); a belief in restoration and perfection of ancestral religion (5.17–48); replacement of family ties with fictive kin (12.46–50); a demand for complete loyalty (10.32–33); a focus on a charismatic leader that returns from the dead (28.1–10; 18–20); an understanding that the fulfillment of their ideals was in part a present reality (10.7; 28.20).[48]

This brief survey of households and voluntary societies in the first century indicates that the Matthean community as a theological or fictive family was defined as a grouping of people not necessarily related by blood but by dependency on a common *paterfamilias* (God the Father) or by a common purpose and reciprocity. The simultaneously permeable and exclusive nature of households and voluntary associations are qualities shared by the fictive family in Matthew. In addition, the Matthean community shares qualities of ideal groups that perceived themselves as fictive kin.

The choice of 'fictive family' over biological family identifies the community of disciples living in 'permanent or normative liminality.'[49]

---

46. Josephus indicates that Essenes who did marry did so only for reprocreative purposes. See Barton, 'Relativisation of Family Ties,' pp. 90–91. For a more complete treatment of Josephus on the Essenes and other religious figures, see Barton, *Discipleship and Family Ties*, pp. 35–44. Even if Philo has largely invented his descriptions of these communities (or even the communities themselves, as some suggest), his idealization of their lifestyle shows that the concept of renouncing biological family to form a fictive family was not invented by Matthew.

47. Barton, 'Relativisiation of Family Ties', p. 99, and Amy-Jill Levine, 'Jesus, Divorce, and Sexuality: A Jewish Critique,' in Leonard Greenspoon, Dennis Hamm, and Bryan LeBeau (eds.), *The Historical Jesus through Catholic and Jewish Eyes* (Harrisburg, PA: Trinity Press International, 2000), pp. 113–29 (esp. p. 121).

48. I have applied to Matthew the general themes discussed by Dale C. Allison, *Jesus of Nazareth: Millenarian Prophet* (Minneapolis: Fortress Press, 1998), pp. 60–64; 78–94. See also his 'The Eschatology of Jesus', in John J. Collins (ed.), *The Encyclopedia of Apocalypticism: The Origins of Apocalypticism in Judaism and Christianity* (3 vols.; New York: Continuum, 1998), I, pp. 267–301, and Carter, *Households and Discipleship*, esp. pp. 46–55; Carter, *Matthew and the Margins: A Sociopolitical and Religious Reading* (Maryknoll, NY: Orbis, 2000); John P. Meier, *A Marginal Jew: Rethinking the Historical Jesus* (3 vols.; New York: Doubleday, 1991–2001), II, pp. 237–455.

49. Carter, *Households and Discipleship*, p. 46, based on Victor Turner's model of liminality in *Ritual Process: Structure and Anti-Structure* (New York: Aldine/Walter de Gruyter, 1969), pp. 94–112.

This liminality has social aspects, in that the Matthean community defines itself against societal norms (e.g., the Matthean Jesus prohibits divorce and recommends that men become 'eunuchs' for the sake of the kingdom [19.3–12]). The Matthean Jesus' descriptions of travails to come (24.3–31), judgment (25.31–46), and his warnings to be alert and watchful (24. 36–44) suggest that the community perceived itself to live in temporal liminality, between the 'already' and 'not yet.'[50] Members of the Matthean community have separated from the economic support and identification with their families of origin (10.35–39; 12.46–50; 19.27–29) in order to join the permanent liminality of the 'communitas' that waits between the world and the kingdom to come. The community lives 'in-between this beginning and this end, in transition to this goal.'[51]

4.4 *The Bridegroom's Fictive Family and Disruption of Kinship Bonds*

In the first century, a bridegroom was closely associated with family, because unlike the modern Western understanding of marrying for companionship and romantic love, the primary reason for marriage in the first century was the formation of the family group or οἶκος.[52] Moxnes summarizes: 'Marriage represents the start of one basic social function of the family: the formation of a group with tasks of production and reproduction, sharing, social protection, worship ... and to transmit wealth.'[53] Maintaining inheritance and kinship bonds was most efficiently achieved by marrying within the familial group or by creating alliances with other groups through marriage for the sake of mutual protection.[54] Continuation of the patrilineal line was very important, so that marriages were arranged toward that purpose. Some (like the Jews) preferred marriage within the community and ideally within the kin-group (endogamy); others (such as the Romans) sought marriage outside the extended family (exogamy), but within the same social class.[55] Non-sanctioned unions (such as between unequal social classes, for instance a

---

50. The 'not yet' is often understood as the eschaton, but could also be interpreted as forthcoming earthly conflicts.

51. Carter, *Households and Discipleship*, pp. 48–55 (quote on p. 55). Cf. Turner, *Ritual Process*, p. 107.

52. Osiek and Balch, *Families*, pp. 41–42; M.L. Satlow, *Jewish Marriage in Antiquity* (Princeton: Princeton University Press, 2001), pp. 12–30. See discussion of the importance of marriage and family in Mediterranean cultures in Carol Delaney, *The Seed and the Soil: Gender and Cosmology in Turkish Village Society* (Berkeley: University of California Press, 1991), pp. 99–146.

53. Moxnes, 'What is Family?', p. 30.

54. Linda Stone, *Kinship and Gender* (Boulder, CO: Westview Press, 1997).

55. Moxnes, 'What is Family?', p. 30.

royal and a freed slave) threatened boundaries.[56] Therefore, the rich attempted to keep inheritance, status, and political power concentrated among members of the elite class.[57] Intermarriages between powerful families of the Herodian and Roman dynasties (cf. Herod and Herodias, Mt. 14.3–4) cemented political alliances and guaranteed that wealth, power, and status remained among the most powerful families.[58] Jesus – a 'bridegroom' who neither chooses a bride nor has a bride chosen for him and who creates a family without marrying or reproducing – flouts these social conventions that consolidate wealth and power within families. Matthew highlights not inheritance and heirs but renunciation of wealth and family (e.g., 12.46–50; 19.27–29).

Jesus' redefinition of family disrupts the cultural expectation of complete loyalty to one's kin, and so the maintenance of family honor (12.46–50):[59] among the poor and wealthy alike, loyalty between family members, especially in times of trouble, was expected for the sake of family honor.[60] Matthew shows an awareness that such kinship ties were important by portraying the irony in the questions people ask upon Jesus' return to his hometown: 'Is this not the carpenter's son? Is not his mother called Mary? And are not his brothers James and Joseph and Simon and Judas? And are not all his sisters with us?' (13.55). This narrative shows that, no matter who his followers (and Matthew's readers) think Jesus is, his people knew him by his family of origin.[61]

Becoming part of the fictive family means for some would-be disciples abandonment of such basic acts of respect as burying a father (8.21–22) and disrupts an 'indissoluble bond of love and kinship between parent and

56. Delaney relates this to cosmological associations between family and agriculture: the family is like the fields from which life comes. One plants familiar seed in familiar soil to ensure a good and healthy crop.

57. Dixon, *Roman Family*, pp. 26–27.

58. Chapman, 'Marriage and Family in Second Temple Judaism', pp. 185–86. See K.C. Hanson's series of articles that illustrate this principle: 'The Herodians and Mediterranean Kinship Part 1: Genealogy and Descent', *BTB* 19 (July, 1989), pp. 75–84; 'The Herodians and Mediterranean Kinship Part 2: Marriage and Divorce', *BTB* 19 (Oct., 1989), pp. 142–51; and 'The Herodians and Mediterranean Kinship Part 3: Economics', *BTB* 20 (Spring, 1990), pp. 10–21.

59. Neyrey, *Honor and Shame*, pp. 52–55; B.J. Malina, *The New Testament World: Insights from Cultured Anthropology* (Louisville: Westminster/John Knox Press, rev. edn, 1993), p. 44.

60. Neyrey, *Honor and Shame*, pp. 53–55; P. Esler, *The First Christians in Their Social Worlds* (New York: Routledge, 1994), pp. 26–27; Dixon, *Roman Family*, p. 30.

61. Moxnes, 'What is Family?', p. 28. In Matthew's narrative world, the question has more to do with the question: who is Jesus' 'father?' Detailed discussion of Jesus' 'real' brothers and sisters can be found in Meier, *A Marginal Jew*, pp. 316–32; Barton, *Discipleship and Family Ties*, pp. 67–107; Bauckham, *Jude and the Relatives of Jesus*.

child.'[62] That disciples were willing to make such an extreme break with first-century conventions[63] represents the urgency they felt to face 'choices about what is most fundamental in life, an ultimate demand more important than family.'[64]

Santiago Guijarro Oporto argues that, given the context of the family as primary social unit, the anti-family gospel sayings in their original setting reflect that such a break with family was often the consequence of following Jesus, but not necessarily a requirement. Oporto cites Jesus' injunctions against divorce (Q 16.18; 1 Cor. 7.10; Mk 10.11–12) and evidence that disciples continued to receive support from families or from disciples who remained at home (Mk 1.29; 2.15; 11.11; 14.3; Mt. 20.20; 27.56; Lk. 10.38–42; Jn 11.1–54) to support his theory that Jesus had nothing against families unless family conflict prevented disciples from doing the work of the Kingdom of Heaven. Therefore, Oporto thinks that Jesus formed a 'fictive family' not to undermine existing families but precisely to provide this important means of support for those would-be followers who had no families of their own.[65] While Oporto's theory may work for discussion of the historical Jesus, the gospel of Matthew reflects more often the actual disruption of families of origin: one seldom sees married couples together, except in the case of Mary and Joseph, and marriage is depicted as full of strife (10.35), so that maybe it is better not to marry (19.10). Matthew depicts women apart from husbands (Mt 15.21; 20.20; 27.55) and men apart from wives (9.18, 23; 19.27). Moreover, while parents seek healing or blessing for their children (e.g., 9.18; 15.21; 19.13), children and parents are in open conflict (10.35–37) or are estranged: the 'sons of Zebedee' have left their father (4.20–22) and appear only with their mother (20.20); Jesus does not acknowledge his mother and brothers (12.46–50).

Oporto's argument, which considers the Jesus movement in general, is challenged by Sheffield's study of family in the gospel of Matthew in particular: she demonstrates how Matthew systematically undermines the role of human father and thus the family of origin in order to replace it with the family headed by God the Father.[66] The fictive household of God is formed by disciples who have chosen to abandon their duty to their family of origin in order to follow Jesus (10.21, 34–37; 12.47–49; 23.9;

---

62. Adele Reinhartz, 'Parents and Children', pp. 61–88 (86).

63. That Jesus should discourage a would-be disciple from burying his father (Mt. 8. 21–22) is described by Hellerman as a 'scandalous saying' unparalleled in Greco-Roman literature (*Ancient Church as Family*, p. 73). Levine suggests that foregoing family ties in a culture where the family is the primary social unit would elicit reactions from surprise to revulsion ('Women in the Q Communit[ies]', p. 159).

64. Osiek and Balch, *Families in the New Testament World*, p. 126.

65. Guijarro-Oporto, 'Kingdom and Family in Conflict', esp. pp. 234–38.

66. Sheffield, 'Father', pp. 52–69.

24.38–44).[67] Thus the Matthean Jesus does not support families of origin but creates situations of extreme conflict, violence, and disloyalty among biological family members: 'Brother will betray brother to death, and a father his child, and children will rise against parents and have them put to death' (10.21). Jesus sets new rules about family allegiance: disciples must subordinate love of parents and children to obedience to God the Father and the brotherhood of the fictive family: 'I have come to set a man against his father, a daughter against her mother, and a daughter-in-law against her mother-in-law; and one's foes will be members of one's own household. Whoever loves father or mother more than me is not worthy of me, and whoever loves son or daughter more than me is not worthy of me' (10.35–58).

The bridegroom's disruption of biological family ties and creation of a fictive family follows a model presented by Moses the bridegroom (חתן, γαμβρός, Exod. 18.1–2), whose role as liberator of his people took a toll on his family life. Both 'bridegrooms' have an adoptive parent who saves them from death, but whom they later abandon: the Pharaoh's daughter rescues and raises Moses as her own son (Exod. 2.10), and Joseph rescues and raises Jesus as his own son.[68] But Moses leaves his fictive mother, and later, as leader of his new family, Israel, he brings misery to Pharaoh's courts with the plagues. Jesus also apparently abandons his adoptive family in order to form a new fictive family (12.46–50). We never hear about Moses' biological mother after the birth narrative; Jesus' mother also fades into obscurity and is replaced by the fictive family (12.46–50).

Moses' birth narrative has gaps that cause disruption in his family: for example, Jonathan Cohen wonders how Moses has a brother (Aaron) if all the boy children were killed,[69] and what happens to the older sister (Exod. 2.4, 7, 8)? Is she the same sister as Miriam?[70] Matthew also leaves the reader wondering about Jesus' brothers and sisters; they appear briefly in 13.55, but because Joseph's role as Jesus' father is known to be adoptive, we do not know if they are to be regarded as biological siblings (or half-siblings, by Mary).[71]

---

67. Osiek and Balch, *Families*, p. 126.

68. Jonathan Kirsch, *Moses: A Life* (New York: Ballantine Books, 1998), pp. 51–52; Nohrnberg, *Like Unto Moses*, p. 136; Jonathan Cohen, *The Origins and Evolution of the Moses Nativity Story* (Leiden: Brill, 1993), pp. 126–27; Gordon F. Davis, *Israel in Egypt: Reading Exodus 1–2* (JSOTSup, 135; Sheffield: Sheffield Academic Press, 1992), pp. 93, 96, 114; George W. Coats, *Moses: Heroic Man, Man of God* (JSOTSup, 57; Sheffield: Sheffield Academic Press, 1988), pp. 43–46; Elias Auerbach, *Moses* (Detroit: Wayne State University Press, 1975), pp. 16–17, 21–23.

69. If Aaron was born several years apart from Moses, he could have escaped the massacre.

70. Cohen, *Origins and Evolution*, pp. 117–19.

71. Moxnes, 'What is Family?', p. 28; Meier, *A Marginal Jew*, I, pp. 316–32; Barton, *Discipleship and Family Ties*, pp. 67–107; Bauckham, *Jude and the Relatives of Jesus*.

Moses' marriage is disrupted by his new role as head of the fictive family of Israel when he sends away his wife Zipporah and two sons (Exod. 18.2–3). Moses' marriage is the cause of family conflict when his sister Miriam and brother Aaron question him about his Cushite wife (Num. 12.1–15); the consequences of this conflict are severe, as Miriam is struck with leprosy and is excluded from the community (Num. 12.10–15) (not unlike the exclusion of the garmentless man and five foolish virgins from the wedding feast in Mt. 22.11–13 and 25.11–12). Boyarin conjectures that Moses, as leader of Israel, was living a celibate life (like Jesus), and that Miriam and Aaron were not speaking *against* the wife (Num. 12.1–9) but rather on her behalf: they were challenging Moses for being overly holy and not having sexual intercourse with her.[72] Thus Moses is a bridegroom who disrupts marriage and family in favor of the fictive family, a role taken up by Jesus the bridegroom in Matthew.

4.5 *The 'Sons of the Bridal Chamber'*

The relationship of the Matthean community to the bridegroom can best be described as 'sons of the bridal chamber' (9.15). In the bridegroom logion, Jesus the bridegroom identifies his followers as 'the sons of the bridal chamber' (οἱ υἱοὶ τοῦ νυμφῶνος)[73] who celebrate Jesus' presence as a bridegroom (9.15). Οἱ υἱοὶ τοῦ νυμφῶνος is related to the Hebrew בני החפה, literally 'the sons of the bridal canopy,' figuratively, the friends of the bridegroom (*b. Sukka* 25b).[74] Another term for the bridegroom's

---

72. D. Boyarin (*Carnal Israel: Reading Sex in Tasmunic Culture* [Berkeley: University of California, 1993], pp. 159–63) discusses a Midrash on Num. 12 that attempts to explain the nature of Miriam and Aaron's complaint to Moses by filling in the 'gaps' in the story.

73. Some manuscripts (D, and the entire Latin tradition based on the same Greek reading) read: 'sons of the bridegroom' (υἱοὶ τοῦ νυμφίου and Latin '*filii sponsi*'). The Vulgate translates *filii nuptiarum* (sons of the bridal chamber). The Latin portion of Codex Cantabrigiensis (Bezae) has *filii sponsi* (sons of the bridegroom) with Jesus the bridegroom as *sponsus*. That the rendering νυμφίου is not likely to be original is evident not only by the scarcity of manuscripts with this reading, but also from the unreliability of Bezae itself. See Bruce M. Metzger, *The Text of the New Testament: Its Transmission, Corruption and Restoration* [Oxford: Oxford University Press, 3rd edn, 1992], p. 50). However, many Church fathers are influenced by the reading '*filii sponsi*' and refer to the sons of the bridegroom in their writing.

74. Ancient scholars tend to interpret the 'sons of the bridal chamber' as sons of David or as Christians in general. For example: Augustine claimed that because the sons of David are the children of the bridegroom, therefore all Christians are his sons (*Expositions on the Psalms*, 47.29). Elsewhere, Augustine said that the sons of Korah are the sons of the bridegroom, who bear the sign of the cross (*Expositions on the Psalms*, 3.2). Arnobius Iunior (fifth century CE), in *Expositiunculae in Mattheaeum*, 12, wrote that the children of the bridal chamber are ourselves; therefore, the person who dwells on this passage will not fast, because the bridegroom is with him, the one who said 'I am the bread of life' (Jn. 6.35) (trans. C.S.

friends is שׁושׁבינים (*Sanh.* 3.5, 27b; *b. Bath* 9.4, 144b), defined as
'friend(s) of the groom'[75] or groomsmen.'[76] The Aramaic שׁושׁבינא ('best
man' or 'close friend') is related to Akkadian *susapinnu*, also meaning
friend of the bridegroom.[77] Most scholars (if they treat the phrase at all)
translate οἱ υἱοὶ τοῦ νυμφῶνος freely as a reference to the groom's
attendants or wedding guests[78] and note that the bridegroom's presence
was an occasion for great joy, celebration, and feasting.[79]

None of the ancient sources refers to the specific tasks of the 'sons of the
bridal chamber'; however, numerous descriptions of bridal chambers
include some clues to attendants or family members' roles.[80] Attendants
to the bridegroom and bride were sometimes responsible for preparing the

---

Kraszewski, *The Gospel of Matthew with Patristic Commentaries* [Studies in Bible and Early
Christianity, 40; Lewiston, NY: Edwin Mellen Press, 1999], p. 301). See Cremer, who argues
that the friends of the bridegroom had no christological significance until the middle ages
('Die Söhne des Brautgemachs [Mk 2.19 parr] in der griechischen und lateinischen
Schrifterklärung', *BZ* 11 [1967], pp. 246–52); see also Davies and Allison, *Matthew*, II, p.
109.

75. '*Hochzeitkamerad,*' according to J. Levy, *Wörterbuch über die Talmudim und
Midraschim* (Berlin: Benjamin Haiz Verlag, 2nd edn, 1924), p. 526, and Marcus Jastrow,
A Dictonary of the Targumim, the Talmud Babli and Yerushalmi, and the Midrashic Literature
(New York: Pardes Publishing House, Inc., 1950), p. 1543.

76. '*Hochzeitsbeistand,*' so G. Dalman, *Aramäisch-Neuhebräisches Handwörterbuch zu
Targum, Talmud und Midrasch* (Hildesheim: Georg Olms Verlagsbuchhandlung, 1967), p.
418.

77. Michael Sokoloff, *A Dictionary of Jewish Babylonian Aramaic of the Talmudic and
Geonic Periods* (Ramat-Gan, Israel: Bar Ilan University Press; Baltimore: Johns Hopkins
University Press, 2002), p. 1124.

78. So Allen, *Matthew*, pp. 91–92; Beare, *Matthew*, p. 229; Davies and Allison, *Matthew*,
II, p. 109. Leon Morris explores the significance of the bridegroom's presence as a time of joy
(*The Gospel According to Matthew* [Grand Rapids, MI: Eerdmans, 1992], p. 45, n. 40).
Schnackenburg thinks the 'sons of the bridal chamber' are not only wedding guests, but 'a
reliable image of Judaism.' He does not explain what he means (*Matthew*, p. 89).

79. Isaiah defines joy and rejoicing (שׂושׂ אשׂישׂ, εὐφροσύνη εὐφρανθήσεται (LXX Isa.
61.10), χαίρων χαρήσομαι (Aquila, Isa. 61.10), or ἀγαλλιάσει ἀγαλλιάσομαι (Symmachus
and Theodotion, Isa. 61.10) as that of a 'bridegroom' (בחתן [Isa. 61.10]). See also the
bridegroom's rejoicing (משׂושׂ) in Isa. 62.5. Flavius Philostratus (*Heroikos* 11.4) similarly
describes the joyful nature (ἱλαρόν) of the bridegroom (νυμφίον); trans. Jennifer K. Berenson
Maclean and Ellen Bradshaw Aitken, *Flavius Philostratus: Heroikos* (Atlanta: Society of
Biblical Literature, 1977), p. 34. In rabbinic tradition, because celebration was inappropriate
during times of catastrophe and mourning, weddings were discouraged (*m. Sot.* 9.14; *t. Sot.*
15.8–9) in echo of the prophets' pronouncement in times of woe: 'the voice of the bridegroom
and bride' will be silent (Jer. 7.34; 16.9; 25.10; Joel 2.16; Bar. 2.23). This tradition does not
mean there were no weddings in difficult times; it simply illustrates the point that weddings
were supposed to be completely joyful.

80. A bridal chamber was variously called a νυμφών (Mt. 9.15; Dioscorides Pedanius, *De
material medica* 3.132.20); νυμφαία (Plutarch, *Rom. Quaes.* 1; Dionysius Halicarnassensis,
Ant. Rom. 2.30.6; Chariton, *Callirhoe*, 1.1.13; 3.2.15; Varro, *Ling.*, 5.61–62; Dioscorides
Pedanius, *De materia medica* 3.132.1, cited in Max Wellmann [ed.], *Pedanii Dioscuridis.*

bridal chamber and bringing the couple together there,[81] but that is not the task of the 'sons of the bridal chamber' in Mt. 9.15, because the Matthean bridegroom has no bride. Indeed, the Matthean bridegroom never enters the bridal chamber. For Matthew, the only designated role of 'the sons of the bridal chamber' (οἱ υἱοὶ τοῦ νυμφῶνος) is to celebrate with the bridegroom.[82]

Such joy in the presence of the bridegroom is illustrated by literary scenes of spontaneous festivity. People came out of their houses to see the bridal party pass.[83] Catullus describes the wedding procession of Peleus and Thetis that drew a crowd from all over the land; everyone abandoned fields and work to join the happy throng (*Poem* 64.32–47; cf. Mt. 22. 1–10).[84] This scene is reminiscent of Simon and Peter abandoning their nets (4.18–22) and Mathew his tax booth (9.9) to follow Jesus. More, Matthew's abandoning his work to join the bridegroom's procession[85] occurs just before the dinner at which Jesus first describes himself as a bridegroom (9.15).

The 'sons of the bridal chamber' are not only wedding guests but have a familial relationship to Jesus the bridegroom. Just as Matthew uses υἱός to identify a group of people or to denote close association, such as 'Son of David' (12.23; 21.15), 'sons of the Pharisees' (12.27), 'sons of the kingdom' (13.38), 'sons of the evil one' (13.38), and 'sons of Gehenna'

Danazarbei De Materia Medica [3 vols.; Berlin: Weidmannsche Verlagsbuchhandlung, 1958], II, pp. 141–42); νυμφικός (Chariton, *Callirhoe*, 3.10.8); θάλαμον (Aelian, *On Animals*, 6.60; Lucian, *Herodotus* 5); κλίνη νυμφική (Lucian, *Herodotus* 5); חפה (Ps. 19.6; Joel 2.16) or παστός (LXX Ps. 18.6; Joel 2.16); *torus genialis* (Pliny, *Panegyric* 8.1); *lectus genialis* (Seneca, *Controversiae* 6.6; Cicero, *Pro Cluentio* 14–15; cf. Juvenal, *Sat.* 6.21–22).

81. The wedding attendants, headed by the *pronuba* (a woman in her first marriage and whose husband was still living, who represents the ideal future for the new bride), would prepare the wedding bed and help the bride prepare (see Susan Treggiari, 'Putting the Bride to Bed' *Echos du Monde/Classical Views* 30 [1994] pp. 314–15, n. 10). Cf. description of bridal bed (κλίνη νυμφική) in Lucian, *Herodotus* 5; Catullus, *Poems* 64.47–52; 265–66; Lucan 2.356–7; Claudius, *Epithalamium de nuptiis Honorii* 10.213–27; Xenophon, *Eph.* 1.8.2–3. In Chariton's account, the *parents* of the bride and groom were expected to prepare the marriage bed (κοίτην) and chamber (νυμφικήν) (*Callirhoe*, 3.10.8). Cf. Tob. 7.12–17. Attendants might bring the bridegroom to the bed (Xenophon, *Eph.* 1.8; Plautus, *Cas.* 891). Aelian (*On Animals*, 6.60) mentions the discretion of the wedding attendants who know to withdraw when the bridegroom and bride enter their wedding chamber (θάλαμον).

82. Mourning or fasting is inappropriate in his presence (Mt. 9.14–15; cf. Isa. 61.10; 62.5; Jer. 33.1; John 3.9).

83. Chariton, *Callirhoe*, 3.2.17.

84. Translation by Thomas Banks, *Diotima*, 1997. That there could be hundreds in the wedding procession is evidenced by Josephus (*Ant.* 13.18, 20). See also Aristides, 78.10.

85. Matthew does not technically join a wedding procession, but Jesus is walking along among crowds of people, as would a bridegroom (9.8–9). Thus, the dinner with tax collectors and sinners at which Jesus calls himself a bridegroom foreshadows the wedding banquet (9.10–15; cf. 22.1–14; 25.1–13).

(23.15), so οἱ υἱοί τοῦ νυμφῶνος (9.15), the 'sons of the bridal chamber,' is a designation for those who are closely associated with Jesus the bridegroom.[86] That the 'sons of the bridal chamber' saying in Mt. 9.15 is sandwiched between two instances in which Jesus addresses someone as a child (τέκνον in 9.2 and θύγατερ in 9.22) is a clue to the identity of the 'sons of the bridal chamber': those who take heart because their sins are forgiven and whose faith has saved them. Jesus says to the paralyzed man: 'Take heart, child (τέκνον), your sins are forgiven' (9.2) and to the hemorrhaging woman, 'Take heart, daughter (θύγατερ), your faith has made you well' (9.22). These 'children' represent the bridegroom's new spiritual family who take heart and cannot mourn, because the bridegroom is with them (9.15).

That those who celebrate with the bridegroom include a faithful 'daughter' (θύγατερ) (9.22), and (if we read allegorically) that ten women go to meet the bridegroom in the Parable of the Ten Virgins (25.1–13), suggests that the 'sons of the bridal chamber' can be understood to be a gender-inclusive term.[87] The generic quality of membership inherent in the term υἱοί (e.g., 'sons of the kingdom' and 'sons of the evil one' [13.38]), would seem to include all those who rejoice with the bridegroom, male or female. Matthew portrays women with great faith (the woman who touched the fringe of Jesus' cloak, 9.20–22; the 'queen of the South,' 12.42; the Canaanite woman, 15.21–28; the women at the cross and tomb, 27.55–57; 28.1–6) and who take active roles as servants to Jesus (Peter's mother-in-law, 8.14–15; the anointing woman, 26.6–13).

---

86. The Greek υἱός can refer to 'a person related or closely associated as if by ties of sonship: a pupil, follower, or one who is otherwise a spiritual son,' or 'one whose identity is defined in terms of a relationship with a person or thing.' In particular, υἱός with the genitive denotes 'one who shares in it or is worthy of it,' and Mt. 9.15 is listed among the examples (BDAG, pp. 1024–25). The Aramaic בר includes also the nuance of 'worthiness' (Sokoloff, *Dictionary of Jewish Babylonian Aramaic*, p. 233) and developed as a definition of membership; for example, the 'son of a mare' (בר סוסתא) describes horses in general (M. Sokoloff, *Dictionary of Jewish Palestinian Aramaic of the Byzantine Period* (Ramat-Gan, Israel: Bar Ilan University; Baltimore: Johns Hopkins University Press, 2nd edn, 2002), p. 97. Hebrew בן denotes a member of group, order, or class, such as 'sons of the prophets' (בני הנביאים, υἱοὶ τῶν προφητῶν) in 2 Kgs 2.3, 5, 7 (LXX 4 Kgs 2.3, 5, 7); or a quality, such as a strong man or valiant warrior who is called a 'son of might' (בני חיל, υἱόν δυνάμεως) in 1 Sam. 14.52 (BDB, p. 121). Eduard Lohse defines υἱός as a member of a society, group, or fellowship (E. Lohse , 'υἱός', *TDNT*, 8, pp. 340–62 (esp. pp. 345–46); E. Schweizer, 'υἱός', TDNT, 8, pp. 363–92 (esp. p. 365), and F. Hahn, 'υἱός', *EDNT*, pp. 381–92 (esp. p. 383). G. Adolf Deissmann observes that in ancient Near Eastern thought, intimate relationship, 'whether of connection, origin or dependence' is a relationship of sonship, 'even in the spiritual sphere' (*Bible Studies* [trans. A. Grieve; Edinburgh: T&T Clark, 1901; repr. Peabody, MA: Hendrickson, 1988], p. 161). Deissmann cites Mt. 9.15 as an example of this intimate relationship (p. 162).

87. שושבינא can also refer to a woman friend, as in *Qid.* 81a. Cited in Michael Sokoloff, *A Dictionary of Jewish Babylonian Aramaic*, 2002, p. 1125.

But there is also evidence to the contrary that suggests the 'sons of the bridal chamber' is an exclusively male group, like the 'Twelve' (οἱ δώδεκα μαθητάς, 10.1; οἱ δώδεκα, 26.14). The term υἱοί normally stands for only male offspring; moreover, while υἱοί can refer to generic group-membership, this does not mean that the group must include female members. Women are portrayed as faithful servants in Matthew, but they are never included among the inner group of twelve disciples, and even with his portrayal of faithful women, gender roles in Matthew remain in place: women are never seen in positions of authority or lasting intimacy with Jesus. Jesus apparently dismisses his mother (along with his brothers, 12.46–50); she is not named among the women at the cross (27.55–56).[88] Women who receive healing (9.18–25; 15.21–28) or who serve Jesus (8. 14–15; 26.6–23) disappear from the narrative. The ten women in the parable who go to meet the bridegroom (25.2) are never portrayed actually eating or celebrating with him. Women who provided for Jesus faithfully follow him to the cross (27.55–56) but look on 'from a distance' (ἀπὸ μακρόθεν); men alone prepare Jesus' body burial (27.57–60).[89] Women see the angel at Jesus' tomb and then see Jesus himself (28.1–10); but they are immediately instructed to go tell the *disciples* (εἴπατε τοῖς μαθηταῖς, 28.7) and the *brothers* (ἀδελφοῖς, 28.10). While going to tell the disciples could be interpreted as the role of an evangelist, Matthew undermines the women's brief authority when he tells us that it is only the 'eleven' who are with Jesus on the mountain in Galilee to receive the Great Commission (28.16–20).[90] Because the Matthean Jesus uses gender-inclusive language to speak of his fictive kin as 'mother and brothers and sisters,' we may well conclude that the 'sons of the bridal chamber' – the most intimate members of the bridegroom's party – do not include women (because the evangelist could have used gender-inclusive language to

---

88. Jesus' mother is among the women at the cross and is given to the care of the beloved disciple in John (19.25–27). She is not among the women named in Mk 15.47; 16.1. Luke mentions 'women' but Mary is not among those specifically named (23.27, 49; 24.10).

89. The extent of the role of women in preparation of the body is ambiguous. Luke portrays women helping to anoint the dead body in Lk. 23.50–24, but men alone prepare Jesus' body in Mk. 15.42–47; Jn 19.38–42 (cf. a man plans to bury his father in Mt. 8.21).

90. Matthew draws attention to women in female-coded roles such as serving men in the home (8.14); making bread (13.33); being called prostitutes (21.32); conceiving and nursing infants (1.18; 24.19); relying on a husband for protection (2.13–23); and intervening to ask a king to honor her son(s) above others (20.20–21; cf. 1 Kgs 1.11–31). In contrast, men are portrayed in positions of authority, such as king, ruler, or governor (2.1; 14.1; 18.23; 22.2–13, 21–22; 27.11–26); 'Lord' (κύριος) and Son of Man (8.23; 11.19; 17.12–14, 22; 20.28; 25.11, 31–46; 26.2); the Twelve (10.1–5; 26.20); the Pharisees, Sadducees, chief priests, scribes (12.2, 14, 24; 15.1; 16.1; 19.3; 21.14, 23; 21.45; 22.23; 23.2–36; 26.3; 26.47; 26.57–66); a centurion (8.5–9); prophets (3.1–17; 13.57; 14.3–4; 17.11–12); the keeper of the keys to heaven (16.19); and householders or landlords (20.1–15; 21.33–41; 24.45–51; 25.14–30). Men are also portrayed in the male-coded roles of sower of seeds (13.1–9); merchant (13.44); fisherman (4.18–22; 13.47); carpenter (13.55); tax collector (9.9–12; 21.31); and soldier (27.27–37).

describe this intimate group as 'sons *and daughters* of the bridal chamber'). Women in the gospel remain in women's roles of mother, sister, and daughter, but while men in the role of 'brothers' can also be 'sons,' the women (literally) cannot be.

Elsewhere in the gospel, those who follow Jesus are generic 'children' (neuter παιδία, 18.2–3) or brothers (ἀδελφοί) and sisters (ἀδελφαί) to Jesus (and presumably to each other) (12.50). Both genders are included as family members or wedding guests in Jesus the bridegroom's wedding feast (22.1–14; 25.1–13). Even though both genders are included, this is not an egalitarian fictive family: the most preeminent group in the gospel remains the Twelve, who are all male, and the gender roles of the ἐκκλησία are the same as those for the οἶκος at large.

4.6 *Joseph as Model for Adoptive Fatherhood*

Because the fictive family claims God as their Father, the 'sons of the bridal chamber' and fictive 'brothers and sisters' are not a product of sexual union. Rather, they are created through mission and incorporation into the family. Matthew's depiction of Jesus' unusual birth and infancy foreshadows the role of fathers who do not reproduce biologically but who adopt others into the fictive family. Matthew is clear that Jesus had no biological father, but as Krister Stendahl has shown, he was 'engrafted' into the theological family and lineage of Abraham and David through his adoptive father, Joseph.[91] Thus, the bridegroom disrupts not only

---

91. Krister Stendahl, 'Quis et Unde? An Analysis of Matthew 1–2,' in Graham N. Stanton (ed.), *The Interpretation of Matthew* (Edinburgh: T&T Clark, 2nd edn, 1995), pp. 69–80. (First published in *Judentum, Urchristentum, Kirche*, ed. W. Eltester [1960], pp. 94–105.) Michael Crosby makes a similar observation in *House of Disciples*, p. 87. Raymond E. Brown discusses the history of tradition about both Joseph and Mary as descendents of David (*The Birth of the Messiah: A Commentary on the Infancy Narratives in the Gospels of Matthew and Luke* [New York: Doubleday, rev. edn, 1993], pp. 86–89, 587–90). Andries van Aarde argues that because Jesus was a fatherless child, he was not part of the family of Abraham (although for Matthew, he clearly is a 'son of Abraham' in 1.1) and so, technically not a child of God, and not a full participant in the social and religious life of the Temple cult, a situation of rejection that led him to befriend other 'sinners' and to put his trust in God as his father. This interpretation ignores Joseph's role as adoptive father and is based on a misunderstanding of the Temple's importance in the lives of diaspora Jews, who would not be affected by whether or not they could enter the inner courts, as a visit to the Temple might be a once-in-a-lifetime event. See Andries van Aarde, 'Fatherless in First-century Mediterranean Culture: The Historical Jesus Seen from the Perspective of Cross-cultural Anthropology and Cultural Psychology', *Hervormde Teologiese Studies* 55 (1999), pp. 97–119. Walter Wangerin ('A Stranger in Joseph's House', *CToday* 39.14 [Dec. 11, 1995], pp. 16–21) suggests that anyone who acknowledges God's fatherhood realizes that all parents are adopters of children, and that parents raise these children in righteousness, like Joseph raised Jesus, to release them for the purpose for which they are born.

marriage and sexuality, but the whole cultural value on procreation and family lineage.[92]

The fictive family starts with Joseph's genealogy, then extends beyond the family of Israel. Because Joseph is not Jesus' biological father, it is only because Joseph adopted Jesus that this genealogy of Israel becomes part of the genealogy of the Church. That Jesus is called 'son of Abraham' and 'son of David' ties him to the founding patriarch and to the king who has messianic prophecies connected to his name, but the genealogy contains both Jews and Gentiles: Ruth the Moabite who chose to stay bonded to Israel rather than return to Moab (Mt. 1.5; cf. Ruth 1.4); Rahab, probably in reference to the Canannite prostitute in Jericho who helped the spies from Israel and claimed the God of Israel as her own (1.5; Josh. 2.1–14); and the wife of Uriah the Hittite, who became wife of David and mother of his children (1.6; 2 Sam. 11.3).[93] These Gentiles are antecedents of the expansion of Israel to form a family that includes those outside Israel. Moreover, by including in the genealogy women who were unmarried, seductresses, adulteresses, and prostitutes, the author demonstrates that the fictive family of God is formed outside the conventional social traditions and through the extraordinary righteousness these women demonstrated.[94] Thus, the bridegroom's birth disrupts conventions of marriage, sexuality, and traditional lineage.

As the women in Jesus' genealogy reproduce in situations outside social acceptability, Joseph also 'reproduces' outside the usual means. He is the model of the non-procreative father who incorporates new members to his family by adoption.[95] The only father begetting children in the new

---

92.   Carter, *Households and Discipleship*, p. 114.

93.   Levine, 'Matthew', p. 253; Jane Schaberg, *The Illegitimacy of Jesus: A Feminist Theological Interpretation of the Infancy Narratives* (Crossroad: New York: 1990), pp. 20–36; M. Crosby, *House of Disciples*, pp. 85–87; Dan O. Via, 'Narrative World and Ethical Response: The Marvelous and Righteous in Matthew 1–2', *Semeia* 12 (1978), pp. 123–49.

94.   Levine, 'Matthew', p. 253.

95.   Matthew does not state that Joseph adopted Jesus, but Joseph's actions are those of an adoptive parent. Levine ('Matthew', p. 254) states that by naming the child, Joseph has become his legal father; also Sheila Klassen-Wiebe, 'Matthew 1.18–25', *Int* 46 (1992), pp. 392–95 (392). Schaberg (*Illegitimacy,* p. 41) argues that the completion of fourteen generations of Joseph's genealogy indicates Joseph's legal adoption of Jesus. Raymond Westbrook ('The Character of Ancient Near Eastern Law', in Westbrook [ed.], *A History of Ancient Near Eastern Law* [2 vols.; Handbook of Oriental Studies, Section One, The Near and Middle East, 72; Leiden: Brill, 2003], I, pp. 1–90 [50–54, esp. p. 53]) demonstrates that adoption laws were in place long before Joseph's time. Roman adoption could be as formal as *adoptio* (requiring legal ratification by public officials), or less formally, *adrogatio* (the transfer of allegiance to someone's *potestas*). *Testamentary* adoption required no legal ratification, and the Romans also recognized affective adoption, that of caring for a child as one's own son or daughter without formally adopting. See Mireille Corbier, 'Constructing Kinship in Rome: Marriage, Divorce, Filiation, and Adoption', in David I. Kertzer and Richard P. Saller (eds.), *The Family in Italy from Antiquity to the Present* (New Haven: Yale

theological family is God the Father, whose method of creating 'children' for the Kingdom of Heaven is not sexual but by the command to 'make disciples of all nations, baptizing them in the name of the Father and the Son and the Holy Spirit' (ἁγίου πνεύματος, 28.19). That Jesus was born by the Holy Spirit (πνεύματος ἁγίου, 1.20) and was claimed as God's son by the spirit of God (πνεῦμα θεοῦ) descending at his own baptism (3. 16–17) indicates that baptism into the Church is a form of being born into the fictive family.[96]

Joseph's role as father is to be protector of the infant Jesus and his mother. He is bridegroom to Mary and raises a child that is not his; he fulfills the nuance of 'protector' in the definition of חתן[97] as he protects the infant Jesus from harm by guiding the mother and child through Egypt and Israel.[98] Just as a former 'Joseph' – himself adopted into the family of Pharaoh and the nation of Egypt – took care of his family in Egypt (Gen. 45–50), Joseph cares for his family.[99]

As a non-procreative but adoptive caretaker, Joseph has made himself a 'eunuch' (at least temporarily) for the sake of the Kingdom of Heaven (19.12).[100] Even though the gospel at least allows for later sexual activity with Mary (1.25) and speaks of Jesus' having brothers and sisters (the

---

University Press, 1991), pp. 127–44. For further discussion of adoption in antiquity, see Kathleen E. Corley, 'Women's Inheritance Rights in Antiquity and Paul's Metaphor of Adoption', in Amy-Jill Levine (ed.), *A Feminist Companion to Paul* (Sheffield: Sheffield Academic Press, 2004), pp. 98–121; Trevor Burke, 'Pauline Adoption: A Sociological Approach', *EvQ* 73.2 (2001), pp. 119–34; Andreas Köstenberger, 'Marriage and Family in the New Testament', in Ken M. Campbell (ed.), *Marriage and Family in the Biblical World* (Downers Grove, IL: InterVarsity Press, 2003), pp. 240–84 (esp. 268–69).

96. That the historical Jesus was born of both biological father and mother is accepted by many scholars today. See in particular the extended arguments offered by Schaberg, *Illegitimacy*, Gerd Lüdemann, *Virgin Birth? The Real Story of Mary and Her Son Jesus* (trans. J. Bowden; Harrisburg, PA: Trinity Press International, 1998), and Robert J. Miller, *Born Divine: The Births of Jesus and Other Sons of God* (New York: Polebridge Press, 2003). I am not arguing against this historical view of a non-miraculous birth but interpreting what I think the evangelist conveys about Jesus' origin.

97. E. Kutsch, 'חתן', *TDOT*, 5, p. 272.

98. Davies and Allison, *Matthew*, I, pp. 260–65; Keener, *Matthew*, pp. 107–109; Harrington, *Matthew*, p. 49; M. Eugene Boring, 'The Gospel of Matthew,' in *The New Interpreter's Dictionary of the Bible* (12 vols.; Nashville: Abingdon Press, 1995), VIII, pp. 89–505 (146–147). Gundry, *Matthew*, p.33; Schweizer, *Matthew*, pp. 42–43.

99. Patte (*Matthew*, p. 37), Carter (*Matthew and the Margins*, p. 83), Gundry (*Matthew*, p. 33), and an extensive treatment by Andries van Aarde ('The Carpenter's Son [Mt. 13.55]: Joseph and Jesus in the Gospel of Matthew and Other Texts', *Neot* 34 [2000], pp. 173–90) note that the flight to Egypt recalls another Joseph, the son of Jacob, who precedes Jesus' adoptive father, and has implications for the Matthean portrayal of salvation history.

100. Keener suggests that Joseph, through his self-control, models the role of eunuch (*Matthew*, p. 472). Allison ('Divorce, Celibacy and Joseph', [Matthew 1.18–25 and 19.1–2]', *JSNT* 49[2003], pp. 3–10) recognizes Joseph's righteousness manifested in his celibacy during Mary's pregnancy.

reader assumes these are fathered by Joseph), Joseph is, during his starring role, a celibate bridegroom and a non-procreative father who prefigures the ideal for non-reproductive masculinity in Matthew.[101]

That Jesus' family are refugees in Egypt is a further example of Jesus' disruption of traditional households.[102] The future bridegroom is shuttled from Bethlehem to Egypt, and though he temporarily has a home in Nazareth, his hometown will eventually reject him (13.53–58).[103] His adult 'household' is not located anywhere; he is a wanderer who had no place to lay his head (8.20)[104] and whose disciples have left houses, fields, and relatives to follow him (19.27–29).[105] The bridegroom's non-geographical household indicates the expansion of the Kingdom of Heaven to include all who are homeless: people who have deserted families or who have been disenfranchised by their families.[106]

4.7 Eunuchs for the Kingdom

Normally, a bridegroom would become a husband by virtue of consummation of the marriage and subsequent reproduction; weddings in the first-century served not only to establish new families and kinship ties but to celebrate fertility and sexuality as valued aspects of life.[107] But Jesus is a bridegroom who does not consummate a marriage, just as his

---

101. Allison, 'Divorce, Celibacy, and Joseph', pp. 3–10; see also Allison's chapter 'Jesus as a Millenarian Ascetic', in Allison, *Jesus of Nazareth Millenarian Prophet* (Minneapolis: Fortress Press, 1998), pp. 172–216. Andries van Aarde ('Social Identity, Status, Envy and Jesus' Abba', *Pastoral Psychology* 45 [1997], p. 459) points out that even a biological father 'adopted' his own children by deciding to include them in the household, but I think there is a difference between acknowledging one's own child and adopting someone else's as one's own. That Joseph disappears from the story after the birth narrative indicates to many interpreters that he must have died; however, van Aarde demonstrates that Jesus transferred his filial allegiance entirely to God the Father ('Social Identity', pp. 451–72, and 'Fatherless in First-Century Mediterranean Culture', *Hervormde Teologiese Studies* 55 [1999], pp. 97–119).

102. Keener, *Matthew*, pp. 107–109; Carter, *Matthew and the Margins*, p. 88. God's rescuing Jesus is a demonstration that the anticipated salvation of God's people is at hand, as an echo of the Exodus event.

103. Carter, *Matthew and the Margins*, p. 88.

104. Keener, *Matthew*, p. 107; following Schweizer, *Matthew*, p. 41.

105. M.A. Powell, *Chasing the Eastern Star* (Louisville: Westminster/John Knox Press, 2001), p. 144.

106. That Jesus fulfills the prophecy 'out of Egypt I have called my son' (11.1) shows that God's planned salvation is not only for those within the bounds of the 'promised land,' but for those outside it, who also are like refugees (Keener, *Matthew*, p. 109; Patte, *Matthew*, p. 38; Guijarro-Oporto, 'Kingdom and Family in Conflict', pp. 234–38).

107. Satlow, *Jewish Marriage*, p. 162, 180. Not all marriages were celebrated with weddings nor were legalized by written documents; the marriage was legitimated by consummation. *P. Oxy.* 2.237 describes the status of the daughter of a man and woman who have a an 'unwritten' marriage (ἀγράφων γάμων).

adoptive father Joseph remains a 'bridegroom' by not consummating his marriage until after Jesus' birth (if ever) (1.24–25).[108] The disciples are not to produce children but are to become children themselves – a celibate and non-procreative role[109] – thus disrupting the expectation of sex and reproduction associated with weddings. Amy-Jill Levine summarizes: 'The eunuch for the kingdom then was one who did not seek children, and this means one who abstained from sexual intercourse.'[110] The bridegroom Jesus disrupts the customary formation of households by saying that those who become 'eunuchs' (εὐνοῦχοι) for the kingdom gather in new members as brothers and sisters and do not act as 'fathers' except in an adoptive sense. If they act as head of the household, they do not create heirs through marriage and sexual intercourse.[111]

Typically, the eunuch saying is taken to mean that disciples are to remain unmarried or to practice voluntary celibacy, because it has been assumed that eunuchs are incapable of marriage.[112] Thus, because Jesus was unmarried and celibate, Meier, Davies and Allison (among others) suggest that the epithet 'eunuch' was hurled as an insult against Jesus. Thereupon, Jesus turned the insult into praise for those who have the gift of celibacy.[113] In this interpretation, becoming a eunuch for the kingdom means remaining celibate in order to dedicate one's self more fully to the work of the Kingdom of Heaven.[114]

---

108. Amy-Jill Levine, 'The Word Becomes Flesh: Jesus, Gender, and Sexuality', in James H. Charlesworth and Walter P. Weaver (eds.), *Jesus Two Thousand Years Later* (Harrisburg, PA: Trinity Press International, 2000), pp. 62–83 (75–76).

109. Levine, 'The Word Becomes Flesh', p. 76.

110. Levine, 'The Word Becomes Flesh', p. 76.

111. Even a 'real' eunuch could be the head of a household (e.g., Potiphar is apparently both a eunuch [סְרִיס, εὐνοῦχος; Gen. 39.1] and head of a household including wife and slaves [Gen. 39.2–7]).

112. My thanks to Brant Pitre for his insights and research in, 'Eunuchs for the Sake of the Kingdom? Rethinking Marriage, Children, Sex, and Celibacy in Matthew 19.1–15', (unpublished seminar paper, Vanderbilt University, 1998).

113. Meier, *A Marginal Jew*, III, pp. 505–507; Davies and Allison, *Matthew*, III, p. 25. Also Jerome Kodell, 'The Celibacy Logion in Matthew 19.12', *BTB* 8 (1978), pp. 19–23.

114. So Harrington, *Matthew*, p. 274; Boring, 'Matthew,' pp. 386–87. Gundry, *Matthew*, p. 383; Davies and Allison, *Matthew*, III, pp. 26–27; Keener, *Matthew*, p. 472; Patte, *Matthew*, p. 267; Schweizer, *Matthew*, p. 383; Beare, *Matthew*, p. 392; Albright and Mann, *Matthew*, p. 227; Francis Moloney, 'Matthew 19.3–12 and Celibacy: A Redactional and Form Critical Study', *JSNT* 2 (1979), pp. 42–60; G. Petzke, 'εὐνοῦχος', *EDNT* 2, p. 81; J. Schneider, 'εὐνοῦχος', *TDNT* 2, p. 768. Celibacy was part of membership in some religious communities, as we have seen with the Theraputae and the Essenes, and self-castration is mentioned in reference to the worshippers of Cybele, sometimes known as '*galli*' (descriptions of the *galli* are in Mary Beard, John North, and Simon Price [eds.], *Religions of Rome* [2 vols.; Cambridge: Cambridge University Press, 1998], II, p. 210). While Jesus does not call for actual castration, there are resonances between a bridegroom who does not marry, who promotes becoming a 'eunuch for the Kingdom of Heaven' (19.12), who dies a

In antiquity it was commonly assumed that eunuchs were necessarily unmarried and celibate (e.g., Philo questions how a eunuch could be married [*Allegorical Interpretation* 3.84.236]). But this understanding was not universal. There is evidence that eunuchs did marry,[115] experienced lust, and were capable of sexual activity.[116] Dio Chrysostom (*Orationes* 4.36.2) describes how a eunuch maintains a love of women (ἐρᾶν τῶν γυναικῶν) and lies with them (καὶ συγκαθεύδουσιν αὐταῖς) all night.

Therefore, what distinguishes eunuchs from intact men is their infertility.[117] Dio says that when the eunuch lies with a woman, 'nothing happens' (γίγνεται δ' οὐδὲν) (which could either mean impotence or lack of sperm).[118] Sirach indicates that the eunuch has lust (Sir. 20.4), but like

---

bloody death, and whose body does not decay with the myth of Cybele and Attis. Catullus describes Attis' self-castration that made him a 'false woman' (*notha mulier*) (Catullus, *Poem* 63 [trans. C.H. Sisson and M. Meyer], cited in Marvin W. Meyer, *The Ancient Mysteries: A Sourcebook of Sacred Texts* [San Francisco: Harper & Row, 1987], pp. 125–28). Also Arnobius of Sicca, *Adversus Nationes*, 5.5–7, 16–17 (trans. G.E. McCracken), cited in Meyer, *The Ancient Mysteries*, pp. 116–19. Attis dies from his wound, but his body does not decay. Lucian of Samosata describes the ritual frenzy and self-castration of worshippers he calls the 'Galli' (attributed to Lucian of Samosta, *De Dea Syria* 49–51 [trans. H.W. Attridge and R.A. Oden], cited in Meyer, *The Ancient Mysteries*, p. 139). Apuleius of Madauros facetiously describes the self-flagellating worshippers (Apuleius of Madauros, *Metamorphoses* 8.27–28 [trans. J. Lindsay], cited in Meyer, *The Ancient Mysteries*, pp. 144–45). That becoming a eunuch did not always entail ritual castration is evidenced in Hippolytus, who wrote that the Naassenes (a Gnostic group) worshiped the mother goddess Cybele but believed in *spiritual* castration (more in keeping with Mt. 19.12). Significantly for interpretation of 'spiritual castration,' such as in Mt. 19.12, Hippolytus reports that they refrained from sexual intercourse in order to transcend the earthly realm of sexuality for the spiritual realm of heaven (Hippolytus, *Refutatio Omnium Haeresium* 7.13–19; 9.10–11 [trans. W. Foerster]), cited in Meyer, *The Ancient Mysteries*, pp. 149–50, 154).

115. Juvenal, *Satire* 1.22. Potiphar is a eunuch (εὐνοῦχος) with a wife (Gen. 39.1, 7–20), although some interpret 'eunuch' here to refer to his office, not his sexuality. In the *Mishnah* (*Yeb.* 8.2), a man whose testicles or whose penis is cut off is allowed to have sexual relations with a female convert or a freed slave girl, and a man who has been made a eunuch can fulfill levirate marriage (*Yeb.* 8.5).

116. Sir. 20.4 ('a eunuch lusting to violate a girl'). While some early Christians believed castration would remove desire, this was not always the case. Men without testicles are still capable of sexual activity; cf. Aline Rouselle, *Porneia: On Desire and the Body in Antiquity* (trans. F. Pheasant; Cambridge, MA: Blackwell, 1988), pp. 122–23; Daniel F. Caner, 'The Practice and Prohibition of Self-Castration in Early Christianity', *VC* 51 (1997), pp. 396–415 (412); Peter Brown, *The Body and Society: Men, Women, and Sexual Renunciation in Early Christianity* (New York: Columbia University Press, 1988), p. 169.

117. Soranus (*Gynaeciorum* 4.2.40.5) describes eunuchs as those whose 'twins' have been compressed or pinched (θλιβόμενοι γὰρ οἱ δίδυμοι). I am guessing that 'twins' or 'the pair' is a reference to the testicles. Rufus (*De partibus corporis humani* 58.4) uses the same terminology (διδύμων) when describing why those who have made themselves eunuchs (οἱ εὐνουχισθεντες) are childless (ἄγονον).

118. γίνομαι and the variant here, γίγνομαι, means to produce or to come into being, as ὃ γέγονεν (Jn. 1.3), but is rarely used for the production of children, so 'impotence' is probably the meaning here. The usual term for 'beget' is γεννάω (e.g., Mt. 1.2–20).

an idol who can neither eat nor smell the food sacrificed to it, the eunuch groans in frustration when embracing a girl (Sir. 30.20).

Thus it is not celibacy or sexuality that determines the eunuch, but the inability to reproduce due to impotence or lack of testicles.[119] Philo distinguishes eunuchs from men (and women) precisely by their inability to reproduce: they are 'barren' (ἀγόνος), because they can neither scatter seed (σπέρματα καταβάλλεσθαι) nor nourish it (*De Ebriate* 210.4–7; 211.6; *De Somniis* 2.184; also *On Joseph*, 12.58). Josephus, who abhors the idea of castration, says that men who have become eunuchs have killed their own children (*Ant.* 40.290).

Because the eunuch saying is embedded between a pronouncement about becoming like a little child and the blessing of children (18.2–3; 19.13–14),[120] the role of 'eunuch' suggests being childlike, that is prepubescent, a non-reproductive role. In fact, eunuchs were regarded as childlike (Claudian, *In Eutropium* 1.333; 342–45; 466–70).[121] Thus, to become a eunuch for the sake of the Kingdom of Heaven is closely linked with becoming like a child to enter the kingdom.[122]

Infertility, whether voluntary or involuntary, promotes the unity of the new fictive family, because there is no longer a need for biological relationships that potentially divide people according to inheritance and class. That the 'eunuch who makes himself one' is most likely to be equated with a man who is celibate – for voluntary infertility is almost tantamount to celibacy – indicates that Matthew does not support new marriages. There is no need for men and women to marry because the new family is made only of 'mothers and brothers and sisters.' Matthew valorizes non-procreative lifestyles (19.10–12) in order to strengthen bonds between fictive kin over and against traditional ties between couples, parents, and children.[123] The community reverts to the status of children (18.1–5; 23.9; cf. 5.45; 7.9–11; 19.14) instead of producing them. Matthew does not forbid reproduction but discourages it with his eunuch saying (9.12) and his reference to the extra difficulty that will be

119.   F. Scott Spencer ('The Ethiopian Eunuch and His Bible: A Social-science Analysis', *BTB* 22 [1992], pp. 155–65) discusses the eunuch's inability to procreate as the reason he was excluded from the community: he could not produce heirs to the covenant and he represented something less than whole. In Acts (as in Matthew's fictive family), the outcast eunuch finds a community.

120.   Keener (*Matthew*, p. 470) recognizes this familial context but does not pursue it.

121.   Trans. Maurice Platnauer, *Claudian* (2 vols.; LCL; Cambridge, MA: Harvard University Press, 1922). Aline Rouselle writes that eunuchs return to a state of childhood (*Porneia*, pp. 122, 127).

122.   Pitre, 'Eunuchs for the Sake of the Kingdom'.

123.   Davies and Allison disagree. They state that the first gospel is 'too Jewish to permit the redemption to eclipse creation' and that 'marriage is a part of the natural order' that is from God, 'despite the coming of the eschatological change' (*Matthew*, III, p. 26).

experienced by those who are pregnant and nursing infants in the last days (24.19). While Jesus heals children (9.22; 15.28) and twice points them out as models of the Kingdom of Heaven (18.2–3; 19.13–15), the gospel is not enthusiastic about 'real' children or reproduction, but about disciples becoming fictive children.

That men would voluntarily call themselves eunuchs disrupts gendered power structures in ancient society. Eunuchs were of ambiguous gender: they were regarded as effeminate men[124] or altogether genderless.[125] Thus, in Arthur Dewey's analysis, eunuchs threatened the 'elitist vision of controlled society' in which men constantly struggled to maintain and prove their virility, which gave them their power.[126] Matthew Kuefler writes that the eunuch was a 'constant reminder of the tentative nature of sexual difference and thus of masculine privilege.'[127] In addition, being made a eunuch was shameful: castration was often used as punishment or as part of enslavement. A conqueror would castrate a king and his sons as prisoners of war (2 Kgs 20.18; Josephus, *Ant.* 10.33.3; cf. *Testament of Judah* 23.4), an act that not only humiliates them, but ensures the end of their dynasty.[128] That Jesus asks his disciples to take on such a shameful role, even voluntarily, means radically redefining their masculinity.

Finally, the cultural role of the eunuch as faithful servant suggests that men of Jesus' fictive family must be loyal servants in the household of God. Becoming a eunuch implies servanthood, a concept congruent with the Matthean depiction of disciples who faithfully serve their master (e.g., Mt. 24.45–51; 25.14–30). That a bond between master and servant could be as strong as family is a logic explained by Xenophon (*Cyropaedia* 7), who writes that eunuchs are the most trusted servants because they have no wives and children to put first in their affections, and so they put the

---

124.   Josephus derides eunuchs as effeminate (*Ant.* 40.291). Dio Chrysostom says they are weaker than females and more effeminate (ἀσθενέστερον τοῦ γυναικείου καὶ θηλύτερον), translation mine (*Orationes* 77–78.36), and describes with disgust the youth that Nero had castrated and made into a woman with a women's name, clothing, and hair style (*Orationes* 62.6). Juvenal ridicules eunuchs as 'flabby' (*Satire* 1.22), perhaps in reference to their impotence or to a softness of body befitting a female. Claudian likens the eunuch to an old woman (*In Eutropium* 1.2). Philo suggests that men devoted to pleasure are barren (ἄγονος) like eunuchs (*Joseph* 153.1) and that to be a slave of passions makes one as unmanly as a eunuch (*Quod Deus Immutabilis* 111.2), who enjoy luxurious meats and drinks (*De Ebriate* 210.4).

125.   Philo, *De Ebriate* 210.4–7.

126.   Arthur J. Dewey, 'The Unkindest Cut of All? Matt. 19.11–12', *Foundations and Facets Forum* 8 (1992), pp. 113–22 (118, 120).

127.   Matthew Kuefler, *The Manly Eunuch: Masculinity, Gender Ambiguity, and Christian Ideology in Late Antiquity* (Chicago: University of Chicago Press, 2001), p. 31.

128.   René Péter-Contesse, 'Was Potiphar a Eunuch?', *BT* 47.1 (1996), pp. 142–46 (143).

master's (and his family's) best interests first.[129] Moreover, though there are examples of eunuchs who betrayed their masters,[130] the eunuch is most often portrayed as extremely loyal.[131] The 'eunuchs' of Matthew's fictive family are loyal to their master, God the Father; and they (ideally) have no wives or biological children that divide their attention from their master's fictive family.[132]

As self-made 'eunuchs,' the disciples could look to the model set by actual eunuchs who performed many important jobs on behalf of their master. Eunuchs are in charge of the household or education of children,[133] serve as bodyguards[134] as trusted royal confidants,[135] and as military leaders.[136] The Hebrew סריס (eunuch or official) comes from the Akkadian *ša-reši*, literally 'he of the head' or 'one who stands at the head,'[137] from which two types of service are indicated: one who stands at the head of the bed (a chamberlain) or one who is head or leading official. Hawkins explains that 'to stand at the head' implies that the one being attended is lying down, and therefore, the attendant is in the bed chamber.[138] This is the literal meaning of the Greek εὐνοῦχος, a 'bed

---

129. Cristiano Grottanelli, 'Faithful Bodies: Ancient Greek Sources on Oriental Eunuchs', in A.I. Baumgarten, J. Assmann, and G.G. Stroumsa (eds.), *Self, Soul and Body in Religious Experience* (Studies in the History of Religions, 78; Leiden: Brill, 1998), pp. 404–16. The eunuch's loyalty as protector of the king's family is illustrated by a eunuch who risked his life to go out to the battle front in order to assure the king that his wife had been unmolested and unharmed during a siege (Arrian, *Ana.* 4.20.1–2).

130. Eunuchs switch allegiance to Jehu and throw Jezebel from the tower (τοῖς εὐνούχοις προσέτακεν αὐτὴν ἀπὸ τοῦ πύργου βαλεῖν, Josephus, *Ant.* 9.123.1; 2 Kgs 9. 32–33). Eunuchs plot against the king (ἐπιβουλευσάντων τῷ βασιλεῖ ... τῶν εὐνούχων), and the king crucifies them (εὐνούχους ἀνεσταύρωσεν, Josephus, *Ant.* 11.207–208). Bogoas the Eunuch was also killed for conspiracy against the king (Josephus, *Ant.* 17.44).

131. C. Grottanelli, 'Faithful Bodies', p. 407–408. Nehemiah calls himself a εὐνούχος in the context of being God's loyal servant and prays for God's favor (Neh. 1.11).

132. If they do have wives and family (e.g., evidently Peter was married, because he has a mother-in-law [πενθεράν; 8.14], but he has left everything to follow Jesus [19.27–29]). Becoming a 'eunuch' for the sake of the Kingdom of Heaven potentially disrupts those relationships.

133. Harpocration, *Lex.* 136.6; Josephus, *Vit.* 429.4; *Ant.* 14.348; 16.230; *War* 1.488.

134. Dio Chrysostom, *Orationes* 6.38.7

135. Josephus, *Ant.* 11.223, 261; 15.226.

136. Josephus, *Ant.* 10.149, 175.

137. J.D. Hawkins, 'Eunuchs among the Hittites' in S. Parpola and R.M. Whiting (eds.), *Sex and Gender in the Ancient Near East* (2 vols; Helsinki: The Neo-Assyrian Text Corpus Project, 2002), I, p. 218; Edwin M. Yamauchi, 'Was Nehemiah the Cupbearer a Eunuch?', *ZAW* 92.1 (1980), pp. 132–42 (135); Johannes Schneider, 'εὐνοῦχος', *TDNT* 2, pp. 765–68 (766).

138. Hawkins, 'Eunuchs among the Hittites', p. 218, n. 15.

keeper' (εὐνή 'bed' and ἔχω 'have, keep').[139] (Perhaps the 'sons of the bridal chamber' can be imagined as 'eunuchs' who keep the bridal bed.) In the capacity of chamberlain, eunuchs are often found in charge of a king's harem caring for women and children,[140] thus providing a role for 'eunuchs for the kingdom' who would care for members of the fictive family. The eunuch's caretaking duties involved feeding and caring for others: cupbearer,[141] cook or food server,[142] personal attendant, or doorkeeper.[143]

The role of the 'eunuch' in an official capacity has led some scholars to argue that the term 'eunuch' did not originally mean 'castrated' (although by the time the Greek εὐνοῦχος was coined, castration was understood). René Péter-Contesse suggests that ša-reši refers to someone highly placed in the court (who may or may not be a castrato).[144] The self-made eunuchs of the Kingdom of Heaven, then, have models for leadership

139. BDAG, p. 409. Danker's first definition of εὐνοῦχος is, without reservation, a castrated man. He adds the meaning of a 'celibate' later in the definition. Gary Taylor discusses why men physiologically incapable of impregnating a woman make ideal guardians against men who can in 'Contest of Males: The Power of Eunuchs', in Taylor, *Castration: An Abbreviated History of Western Manhood* (New York: Routledge, 2000), pp. 33–47 (33–35).

140. A harem included not only wives, but also children and concubines: γυναῖκα καὶ τέκνα καὶ παλλακάς (*Testament of Joseph* 13.5). Cf. eunuchs are listed among women, children, and soldiers taken captive (Jer. 41.16).

141. Nehemiah calls himself both a cupbearer to the king and a εὐνοῦχος (Neh. 1.11). Cf. also Gen. 40.2.

142. In Gen. 40.2, 'Pharaoh was angry with his two eunuchs [סריס , εὐνοῦχοι], the head cupbearer and the head baker' (cf. Philo, *Jos.* 27.7; 37.2). Josephus (*Ant.* 16.230.1; *War*, 1.488.2) describes eunuchs whose task is to bring the king's drink and supper and put him to bed. Eunuchs bearing food are also noted in *Testament of Judah* 23.4

143. Bagoas the eunuch (εὐνοῦχος) is Holofernes' personal attendant (Judg. 12.11; 13.1; 14.14–18) and serves as a doorkeeper (Judg. 13.1; 14.14–18). Karlheinz Deller notes many examples of the eunuchs' duties in 'The Assyrian Eunuchs and Their Predecessors', in Kazuko Watanabe (ed.), *Priests and Officials in the Ancient Near East* (Heidelberg: Universitätsverlag, 1999), pp. 303–11 (308).

144. Péter-Contesse ('Was Potiphar a Eunuch?', p. 146) concludes that the term εὐνοῦχος should be translated 'eunuch' or 'official' according to the context; however, the context does not always make such a distinction clear. J.D. Hawkins ('Eunuchs among the Hittites', in I, pp. 217–33 [218]) demonstrates that ἐκτομίας, 'cut out,' is a sometimes used with εὐνοῦχος and therefore makes their castration clear. In the first-century, Apollonius (*Lexicon Homericum* 91.19) also uses ἐκτομίας and εὐνοῦχος synonymously. Karlheinz Deller ('The Assyrian Eunuchs and Their Predecessors', pp. 309–10); Hayim Tadmor ('The Role of the Chief Eunuch' and the Place of Eunuchs in the Assyrian Empire,' in Parpola and Whiting [eds], *Sex and Gender in the Ancient Near East*, II, pp. 604–606), Hawkins, 'Eunuchs among the Hittites', p. 219, and Yamauchi ('Was Nehemiah the Cupbearer a Eunuch?', p. 139) study references to both bearded and unbearded eunuchs as possible evidence of uncastrated and castrated men, respectively, who serve in official capacities. Hawkins argues that the eunuch is a *castrato* because of examples of the ša-reši who does not beget and whose semen is dried up; moreover, while courtiers specifically had sons and grandsons, the ša-reši had unspecified and ambiguous successors (Hawkins, 'Eunuchs among the Hittites', p. 219).

roles outside the domestic sphere: they serve as governors, court officials,[145] charioteers, guards, army officers,[146] and envoys.[147] The Ethiopian eunuch (Acts 8.27) is an envoy of a queen and possibly also a charioteer.[148] Eunuchs served not only royalty: Harpocration (*Lexicon* 136.6) describes a eunuch (εὐνοῦχος) who ordered the domestic affairs of Aristotle (οἰκείως δὲ διέκειτο πρὸς Ἀριστοτέλην), and Josephus writes that he himself had a eunuch servant who served as a teacher for his child (δοῦλον εὐνοῦχον παιδαγωγὸν τοῦ παιδὸς μου) (Josephus, *Vit.* 429.4).

Jesus' injunction that his disciples make themselves 'eunuchs' in the household of God is a demonstration of loyalty and servanthood. They are an example of the role expected of men in the bridegroom's family as they adopt members and take care of fictive family.[149] By the formation of fictive family with adoptive fatherhood, Matthew illustrates how eunuchs need not fear being like 'dry trees' whose names will die out (because of childlessness). Rather, to the faithful eunuch the deity will give a reward better than household, sons, and daughters: 'I will give to them in my house and in my walls a monument (ἐν οἴκῳ μου καὶ ἐν τῷ τείχει μου τόπον ὀνομαστόν) better than sons or daughters (κρείττω υἱῶν καὶ θυγατέρων), and an everlasting name (ὄνομα αἰώνιον) ... that will not be lost' (οὐκ ἐκλείψει; Isa. 56.3–5; cf. Wis. 3.14).

Becoming a 'eunuch' resonates with the warning that it is better to cut off (ἐκκόπτω) one's hand or foot[150] than to stumble (18.8; cf. 5.10) or become a stumbling block for these little ones (τῶν μικρῶν τούτων) (18.6). Matthew uses the same term 'cut off' (ἐκκόπτω) for the tree that does not produce good fruit (3.10; 7.19). Production of fruit is applied

145. P. Kyle McCarter, 'Biblical Detective Work Identifies the Eunuch', *BAR* 28.2 (2002), pp. 46–48, 61; Hayim Tadmor, 'Was the Biblical *saris* a Eunuch?', in Ziony Zevit, Seymour Gitin, and Michael Sokoloff (eds.), *Solving Riddles and Untying Knots: Biblical, Epigraphic, and Semitic Studies in Honor of Jonas C. Greenfield* (Winona Lake, IN: Eisenbrauns, 1995), pp. 317–25 (317); Tadmor, 'The Role of the Chief Eunuch', pp. 603–11; Yamauchi, 'Was Nehemiah the Cupbearer a Eunuch?', p. 135.

146. Deller, 'The Assyrian Eunuchs', p. 308. A eunuch (εὐνοῦχος) is in command of soldiers (Jer. 52.25).

147. Deller, 'The Assyrian Eunuchs', p. 308. Josephus describes eunuchs who managed government affairs (Josephus, *Ant.* 16.230.1). Eunuchs are listed among the royal court and artisans who departed from Jerusalem (Jer. 29.2).

148. The eunuch becomes part of the Church's fictive family (Spencer, 'The Ethiopian Eunuch', pp. 16–63). Eunuchs serve as bodyguards to the king (Dio Chrysostom, *Orationes* 6.38.7) and as military officers, as in the case of Batis the Eunuch who resisted Alexander's armies at Gaza (*Arrian*, Ana. 2.25.4).

149. Harpocration (1 CE) recounts that a eunuch named Hermias had an adopted daughter (τὴν θετὴν αὐτοῦ θυγατέρα ἔδωκε τῷ φιλοσόφῳ). Hawkins gives examples of eunuchs who use the legal formula 'Be made my son' as evidence of eunuch adoption ('Eunuchs among the Hittites', pp. 220, 231).

150. 'Foot' or 'feet' is sometimes a euphemism for genitalia (e.g., Ruth 3.7; Isa. 7.20; and possibly Exod. 4.25).

also to human fertility: Soranus (*Gynaeciorum* 4.2.40.5) describes eunuchs as having 'unripe fruit' (τῶν ὤμων). Therefore, Matthew hints that the eunuch does not produce good fruit by *reproductive* means, but instead cuts off that which does not produce 'good fruit.' Such metaphorical self-mutilation (19.12) is sandwiched between two injunctions about the importance of and care for the 'children' (18.2–14; 19.13–14). Therefore, Matthew indicates that the fictive family members must prefer to become like children and to 'cut off,' to become like eunuchs, rather than fall into behaviors that might lead 'little ones' astray and therefore damage the community. Matthew's warning that looking upon a woman with lust is in itself adultery and a reason for plucking out the offending eye (5.27–29; cf. 18.9) indicates that Matthew targets sexual relations (except within marriage) as a primary behavior that leads people astray and poses a threat to the 'little ones' of the fictive family.

Jesus' saying to become like children (γένησθε ὡς τὰ παιδία) (18.3–4) precedes a long exhortation about taking care of 'these little ones' (τῶν μικρῶν τούτων) and welcoming them (δέχεται) (18.5–14). Matthew also refers to the missionaries as 'little ones' (τῶν μικρῶν τούτων), who should be welcomed (δέχεται) (10.40–42), and refers to recipients of good deeds (including being welcomed; συνάγετε) as 'of these my brothers, the least ones' (τούτων τῶν ἀδελφῶν μου τῶν ἐλαχίστων) (25.40).[151] Because Jesus enjoined the disciples to become like children (18.3–4), I interpret the 'little ones' as including those who have become fictive 'children' of the community as both missionaries and recipients of missionary work, thus inclusive of the entire fictive family and its potential new members.

4.8 *Fatherhood and Motherhood in Matthew*

As becoming a eunuch for the Kingdom of Heaven means taking on a non-procreative but adoptive and caretaking role, Matthew consistently reinforces the unimportance of biological fathers. Moreover, he replaces fathers with God the Father.[152] Moxnes observes that fathers are not included among those who follow Jesus: the lack goes against one of the most important relationship ties in the first century and reinforces the Matthean insistence that Jesus has no human father.[153]

Julian Sheffield demonstrates how the Matthean Jesus systematically subordinates the role of fathers, first by discounting the importance of

---

151. The 'little ones' is also a reference to the missionaries, who should be welcomed (in the same way the children are welcomed) (10.40–42)

152. Moxnes, 'What is Family', pp. 34–35; J. Sheffield, 'The Father in the Gospel of Matthew', pp. 52–69.

153. Moxnes, 'What is Family,' pp. 34–35.

ancestral fathers: 'Do not presume to say among yourselves, "The father we have [is] Abraham," for I tell you, God is able out of these stones to raise up children for Abraham"' (3.9); and Jesus says that fathers of the scribes and Pharisees are murderers (23.31).[154] Jesus instructs his followers: 'call no one on earth your father, for you have one Father, the one in heaven' (23.9). He tells a would-be disciple that he cannot first bury his father (8.21–22). James and John act out this injunction when they abandon their father to follow Jesus (4.21–22).[155] In the formation of Jesus' fictive family, Matthew replaces biological fathers with the Father in heaven when he does not include 'fathers' in the fictive family: 'Whoever does the will of my *Father* in heaven is my *brother, sister*, and *mother*' (12.50). He replaces genealogical fatherhood with adoptive fatherhood by tracing the genealogy of Jesus through Joseph, a man who did not sire him (1.1–17).

Matthew depicts biological fathers as sometimes cruel (Herod, father of Archelaus [2.22] and of Herod Antipas [14.1], slaughters children [2.16]), or inadequate: for example, Jesus praises 'Simon *son of Jonah*' (Σίμων Βαριωνᾶ) for recognizing he is the Christ, but immediately indicates that 'flesh and blood' (σὰρξ καὶ αἷμα) did not reveal this to Simon, but the Father in heaven, and then renames him 'Peter' (σὺ εἶ Πέτρος). Thus, Jesus removes not only the blood father's authority and influence, but even the name Simon's father gave him (16.17). By naming Simon Peter, Jesus extracts him from his relationship to his father Jonah and adopts him into the fictive family, just as Joseph's naming Jesus made him a member of his family (1.25).

Where Matthew does mention men *acting* as fathers and caring for children, he avoids identifying them specifically as 'father.'[156] Matthew thus separates the fatherly role of caretaker from that of progenitor. For example, Joseph cares for Mary and the infant Jesus (1.18–21, 24–25; 2.13–15; 19–23), but Matthew takes pains to show that Joseph is not Jesus' biological father (1.18–20, 25). Matthew reinforces this depiction of Joseph's non-progenitive relationship to Jesus when the crowd poses an ironic question upon Jesus' return to his hometown. When they ask, 'Is

---

154. Sheffield, 'The Father in the Gospel of Matthew,' p. 59. Sheffield argues that the Pharisees are 'criminally irresponsible fathers' because they represent the people who say, 'His blood be on us and upon our children' (27.25). However, as Sheffield herself concedes, this text nowhere mentions the Pharisees. Matthew says that the chief priests and elders persuade the crowd to choose Barabbas and let Jesus be killed (25.20), but they do not have anything to do with the people's condemning statement.

155. Sheffield ('The Father in the Gospel of Matthew', pp. 60–63) notes that they are called the 'sons of Zebedee' only when they act inappropriately toward the fictive family (e.g., 20.20–28).

156. Sheffield, 'The Father in the Gospel of Matthew', p. 64.

this not the carpenter's son?' (13.55), the audience, of course, knows that Jesus is *not* the carpenter's (biological) son.[157]

Men seek healing for children (9.18–26; 17.14–15) but are not called 'father' (8.5–13); they act as fathers (as did Joseph) without receiving the designation. For example, the centurion who seeks a cure for his παῖς, which is sometimes translated as 'servant' (so, the NRSV), but also means 'child' (8.5–13), is not called 'father.'[158] Men who model fatherly responsibility know how to give good things to their children (υἱοί), as does the heavenly Father (7.9–10), but Matthew leaves the specific title of 'father' to the Father in Heaven alone.[159] And, the heavenly Father, even more than earthly fathers, gives good things to those who ask him (7.11; cf. 6.7, 25–32).

In the midst of a systematic demotion of earthly fathers, Matthew maintains the role of mother in the fictive family, with certain limitations. There is no 'heavenly mother' to whom earthly mothers need to defer, but Matthew does give clues to the role of earthly mothers. Mary is frequently designated as Jesus' mother; the role is so important that it is used even when a personal pronoun would suffice (2.11, 13, 14, 20, 21). Moreover, Matthew includes four mothers in addition to Mary in Jesus' genealogy (1.1–16). Matthew depicts a Canaanite woman's persistence in seeking healing for her child (15.21–28), although she is not designated as 'mother' (like the centurion who acted as father but was not called 'father'). This mother models a way in which the community ought to be zealous for the welfare of the 'children' of the fictive family, even those who have been considered to be outsiders.

As he does with biological fatherhood, Matthew subordinates biological motherhood to fictive parenthood in the Kingdom of Heaven. On the one hand, Mary is named several times as Jesus' biological mother, but on the other hand, her pregnancy is highly unusual (1.18–20). She is apparently not pregnant by sexual relations with a human male but is mysteriously with child by the Holy Spirit, and her pregnancy is the means by which 'the beginning/origin (γένεσις) of Jesus the Messiah took place' (1.18). Γένεσις echoes the title of the first book of the Greek Old Testament, where 'in the beginning, *God* created.'

Matthew subordinates Mary's role of biological motherhood to that of

---

157. Harrington, *Matthew*, p. 192; Senior, *Matthew*, pp. 144–45; Boring, 'Matthew,' p. 298; Davies and Allison, *Matthew*, II, pp. 364–65; Keener, *Matthew*, p. 370; Patte, *Matthew*, p. 182; Long, *Matthew*, pp. 143–44; Hare, *Matthew*, p. 146; Gundry, *Matthew*, p. 250; Schweizer, *Matthew*, p. 295; Albright and Mann, *Matthew*, p. 162; Luz, *Matthew*, II, pp. 225–26; Beare, *Matthew*, p. 285; Schnackenburg, *Matthew*, p. 120.

158. παῖς is the term for 'child' that Matthew uses to exhort the disciples to become like children (18.2–3).

159. Sheffield, 'The Father in the Gospel of Matthew', p. 64.

the *adoptive* parent, Joseph.[160] In stark contrast to Luke's version, with the angel's appearance to Mary and her song of praise (Lk. 1.26 – 2.51), it is not Mary but Joseph who is the main subject of the Matthean birth narrative. An angel appears to Joseph (1.20), not to Mary (cf. Lk. 1. 26–56). She has no function in the narrative beyond the fact that she 'was found to be having in the womb' (εὑρέθη ἐν γαστρὶ ἔχουσα). The passive voice reinforces the sense that all is done to her or for her on behalf of the infant Messiah. She gives birth (ἔτεκεν υἱόν) (2.25), but her role, unlike in Luke, remains passive (there is no wrapping the infant in a cloth, placing him in a manger, or treasuring the events in her heart [cf. Lk. 2.6, 19, 51]). Matthew does not tell the reader what the biological mother does after her child's birth because for Matthew, biological motherhood is problematic. Mary remains in narrative silence under the fictive father and bridegroom as he protectively shuttles his family from Bethlehem to Egypt and then to Nazareth to escape those that would kill the infant Jesus.

Mary's next appearance in the gospel is literally 'outside' (ἔξω) the house, while the group of disciples is within.[161] Jesus does not acknowledge her. Moreover, he takes her title of 'mother' and gives it to his disciples (12.46–50).[162] Mary's neighbors remember that she is Jesus' mother (13.55), but being his mother in this context is a dubious relationship, because they are offended by him. That she does not reappear in the gospel is not surprising, since Jesus finds biological mothers to be obstacles to faithful discipleship: 'Whoever loves father or *mother* more than me is not worthy of me' (10.37), and 'Whoever leaves … father and *mother* … for the sake of my name will receive a hundredfold, and will inherit eternal life' (19.29). Here, to receive one hundredfold means one hundredfold members of the bridegroom's fictive family.[163]

The Matthean Jesus shows that biological motherhood is overshadowed by the kingdom: 'Among those born of women no one has arisen greater than John the Baptist; yet the least of the Kingdom of Heaven is greater than he' (11.11). Matthew depicts Herodias as a 'bad' mother who involves her daughter in the gruesome death of John (14. 8–11).[164] A mother weeps for children she is unable to save (2.18), and mothers are mentioned specifically among those who will suffer greatly in the last days ('woe to those who are pregnant and nursing infants in those days' [24.19]).

---

160. Osiek and Balch, *Families in the New Testament World*, p. 135.

161. Crosby, *House of Disciples*, p. 58.

162. Jerome Neyrey explains the significance of Jesus' action as a deliberate separation of 'insiders' from 'outsiders,' as Jesus' biological family is literally standing outside, while the disciples are gathered inside around him. See Neyrey, *Honor and Shame*, p. 53.

163. Sheffield, 'The Father in the Gospel of Matthew,' pp. 65–67.

164. Osiek and Balch, *Families in the New Testament World*, p. 136.

When Matthew specifically mentions a parent with child, the children are portrayed as medical liabilities: the children are sick (8.5–8), demon-possessed (15.22), epileptic (17.14), or dead (9.18). In other scenes where children appear and their health is not an issue, no parents appear: 'children were brought to him' (προσηνέχθησαν αὐτῷ παιδία) to be blessed (προσεύξηται). But the passive construction makes it unclear who was bringing them; readers assume it was their mothers or fathers, but Matthew leaves the them out of the picture. When Matthew depicts the children calling to one another in the marketplace (11.16) or crying out 'Hosanna' in the temple (21.15), he does not mention accompanying parents.

While biological mothers are honored by their inclusion in the genealogy, their stories show that they are subject to violence and death. Tamar is in danger of being burned to death when she is found to be pregnant (Gen. 38.12–26). Rahab risks her life to betray her city to the Israelites (Josh. 2.1–24, esp. vv. 18–22; cf. 6.22–25). Until Boaz steps in, Ruth is homeless and in danger of being molested (literally 'grasped' [ἄψασθαί] or 'meddled with, touched, struck' [נגע]) by young men (παιδάριοι) while she gleans in the fields (Ruth 2.9). Bathsheba's husband is killed to cover her and David's adultery (2 Sam. 11.14–26), and the Lord causes their child to die (2 Sam. 12.14–19). Mary faces being divorced (until the angel instructs Joseph); then she must flee those who would kill her child.

Matthew offers an example of a woman who *exchanges* her role as biological mother to that of 'fictive' mother. The mother of the sons of Zebedee first comes to Jesus as a biological mother attempting to gain special favor for her sons in the kingdom (20.20–21; cf. Bathsheba petitioning King David to make her son Solomon his successor [1 Kgs 15–21]).[165] But this mother does not know what she is asking; it is the Father, not the son, who will decide who sits at his right and left, and moreover, the way to the kingdom involves drinking the cup that Jesus drinks (20.20–22; cf. 20.18–19). This birth mother, through her misunderstanding of the kingdom, manages only to draw the other disciples' ire against her sons (20.24). However, she is one of the women who stood vigil at the crucifixion (27.56), a detail that shows that she did, in the end, have some understanding of the 'cup' that Jesus had to drink and was part of the faithful group at the cross. Her role as biological mother thus figuratively ends as she stands without her biological sons but

165. Other examples of mothers who attempt to elevate a son or most-favored son into becoming the heir apparent include Sarah and Rebekah. Sarah drives her son's rival and his mother into the wilderness (Gen. 21.8–14); Rebekah maneuvers her favorite son Jacob into position to receive his older brother's blessing (Gen. 27.5–17).

near to Jesus, and her role as a mother in the *fictive* family of Jesus comes to the fore.

4.9 *'The Slaughter of the Innocents' and Violence in the Matthean Family*

A violent aspect of the birth of Jesus and the establishment of his fictive family is the episode of Herod's slaughter of the children of Bethlehem (2.13–18).[166] Matthew models Jesus' nativity on that of Moses, a savior whose story involves the deaths of many children (Exod. 1.22–2.5; 11.1–10; 12.29–32).[167] As Moses is rescued from a brutal king (Exod. 1.22–2.5) and later rescues his people (Exod. 12.29–32), so also Jesus is rescued from a brutal king and later saves his people from their sins (cf. Mt. 1.21).[168] This story has horrifying connotations for what sort of fictive family the gospel of Matthew describes: a family in which some children die so that others may be included in the new family.[169] The 'slaughter of the

---

166. Carter, *Matthew and the Margins*, p. 89.

167. Discussions of the thematic connection between Pharaoh's decree to kill the infant boys (Exod. 1.22–2.5) and Herod's slaughter of the children of Bethlehem in Mt. 2.13–19 are found in Allison, *The New Moses*, pp. 140–65; Davies and Allison, *Matthew*, I, pp. 260–65; Keener, *Matthew*, pp. 107–109; Harrington, *Matthew*, p. 49; Kirsch, *Moses: A Life*, pp. 48–49; Boring, 'Matthew', pp. 146–47. Gundry, *Matthew*, p.33; Donald Senior, 'Matthew 2.2–12', *Int* 46 (1992), pp. 395–98 (esp. p. 398); Luz, *Matthew*, I, pp. 144–45; Schweizer, *Matthew*, pp. 42–43. Cf. Davis, *Israel in Egypt*, p. 96, 106, 110; Richard T. France, 'The Massacre of the Innocents – Fact or Fiction?', in E.A. Livingstone (ed.), *Studia Biblica 1978* (JSNTSup, 2; Sheffield: Sheffield Academic Press, 1980), pp. 83–94; Richard T. France, 'Herod and the Children of Bethlehem', *NovT* 21 (1979), pp. 98–120 (esp. pp. 105–106, 108–10); G.M. Soares Prabhu, *The Formula Quotations in the Infancy Narrative of Matthew* (Rome: Biblical Institute Press, 1976), pp. 6–10.

168. Keener, *Matthew*, pp. 106–108; Boring, 'Matthew', p. 149; Patte, *Matthew*, pp. 36–37. With the parallel to Moses, Matthew sets up a fulfillment citation: 'Out of Egypt I have called my son' (Mt. 2.15; cf. Hos. 11.1 and Exod. 4.22). Richard J. Erickson, 'Divine Injustice? Matthew's Narrative Strategy and the Slaughter of the Innocents (Matthew 2.13–23)', *JSNT* 64 (1996), pp. 5–27 (esp. pp. 13–15). Erickson also notes the similarity between Joseph's receiving a dream instructing him that the men who seek the life of the child are dead and Moses' receiving information that the men seeking his life are dead. Moses takes his wife and children back to Egypt (Exod. 4.20), while Matthew takes his wife and child from Egypt back to Israel (Mt. 2.21). Erickson recognizes that here, Moses is being compared to Joseph, not Jesus, but does not think this spoils the typology ('Divine Injustice', p. 16).

169. Several interpreters conclude that even if there is no outside historical evidence of the Matthean 'slaughter of the innocents,' given Herod's reputation, it certainly could have happened. Josephus tells us that Herod became increasingly paranoid in the last four years of his reign and eliminated anyone he suspected of plotting against him, including his own wife and children (*Antiquities* 15.213–36; 16.356–94; 17.32–82; 164–67). See Keener (*Matthew*, pp. 110–11); France ('The Massacre of the Innocents', pp. 89–90, and 'Herod and the Children', pp. 114–15); Davies and Allison (*Matthew*, I, pp. 264–65).

innocents' informs the future bridegroom's identity as Moses-like savior but also foreshadows the disruption of families (e.g., 10.34–38; 12.46–50; 19.29). Moreover, Jesus himself dies as an innocent son (cf. Mt. 26.24, 39–42, 53–54, 59–60; 27.21, 24); after his death (and resurrection), the fictive family expands into all the world as new members are 'born' by baptism and obedience to the Father's will (28.19–20).

While Matthew blames the murders of the children on Herod, behind the divine rescue of one child lurks the question of divine abandonment of the other children. As George Nicol writes of the Mt. 2.1–18, 'what blemishes the story is the way this child escapes. This is no chance escape, but God intervenes and rescues this one child while leaving the others to perish. And we, so far removed from the event and story alike, can be struck by the horror of this most scandalous intervention ... why should God intervene to save this one child, while abandoning the others to the fate brought upon them by his birth?'[170] Richard Erickson suggests that the infant Jesus' escape is not only offensive but cowardly: 'How could a truly good God permit the Innocents to suffer because of the birth of his Son, whom he hustles off to safety, leaving the others to die? Could he not have spared them all?'[171]

Interpreters deal with this issue of theodicy in several ways. Eugene Boring asks 'what kind of deity warns only one family of impending disaster and allows other innocent children to be killed?' His solution – to categorize the story as 'confessional,' that is, not an account of a real historical event but an expression of the Church's faith that God was active in providing and preserving the Messiah[172] – is not helpful, because it does not deal with God's violence even on a figurative level. Eduard Schweizer, Raymond E. Brown, and Ulrich Luz argue that Matthew does not implicate the deity in the murder of the children because the evangelist carefully uses the passive voice ('in this way was fulfilled what the prophet Jeremiah had said') to explain the event.[173] According to Schweizer, Matthew 'escapes any suggestion that God willed the slaughter of the infants.' Luz and Brown point out that the fulfillment citation deliberately avoids the words found in other fulfillment citations ('in order that the scripture is fulfilled'), so that the passage 'does not speak of the direct responsibility of God for the death of the children.'[174] Brown concedes

---

170. George G. Nicol, 'The Slaughter of the Innocents', *ExpTim* 97 (1985), pp. 55–56 (55).

171. Erickson, 'Divine Injustice', p. 18. Erickson observes that Moses flees for his life in cowardice after killing an Egyptian (in response to 'his first sense of the call to deliver his own people') and so deserts his people to suffer more years of bondage (p. 18).

172. Boring, 'Matthew', p. 149.

173. Schweizer, *Matthew*, p. 41; Raymond E. Brown, *The Birth of the Messiah* (New York: Doubleday, rev. edn, 1993), p. 205; Luz, *Matthew*, p. 147.

174. Luz, *Matthew*, p. 147.

that the passive construction 'probably reflects Matthew's reluctance to attribute to God an evil purpose.'[175] Matthew's use of the passive may be an attempt not to implicate the deity, but Matthew's portrayal of God's activity behind the *other* events in the nativity story – such as Mary's pregnancy, angel visitations to Joseph and the magi – belies God's passivity.

Craig Keener appeals to a theology of unknowable divine intent: we cannot explain the deity's actions. Keener observes that Matthew does not *attempt* to portray a perfect world in which no children die. Instead, Matthew shows that God sometimes intervenes, but not always. The story laments the injustice and brutality of the world, then promises a new king who will restore justice.[176] But the Matthean Jesus never gets around to restoring justice. He is a bridegroom who never weds, and he is a judge who promises vindication of the righteous (25.31–46) but has not brought it about. Meanwhile, the infants of Bethlehem are still dead and remain unvindicated, and Rachel still weeps and will not be comforted.

Daniel Patte offers an explanation that qualifies God's activity in the world: 'God does not interfere with the natural course of events.'[177] For Patte, divine power is not expressed directly, but manifests itself through history: ultimately it is God and not Herod who has power over life and death. While I agree that the story validates the eventual triumph of God's power, I cannot agree that the *Matthean* author portrays God as non-active in the natural course of events, because the birth narrative is all about God's intervention in the events, from Jesus' birth to the flight to Egypt.

Davies and Allison suggest that Matthew's use of τότε (2.17) links this story to Judas' betrayal and hanging (27.9). Just as Judas, not God, is responsible for his demise, Matthew signals that God is not responsible for the slaughter of the innocents, but that those who seek to do away with Jesus bring violence on themselves.[178] The flaw in this argument is that it was not the children that sought to kill Jesus, but Herod; these children did not bring down violence on themselves. This interpretation blames the innocent for their suffering and begs the question: if the children don't bring violence on themselves, who does? Davies and Allison's linking the slaughter of the innocents to the events of the passion narrative, plus their suggestion that those who would kill Jesus bring violence on themselves, immediately reminds me of Matthew's infamous

---

175. Brown, *Birth*, p. 205.
176. Keener, *Matthew*, p. 110.
177. Patte, *Matthew*, pp. 36–37. Patte notes that Matthew announces Herod's death three times (2.15, 19, 20) in order to reinforce God's greater but non-aggressive power. Donald Senior agrees that Matthew contrasts Herod's use of violent power against Jesus' 'life-giving' power ('Matthew 2.2–12', p. 398).
178. Davies and Allison, *Matthew*, I, p. 266.

line: 'His blood be on us and on our children' (27.25). I resist this implication. In the end, there is no satisfactory explanation for the deaths of these children who do not intend to harm the infant Jesus and who do not yet – and indeed cannot – accept or reject him as Messiah. What the story does support is the Matthean fictive family model: biological parents are powerless to protect their children, and biological children die. Fictive parents, however, are able to rescue children to form a fictive family.

Matthew contrasts the violent King Herod with Jesus, the rightful King of the Jews, and he contrasts the bad father Herod with the good divine Father. And yet the contrast is not as distinct as Matthew might have the reader believe, because just like Herod, the divine king and Father of the bridegroom cuts off or throws into the fire those who do not accept his reign (e.g., 22.7; 24.51). The only 'father' in the nativity story who shows no violent intent is Joseph, the adoptive father, whose only concern is to escape the powers that be and keep his family safe. But not even Joseph represents a father figure who consistently acts responsibly, because he does not warn any other families of the impending slaughter. And thus Matthew unwittingly makes the adoptive father-hero Joseph complicit in the massacre. The divine father and fictive father both act to protect their 'sons,' but in not sharing news of the impending massacre with others outside their small fictive family enclave, they both allow other children to die.

For Matthew, the infant Jesus escapes evil on *this* occasion in order to fulfill his role as savior of all on a *later* occasion. In Matthew's reasoning, because Jesus lived to adulthood, he was able to 'save his people from their sins' (1.21). Wendy Zoba writes that the 'gospel logic asserts that in saving the One, God *did* save them all,'[179] and Richard Erickson asserts, 'The evader evades only long enough that he may grow up and bear it all on behalf of his people.'[180] Not clear is why the sacrifice of the children must be part of this salvation.

The sacrifice of a few (or one) for the eventual good of the many is a theology of sacrificial atonement that accepts violence as a necessary part of God's salvific plan: Jesus gives his life as a ransom for many (20.28). This theology accepts the deaths of the children as a necessary sacrifice for the eventual salvation of many. The early Church regarded these children as *participants* in this sacrifice and salvation: they are martyrs who shared the suffering of Christ.[181] Because of this theology, violence becomes a necessary part of the life of the Matthean bridegroom's life and the

179. Wendy Murray Zoba, 'How Shall We Reconcile the Glorious Birth of the Savior with the Bloody Deaths of the Boys of Bethlehem?', *CToday* 41 (Dec. 8, 1997), pp. 24–26.
180. Erickson, 'Divine Injustice?', p. 24.
181. Their feast day (the Feast of the Holy Innocents) is celebrated Dec. 28 (Luz, *Matthew*, I, pp. 147–48).

foundation of his fictive family. Therefore, in Matthew, there is an integral irony that the bridegroom dies so that others may live, but the bridegroom (and his community) lives because others die.

4.10 *Conclusion*

Matthew establishes a 'fictive family' that replaces the traditional 'οἶκος.' The fictive family is not anomalous in this period, as it can be compared to voluntary associations, but adds one more layer onto the typical voluntary association by the gospel's concern for liminality: one leaves the family and joins the Church, unlike most other associations, where one can be a member of the association as well as of the family.

Finally, in antiquity, while the voluntary society could be a place of support, it could also be a site of persecution; just so, the fictive family of Jesus could be a place of acceptance and support, but affiliation with this fictive family could, and did, lead to conflict and danger.

In this family there are mothers and brothers and sisters, but no fathers; Jesus disrupts the household with *paterfamilias*. Matthew, as Julian Sheffield shows, marginalizes the biological fathers in the text: fathers are not included in the depiction of the fictive family of mothers, brothers, and sisters, and Jesus tells disciples to call no one on earth their father. Mothers, too, are marginalized. Mothers who seek the advancement of their sons are silenced, and even Mary is replaced as Jesus' mother. The least in the Kingdom of Heaven are those 'born of women,' and those who are pregnant and nursing will suffer most greatly when catastrophic events occur. These disruptions of biological family ties can be seen as part of the Matthean 'new Moses' motif.

The community members are best described as 'sons of the bridal chamber,' relationships perhaps restricted to men, for Matthew's is no egalitarian community. Male and female roles remain intact, and while women are prominently featured in Matthew – and while the *paterfamlias* has been replaced – they still lack the more intimate role enjoyed by the inner circle of the Twelve or of the 'sons of the bridal chamber.' Just as the Matthean bridegroom has no bride, there are no 'daughters of the bridal chamber' either.

The fictive family is established by Joseph when he adopts Jesus and engrafts him onto his genealogy. Joseph models the new kinship group by agreeing to raise and protect a child he did not father. The genealogy foreshadows the break in the traditional family lineage by the inclusion of the four women. But the adoptive family is founded in the context of violence: Herod murders the children of Bethlehem when he seeks to kill the newborn Jesus. The problem of theodicy arises when it appears that God, who orchestrates all the other events in the birth narrative, is also responsible for the deaths of the children because the warning came to only one father; and Joseph, who received the warning, failed to notify other families of impending doom.

Violence is part of the fictive family, in its establishment, and in its maintenance. I reluctantly conclude that the fictive family is a dangerous affiliation. Those who affiliate with Jesus, who join his new voluntary family, are themselves likely victims of persecution: Joseph and Mary have to flee, and the 'brothers, sisters, and mothers' are expected to suffer and even to die for Jesus' sake (10.32–39; 20.22–28; 24.9–21).

Chapter 5

THE ABSENT BRIDE, ANGELS, AND ANDROGYNY:
SEXUALITY IN MATTHEW

Ἐρρέθη δέ, Ὃς ἂν ἀπολύσῃ τὴν γυναῖκα αὐτοῦ, δότω αὐτῇ ἀποστάσιον. ἐγὼ δὲ λέγω ὑμῖν ὅτι πᾶς ὁ ἀπολύων τὴν γυναῖκα αὐτοῦ παρεκτὸς λόγου πορνείας ποιεῖ αὐτὴν μοιχευθῆναι, καὶ ὃς ἐὰν ἀπολελυμένην γαμήσῃ, μοιχᾶται.

It was also said, 'Whoever divorces his wife, let him give her a certificate of divorce.' But I say to you that anyone who divorces his wife, except for a deed of sexual immorality, causes her to commit adultery; and if the one divorced remarries, he commits adultery.' (5.31–32)

καὶ προσῆλθον αὐτῷ Φαρισαῖοι πειράζοντες αὐτὸν καὶ λέγοντες, Εἰ ἔχεστιν ἀνθρώπῳ ἀπολῦσαι τὴν γυναῖκα αὐτοῦ κατὰ πᾶσαν αἰτίαν; ὁ δὲ ἀποκριθεὶς εἶπεν, Οὐκ ἀνέγνωτε ὅτι ὁ κτίσας ἀπ᾽ ἀρχῆς ἄρσεν καὶ θῆλυ ἐποίησεν αὐτούς; καὶ εἶπεν, Ἕνεκα τούτου καταλείψει ἄνθρωπος τὸν πατέρα καὶ τὴν μητέρα καὶ κολληθήσεται τῇ γυναικὶ αὐτοῦ, καὶ ἔσονται οἱ δύο εἰς σάρκα μίαν. ὥστε οὐκέτι εἰσὶν δύο ἀλλὰ σὰρξ μία. ὃ οὖν ὁ θεὸς συνέζευξεν ἄνθρωπος μὴ χωριζέτω. λέγουσιν αὐτῷ, Τί οὖν Μωυσῆς ἐνετείλατο δοῦναι βιβλίον ἀποστασίου καὶ ἀπολῦσαι αὐτήν; λέγει αὐτοῖς ὅτι Μωυσῆς πρὸς τὴν σκληροκαρδίαν ὑμῶν ἐπέτρεψεν ὑμῖν ἀπολῦσαι τὰς γυναῖκας ὑμῶν, ἀπ᾽ ἀρχῆς δὲ οὐ γέγονεν οὕτως. λέγω δὲ ὑμῖν ὅτι ὃς ἂν ἀπολύσῃ τὴν γυναῖκα αὐτοῦ μὴ ἐπὶ πορνείᾳ καὶ γαμήσῃ ἄλλην μοιχᾶται.

And Pharisees came to him, testing him and saying, 'Is it permitted for a man to divorce his wife for any cause?' And answering, he said, 'Have you not read that the one who created from the beginning made them male and female?' He said, 'For this reason a man leaves father and mother and is joined to his wife, and they become, the two, one flesh. So no longer are they two, but one flesh. Therefore what God joined together, let no man separate.' They said to him, 'Why then did Moses command to give a written statement of divorce and to divorce her?' He said to them, 'Because Moses – for the sake of your hard heart – allowed you to divorce your wives, but from the beginning it was not so. And I say to you, that whoever divorces his wife, except for sexual immorality, and marries another commits adultery. (19.3–9)

ἐν γὰρ τῇ ἀναστάσει οὔτε γαμοῦσιν οὔτε γαμίζονται, ἀλλ᾽ ὡς ἄγγελοι ἐν τῷ οὐρανῷ εἰσιν.

For in the resurrection neither do they marry, nor are they given in marriage, but they are like angels in heaven (22.30).

5.1 *Introduction*

Given the previous chapter's review of the non-procreative fictive family, it is a strong possibility that the Matthean bridegroom discourages sexual activity, even in marriage, because Matthew does not want people to have children. Instead, they are to become *like* children, that is, incapable of procreation.[1] The Matthean Jesus is a bridegroom who never marries, never enters the bridal chamber, and does not procreate. He represents Matthew's ideal, that it is better to become a 'eunuch for the kingdom' than marry (19.10–12) and that there will be no marriage in the resurrection (22.30). While the Matthean bridegroom does not forbid marriage – indeed, he exhorts his community against divorce (5.31–32; 19.3–9) – his own celibacy and promotion of a fictive family over a biological family suggest he prefers celibacy even within marriage.

5.2 *The Absent Bride*

The Matthean bridegroom has no bride. A common explanation for this striking omission is that Matthew drew upon the tradition of Israel as bride and so considered the feminine Church (ἐκκλησία) as bride to Jesus the bridegroom. Matthew would not be unique in associating the Church with the bride: Paul wanted to present his nascent Christian community as a 'bride' for Christ (2 Cor. 11.2; cf. Eph. 5.23–25), and later tradition would make similar claims (e.g., Rev. 22.1–9; *Odes of Solomon* 3, 42;

---

1.   The Matthean logia about becoming like children are discussed in Ch. 4. *G. Thomas* uses a common tradition about becoming like children (*G. Thom.* 21–22; cf. Mt. 18.2–3; 19.13–15) but adds the notion of unashamed nakedness. Like the first couple in the Garden of Eden, those who wish to enter the kingdom must become like innocent children unaware of their nakedness; removal of garments is to ascend to a spiritual level. S.D. Fohr (*Adam and Eve: The Spiritual Symbolism of Genesis and Exodus* [New York: University Press of America, 1986], p. 125) argues that children lose their primordial perfection at puberty when they gain sexual awareness.

Tertullian, *De Monog.* 5, *De Fuga* 15; Origen, *Commentary on St. Matthew*, Bk. 14; cf. also *Shepherd of Hermas,* Vision 3; 2 Clement 15).[2]

Yet there are reasons to question that the community is 'bride' in the first gospel. The Matthean Jesus states it is better not to marry but to become eunuchs for the sake of the kingdom (19.10–12), and that there is no marriage in the resurrection (22.30): these clues indicate that for Matthew, the higher calling is virginity or celibacy.[3] Further, that Matthew forbids divorce does not mean the evangelist encourages marriage *per se*; rather, he wants married couples to be models of the 'one flesh' of Adam and Eve (Gen. 2.24), that is, members of a new family, or better, to be 'like the angels' (22.30).

The bridegroom's teachings concerning marriage and divorce impact the lives of disciples in the present (5.31–32; 19.3–12) as well as pointing to the resurrection (22.23–30). The Matthean bridegroom indicates his expectation that there will be no marriage and sexuality in the resurrection by strictly defining the sexual ethics of his community in the present. For the bridegroom, marriage belongs to the present age. He compares the current age to the time of Noah: 'For as the days of Noah were, so will be the coming of the Son of Man. For as in those days before the flood they were eating and drinking, marrying and giving in marriage, until the day Noah entered the ark, and they knew nothing until the flood came and swept them all away, so too will be the coming of the Son of Man' (24. 36–39; cf. Gen. 6.1–7.24). The Matthean bridegroom thus urges that it is better not to marry (24.36–39; cf. 19.3–12; 22.30) but to look forward instead to eating and drinking at the eschatological banquet (8.11).

The Matthean bridegroom disrupts the institutions of marriage and family in a culture that valued these institutions highly. For example, Ben Sira 36.30 reads, 'Where there is no fence, the property will be plundered; and where there is no wife, a man will become a fugitive.'[4] Although it is always problematic to read Talmudic texts back into Second Temple Judaism, we do know that the rabbinic tradition regarded marriage as both divine command and blessing. Within early Judaism itself, we have

---

2. The allegory of the Church or individual Christian as 'Bride of Christ' was developed through the Middle Ages and into the Reformation. For discussion, see Claude Chavasse, *The Bride of Christ* (London: Faber and Faber, 1940), pp. 196–97.

3. Davies and Allison concede that this interpretation is implicit in Matthew, even though they interpret the thrust of the marriage and divorce teachings to point toward monogamy, not celibacy (*Matthew*, III, pp. 4–27). Matthew certainly promotes monogamy, with his prohibition of divorce and remarriage, but he is also interested in elevating the fictive family over the biological family (thus precluding the need for marriage and sex) and looking toward the non-married perfection of the angels. Thus, I think Matthew points to celibacy, even within marriage.

4. For additional citations, see T. Ilan, *Jewish Women in Greco-Roman Palestine* (Peabody, MA: Hendrickson, 1996), p. 57.

marriage contracts (*Ketubot*) as well as divorce documents (*Gittin*).[5] Among a number of extant Aramaic and Greek marriage contracts from the late first century and early second century CE is a dowry settlement (dated 94 CE) belonging to Babatha, and a marriage contract for Salome Komaise that states the amount to which she is entitled in case of divorce.[6] While probably not a Jewish marriage contract, the following first-century document (*BGU* 4.1050) from Alexandria for a couple named Isodora and Dionysios may well provide a model for what Jews in the Diaspora, or those of Jewish background in Matthew's community, might have utilized. This is because Jews under Roman rule could avail themselves of Roman as well as Jewish courts. This particular text includes the amount of dowry and conditions under which the marriage contract would be violated: the husband would have to pay back one and a half times the dowry if he were to become 'wanton' (ὑβρίζειν), throw out his wife, or bring in another woman. For the wife's part, she must not sleep away from him (ἀπόκοιτον), be absent for a day from the house without her husband's knowledge nor be together with another man. The couple and/or their families agree to the contract with the ending phrase 'we consent' (ἀξιοῦμεν).[7]

Both Jews and Greeks valued marriage. The following texts are a few examples of many. According to *b. Yeb.* 61b, an unmarried man was believed to have no happiness, blessing, or good.[8] Plutarch (*Advice to the*

---

5. See Ilan, *Jewish Women*, passim.

6. A.-J. Levine, 'Matthew', p. 255. See Anthony J. Saldarini, 'Babatha's Story: Personal Archive Offers a Glimpse of Ancient Jewish Life', *BAR* 24 (1998), pp. 29–37, 72–74, and Tal Ilan, 'How Women Differed', *BAR* 24 (1998), pp. 38–39. For discussion of marriage contracts, see also Leonie J. Archer, *Her Price Is Beyond Rubies: The Jewish Woman in Graeco-Roman Palestine* (JSOTSup 60; Sheffield: JSOT Press, 1990), pp. 171–88; Mordechai A. Friedman, *Jewish Marriage in Palestine: A Cairo Geniza Study*, vol. 1: *The Ketuba Traditions of Eretz Israel* (Tel-Aviv/New York: The Jewish Theological Seminary of America, 1980); and John J. Collins, 'Marriage, Divorce, and Family in Second Temple Judaism', in Leo G. Perdue, Joseph Blenkinsopp, John J. Collins, and Carol Meyers (eds.), *Families in Ancient Israel* (Family, Religion, and Culture series; Louisville: Westminster/John Knox Press, 1997), pp. 104–62, esp. 111–12.

7. Text from *Perseus* website (www.perseus.tufts.edu/), translation mine. Similar details are recorded in two second-century Greek marriage contracts from Egypt in Mary R. Lefkowitz and Maureen B. Fant, *Women's Life in Greece and Rome: A Sourcebook in Translation* (Baltimore: Johns Hopkins University Press, 2nd edn, 1992), pp. 149–50. Marriage contracts are discussed in Ilan, *Jewish Women in Greco-Roman Palestine*, pp. 89–94; J.J. Collins, 'Marriage, Divorce', pp. 104–62 [see pp. 107–109]; Saldarini, 'Babatha's Story', pp. 29–37, 72–74, Ilan, 'How Women Differed', pp. 38–39, 68; and Archer, *Her Price is Beyond Rubies*, pp. 171–88; and Friedman, *Jewish Marriage in Palestine*, S. Treggiari, *Roman Marriage*, pp. 125–60; Mireille Corbier, 'Divorce and Adoption as Roman Familial Strategies', in Beryl Rawson (ed), *Marriage, Divorce, and Children in Ancient Rome* (Oxford: Clarendon Press, 1996), pp. 47–78, esp. p. 52.

8. Satlow discusses the myriad rabbinic writings on the purpose and good of marriage in *Jewish Marriage*, pp. 4–41.

Bride and Groom) discussed the importance of marriage: 'In philosophy too there are many fine subjects of discourse, but none more important than this discourse of marriage, whereby philosophy charms those who come together to share their lives, and makes them gentle and amenable to each other.'[9] Inscriptions on Roman tombstones extol the long-married couple; the *univera* or 'once-married' woman represented the highest standard of womanhood.[10] The orator Cicero (*Pro Cluentio*, 175) uses lofty terms to idealize the 'chaste and legal right of marriage.'[11] A bridegroom who never becomes a husband obviously undermines these cultural expectations.

The bridegroom's not having a bride also disrupts the family's role in its own continuity: the family has failed to perform the expected role of arranging the marriage.[12] Already in biblical tradition, Abraham arranges for a bride for Isaac (Gen. 24.3–4); Isaac arranges for a bride for Jacob (Gen. 28.1–2); Samson's father and mother arrange a marriage for Samson (Judg. 14.1–10). This value continues in Ben Sira 7.33: 'Do you have sons? Discipline them, and marry them off to women while they are still youths.' Jesus' having no father (if Joseph has died) is not an excuse for the failure of the family to find him a bride; a friend of the family, female head of household, or other agent could arrange a marriage for him.[13] (Or, he could have found his own bride, and so fulfilled familial expectations.) In the fictive family created by the bridegroom, God the Father does not find

---

9. Translated by Donald Russell in Sarah B. Pomeroy (ed.), *Plutarch's Advice to the Bride and Groom and A Consolation to His Wife* (Oxford: Oxford University Press, 1999), p. 5. See also Lisette Goessler, 'Advice to the Bride and Groom: Plutarch Gives a Detailed Account of His Views on Marriage', in Pomeroy, *Plutarch's Advice*, pp. 97–115, esp. p. 110.

10. Treggiari, *Roman Marriage*, pp. 471–82. Treggiari argues that the seeming increase in the rate of divorce in the Augustan period can be explained by the unusually plentiful written sources about the political machinations of a statistically small group of elite families, but it does not necessarily represent the empire as a whole.

11. Cicero, *Pro Cluentio Oratorio*, as translated by Treggiari, *Roman Marriage*, p. 270.

12. For examples of parental roles in arranging marriages in Second Temple Judaism, see Ilan, *Jewish Women*, pp. 65–67.

13. Pharaoh gave Joseph Asenath as his wife (Gen. 41.45). According to the late first-century historian Arrian, Alexander acted as the head of family for his men by providing them with brides (*Anabasis of Alexander*, 7.4.4–7). Sometimes other family members, friends, or agents made the match: Phalaridis (second century CE) writes of a mother finding a bridegroom for her daughter (εὕρηται νυμφίον ἡ μήτηρ τῆς παιδός) (*Epistulae* 142.2.5). Rudolphus Hercher (ed.), *Epistolographi Graeci* (Paris: Institute Franciae Typographo, 1873), p. 454. Philo recounts the story of Sarah finding a second bride for her husband for the production of children (*Abr.* 250.1; *Cong.* 72.4). A rabbinic tale reveals that the mother of the bride-to-be could have a great deal of influence in the choice of bridegroom (*b. Qid* 45b). A servant negotiated the betrothal of Antony's daughter to Lepidus's son in 37 CE (Appian, *Bellum civile* 5.93). For detailed discussion and examples, see Treggiari, 'From Negotiation to Engagement', in *Roman Marriage*, pp. 125–60.

the Son a bride, because Jesus the bridegroom needs no bride and because there is no longer any need for brides and bridegrooms.

5.3 *Like the Angels: No Marriage in Heaven*

The Matthean bridegroom's ideal is that community members remain single because the resurrected 'are like angels in heaven' (ὡς ἄγγελοι ἐν τῷ οὐρανῷ εἰσιν), who neither marry nor are given in marriage' (22.30). Matthew treats the meaning of 'like the angels' as self-evident: they are not married and therefore celibate or virginal (22.30). According to Matthew angels belong to the realm of heaven (18.10), and their role is to serve as intermediaries between heaven and earth (Mt. 1.20, 24; 2.13, 19). Thus, in effect, the angels have a liminal role comparable to that of the fictive family of the Matthean community. To use the English idiom, both angels and the community might be regarded as indicators of 'heaven on earth.' The angels wait to minister to Jesus (4.11; 26.53), just as his disciples do. They participate in the last judgment (13.39; 16.27; 24.31; 25.31), just as his disciples will: 'Jesus said to them, "Amen, I tell you, at the renewal of all things, when the Son of Man is seated on the throne of his glory, you who have followed me will also sit on twelve thrones, judging the twelve tribes of Israel" '(19.28). They roll back the stone from the tomb and speak to the women seeking Jesus (28.2, 5); although there is no precise parallel for the disciples to this angelic role, Jesus' male and female followers nevertheless also proclaim the news of the resurrection.

Matthew had good cause to presume that references to angels would be self-evident, for they are mentioned frequently in both early Jewish and early Christian texts. Although discussions of angels do have individual emphases, we can nevertheless draw a composite picture. Angels sometimes take human form, but seem to have no physical needs: they do not eat or drink (Tob. 12.19; *Apoc. Ab.* 13.4; *Test. Ab.* 4.9–10; Josephus, *Ant.* 1.11.2 or 197; *1 Enoch* 17.1; 86.3).[14] Here of course we have a distinction from Matthew, in that the members of the fictive family demonstrate their relational status by means of table fellowship (the

---

14.   In Gen. 18.1–8 and 19.1–3, the angelic visitors appear to eat. Angels can appear to be ordinary men (e.g., Gen. 18.1–8; 19.1–3; Judg. 13.3–21; Tob. 5.4) or have a supernatural, shining or fearful appearance (Mt. 28.3; cf. Dan. 10.6; *Apoc. Zeph.* 6.11–12; Rev. 10.1; 15. 5–6). They serve God as heavenly messengers (Mt. 1.20–21; Rev. 1.12–20; 5.2–9; Gen. 16.7–14; *Jub.* 32.24; Judg. 6.23; *Jos. Asen.* 14.11; 26.2; 28.7; *Hist. Rech.* 4.2–3) and can be sent to judge or mete out divine punishment (Gen. 19.1–26; Mt. 13.39; 16.27; 24.31; 25.31; Rev. 15.6; *Apoc. Zeph.* 6.15–17). They serve humans as guardians and guides (Mt. 1.20, 24; Tob. 11.14–15; Rev. 21.9; 11QBer 11.13–14) and mediate prayers to heaven (*1 Enoch* 9.1–11; 40.6, 9; Tob. 12.12–15; *Test. Levi* 3.5–7; 5.5–6). For a study of angels in the first century, see Maxwell J. Davidson, *Angels at Qumran: A Comparative Study of 1 Enoch 1–36, 72–108 and Sectarian Writings from Qumran* (JSPSup, 11; Sheffield: JSOT Press, 1992), esp. pp. 288–93.

members of the community are not angels; they are *like* angels). Angels are immortal, which means they have no need to marry or be given in marriage (Mt. 22.30); some sources explicitly state that they do not have sexual intercourse (Lk. 20.36; *1 Enoch* 15.4, 6),[15] and a rabbinic teaching claims that 'in the world to come there is no propagation' (*b. Ber.* 17a). To be like angels, then, means to belong to the heavenly realm and to mediate God's will (cf. Heb. 2.2–9); this role does not include marriage (or procreation).

Marriage belongs to those who live on earth; for those who live in heaven there will be no more marriage. Heavenly existence is like Edenic existence: Adam and Eve were like angels before their disobedience (*Apoc. Zos.* 7.2; *2 Enoch* 30.11; *Apoc. Adam* 5.64.15–20; 76.4–6).[16] Josephus affirms that those who depart from this life and go to heaven are given chaste bodies (*War* 3.374). Therefore, someone who strives for the perfected angelic way of life in the resurrection imitates the first couple's Edenic chastity.[17]

Indeed, only 'fallen' angels marry and have sexual relations. Genesis 6.1–4 tells about the 'sons of God' (οἱ υἱοὶ τοῦ θεοῦ; בְּנֵי־הָאֱלֹהִים)[18] who take wives and beget a race of heroes.[19] By Matthew's time, this story was not (as it appears to be in Genesis) a benign etiological tale: rather, the angels' actions bring evil into the world, and their offspring are not heroes but giants who destroy and cannibalize the people (*Jub.* 5.1–11; 7.21–25;

---

15. Keener, *Matthew*, p. 528; Davies and Allison, *Matthew*, III, pp. 227, 229; Allison, *Jesus of Nazareth*, pp. 177–78; Meier, *A Marginal Jew*, III, pp. 507–508.

16. Davies and Allison, *Matthew*, III, p. 228.

17. Allison, *Jesus of Nazareth*, pp. 189, 209.

18. The Hebrew for 'gods' here is plural (אֱלֹהִים) but refers to one God and therefore is translated as singular in Greek.

19. Victor P. Hamilton, *The Book of Genesis: Chapters 1–17* (New International Commentary on the Old Testament; Grand Rapids, MI: Eerdman's, 1990), p. 262. Hermann Gunkel argues convincingly that the story has its beginning in older, polytheistic religions, in which 'sons of the gods' were lesser deities, like gods and goddesses in Greek mythology. See Hermann Gunkel, *Genesis* (trans. M.E. Biddle; Macon, GA: Mercer University Press, 1997; reprint of Gunkel's *Genesis*, 3rd edn [Göttingen: Vandenhoeck and Ruprecht, 1977]), pp. 56–57. This passage seems to be a remnant from an older story about a pantheon of lesser deities, perhaps the Canaanite 'sons of El.' Neither the Hebrew nor Greek text of Gen. 6.1–4 refers to angels, but instead each preserves the ancient reference to 'sons of the gods' (except *Codex Alexandrinus*, which reads ἄγγελοι τοῦ θεοῦ). The term 'sons of god' (בְּנֵי־הָאֱלֹהִים) had been translated 'angels' (ἄγγελοι) in the LXX (Job 1.6; 38.7) and so may be regarded as equivalent. The heavenly host is made up of 'gods' (θεῶν; Ps. 82.1, 6) or 'angels, messengers' (מַלְאָכַי, ἄγγελοι; Pss. 91.11–12; 103.19–22; 148.2), and the angels descend (κατέβαινω) from heaven (οὐρανός, Gen. 28.12), just as the 'the sons of heaven' (οἱ υἱοὶ οὐρανοῦ) descend (κατέβαινω) from heaven (*1 Enoch* 6.2). Matthew Black presents J.T. Milik's argument that the story of the angels descending to marry human women in *1 Enoch* 6 may in fact be the source of Gen. 6.1–4, and not vice versa. He also links the story to Gnostic mythology about divine beings descending from the heavens to bring or find corruption on earth. See Matthew Black, *The Book of Enoch or I Enoch* (Leiden: E.J. Brill, 1985), p. 14, and n. 37.

1 Enoch 6.1–8.4; *4Q Book of the Giants*[c] [4Q531];[20] 4QAges of Creation [4Q180] frag. 1.7–10;[21] *Testament of Reuben* 5.6). Angel-human pairings are an aberration and a defilement; as a result of their contact with human women, these angels are banished from heaven forever (4Q*Enoch* [4Q201] 3.13–23; CD-A, 2.18–21]). The apostle Paul seems to refer to potentially predatory heavenly beings when he instructs women in the congregation to cover themselves 'because of the angels' (1 Cor. 11.2–16).[22]

The Matthean community would not have been alone in its understanding of human striving for angelic perfection. Transcendence of earthly existence by imitation of the angels is an ideal signaled by numerous pseudepigrapha, and it is continued into Gnostic texts.[23] The Dead Sea Scrolls reveal that some groups of people believed that they were living in the presence of angels (for example, 1QS 11.5–8; 1Qsa; 4Q491). Texts give evidence that their communities maintained certain standards of purity in order to join the angels' council and to worship with them: 'angels of holiness are among the congregation' (1QSa II.8–9); 'you shall be serving in the temple of the kingdom, sharing the lot with the angels' (1QSb 4.26; cf. also 1QH 3.21–23; 6.13, 11.11–14; 4Q181 frg.

20.   Trans. P.G. Martínez, *The Dead Sea Scrolls Translated: The Qumran Texts in English* (Leiden: Brill, 2nd edn, 1996), p. 262.

21.   Trans. Martínez, *Dead Sea Scrolls*, p. 212. Davidson, *Angels at Qumran,* pp. 288–93; L.J. Peerbolte, 'Man, Woman, and the Angels in 1 Cor. 11.2–16', in G. Luttikhuizen (ed.), *The Creation of Man and Woman: Interpretation of Biblical Narratives in Jewish and Christian Traditions* (Themes in Biblical Narrative, 3; Leiden: Brill, 2000), pp. 76–92. The women gave birth to giants who ate all the available food, then each other and the people themselves (*1 Enoch* 7.1–6; *Jub.* 5.2–3; 4Q*Enoch*[a] [4Q201] 3.18–21). The angels taught their wives magic and herbal lore (*1 Enoch* 7.2; 4Q201 3.16–23; 4.1–5) as well as how to make jewelry and cosmetics (4Q202 2.18–29), manufacture weapons, and how to do astrology (*1 Enoch* 8.1–4; 4Q*Enoch*[b] [4Q202 3.1–6]). The angels are accused of adultery (Bitenosh tries to persuade her husband Lamech that the child she carries is his, because he suspects the 'Watchers' have impregnated her [1Q*Genesis Apocryphon* [1Q230] 2.1–18]). For these crimes, the angels were punished and their offspring exterminated (*1 Enoch* 10.1–16; 12.4–6; *Jub.* 5.6–11; 10.1–12; 4Q*Enoch*[c] [4Q202] 4.6–11; 5.3). All Qumran texts translated by Martínez, *Dead Sea Scrolls*, pp. 34, 230, 247–51.

22.   Dale Martin, *The Corinthian Body* (New Haven: Yale University Press, 1995), pp. 242–43.

23.   The practice of angel-imitation was a sign of a higher spiritual state. For example, the sons of Levi were chosen for priesthood to minister as the angels do (*Jub.* 30.18). The *Prayer of Jacob* beseeches the deity to fill his heart with good things, so that he can be an 'earthly angel, as an immortal' (*Prayer of Jacob* 18–19). In a vision, Zephaniah sees himself putting on the garments of angels, praying, and conversing in their language (*Apoc. Zeph.* 8.3–4). One of Job's daughters speaks in the dialect of the angels and no longer cares for earthly things (*Test. Job* 48.2–3; 52.7), and all of Job's daughters obtain heavenly cords that allow them to transcend earthly concerns and live in the heavens (*Test. Job* 47.2). The concept of becoming like an angel survived in Gnostic bridal chamber imagery from the second and third centuries (cf. *G. Phil.* 65): see Jorunn Jacobsen Buckley, *Female Fault and Fulfillment in Gnosticism* (Chapel Hill: University of North Carolina Press, 1986), pp. 120–21.

1,1.3–4; 4Q511 2 1.8).[24] John J. Collins describes this intermingling of heavenly and earthly beings as a realized eschatology: some of the communities represented in the Dead Sea Scrolls 'believed that they were already living the risen life with the angels' and that 'the goal of the Qumran community ... was an angelic form of life.'[25]

Collins notes that a celibate lifestyle is 'compatible with the desire to live an angelic life,' and that there may have been elite celibate groups who, as the Cairo-Damascus document puts it, 'separate from the habitation of unjust men and go into the wilderness to prepare the way ...' and who 'walk in perfect holiness' as opposed to those who married (CD 7.5–6).[26] These sectarian groups sought to find heaven on earth and life with the angels. John Meier argues that Qumran communities who practiced celibacy may have anticipated the end times and so imitated the celibate angels as preparation for 'holy war' (since men engaged in holy war were to keep away from women [1 Sam. 21.4–5]; Jesus cites this pericope in Mt. 12.3–4, but in a different context). Jesus' apparent commitment to celibacy in Matthew is not preparation for holy war, but it does resonate with the anticipation of being like the angels (22.30).

Not clear is whether Matthew thinks that 'being like the angels' means becoming male-like. Angels are portrayed as male[27] and in male-gendered roles: they serve in the innermost sanctum at the divine throne as priests, a position reserved for males (4Q400 [4QShirShabba] 1.1.1–17).[28] *Jub.* 15.27–28 states that the angels were created circumcised, and all the angels in this pseudepigraphon, as well as throughout the rest of the ancient literary corpus, have masculine names.[29] Clement of Alexandria indicates

24. See Loren T. Stuckenbruck's discussion of the angels and the Qumran community in *Angel Veneration and Christology: A Study in Early Judaism and in the Christology of the Apocalypse of John* (WUNT, 2. Reihe; Tübingen: J.C.B. Mohr, 1995), pp. 154ff.

25. John J. Collins, *The Apocalyptic Imagination: An Introduction to Jewish Apocalyptic Literature* (Grand Rapids: Eerdmans, 2nd edn, 1998), pp. 174–76. Also Stuckenbruck, *Angel Veneration*, p. 159. See discussion of the angels' priestly function in Devorah Dimant, 'Men as Angels: The Self-Image of the Qumran Community', in Adele Berlin (ed.), *Religion and Politics in the Ancient Near East* (Bethesda, MD: University Press of Maryland, 1996), pp. 93–103.

26. Collins, *The Apocalyptic Imagination*, p. 176. Josephus mentions both celibate and married 'Essenes' (*War*, 2.8.2, 13; *Ant.* 18.1.5). Wives and children are mentioned in CD 7. 6–9 and 19.2–5; in 1QSa 1.9–10, men may not have sexual relations until they are of a certain age.

27. Davies and Allison, *Matthew*, III, p. 229.

28. Allison, *Jesus of Nazareth*, p. 177.

29. See Gunnar Berefelt, *A Study on the Winged Angel: The Origin of a Motif* (Stockholm: Almqvist and Wiksell, 1968), esp. pp. 21–36, 57–62, 110–111. Davies and Allison (*Matthew*, III, p. 229) note that the Gnostic aeons included female names, but these most likely post-date Matthew, and it is not clear that the aeons are the same thing as angels. See also Jorunn Jacobsen Buckley, *Female Fault and Fulfillment*, pp. 62–63.

that the maleness of angels was assumed (*Ex. Theod.* 21). If the prevailing view of angels was that they are all male, then to be 'like the angels' (22.30) means becoming male-like – as in the *Gospel of Thomas* (logion 114). The implication would be that women must somehow abandon female gender in order to remain in the company of disciples when they are resurrected (if not before).[30]

In my reading, Matthew does not negate female gender, at least for the liminal community on earth. In the earthly community, Matthew encourages members to be like the angels and so neither to marry nor to be given in marriage (22.30).[31] The description itself presumes gender roles. Further, even among those who will be saved gender roles are preserved: in 24.40–41 Jesus states that 'two men will be in the field, one will be taken and one will be left. Two women will be grinding meal together; one will be taken and one left.' Therefore, Matthew implies that both males (who work in the field) and females (who grind meal) are present in the community, but that they will no longer need to marry or be given in marriage.

Jesus' response to the Sadducees' question ('whose wife of the seven will she be?' [28.27]) sets up the hypothetical scenario in which both men and women are 'in' the resurrection. But because the Sadducees did not believe in resurrection (Mk. 12.18; Acts 4.1–2; 23.8; Josephus, *Ant.* 18.11; *War* 2.164–66),[32] their question to Jesus was meant to challenge him, not describe a situation they thought likely or even possible.[33] The Matthean Jesus' dismissal of the Sadducees' scenario proves Jesus' superiority over his opponents and defends the Matthean theology of resurrection (cf. 28.11–15), but it also implies that, for Matthew, gender roles are no longer

---

30. Kari Vogt discusses the development of the metaphor of gender transcendence in Hellenistic religious thought in '"Becoming Male": A Gnostic and Early Christian Metaphor', in Kari Elisabeth Børresen (ed.), *Image of God and Gender Models in Judaeo-Christian Tradition* (Oslo: Solum Forlag, 1991), 172–87.

31. Males have the active role as they *take* wives (Joseph *took* his wife; παρέλαβεν τὴν γυναῖκα αὐτοῦ [Mt. 1.25; cf. 1.20]; cf. Isaac *took* Rebekah [ἔλαβεν τὴν Ρεβεκκαν ... καὶ ἠγάμησεν αὐτήν; Gen. 24.67]; Tobias *takes* Sarah [λαμβάνω; Tob. 8.7]). Females have a passive role, as they are *promised* or *given* in marriage (Mary *was promised* to Joseph; μνηστευθείσης τῷ Ἰωσήφ [Mt. 1.18–19]; Laban *gives* Rachel to Jacob [ἔδωκεν; Gen. 29.29]; Sarah's father *gives* her to Tobias as a wife [παρέδωκεν αὐτὴν τῷ Τωβια γυναῖκα; Tob. 7.11–12]). The Mishnah also uses active voice to describe men's actions in arranging a marriage and passive to describe women's, even when the woman is her own agent: 'A man *effects betrothal* on his own or through his agent. A woman *becomes betrothed* on her own or through her agent. A man *betrothes* his daughter when she is a girl on his own or through his agent' (*m. Qid.* 2.1) (trans. Jacob Neusner, *The Mishnah: A New Translation* [New Haven: Yale University Press, 1988], p. 489).

32. Davies and Allison, *Matthew*, I, pp. 302–303.

33. Davies and Allison (*Matthew*, III, p. 223) say that the Sadducees' question was 'insincere and malicious.'

important in heaven; they may well be non-existent. Therefore, 'being like the angels' in Matthew means that within the liminal community, male and female gender roles remain, but one principal determinant of gender roles – the institution of marriage – is mitigated if not erased. The family consists of mothers, brothers, sisters, and a bridegroom; there are no husbands and no wives *and no brides*. Finally, just as there are celibate men and women in the fictive family, both males and females (if these terms are even relevant in the Kingdom of Heaven) will be celibate in the resurrection.[34]

5.4 *One Flesh: Gender and Sexuality in Matthew*

While the Matthean ideal is that those who are single remain unmarried (19.10–12), the evangelist does not condemn marriages already contracted. Indeed, the Matthean Jesus twice forbids divorce (5.32; 19.3–9) on the grounds that 'the two become one flesh' (ἔσονται οἱ δύο εἰς σάρκα μίαν) and cannot be divided (19.5–6; cf. Gen. 2.24). Interpreters offer numerous explanations for 'one flesh': Matthew refers to sexual union or conception of children,[35] to God's desire for lifelong marriage,[36] to a relationship that becomes as strong as a blood relationship,[37] or to Adam and Eve.[38] As I have argued in the previous chapter, Matthew does not care about the conception of children (and in fact discourages it). Consequently, I do not agree that 'one flesh' refers to sexual union, let alone conception. (Indeed, whereas marriage is the permanent state, sexual intercourse is not.) Lifelong marriage, the second explanation, comports with the Matthean prohibition of divorce and remarriage, and marriage that becomes as strong as a blood relationship fits the Matthean ideal of a fictive family of non-related people (if the purpose of that

---

34. Several Christian texts from the second to the fourth centuries liken virginity to angelic perfection. A few examples: Ambrose attributes virginal chastity to the angels, who in turn guard virgins on earth (*Concerning Virgins*, 1.9.2); Serapion praises the virginity of the angels and Christians who imitate them (*The Eight Principal Faults*, 19); Jerome refers to angelic virginity (*Against Jovinianus*, 1.40–41); John of Damascus proclaims that virginity and celibacy are an imitation of the angels (*Concerning Virginity*, 4.24); and Methodius says that virginity is akin to the life of angels ('Concerning Chastity', *Discourse* 8.2).

35. Davies and Allison, *Matthew*, III, p. 13.

36. So Davies and Allison, *Matthew*, III, p. 3, 9; Levine, 'Matthew', p. 255; Boring, 'Matthew', p. 386; Schnackenburg, *Matthew*, pp. 183–94.

37. Davies and Allison, *Matthew*, III, p. 13.

38. Levine, 'Matthew', p. 255. See also Harrington, *Matthew*, p. 276; Patte, *Matthew*, pp. 264–65; Boring, 'Matthew', p. 386; Beare, *Matthew*, p. 155; Albright and Mann, *Matthew*, p. 226; Schnackenburg, *Matthew*, p. 184. 'The appeal to Genesis, to the golden age, is typical of millenarian piety' (Levine, 'Jesus, Divorce, and Sexuality: A Jewish Critique', in L. Greenspon, D. Hamm, and B. LeBeau [eds.], *The Historical Jesus through Catholic and Jewish Eyes* [Harrisburg, PA: Trinity Press International, 2000], p. 121).

marriage is not procreation or consolidation of wealth and power, as discussed in Chapter 4 on the fictive family). That the Matthean Jesus alludes to Gen. 2.24 to explain the marital relationship clearly invokes Adam and Eve, the two made from one flesh. But Matthew's understanding of the story of Eden must be examined in light of the tradition-history of his time. Adam and Eve attracted the attention of numerous exegetes, in part because of the questions the Genesis text does not answer. For example, did Adam and Eve have sexual relations while they were in Eden? Was the first human being both 'male and female' (as Genesis 1 might imply) or a male from whom the female was created (so the story in Genesis 2)? What does the 'two becoming one flesh' mean in terms of gender and sexual activity?

5.4.1 *Rabbinic and Philonic Interpretations of 'One Flesh'*

The different interpretations of the nature of the first human stems from the two creation stories in Genesis. The first story (Gen. 1.26–27) weaves single and plural verbs and pronouns in describing the divine image and created humanity: 'Then God said, "Let *us* make (נעשה; ποιήσωμεν [plural]) humankind in *our* image (בצלמנו; εἰκόνα ἡμετέραν) according to *our* likeness (כדמותנו; ὁμοίωσιν [plural])" ... So God created the human (האדם; τὸν ἄνθρωπον [singular]) in *his* image (בצלמו; εἰκόνα θεοῦ [singular]), male and female he created *them'* (זכר ונקבה ברא אתם; ἄρσεν καὶ θῆλυ ἐποίησεν αὐτούς [plural]; Gen. 1.26–27). Genesis 1 suggests that the first human was *both* male and female in one being. The second story says that God made the man (Gen. 2.7; the Hebrew '*ha-adam*' can be translated 'the earthling'), and then made the woman from the man: 'And the rib (or side) that the Lord God had taken from the man he made into a woman and brought her to the man' (Gen. 2.27). Genesis 2 suggests that the first human being was male or at best indeterminate, and that the female did not exist until she was taken from his side and given to him.

From the first creation story (1.26–27), Philo imagined an incorporeal human being who was both male and female, a primordial androgyne.[39]

---

39. The apostle Paul, who also reflects the influence of Platonic dualistic thinking in his 'spirit vs. flesh' rhetoric, may be alluding to the primordial androgyne when he claims that in Christ Jesus, gender difference is nullifed: 'there is no male nor female' (οὐκ ἔνι ἄρσεν καὶ θῆλυ [Gal. 3.27–28]). See Dennis Ronald MacDonald, *There Is No Male or Female: The Fate of a Dominical Saying in Paul and Gnosticism* (HDR, 20; Philadelphia: Fortress, 1987), pp. 11, 38. Alan F. Segal suggests that Paul believed the resurrected body recovered its original androgynous nature (1 Cor. 15.39–49) and that the Body of Christ is itself androgynous (Gal. 3.26–28) in 'Paul's "Soma Pneumatikon" and the Worship of Jesus', in Carey C. Newman, James R. Davila, and Gladys S. Lewis (eds.), *The Jewish Roots of Christological Monotheism* (Leiden: Brill, 1999), pp. 265–66. See also Frédéric Monneyron, *L'Androgyne romantique: du mythe au mythe littéraire* (Grenoble: Ellug, 1994), pp. 34–39. The second-century account

This first male/female human lived as a 'solitary' (ἑνός) until God divided 'him' into two beings (*Opif. Mun.* 53.152). As a solitary, before Adam was divided into two beings, this first human reflected the image of God and enjoyed immortality.[40] Philo interprets the second story (Gen. 2.18–24) to mean that the first human being was completely male or genderless. It was not until God divided the flesh of this male human into two parts that two genders came into existence (*Quaes. Gen.* 1.25),[41] and this bifurcated 'Adam' was less perfect than the 'first Adam,' the primordial androgyne.

Matthew's portrayal of marriage does not fit either of Philo's scenarios exactly. Perhaps for Matthew, there are two levels of existence, represented by married and unmarried states: marriage belongs on earth, where

---

of creation called the *Poimandres* borrows the seven-fold creation story from Genesis, and like Philo, describes the first human being as androgynous and immortally perfect. For detailed discussion of creation and the 'fall' of man from immortal perfection in Genesis 1–3 and the Poimandres, see C.H. Dodd, *The Bible and the Greeks* (London: Hodder & Stoughton, 1935), pp. 99–103, 145–69.

40.   David M. Hay, 'The Veiled Thoughts of the Therapeutae', in Robert M. Berchman (ed.), *Mediators of the Divine* (South Florida Studies in the History of Judaism, 163; Atlanta, GA: Scholars Press, 1998), pp. 175–76. Some Greek and Jewish philosophers construed the primordial human being as an 'androgyne' (ἀνδρόγυνον), literally 'man-woman,' male-female duality in one body. See Plato (*Symposium* 189–93). A history of androgyny in religious thought is offered by Jan Zandee, 'Der Androgyne Gott in Ägypten: Ein Erscheinungsbild des Weltschöpfers', in Manfred Görg (ed.), *Religion im Erbe Ägyptens* (Wiesbaden: Otto Harrassowitz, 1988), pp. 240–78, and Carl H. Kraeling, *Anthropos and Son of Man: A Study of Religious Syncretism of the Hellenistic Orient* (New York: Columbia University Press, 1927). See also discussion in Boyarin, *Carnal Israel*, p. 38, and 'Paul and the Genealogy of Gender', *Representations* 41 (1993), pp. 1–33 (9–11); Thomas Tobin, *The Creation of Man: Philo and the History of Interpretation* (CBQMS; Washington: Catholic Biblical Association of America, 1983), p. 32; Monneyron, *L'Androgyne romantique*; E. Benz, *et al.* (eds.), *Cahiers l'Hermétisme: L'Androgyne dans la littérature*, Paris: Éditions Albin Michel, 1990); MacDonald, *There Is No Male or Female*; Wayne A. Meeks, 'The Image of the Androgyne: Some Uses of a Symbol in Early Christianity', *HR* 13 (1974), pp. 165–208; Jorunn Jacobsen Buckley, 'An Interpretation of Logion 114 in the *Gospel of Thomas*,' *Novum Testamentum* 27.3 (1985), pp. 245–72, esp. p. 246. Daniel Boyarin explains: 'According to [the myth of the primal androgyne], the first human being was an androgyne who was later split into the two sexes. However, and this is the catch, in the Hellenistic world and late antiquity the primal androgyne was almost always imagined as disembodied, so that the androgyne was really no-body, and dual-sex was no-sex. This myth, I suggest, encodes the dualist ideology whereby a spiritual androgyny is contrasted with the corporeal (and social) division into sexes' (Boyarin, 'Genealogy of Gender,' p. 18).

41.   This bifurcation differs from Plato's understanding that the first human beings were literally two-sided, some being male-male, some female-female, and some having both a male and a female side in one body. Philo laments that when the woman was created, the human was no longer 'one.' See Annewies Van den Hoek, 'Endowed with Reason or Glued to the Senses: Philo's Thoughts on Adam and Eve', in Luttikhuizen (ed.), *The Creation of Man and Woman*, pp. 63–75. For Philo, the woman is completely derivative and unnecessary, less perfect than the male (*Quaes. Gen.* 1.25, 27). Though Philo writes elsewhere that becoming 'one flesh' can have the happy result of affection and shared pleasures (*Quaes. Gen.* 29), he

couples imitate the reunion of Adam and Eve as 'one flesh' from which they were divided; but in the resurrection, they will more perfectly resemble the primordial androgyne, who is both male and female (or, as Boyarin would have it, neither), and who, like the angels, has no need for marriage.

Rabbinic Judaism also reflects the androgyne myth in interpretations of the Genesis creation stories (*b. Megilla* 9a; *Gen. Rab.* 8.1; *Lev. Rab.* 14): God's taking the woman from the man's side was perceived as an actual bifurcation of the male, resulting in male and female. But the rabbis did not treat this division of the sexes or the creation of sexuality as a fallen or less perfect state, as did Philo. For the rabbis, the creation of male and female was good. Marriage completed the original human, while fulfilling human creation in the image of God.[42] To be 'one flesh' (Gen. 2.24) was fully to embrace sexuality as the restoration of the image of God in the first created human. Rabbinic Judaism imagined the eschaton to *be like* marital joy, not an annulment of it (as Matthew does). Gary Anderson cites the marriage blessing over the bride and bridegroom as evidence that creation, Eden, and marital joy are linked to eschatological fulfillment: the blessing alludes to the creation of human kind in God's image, the joy of creatures in the primordial Eden, and the rejoicing of the bride and bridegroom, then asks that the 'voice of the bridegroom and bride' be heard quickly in the streets of Judah and Jerusalem (*b. Ketub.* 8a).[43]

From these brief descriptions of Philonic and rabbinic interpretations of the creation story and the place of marriage, we can see that Matthew more closely resembles Philo. In his description of the resurrection where the angels do not marry, Matthew apparently affirms that human beings will return to the primordial perfection of the immortal first human who was both male and female and had no need of marriage (represented by

---

warns that the man's desire for the woman is the source of unhappiness and death (*Opif. Mun.* 53.151). Philo leaves out Plato's male-male and female-female pairs altogether. Jacob Jervell, *Imago Dei: Gen 1,26 im Spätjudentum, in der Gnosis und in den paulinischen Briefen* (Göttingen: Vandenhoeck & Ruprecht, 1960), pp. 66–68. John J. Collins discusses a Qumran text, 'The Vision of Hagu,' that parallels Philo's description of the creation of two types of human beings ('In the Likeness of the Holy Ones: The Creation of Humankind in a Wisdom Text from Qumran', in Donald W. Parry and Eugene Ulrich [eds.], *The Provo International Conference on the Dead Sea Scrolls* [Leiden: Brill, 1999], pp. 609–18).

42.   For a thorough treatment of various Jewish and early Christian interpretations of sexuality, see Gary A. Anderson, *The Genesis of Perfection: Adam and Eve in Jewish and Christian Imagination* (Louisville: Westminster/John Knox Press, 2001).

43.   Gary Anderson, 'The Garden of Eden and Sexuality in Early Judaism,' in Howard Eilberg-Schwartz (ed.), *People of the Body: Jews and Judaism from an Embodied Perspective* (New York: State University of New York Press, 1992), pp. 47–68 (esp. 56–59). However, even with the rabbis' positive view of sexuality, Daniel Boyarin (*Carnal Israel*, pp. 45–56) notes that a certain degree of sexual asceticism was still possible for *some* who regarded sex much in the same way as did the Christian Church fathers: that it was only for procreation and not a thing to be enjoyed.

the story in Genesis 1). That Matthew speaks of the married couple as 'the two become one flesh,' however, refers to the story in Genesis 2, where the man and woman are separate beings. Their marriage reunites the two parts that had been separated.

A final question is whether Matthew imagines that the couple in Genesis 2 was sexually active or not. Certainly there were those who claimed that Adam and Eve were chaste until they were expelled from Eden. 'For when [Adam] transgressed ... the conception of children came about, the passion of the parents was produced' (*2 Bar.* 56.6).[44] The Genesis story does not mention intercourse and procreation until Gen. 4.1 (cf. *Jub.* 3.32–35). (However, the *Life of Adam and Eve* (18) indicates that Eve was three months pregnant when the couple were expelled from Eden.) While Matthew does not forbid sexual activity, his 'eunuch' saying (19.10–12) suggests an opportunity to participate in a higher calling: that of Adam and Eve, who were chaste in the garden before they were expelled. The couple's chastity in earthly life was lived in expectation of achieving an even higher status, that of the perfectly united primordial androgyne described in Genesis 1.

For Matthew, Adam and Eve represent the ideal of male and female who are bonded as a fictive family but do not have sex or reproduce, like Joseph and Mary, a married couple who, while they are representing righteousness, do not have sexual intercourse and so do not procreate. Mary remains a virgin, and the child is by the Holy Spirit. When Joseph and Mary no longer fulfill the non-reproductive role, they fade from the story: Mary is replaced by fictive mothers (12.46–50), and Joseph disappears altogether. Married couples (as well as singles) can aspire to a more perfect life, without marriage, in the resurrection.

Philo of Alexandria in *De Vita Contemplativa* and *Hypothetica* described an earthly community called the Therapeutae and Therapeutrides that lived out just such heavenly perfection.[45] Though there is some question as to whether the Therapeutae actually existed – they could be Philo's utopian invention – Philo's account is nevertheless valuable for providing a context within which Matthew's own community construction may be understood.

According to Philo, the Therapeutae and Therapeutrides chose to leave their possessions and families and to give up their inheritance in order to live free of earthly desires and passions and to pursue service to the one God (*De Vita. Cont.* 2.13). Philo says that they lived both in heaven and

---

44. Translation by A.F.J. Klijn, '2 (Syriac Apocalypse of) Baruch', in J.H. Charlesworth (ed.), *The Old Testament Pseudepigrapha* (2 vols.; New York: Doubleday, 1983), I, pp. 615–652 (641).

45. Parts of Philo's lost work, *Hypothetica*, are quoted by Eusebius in his *Praeparatio Evangelica* (8.6.1–11.18).

the world (*De Vita. Cont.* 11.90). Men and women lived separately but in the same community. Philo does not say if they were married, celibate, or if they practiced celibacy within marriage, but he does indicate that many of the women had been virgins all their lives (*De Via Cont.* 8.68).

Daniel Boyarin describes the way in which the Therapeutae and Therapeutrides exemplified a symbolic return to primal androgyny, and how similar ideal communities might have done the same (Boyarin refers specifically to Paul's Corinthians, but the same argument holds for Matthew):

> Once a year (or once in seven weeks), the community came together for a remarkable ritual celebration. Following a simple meal and a discourse, all of the members begin to sing hymns together. Initially, however, the men and the women remain separate from each other in two choruses. The extraordinary element is that as the celebration becomes more ecstatic, the men and the women join to form one chorus, 'the treble of the women blending with the bass of the men'. I suggest that this model of an ecstatic joining of the male and the female in a mystical ritual recreates in social practice the image of the purely spiritual masculo-feminine first human of which Philo speaks in his commentary – indeed, that this ritual of the Therapeutae is a return to the originary Adam. This point is valid whether or not the community of Therapeutae ever really existed or not. In either case the description is testimony to the translation of anthropology into social practice in Philo's writing. If they did exist, moreover, we have further strong evidence that Philo is representative of larger religious traditions and groups. Although, obviously, the singing and dancing are performed by the body, the state of ecstasy (as its etymology implies) involves a symbolical and psychological condition of being disembodied and thus similar to the primal androgyne. The crux of my argument is that a distinction between androgyny as a mythic notion and one that has social consequences is a false distinction. The myth of the primal androgyne, with all of its inflections, always has social meaning and social significance, for Paul no less than for Philo, for rabbis and for Corinthian Christians.[46]

That Matthew was familiar with the androgyne myth cannot be proven; nor can it be proven that the Matthean community would have taken such a myth to heart and practiced celibacy even within marriage. However, it can be shown that the myth was well known and influential in Matthew's time and across great distances by its survival from Philo's Egypt to Paul's

---

46.   Boyarin, 'Paul and the Genealogy of Gender', pp. 28–29.

Mediterranean world,[47] to later rabbinic interpretations of the Genesis creation stories (*b. Megilla* 9a; *Gen. Rab.* 8.1; *Lev. Rab.* 14).[48] The rabbis did not follow Philo's Hellenistic dualism that treated the division of the sexes as the beginning of suffering (*Opif. Mun.* 53.152); rather, they taught that marriage completed the original human and at the same time fulfilled human creation in the image of God. But Matthew, who favors the celibate angelic existence as the more perfect state, is closer to Philo than to the later *midrashim*. For Matthew, the union of male and female in one flesh is a status that will be surpassed by angelic singleness in the resurrection (22.30).

5.4.2 *The Essenes and the Rechabites*

Other ideal groups present possible models for Matthew's understanding of marriage and the place of sexual activity and procreation within marriage: the Essenes and the Rechabites. Philo and Josephus describe the Essenes as forming utopian communities in which people gave up family connections and all luxuries (Philo, *Hyp.* 11.10–12; Josephus, *Ant.* 18.5.20), a description reminiscent of the Matthean community. Philo states explicitly that the Essenes were celibate and did not marry (*Hyp.* 11.14). But Josephus reports that an order of the Essenes married for the purpose of having children to continue the community (*War* 2.8.121). Josephus clarifies that an Essene man did not marry a woman until he was sure she was fertile (unclear is how one would know), and he had no relations with her while she was pregnant in order to prove that his sexual relations were for propagation only (*War* 2.8.13; cf. Tob. 8.7). Philo and Josephus's accounts indicate that different groups of Essenes followed different sexual patterns, but both descriptions agree that sexual relations were for the purpose of procreation, not for pleasure. While a minority of scholars question whether the Essenes of Philo and Josephus correspond to communities represented by the Dead Sea Scrolls, documents associated with them confirm the ascetic value expressed in Philo and Josephus's accounts: a man who approaches his wife for lust and not in

---

47. Kari Elisabeth Børresen, 'God's Image, Man's Image? Patristic Interpretation of Gen. 1.27 and 1 Cor. 11.7', in Børresen (ed.), *Image of God and Gender Models in Judaeo-Christian Tradition* (Oslo: Solum Forlag, 1991), pp. 188–207. Indeed, the myth has continued to inspire religious thought and has been studied by modern scholars of the history of religion and psychology such as Mircea Eliade, Henry Corbin, Gershom Scholem, and C.G. Jung (Steven M. Wasserstrom, 'Uses of the Androgyne in the History of Religions,' *SR* 27/4 [1998], pp. 437–53).

48. See L. Teugels, 'The Creation of the Human in Rabbinic Interpretations', in Luttikhuizen (ed.), *The Creation of Man and Woman*, pp. 107–27, esp. 110–113.

accordance with regulation shall leave the community and never return (4QDd 12).[49]

5.4.3 *The Apocalypse of Zosimus*

The Apocalypse of Zosimus describes an ideal community called the 'Rechabites,' who lived as angels but who remained married.[50] Zosimus's Rechabites were already married when they were transported by angels to live without sin in an island paradise. When they arrived in their new home they did not divorce, but lived separately (*Apoc. Zos.* 10.5–7); thus they offer a model of how Matthew perceived married couples could live in a celibate state (Mt. 5.31–32; 19.3–12). The Rechabite couples had intercourse only once; then they remained celibate for the rest of their lives. The wife conceived two children, one who would marry, and one who would remain a virgin (*Apoc. Zos.* 11.6–8).[51] To complete the portrayal of paradise on earth, they were clothed in glory as were Adam and Eve before they sinned (*Apoc. Zos.* 12.3); we might recollect here the Matthean Jesus' exhortation, 'Consider the lilies of the field, how they grow ... yet I tell you, even Solomon in all his glory was not clothed like one of these ... Therefore do not worry, saying "What will we eat" or "What will we drink?" or "What will we wear?"' [6.28–31]). Thus, the *Apocalypse of Zosimus* portrays earthly marriage in terms of the Edenic existence of Adam and Eve and offers a picture of how Matthew could have imagined ideal marriage (albeit without reproduction) in his community.

Celibacy as a demonstration of piety, even within marriage, was an ideal known and perhaps practiced by Jews in Matthew's time. The difference between the Matthean portrayal of celibacy and that of the Rechabites, Essenes, and Therapeutae is that Matthew did *not* promote sexual intercourse for the purpose of procreation. There is no indication in

---

49. See Martínez, *Dead Sea Scrolls*, p. 62 for more versions of this statement. 1Qsa 1.10 directs that a man may not have intercourse with a woman until he is twenty years old 'when he knows good and evil.' The reference to good and evil may also be a warning against intercourse for lust, but there are many other possible interpretations of what may have deemed 'evil' sexual matters.

50. The biblical Rechabites were descendents of Rechab, ancestor of Jonadab, who commanded his household not to drink wine, build houses, sow, or plant, but to live in tents. Jeremiah cites their perfect obedience to their patriarch in order to shame Judah for disobedience to the Lord (Jer. 35.2–19). Jeremiah's Rechabites, with their perfect obedience and apparently ascetic way of life, inspired the pseudepigraphon.

51. The Rechabites protested that the purpose of sexual union had nothing to do with pleasure or lust (cf. Tob. 8.7), but merely served to maintain the community's population. According to the Rechabites. 'The memory of the desire does not arise in the heart of any and they remain like virgins for the rest of their days' (*Apoc. Zos.* 11.7).

Matthew that couples needed to be having sexual relations, because Matthew promoted instead a fictive family.

5.4.4 *Gospel of Thomas.*
The *Gospel of Thomas* provides a parallel to the Matthean bridegroom tradition and the theme of 'two becoming one,'[52] but with an important difference: while *Thomas* apparently erases gender, Matthew does not.[53] Like Mt. 9.14–15, *Thomas* includes Jesus as the bridegroom in the context of a controversy about fasting (*G. Thom.* 104).[54] *Thomas* emphasizes

---

52. *Thomas* and Matthew may share similar origins and sources, most likely Syrian. See Helmut Koester, 'Introduction', in Bentley Layton (ed.), *Nag Hammadi Codex II, 2–7* (NHS, 20; Coptic Gnostic Library; Leiden: E.J. Brill, 1989), pp. 40–41; P. Perkins, 'The Gospel of Thomas', in E. Schüssler Fiorenza (ed.), *Searching the Scriptures*, II, pp. 534–60 (537–38); Helmut Koester, 'The Gospel of Thomas,' in J.M. Robinson (ed.), *The Nag Hammadi Library* (San Fransisco: Harper San Francisco, 3rd edn, 1990), pp. 124–138 (p. 125); Stevan Davies, *The Gospel of Thomas and Christian Wisdom* (New York: Seabury, 1983), p. 145. Because it shares a sayings source that may be earlier than Q, *Thomas* has been dated by some scholars to the first century CE. See Bentley Layton, *Nag Hammadi Codex II, 2–7* [NHS, 20; Coptic Gnostic Library; Leiden: E.J. Brill, 1989], p. 28; Stephan J. Patterson, *The Gospel of Thomas and Jesus* (Sonoma, CA: Polebridge Press, 1993), pp. 113–120. But others date *Thomas* to the second century: Robert M. Wilson, *Studies in the Gospel of Thomas* (London: A.R. Mowbray and Co., 1960), pp. 7–8; Marvin Meyer, *The Gospel of Thomas: The Hidden Sayings of Jesus* (San Francisco: HarperSanFrancisco, 1992), p. 10; K.O. Schmidt, *Die geheimen Herren-Worte des Thomas-Evangeliums: Wegweisungen Christi zur Selbstvollendung* (Pfullingen/Würt: Baum-Verlag, 1966), pp. 6–7.

53. Buckley, 'An Interpretation of Logion 114', pp. 252–56; Meyer, 'Making Mary Male: The Categories of "Male" and "Female" in the Gospel of Thomas', *NTS* 31 (1985), pp. 554–70 (557–58); Perkins, 'Gospel of Thomas', pp. 558–59; Meeks, 'Image of the Androgyne', pp. 186–89; Bruce Lincoln, 'Thomas-Gospel and Thomas-Community: A New Approach to a Familiar Text', *NovT* 19 (1977), pp. 65–76; Sasagu Arai, '"To Make Her Male": An Interpretation of Logion 114 in the Gospel of Thomas', *Studia Patristica* 24 (1993), pp. 373–76; Wilson, *Studies in the Gospel of Thomas*, p. 31.

54. When asked about fasting, Jesus replies, 'When the bridegroom leaves the bridal chamber, then let them fast and pray' (*G. Thom.* 104) (cf. Mt. 9.14–15). *Thomas* hints at the bridal chamber in Valentinian Gnostic texts, where the bridal chamber restored initiates to a primordial unity that transcended gender and could never be separated (e.g., *G. Philip* 65. 1–13; 68.16–26; 70.10–23; 71.4–15; 72.20–24; 76.3–9; cf. 81.30–82.25; 86.1–9; *Gospel of the Egyptians* in Clement, *Strom.* 3.9.63; *Dialogue of the Savior* 138.15–20, 144.15–145.5). For a summary of the Gnostic bridal chamber ritual as a means of reuniting the male and female for the purpose of creating a 'living spirit,' see Buckley, *Female Fault and Fulfillment*, pp. 91–106; Meyer, 'Male and Female in the Gospel of Thomas', esp. pp. 557–58; and Meeks, 'Image of the Androgyne', pp. 189–91. *Thomas* locates the bridegroom *in* the bridal chamber (compare Matthew's 'how can the sons of the bridal chamber mourn and fast while the bridegroom is *with* them' [Mt. 9.15], with no clear indication of where they are together, that is, in or outside the bridal chamber). The difference alerts the interpreter to the greater importance of the bridal chamber in *Thomas*: while Matthew's bridegroom will passively 'be taken away,' Thomas' bridegroom actively 'leaves the bridal chamber.'

becoming a 'solitary' as a prerequisite for entering the bridal chamber and
the Kingdom of Heaven: 'Many are standing at the door, but it is only the
"solitary" [Greek μοναχός and Coptic *monoxos*, 'alone,' 'single,' or
'solitary'] who will enter the bridal chamber' (*G. Thom.* 75), and 'Blessed
are those who are alone (*monoxos*) and chosen, for you will find the
kingdom' (*G. Thom.* 49).[55] A 'solitary' is one of God's elect who (in
Thomas) incorporates both genders into one, or who transcends gender
distinction altogether: 'Jesus said to them, 'When you make the two one
[Coptic: *ouwt*, 'single, sole, one'],[56] and when you make the inside like the
outside and the outside like the inside, and the above like the below, and
when you make the male and the female one and the same, so that the
male not be male nor the female be female, when you make eyes in place
of an eye, a hand in place of a hand, a foot in place of a foot, an image in
place of an image, then will you enter the kingdom' (*G. Thom.* 22b; cf.
Gal. 3.28).[57]

Jorunn Buckley suggests that the 'solitary' is 'a prototype of Adam who
needs to be reunited to himself ... going into the bridal chamber, he (or as
the case may be, she) is imaged as bride.'[58] Perkins writes that the one who
enters the bridal chamber returns to the 'primordial beginning' and 'seeks
to recover the immortal image of the heavenly Adam.'[59] The Matthean
bridegroom is solitary, in the sense that he does not have a bride, but
he does not erase gender roles: the two becoming one is a return not
to primordial perfection (one Adam) but to Adam and Eve before
they left the garden. The disciples are not 'bridegrooms' or 'brides' and do
not enter the bridal chamber; by extension, they never achieve the
androgynous state. Gender roles of male and female, in Matthew, are not
erased; but because no one, not even the bridegroom, actually enters the
Matthean bridal chamber, the implication is that there is no need

---

55. Monoxos is a Greek loan word (from μόνος, alone, forsaken, solitary). Marvin
Meyer translates monoxos as 'alone' (*The Gospel of Thomas*, pp. 43, 55); Risto Uro translates
'solitary' in *Thomas at the Crossroads: Essays on the Gospel of Thomas* (Edinburgh: T&T
Clark, 1998), pp. 156; R.M. Wilson translates 'solitary' or 'single one' in *Studies in the Gospel
of Thomas*, p. 33. K.O. Schmidt translates '*Einsamen*' ('lonely, solitary, isolated') in *Die
gehemien Herrenworte*, p. 173. Patterson argues that *monoxos*/μοναχός is the source of the
word 'monk' and the practice of parting from family and devoting one's self to singleness
(*The Gospel of Thomas*, p. 152, n. 124, in the context of pp. 152–53). Meeks offers the same
observation in 'Image of the Androgyne', p. 196, n. 138.

56. Thomas Lambdin, *Introduction to Sahidic Coptic* (Macon, GA: Mercer University
Press, 1988), p. 298.

57. Lambdin, *Sahidic Coptic*, p. 293. The *Gospel of Thomas* expounds on the theme of the
two becoming one, although no longer in gendered terms (*G. Thom.* 23, 48–29). Koester
suggests that the 'solitary' refers to someone who has left worldly things behind ('The Gospel
of Thomas', p. 126).

58. Buckley, *Female Fault and Fulfillment*, p. 99.

59. Perkins, 'The Gospel of Thomas', p. 558.

for sexuality. Becoming a 'solitary' has connotations for celibacy for already married couples, confirmed by the Thomasian tradition of the bride and bridegroom who are persuaded to abstain from sexual relations (*Acts of Thomas* 12).

5.5 *Except for Porneia: Marriage and Divorce in Matthew*

The 'two become one flesh' also provides the reason for Matthew's prohibition of divorce (19.4–5; cf. Gen. 2.24). Matthew's reference to the creation story offers a vision of marriage that is the 'beginning of the restoration of paradise' and a 'final realization of what God intended from the beginning.'[60]

Matthew presents indissoluble marriage as part of the created order (19.4–5) but also provides an exception clause to the prohibition of divorce: παρεκτὸς λόγου πορνείας (5.32) or μὴ ἐπὶ πορνείᾳ (19.9). Matthew's exception clause, 'except in the case of *porneia*,' treats only the husband's action in divorcing a wife (5.31–32; 19.3–9) and is less strict than Mark's version (Mk 10.11–12: 'Whoever divorces his wife and marries another commits adultery against her, and if she divorces her husband and marries another, she commits adultery'; Mark offers no exceptions and forbids divorce for both husband and wife).[61] Matthew may have allowed exceptions because of circumstances the community faced, such as consanguineous marriages[62] or in response to Roman law that made it a crime *not* to divorce an adulterous wife (5.31–32; 19.9; cf.

60. Davies and Allison acknowledge that this theme of reunification also stated in Gal. 3.28 could point to the myth of the androgyne, but they do not think that this was so in Matthew's understanding (*Matthew*, III, p. 10, n. 35; p. 14).

61. Davies and Allison, *Matthew*, III, pp. 4–5; Long, *Matthew*, p. 59; Levine, 'Word Becomes Flesh', p. 74; Hare, *Matthew*, p. 219; Schnackenburg, *Matthew*, pp. 57, 183; Albright and Mann, *Matthew*, p. 225. Mary Rose D'Angelo argues that divorce and remarriage would compromise the community's commitment to 'perfection' and asceticism ('Remarriage and the Divorce Sayings Attributed to Jesus', in W. Roberts (ed.), *Divorce and Remarriage* [Kansas City: Sheed and Ward, 1990] pp. 78–106 [95–99]).

62. Levine, 'Word Becomes Flesh', p. 82, n. 30; Levine, 'Jesus, Divorce, and Sexuality', pp. 117–19; R. Hays, *The Moral Vision of the New Testament: Community, Cross, New Creation* (Edinburgh: T&T Clark, 1997), p. 354; John Nolland, 'The Gospel Prohibition of Divorce', *JSNT* 58 (1995), pp. 19–35 (22); John Kampen, 'The Matthean Divorce Texts Re-examined,' pp. 166–67; Michael Goulder, 'Devotion, Divorce, and Debauchery,' in Lone Fatum and Mogens Müller (eds.), *Tro og Historie: festskrift til Niels Hyldahl i anledning af 65 års fødselsdagen den 30. december 1995* (Copenhagen: Museum Tusculanums Forlag, 1996), pp. 107–17 (113).

1 Cor. 7.11).[63] Kathy Gaca suggests that in some contexts a Jew's marriage to a Gentile constituted 'fornication' or 'adultery' (πορνεία) because women who worship other gods are harlots (πόρναι) whether or not their sacred rituals involve sex.[64] Alternatively, Matthew may have included the loophole because the eschaton had not come: what can be tolerated in light of the imminent end of the world is not necessarily comparable to a lifetime of marriage marked by incompatibility, or desertion, or violence.

For Matthew, married couples should not divorce except in the case of πορνεία (unspecified sexual sin), because they represent on earth the 'one flesh' of Adam and Eve in the Garden of Eden.[65] While for Matthew, *gender* is not the issue – both male and female have a place in the restored perfection of the kingdom – *sexual activity* can pose a problem to that perfection, because sexuality risks *porneia*.

Jesus' response to the Pharisees' question, 'Is it lawful for a man to divorce his wife *for any cause?*' (19.3) places him squarely in an ongoing debate over the legal and moral grounds for divorce represented by rabbinic schools (Hillel and Shammai; *m. Git.* 9.10)[66] centered on interpretation of Deut. 24.1, where the only acceptable cause for divorce is ערות דבר (literally 'a word/deed of nakedness,' with the implication of

63. Levine, 'Word Becomes Flesh', p. 82, n. 30. The *Lex Julia de adulteries* (18 BCE) outlined penalties for both men and women who commit *adulterium* (adultery). This was defined as a man having sexual relations with someone else's wife or a married woman having any extramarital sexual encounter. A closely related offense was *stuprum* (a man having sexual relations with a boy, a virgin from a good family, a divorced woman, or a widow). *Stuprum* was sometimes used interchangeably with *adulterium*. There were penalties and disgrace for adulterous men as well as for women, and adultery was very often the cause of divorce. See Aline Roussell, *Porneia: On Desire and the Body in Antiquity* (trans. Felicia Pheasant; Cambridge, MA: Blackwell, 1988), pp. 78–92; and Treggiari, *Roman Marriage*, pp. 270–309.

64. Kathy L. Gaca, *The Making of Fornication: Eros, Ethics, and Political Reform in Greek Philosophy and Early Christianity* (Berkeley: University of California Press, 2003), pp. 160–89.

65. Luz emphasizes that divorce cannot actually dissolve the marital bond established by God (*Matthew*, III, p. 494). Albright and Mann (*Matthew*, p. 226) agree that the couple are now one body and separation is unthinkable. Patte compares divorce to depriving oneself a part of oneself (*Matthew*, pp. 264–65).

66. Whether the disputes between the Houses of Hillel and Shammai actually took place at the time of Jesus, or whether they are later retrojections remains unresolved. Nevertheless, the Matthean discussion as well as whatever may originate with Jesus himself is clearly part of an ongoing Jewish trajectory. Davies and Allison, *Matthew*, III, pp. 3–4, 9; Overman, *Matthew's Gospel*, pp. 278–79; Luz, *Matthew*, II, p. 488; Senior, *Matthew*, p. 78; Beare, *Matthew*, p. 54; Boring, 'Matthew,' p. 395. In first-century Rome, a primary cause of divorce was a man's suspicion of his wife's adultery (for example, Pompey's divorce of Mucia [Cicero, *A..* 1.12.3]). Other reasons for a man to divorce his wife were if she drank wine (Pliny, *Natural History* 14.90; also Plutarch, *Roman Questions* 6) or went out with improper head covering, talked to vulgar persons, or went out without telling her husband (Plutarch, *Roman Questions* 14; Plautus, *Mercator* 821–22).

indecency).[67] The LXX translates עֶרְוַת דָּבָר as ἄσχημον πρᾶγμα ('shameful deed'). The Hillelites interpreted the 'nakedness' or 'shameful deed' symbolically and broadly: a man could divorce his wife for anything that displeased him, while the Shammaites argued that only sexual impropriety was cause for divorce: 'The House of Shammai say, "A man should divorce his wife only because he has found grounds for unchastity," since it is said, "Because he has found in her indecency in anything." And the House of Hillel say, "Even if she spoiled his dish," since it is said, "Because he has found in her indecency in anything." And R. Aqiba says "Even if he found someone else prettier than she," since it is said, "And it shall be if she find no favor in his eyes"' (*m. Git.* 9.10).[68] Jesus' answer to the Pharisees, that 'whoever divorces his wife, except for πορνεία, and marries another, commits adultery' (Mt. 19.9; cf. 5.31–32) is almost identical to Shammai's.[69]

What πορνεία means is not easy to ascertain; the term covers a range of meanings, not always sexual. Besides the divorce exception clauses (5.32 and 19.9), the only other place the word πορνεία appears in Matthew is in a vice list of things that defile (15.19), but its meaning is not clear.[70] The word commonly appears in vice lists but without context for accurate definition (Mk 7.21; 2 Cor. 12.21; Gal. 5.19; Eph. 5.3; Col. 3.5; Rev. 9.21;

---

67. Other passages discouraging divorce include Mal. 2.14–16 and a Wisdom tradition that says it is wise to remain with the wife of one's youth (Prov. 5.18). See D. Warden, 'The Words of Jesus on Divorce', *ResQ* 39 (1997), pp. 141–53 (146–490). David Instone Brewer ('Deuteronomy 24.1–4 and the Origin of the Jewish Divorce Certificate,' *Journal of Jewish Studies* 49 [1998], pp. 230–43) suggests that עֶרְוַת does not refer to adultery but to a condition that made it 'too distasteful for [a husband] to continue in marriage [with his wife],' because the only other place the exact phrase עֶרְוַת דָּבָר occurs is Deut. 23.15 (LXX Deut. 23.14, ἀσχημοσύνη πράγματος), where it refers to the cleanliness of the camp. Deuteronomy 23.12–13 describes a designated area outside the camp and instructions for burying excrement. Such 'indecency' applied to marriage could refer to bodily or household uncleanliness that the husband finds disgusting.

68. Neusner, *The Mishnah: A New Translation* (New Haven: Yale University Press, 1998), p. 487. See discussion by Judith Romney Wegner, *Chattel or Person? The Status of Women in the Mishnah* (Oxford: Oxford University Press, 1988), pp. 45–50.

69. CD 4.20–21 mentions that one who takes two wives in his lifetime is guilty of fornication, because 'male and female he created them' (Martínez, *Dead Sea Scrolls*, p. 36), but it is not clear if this means remarrying after divorce or bigamy (cf. *Jub.* 20.3–6). The Mishnah prohibits a man from remarrying a woman he has divorced if she wed someone else and was subsequently divorced or widowed (*m. Yeb.* 4.12). In the early Church, some people evidently turned to divorce in order to live a life of devotion to the Lord's work in celibacy (Hermas, *Mandate* 4.1.5). Goulder writes that divorce for ascetic purposes was widespread in the early Church ('Devotion, Divorce, and Debauchery', p. 109). D'Angelo agrees that in many cases, divorce reflects the development of asceticism in the early Church ('Remarriage and Divorce Sayings', pp. 93–94).

70. πονηροί (evil), φόνοι (murder), μοιχεῖαι (adultery), πορνεῖαι (unspecified immorality), κλοπαί (thievery), ψευδομαρτυρίαι (false witness, slander), and βλασφημίαι (blasphemy, slander).

Didache 5.1; *Barnabas* 19.4; Clement, *Hom.* 1.18.2; *Ps. Clem.* 17.4; Hermas, *Mandate* 8.3; Dionysius of Halicarnassus, *Antiq. Rom.* 4.24.4).[71] Πορνεία is sometimes interpreted as sexual unchastity on the part of the wife (e.g., Philo, *Spec. Leg.* 3.30; Josephus, *Ant.* 4.253).[72] Πορνεία might include adultery but cannot be limited to adultery, because it is listed with but distinguished from μοιχεία (the usual word for adultery) in other contexts (Mt. 15.19; Mk 7.21; Philo, *Vit. Mos.* 1.300; Hermas, *Mandate* 8.3; *Didache* 5.1).[73]

Paul also prohibits divorce and remarriage after divorce (1 Cor. 7. 10–11), except in the case of marriage to an unbeliever (7.12–15). But Paul uses πορνεία to describe several types of sexual immorality: incest (a man is living with his father's wife [1 Cor. 5.1]); sexual activity outside of marriage (1 Cor. 7.2–5); defilement of the body (1 Cor. 6.13,18; 1 Thess. 4.3); and sexual intercourse with a prostitute (πόρνη) (1 Cor. 6.15–16).[74] Paul also lists πορνεία among sins of impurity (ἀκαθαρσία) and licentiousness (ἀσελγεία). The second-century *Acts of Peter* (30.16) describes a woman who had sexual intercourse with many men and even her own houseboys as having a reputation for πορνεῖα. Demetrius Rhetor (1 BCE) describes πορνεία as a characteristic (χαρακτῆρες) of flute-players (αὐλοῦντας), dancers (ὀρχουμενους), and singers (ᾄδοντας) (*De eloc.* 240.5), perhaps because entertainers were likely to be either slaves whose sexual services could be demanded by their masters, or itinerate performers whose lack of a settled home put them under suspicion of promiscuity.

Πορνεία is not always sexual sin but could refer to any number of wrongful behaviors including idolatry, corruption, and evil that resemble, in the minds of those who call these things πορνεία, someone who is corrupt, unfaithful, and unworthy. The Septuagint uses πορνεία as a metaphor for Israel's idolatry against God and commerce in the luxuries of foreign nations (Hos. 6.10; Jer. 3.2, 9).[75] Philo uses πορνεία to describe the 'harlotry of the soul' (ψυχῆς δὲ πορνείαν) in *Spec. Leg.* 1.282.4, and

---

71. For example, Clement of Rome (1 CE) lists πορνεία among the dangerous influences of evil friends and bad company, including irreverence (ἀφοβία), unbelief (ἀπιστία), avarice (φιλαργυρία), and boastfulness (κενοδοξία) (*Hom.* 1.18.2). The first-century BCE historian Dionysius of Halicarnassus lists πορνεία beside robbery and burglary (λῃστείας καὶ τοιχωρυχίας καὶ πορνείας) and 'all the other evils' (παντὸς ἄλλου πονηροῦ) that have made Rome 'filthy' (ῥυπαρά γέγονεν) (*Antiq. Rom.* 4.24.4).

72. Long, *Matthew*, p. 59; Davies and Allison, *Matthew*, III, p. 530; Schweizer, *Matthew*, p. 125; Senior, *Matthew*, pp. 78, 215; Boring, 'Matthew,' p. 192.

73. Hays, *Moral Vision*, pp. 354–55.

74. See Gaca, *Making of Fornication*, esp. pp. 170–72. Josephus refers to brothels as πορνεῖα (*Ant.* 19.357).

75. See discussion of the prophets' (and Paul's) construction of 'spiritual fornication' and 'spiritual adultery' in Gaca, *Making of Fornication*, pp. 170–89.

Ignatius of Antioch (1 CE) to refer to a whoring spirit (πορνείας πνεῦμα) in *Epistulae interpolatae et epistulae suppositiciae* 5.6.3. The corruption of Rome is described in terms of πορνεία, the sinful actions of Babylon the Great (Rev. 14.8; 17.1–6, 15–18; 18.2–24; 19.2). The great Whore (πόρνη, 17.1, 5, 16) is drunk with the blood of the saints, the prophets, and of Jesus (17.6; 18.24), corrupts the kings of the world with power and luxury (18.3, 9), and supplies merchants with costly goods, slaves, and human lives (18.11–13). If πορνεία refers both to sexual sin and to a metaphorical state of corruption, unfaithfulness and unworthiness, the Matthean legislation includes not only sexual sin but corrupt or disloyal behavior.

Matthew does not tell us exactly what πορνεία is, who decides that it has occurred, or what the consequences should be. That the judgment is subjective leaves cases open for interpretation. Dale Allison suggests that Matthew included the exception clause to his divorce teachings precisely because of the example of Joseph; Matthew wanted to retain the image of Joseph as a righteous man and therefore had to give him a reason he could divorce Mary, but was not obligated to do so.[76] That Joseph chooses not to divorce Mary indicates Joseph's marital resolve to 'commit his life without reservation' as a binding covenant according to the will of God.[77] Conversely, it may equally be the case that God directs Joseph not to divorce her because no acceptable cause of divorce, by Matthew's definition, actually has occurred. Indeed, the reason Joseph does not divorce Mary may well have more to do with Matthew's desire to portray Joseph and Mary as the model of non-reproductive marriage and fidelity to the fictive family. Mary has not committed an act of πορνεία but serves the fictive family.

5.6 *Conclusion*

That Jesus is a bridegroom with no bride signals that marriage is part of the present world (as in the time of Noah, when they married and were given in marriage until they were swept away from the flood), and that there is no longer any need for bridegrooms and brides. The Matthean bridegroom's ideal is singleness and celibacy, because in the resurrection, everyone will be like the angels who do not marry. Angels have no physical needs and exist to serve the deity; only 'fallen' angels marry and procreate. While the angels are portrayed as male beings, Matthew does not negate gender, at least in the present community. The Matthean Jesus preserves gender roles in teachings, including teachings about eschatology. Further, that there are 'mothers and brothers and sisters' in the fictive

76. Dale C. Allison, 'Divorce, Celibacy and Joseph (Matthew 1.18–25 and 19.1–12)', *JSNT* 49 (2003), pp. 3–10, esp. pp. 4–5.
77. Hays, *Moral Vision*, p. 365.

family indicates that certain gender roles are retained. But Matthew does seek to eliminate procreation and does not give an endorsement to the contracting of new marriages. Thus, the gospel removes one of, if not *the* major, social indicator of gender: marriage with its attendant concern for procreation.

The Matthean ideal is singleness, but rather than directly condemning marriage, the Matthean bridegroom actually forbids divorce. The Genesis citation that 'the two have become one flesh' is a reference to the Edenic existence of Adam and Eve. Here Matthew participates in a conversation about Eden that takes place in various early Jewish and Christian circles. According to Philo, differentiation of the original being is the cause of humanity's 'fallen' state; according to the rabbinic tradition, differentiation is an affirmation of the Creator's goodness, desire for human fertility, and restoration of the male and female as one in marriage. Matthew's interpretation is closer to Philo than to the rabbis, because Matthew seems to prefer the celibate state over marriage and discourages procreation.

Matthew's community was not alone in striving to live an angelic or Edenic example: some of the Dead Sea communities, Philo's Essenes and Therapeutae, and the Rechabites described in the *Apocalypse of Zosimus* provide examples of celibate communities that believed they lived in the presence of angels, or communities that included marriage only for procreation. The Matthean bridegroom's promotion of fictive family over biological family suggests he prefers celibacy even within marriage.

CONCLUSION

When the Matthean bridegroom is read in the context of Old Testament bridegrooms (חתנים, νυμφίοι, γάμβροι) a pattern becomes evident: as Old Testament bridegrooms are associated with violence as victims or as perpetrators, so Jesus the bridegroom is victim of violence and associated with the deity's perpetration of violence. As Old Testament bridegrooms lose or abandon their brides, Jesus the bridegroom has no bride. In the examples of Old Testament bridegrooms, marriage is not a secure institution, and reproductive roles are disrupted; this insecurity and disruption prefigure the way Matthew, while not overtly condemning marriage and reproduction, undermines the efficacy of weddings and production of children.

Violence associated with marriage is a common theme in ancient literature that prefigures violence associated with the Matthean bridegroom, especially in the two wedding parables. The Roman institution of marriage was founded, according to myth, on the rape and abduction of the Sabine women; the deity's role as retributive husband to Israel in prophetic rhetoric is tainted with images of domestic violence; the bridegroom in Revelation captains bloody destruction. Death and separation of the couple is so frequently depicted in the Classical sources that it becomes a trope: Greek playwrights associated marriage with death, and bridegrooms and brides frequently die before their weddings. Reading the Matthean bridegroom in the context of this literature suggests that the bridegroom is something of a stock character who is *expected* to be brideless, and whose presence means joy turned to sorrow, destruction and death.

As Matthew's narrative progresses toward the passion, images of violence escalate. The joyful scenes are disrupted as the bridegroom warns of the days of mourning and fasting and as the wedding feast becomes the site of separation and death. Accompanying this shift in imagery is a change in exhortation. After the Sermon on the Mount promotes idealized instruction for peaceful and vital relationships, community-building, forgiveness, and aspirations to a higher righteousness, Matthew's rhetoric progressively emphasizes division and conflict and threatens exclusion, retribution, punishment, and suffering.

Matthew establishes stark polarities between 'bad and good' and 'wise and foolish,' but the attempts to police the boundary between those who will enjoy the wedding feast – allegorically, entry into Jesus' Kingdom of Heaven – and those who will not are formed not by the language of voluntary association but by the rhetoric of coercion. The parables indicate that no one can rest assured of salvation. Indeed, they can be read 'against the grain' (although definitively determining Matthean intent remains an impossibility) as indicating that those who are apparently 'good' or 'wise' – those who wear festal robes and rejoice when the cities are burned; those who do not share with others in need – are in fact *not* loyal to the Kingdom of Heaven but to earthly tyranny. These ambiguities in the text, created by the disjunctions between the instructions in the Sermon on the Mount and what the wedding parables appear to advocate, blur the sharp distinction between 'bad and good,' 'wise and foolish' and call into question the justification for violence.

A non-allegorical reading of the parables challenges the eschatological setting of the wedding feast at the parousia; the king may just be a king who is also a tyrant; the bridegroom may just be a rude man late to his own wedding. A non-allegorical, resisting approach to what Matthew probably wanted to convey eliminates or at least tones down the associations of the Divine King and the Bridegroom Son with retributive violence.

To counter implications of violence associated with the Kingdom of Heaven, I offer a resisting reading of the Parable of the Wedding Feast. I suggest that the 'king' does not represent God or the Kingdom of Heaven but an earthly tyrant. The guests who refuse to come to the feast are just as evil as the 'king,' and the murder and destruction waged by the king fit expected patterns of violence associated with worldly evil. The parable's 'king' is thus no better than the 'earthly kings' such as 'King' Herod. The garmentless man has been 'dragged before governors and kings,' just as Jesus before the authorities; he is, like Jesus, a silent resistor to the tyrant. The parable's subversive message is that this man *should* resist the tyrant, even though his loyalty to the values of the Kingdom of Heaven means he faces violent consequences.

Similarly, I offer a resisting reading of the Parable of the Ten Virgins by suggesting that the 'bridegroom' in this parable is not Jesus and the delay not the parousia; this is an ordinary wedding with a rude and tardy bridegroom as host. The five so-called 'wise' virgins have violated key Matthean teachings presented in the Sermon on the Mount by not aiding the five 'foolish' virgins. The five 'wise' are shrewd instead of sharing, prepared with extra oil instead of relying on providence, and they do not worry about the gospel exhortation to 'stay awake.' The Parable of the Ten Virgins, constructed as a warning against complacency, deconstructs as the five wise virgins complacently sleep, rely on their own resources rather than on providence, and refuse to share with those in need. I read a subversive message in the deconstruction, that perhaps entering this wedding feast is not desirable; the foolish virgins should instead aspire to entering the Kingdom of Heaven, where people share with those in need, rely on providence, and do not call one another 'fool.'

Images of bridegroom, wedding feast, and the creation of a new family in the gospel of Matthew have life-affirming and joyous potential. The text opens with a genealogy that includes unexpected figures: Tamar (a widow who becomes pregnant by her father-in-law), Rahab (a Canaanite prostitute), Ruth (a Moabite widow who procures levirate marriage), and Uriah's widow (Bathsheba, taken in adultery to become mother of Solomon). These women prove their worthiness as mothers in the fictive family, not by procreation but by the extraordinary righteousness or allegiance to the house of Israel that their actions represent.

The text then introduces a new type of family – a virgin mother, a protective non-biological father who agrees to take the pregnant Mary as his wife and raise her son as his own, and a child who 'will save his people from their sins.' The child, soon identified as the 'bridegroom,' (9.15), begins the formation of his own 'fictive family' of mothers and brothers and sisters (12.46–50). Biological fathers are systematically excluded as procreation and marriage contracts yield to voluntary association (e.g., 19.10–12).

Yet each image of the new family contains the threat of disruption and violence. Tamar risks death by fire; Rahab the destruction of family and city; Ruth the loss of her natal family; Bathsheba the death of her husband Uriah and the child she and David conceive. Joseph and Mary form their family in the context of a threat of murder, and the family's preservation comes at the cost of the lives of the children of Bethlehem. Those who choose to affiliate with Jesus the bridegroom face conflict in their own households, between sons and fathers, daughters and mothers, daughters-in-law and mothers-in-law (10.34–39). The traditional family or 'household' is not, for Matthew, a place of *Shalom*.

To a great extent, theologians have resisted the implication that divine orchestration lies behind such disruption; when divine involvement is acknowledged, it is accompanied by theological apologetic. For example, the sacrifice of a few (or one) for the eventual good of the many is a theology of sacrificial atonement that accepts violence as a necessary part of God's salvific plan: Jesus gives his life as a ransom for many (20.28). This theology accepts the deaths of the children as a necessary sacrifice for the eventual salvation of many. The early Church regarded these children as *participants* in this sacrifice and salvation: they are martyrs who shared the suffering of Christ. But because of this theology, violence becomes a necessary part of the life of the Matthean bridegroom and the foundation of his fictive family. Therefore, in Matthew, there is an integral irony: the bridegroom dies so that others may live, but the bridegroom (and his community) lives because others die. I was unable to develop to my satisfaction a resisting reading of the Matthean infancy narrative, in which Joseph, Mary, and Jesus escape the slaughter of the innocents and the subsequent mourning not only of Rachel, but of all those now-bereaved Jews in Bethlehem. In this story, the deity is implicated in the violence; the human king may be the direct cause of the murders, but the deity is equally culpable by failing to stop it while orchestrating the salvation of one family. I resist Matthew's implication that the Bethlehem families – biological families, traditional families, Jews who did not follow the star or worship the Christ – are fated for destruction.

I reluctantly conclude that the fictive family, at least as Matthew depicts it, is a dangerous affiliation. Jesus' birth and incorporation into Joseph's family is overshadowed by death. That Jesus insists his disciples become like little children (18.1–2) and exhorts them to let the children be blessed by him (19.12–13) is a situation fraught with danger, because children associated with Jesus do not always live; in fact allegiance to the fictive family exposes the 'children' to danger: they are expected to suffer and even to die for Jesus' sake (10.32–39; 20.22–28; 24.9–21).

Matthew promises divine judgment as reassurance that God will eventually bring justice; thus humans need not engage in violence. However, a violent deity also implies that the use of coercion is an acceptable means of resolving problems. Certainly the threat of violence has the function of keeping community members in line.

The ideal of the fictive family also has potential to disrupt actual families. Even with his injunctions against divorce, the Matthean bridegroom disrupts the institutions of marriage and family in a culture that valued these institutions highly. A bridegroom who never becomes a husband obviously undermines these cultural expectations. While I am not inclined to take a 'family values' stance comporting with those of people like James Dobson or Jerry Falwell, I am also distrusting of Matthew's alternative ethos where the family (defined according to first-century configurations) is the locus of dissention and where celibacy is the preferred way of life.

I have identified literary images of bridegrooms that anticipate the violence associated with Jesus the bridegroom, and I have both detailed elements of violence in the gospel itself and explored how that rhetoric may have shaped Matthew's community. Matthean violence and rhetoric of 'good' and 'bad' continue to influence life in the Church, as well as attitudes toward the 'other' in the world. The fictive family can be a new home, especially to those without support, but families of origin are broken. Moreover, the members of this family appear to be without support: Peter's mother-in-law who is left without his support; James and John along with their mother leave Zebedee with the boats. Matthew's gospel may well be less interested in providing families for those who have none than in disrupting intact relationships.

Matthew's interest in celibacy can have a helpful function today, especially in the context of American society's fascination with sexual activity of all sorts. The Protestant churches in general lack a place for the celibate or the unmarried, as most single persons in churches can attest. But privileging of one way of life over another – of celibacy over marriage, or, as today's 'family values' groups would have it, of heterosexual marriages that produce children over the choice to remain single or the choice to live in a same-sex relationship – is similarly unhealthy. The Matthean bridegroom and his celibate attendants provide one way of living, but I hope it is not the only way.

If we are to be like angels, then we must carefully judge what the image conveys. On the one hand, the notion that women are 'given in marriage' as if they are a commodity is one I am happy to reject. On the other hand, the erasure of certain gender roles may well be welcome news: women *qua* women should not be excluded from the inner group of disciples, the 'sons of the bridal chamber.'

The wedding feast can function as an inclusive image of joy, but in Matthew's hands it ultimately conveys a message of violence, separation, and death. Some might rejoice when the bridegroom comes, but I must conclude that we might be better off resisting the 'wedding feast' as Matthew describes it. The feast offers nothing to celebrate when doors are barred, guests are tortured, and cities are burned. This is not the image of Christianity I wish to present to my children, or to the world. If parables are designed to call into question the world 'as it is,' and if they are to function as alternative visions, then let them function as such. It may be time we identified with the garmentless man and with the foolish virgins.

Like Barbara Reid, I find that the gospel of Matthew contains models of both peaceful resolution through forgiveness and prayer for enemies, and conflict exacerbated by labeling others and by using violent retribution.[1] Like Reid, I fear interpretations concluding that if 'God punishes evildoers violently, human beings in positions of power may understand the Gospel as giving divine approval for their meting out violent punishment, even execution, to those they judge to be evildoers.'[2] I affirm Reid's suggestion that readers privilege aspects of the gospel that imitate Jesus' example of non-violence over the violence Matthew adds to the parables and come up with non-violent metaphors to express peaceful solutions to conflict and correction of evil.[3]

In response to Reid, I would like to suggest – from my own study – that

---

1. Reid, 'Violent Endings', pp. 237–55. Reid's article was published as I was writing this conclusion. I had read an earlier version of her article presented to the Matthew Section at the annual SBL meeting (Denver, CO; Nov. 17–21, 2001).
2. Reid, 'Violent Endings', p. 253.
3. Reid, 'Violent Endings', pp. 254–55.

readers can find at least a partial peaceful alternative to conflict in the Matthean example of the fictive family. By identifying and resisting violent features, such as the slaughter of the innocents, readers can focus on how the model of adoptive fatherhood and motherhood promotes care for the homeless and the refugee and undermines human tendencies to hoard wealth and crave social status. The Matthean fictive family, while unfortunately disruptive of families of origin, reflects a social reality that sometimes making choices for the sake of the Kingdom of Heaven conflicts with religious establishments, and our choice to follow Jesus the bridegroom may mean eschewing common social expectations and roles.

The Matthean fictive family is a model of families of choice that grow by incorporation rather than by biological reproduction. The gospel is supportive of churches, synagogues, missions, and the many associations for social justice that represent voluntary societies dedicated to furthering peaceful resolution of conflict, economic justice, and protection of the marginal. Though I am fairly certain that Matthew would not approve of my reading, I think Matthew's portrayal of the fictive family also supports today's gay and lesbian families who fit the model of a family of choice headed by (often non-reproductive) mothers and fathers who protect each other and their children from the hostile powers that be in dominant society.[4] Their sexuality often is deemed, especially by the Church, to be on the fringes or outside the bounds of acceptance (like the socially questionable actions of Tamar, Rahab, Ruth, and Bathsheba). However, in the context of the ongoing 'genealogy' of Jesus' fictive family, they may prove someday to be the 'mothers, brothers, and sisters' who have demonstrated extraordinary righteousness.

I want to affirm, with Reid, that non-violent resistance is a viable means of countering violence.[5] My reading of the Parables of the Wedding Feast and Ten Virgins shows that violence is the result of human tyranny, not God's, and that we should not accept a portrayal of the Kingdom that is no better than violent governments and evil coalitions. My reading also shows that loyalty to the ideals of the Kingdom of Heaven can result in becoming the victim of human violence. This sort of resistant reading is certainly not new – as the example of Jesus clearly shows – but is worth reiterating in the context of today's violent world.

Perhaps the time will come when we can all be members of a new family that can embrace more than those of a particular nationality, race, class, or theological perspective; perhaps then we can celebrate at the wedding in which there is a banquet for all, and no one is cast into the outer darkness.

---

4. I thank Emily Askew for this insight.
5. Reid, 'Violent Endings', pp. 242–48.

BIBLIOGRAPHY

Aarde, A. van, 'The Carpenter's Son (Mt. 13.55): Joseph and Jesus in the Gospel of Matthew and Other Texts', *Neot* 34 (2000), pp. 173–90.

—'Fatherless in First-century Mediterranean Culture: The Historical Jesus Seen from the Perspective of Cross-cultural Anthropology and Cultural Psychology', *Hervormde Teologiese Studies* 55 (1999), pp. 97–119.

—*God-with-Us: The Dominant Perspective in Matthew's Story* (Hervormde Teologiese Studies, Supplementary 5; Pretoria: University of Pretoria, 1994).

—'Social Identity, Status Envy and Jesus' Abba', *Pastoral Psychology* 45 (1997), pp. 451–72.

Aitken, E.B., 'At the Well of Living Water: Jacob Traditions in John 4', in C.A. Evans (ed.), *The Interpretation of Scripture in Early Judaism and Christianity* (Sheffield: Sheffield Academic Press, 2000), pp. 342–52.

Albert the Great, *On Matthew* (ed. Auguste Borgnet; 38 vols.; *Opera Omnia*, 10; Paris: Ludovicum Vivès, 1890–99).

Albright, W.F., and C.S. Mann, *Matthew* (AB, 26; New York: Doubleday, 1971).

Allen, W.C., *A Critical and Exegetical Commentary on the Gospel According to S. Matthew* (ICC; New York: Charles Scribner's Sons, 1907).

Allison, D.C., 'Divorce, Celibacy and Joseph (Matthew 1.18–25 and 19.1–12)', *JSNT* 49 (2003), pp. 3–10.

—'The Eschatology of Jesus', in J.J. Collins (ed.), *The Encyclopedia of Apocalypticism: The Origins of Apocalypticism in Judaism and Christianity* (3 vols.; New York: Continuum, 1998), I, pp. 267–301.

—*Jesus of Nazareth: Millenarian Prophet* (Minneapolis: Fortress Press, 1998).

—'Matthew', *The Oxford Bible Commentary* (Oxford: Oxford University Press, 2000), pp. 844–86.

—*The New Moses: A Matthean Typology* (Minneapolis: Fortress Press, 1993).

Alter, R., 'Characterization and the Art of Reticence', in D.J.A. Clines and T.C. Eskenazi (eds.), *Telling Queen Michal's Story*, pp. 64–73.

Anderson, G.A., 'The Garden of Eden and Sexuality in Early Judaism', in H. Eilberg-Schwartz (ed.), *People of the Body: Jews and Judaism from an Embodied Perspective* (New York: State University of New York Press, 1992), pp. 47–68.

—*The Genesis of Perfection: Adam and Eve in Jewish and Christian Imagination* (Louisville: Westminster/John Knox Press, 2001).

Anderson, J.C., 'Matthew, Gender, and Reading', *Semeia* 28 (1983), pp. 3–27; repr. in A.-J. Levine (ed.), *A Feminist Companion to Matthew*, pp. 25–52.

Anderson, J.C., and S.D. Moore (eds.), *Mark and Method: New Approaches to Biblical Studies* (Minneapolis: Fortress Press, 1992).

Aquinas, T., *Catena Aurea: Commentary on the Four Gospels Collected Out of the Works of the Fathers* (trans. John Henry Cardinal Newman; London: Saint Austin Press, 1997).

—*Opera Omnia* (eds. S.E. Fretté and Paul Maré; 34 vols; Paris: Ludovicum Vivès, 1871–80).

Arai, S., ' "To Make Her Male": An Interpretation of Logion 114 in the Gospel of Thomas', *Studia Patristica* 24 (1993), pp. 373–76.

Archer, L.J., *Her Price Is Beyond Rubies: The Jewish Woman in Graeco-Roman Palestine* (JSOTSup, 60; Sheffield: JSOT Press, 1990).

Ardens, R., *Homilies on the Gospels* (ed. J.-P. Migne; 221 vols.; *Patrologiae cursus completus*, 155; Paris: Garnier Frères, 1844–64).

Ashby, G.W., 'The Bloody Bridegroom: The Interpretation of Exodus 4.24–26', *ExpTim* 106 (Ap. 1995), pp. 203–205.

Attridge, H., 'Don't Be Touching Me: Recent Feminist Scholarship on Mary Magdalene', in A.-J. Levine (ed.), *A Feminist Companion to John*, II, pp. 140–66.

Atwood, M., *Good Bones and Simple Murders* (New York: Doubleday, 1994).

Auerbach, E., *Moses* (Detroit: Wayne State University Press, 1975).

Augustodunensis, H., *Speculum ecclesiae* (ed. J.-P. Migne; 221 vols.; *Patrologiae cursus completes*, 172; Paris: Garnier Frères, 1844–64).

Avis, P., *God and the Creative Imagination: Metaphor, Symbol, and Myth in Religion and Theology* (London and New York: Routledge, 1999).

Bacon, B.W., *Studies in Matthew* (New York: H. Holt, 1930).

—'Two Parables of Lost Opportunity', *Hibbert Journal* 21 (1922–23), pp. 337–52.

Bailey, D.R.S. (trans.), *Cicero: Letters to Atticus* (4 vols.; LCL, 8; Cambridge, MA: Harvard University Press, 1999).

Bailey, K.E., *Poet and Peasant and Through Peasant Eyes: A Literary-cultural Approach to the Parables in Luke* (Grand Rapids: Eerdmans, combined edn, 1983).

Baird, A., *The Justice of God in the Teaching of Jesus* (Philadelphia: Westminster Press, 1963).

Bal, M., 'The Anthropological Code', in M. Bal, *Murder and Difference*, pp. 51–73.

—*Death and Dissymmetry: The Politics of Coherence in the Book of Judges* (Chicago: University of Chicago Press, 1988).

—*Murder and Difference: Gender, Genre, and Scholarship in Sisera's Death* (trans. M. Gumpert; Bloomington, IN: Indiana University Press, 1992).

Balabanski, V., 'Opening the Closed Door: A Feminist Rereading of the "Wise and Foolish Virgins" (Mt. 25.1–13)', in M.A. Beavis (ed.), *The Lost Coin*, pp. 71–97.

Baldick, C., *The Concise Oxford Dictionary of Literary Terms* (Oxford: Oxford University Press, 1990).

Ballard, P., 'Reasons for Refusing the Great Supper', *JTS* 23 (1972), pp. 341–50.

Banning, J. van (ed.), *Opus Imperfectum in Matthaeum* (Corpus Christianorum, Latin Series 87B; Turnholt: Brepols, 1988).

Barclay, J.M.G., 'The Family as the Bearer of Religion in Judaism and Early Christianity', in H. Moxnes (ed.), *Constructing Early Christian Families*, pp. 66–80.

Barton, S.C., *Discipleship and Family Ties in Matthew and Mark* (Cambridge: Cambridge University Press, 1994).

—'Historical Criticism and Social-scientific Perspectives in New Testament Study', in J.B. Green (ed.), *Hearing the New Testament: Strategies for Interpretation* (Grand Rapids: Eerdmans, 1995), pp. 61–89.

—'The Relativisation of Family Ties in the Jewish and Graeco-Roman Traditions', in H. Moxnes (ed.), *Constructing Early Christian Families*, pp. 81–99.

Batey, R.A., *New Testament Nuptial Imagery* (Leiden: Brill, 1971).

Bauckham, R., *Jude and the Relatives of Jesus in the Early Church* (Edinburgh: T&T Clark, 1990).

—'The Parable of the Royal Wedding Feast (Matthew 22.1–14) and The Parable of the Lame Man and the Blind Man (*Apocryphon of Ezekiel*)', *JBL* 115/3 (1996), pp. 471–88.

Baumbach, G., *Das Verständnis des Bösen in den synoptischen Evangelien* (Berlin: Evangelische Verlagsanstalt, 1963).

Beard, M., J. North, and S. Price (eds.), *Religions of Rome* (2 vols.; Cambridge: Cambridge University Press, 1998).

Beare, F.W., *The Gospel According to Matthew* (San Francisco: Harper & Row, 1981).

—'The Parable of the Guests at the Banquet', in S.E. Johnson (ed.), *The Joy of Study: Papers on the New Testament and Related Subjects Presented to Honor Frederick Clifton Grant* (New York: MacMillan, 1951), pp. 1–14.

Beasley-Murray, G.R., *Jesus and the Kingdom of God* (Grand Rapids: Eerdmans, 1986).

Beavis, M.A. (ed.), *The Lost Coin: Parables of Women, Work, and Wisdom* (Sheffield: Sheffield Academic Press, 2002).

Bekker, I. (ed.), *Apolloni Sophistae Lexicon Homericum* (Hildesham: Georg Olms Verlagsbuchhandlung, 1967).

Ben-Barak, Z., 'The Legal Background to the Restoration of Michal to David', in D.J.A. Clines and T.C. Eskenazi (eds.), *Telling Queen Michal's Story*, pp. 74–90.

Benner, A.R., and F.H. Fobes (trans.), *The Letters of Alciphron, Aelian, and Philostratus* (LCL, 383; Cambridge, MA: Harvard University Press, 1949, repr. 1990).

Bennett, L.K., and Tyrrell, W.B., 'What Is Antigone Wearing?', *Classical World* 85 (1991), pp. 107–109.

Benz, E., *et al.* (eds.), *Cahiers l'Hermétisme: L'Androgyne dans la littérature* (Paris: Éditions Albin Michel, 1990).

Berefelt, G., *A Study on the Winged Angel: The Origin of a Motif* (Stockholm: Almqvist and Wiksell, 1968).

Biale, D., *Eros and the Jews* (Berkeley and Los Angeles: University of California Press, 1997).

Bird, P., 'To Play the Harlot: An Inquiry into an Old Testament Metaphor', in P.L. Day (ed.), *Gender and Difference* (Minneapolis: Fortress Press, 1989), pp. 75–94.

Black, M., *The Book of Enoch or I Enoch* (Leiden: E.J. Brill, 1985).

—'Metaphor', in M. Johnson (ed.), *Philosophical Perspectives on Metaphor* (Minneapolis: University of Minnesota, 1981), pp. 63–82.

—*Models and Metaphors: Studies in Language and Philosophy* (Ithaca: Cornell University Press, 1992).

Blomberg, C.L., *Interpreting the Parables* (Downers Grove, IL: InverVarsity Press, 1990).

—'Marriage, Divorce, Remarriage and Celibacy: An Exegesis of Matthew 19.3–12', *Trinity Journal* 11 (1990), pp. 163–66.

Boissard, E., 'Note sur l'interpretation du texte "Multi sunt vocati, pauci vero electi",' *Revue Thomiste* 60 (1952), pp. 569–85.

Bonnard, E. (ed.), *Saint Jerome: Commentarie sur S. Matthieu* (2 vols.; Sources Chrétiennes, 259; Paris: Les Éditions du Cerf, 1979).

Booth, W., 'Metaphor as Rhetoric: The Problem of Evaluation', in S. Sacks (ed.), *On Metaphor*, pp. 47–70.

Boring, M. Eugene, *The Gospel of Matthew: Introduction, Commentary, and Reflection* (*NIB*, 8; Nashville: Abingdon Press, 1995), pp. 89–505.

Bornkamm, G., 'Die Verzögerung der Parusie', in W. Schmauch (ed.), *In Memoriam Ernst Lohmeyer* (Stuttgart: Evanglisches Verlagswerk, 1951), pp. 116–26.

Børresen, K.E., 'God's Image, Man's Image: Patristic Interpretation of Gen. 1.27 and 1 Cor. 11.7', in K.E. Børresen (ed.), *Image of God and Gender Models in Judaeo-Christian Tradition*, pp. 188–207.

Børresen, K.E. (ed.), *The Image of God and Gender Models in Judaeo-Christian Tradition* (Oslo: Solum Forlag, 1991).

Borsch, F.H., *Many Things in Parables: Extravagant Stories of New Community* (Philadelphia: Fortress Press, 1988).

Boucher, M., *The Parables* (New Testament Message, 7; Dublin: Veritas, 1981).

Bowman, R.G., and R.W. Swanson, 'Samson and the Son of God or Dead Heroes and Dead Goats: Ethical Readings of Narrative Violence in Judges and Matthew', *Semeia* 77 (1997), pp. 59–73.

Boyarin, D., *Carnal Israel: Reading Sex in Talmudic Culture* (Berkeley: University of California, 1993).

—'Paul and the Genealogy of Gender', *Representations* 41 (1993), pp. 1–33; repr. in A.-J. Levine (ed.), *A Feminist Companion to Paul*, pp. 13–41.

Brenner, A., 'Come Back, Come Back the Shulammite: A Parody of the *wasf* Genre', in A. Brenner (ed.), *A Feminist Companion to The Song of Songs* (Sheffield: Sheffield Academic Press, 1993), pp. 234–57.

—'On Prophetic Propaganda and the Politics of "Love": The Case of Jeremiah', in A. Brenner, (ed.), *A Feminist Companion to the Latter Prophets* (Sheffield: Sheffield Academic Press, 1995), pp. 256–74.

Brett, M.G., 'Reading the Bible in the Context of Methodological Pluralism: The Undermining of Ethnic Exclusivism in Genesis', in M.D. Carroll (ed.), *Rethinking Contexts*, pp. 48–74.

Brewer, D.I., 'Deuteronomy 24.1–4 and the Origin of the Jewish Divorce Certificate', *Journal of Jewish Studies* 49 (1998), pp. 230–43.

Brooks, S.H., 'Apocalyptic Paraenesis in Matthew 6.19–34', in J. Marcus and M.L. Soards (eds.), *Apocalyptic and the New Testament: Essays in Honor of J. Louis Martyn* (JSNTSup, 24; Sheffield: Sheffield Academic Press, 1989), pp. 95–112.

Brown, F. (ed.), *The New Brown–Driver–Briggs–Gesenius Hebrew and English Lexicon* (Peabody, MA: Hendrickson, 1979).

Brown, P., *The Body and Society: Men, Women, and Sexual Renunciation in Early Christianity* (New York: Columbia University Press, 1988).

Brown, R.E., *The Birth of the Messiah: A Commentary on the Infancy Narratives in the Gospels of Matthew and Luke* (New York: Doubleday, rev. edn., 1993).

—'Parable and Allegory Reconsidered', in Brown, *New Testament Essays* (Milwaukee: Bruce, 1965), pp. 254–64.

Browning, D.S., and I.S. Evison, 'Series Forward', in C. Osiek and D.L. Balch, *Families in the New Testament World*, pp. vii–viii.

Brumfield, A.C., *The Attic Festivals of Demeter and Their Relation to the Agricultural Year* (Monographs in Classical Studies; Salem, NH: The Ayer Company, 1981).

Buckley, J.J., *Female Fault and Fulfillment in Gnosticism* (Chapel Hill, NC: University of North Carolina Press, 1986).

—'An Interpretation of Logion 114 in the *Gospel of Thomas*', *NovT* 27.3 (1985), pp. 245–72.

Bultmann, R., *The History of the Synoptic Tradition* (trans. J. Marsh; Peabody: Hendrickson, 5th edn, 1963).

Burke, T., 'Pauline Adoption: A Sociological Approach', *EvQ* 73 (2001), pp. 119–34.

Burkitt, F.C., 'The Parable of the Ten Virgins', *JTS* 30 (1929), pp. 267–70.

Burrus, V., and S.D. Moore, 'Unsafe Sex: Feminism, Pornography, and the Song of Songs', *BibInt* 11 (2003), pp. 24–52.

Buttrick, D., *Speaking Parables: A Homiletic Guide* (Louisville: Westminster/John Knox Press, 2000).

Buttrick, G.A., *The Parables of Jesus* (New York: Harper and Brothers Publishers, 1928).

Calvin, J., *Commentary on a Harmony of the Evangelists, Matthew, Mark, and Luke* (trans. W. Pringle; 10 vols.; Grand Rapids, MI: Eerdmans, 1956–57).

Campbell, D.A. (trans.), *Greek Lyric* (5 vols.; LCL, 143; Cambridge, MA: Harvard University Press, 1982).

Caner, D.F., 'The Practice and Prohibition of Self-Castration in Early Christianity', *VC* 51 (1997), pp. 396–415.

Capon, R.F., *Kingdom, Grace, and Judgment: Paradox, Outrage, and Vindication in the Parables of Jesus* (Grand Rapids: Eerdmans, 2002).

—*The Parables of Judgment* (Grand Rapids: Eerdmans, 1989).

Carey, G., 'Women, Men, and the Book of Revelation: Ethics and Exegesis', in A.-J. Levine (ed.), *A Feminist Companion to Early Christian Apocalyptic Literature* (London: Sheffield/Continuum, forthcoming).

Carmichael, C., 'Marriage and the Samaritan Woman', *NTS* 26 (1980), pp. 332–46.

Carroll, M.D. (ed.), *Rethinking Contexts, Rereading Texts: Contributions from the Social Sciences to Biblical Interpretation* (JSOTSup, 299; Sheffield: Sheffield Academic Press, 2000).

Carter, W., *Households and Discipleship: A Study of Matthew 19–20* (JSNTSup, 103; Sheffield: Sheffield Academic Press, 1994).

—*Matthew and the Margins: A Sociopolitical and Religious Reading* (Maryknoll, NY: Orbis, 2000).

Carter, W., and J.P. Heil, *Matthew's Parables: Audience-oriented Perspectives* (CBQMS, 30; Washington, DC: The Catholic Biblical Association of America, 1998).

Chapman, D.W., 'Marriage and Family in Second Temple Judaism', in K.M. Campbell (ed.), *Marriage and Family in the Biblical World* (Downers Grove, IL: InterVarsity Press, 2003), pp. 183–239.

Chappell, F. (trans.), 'Alcestis', in D.R. Slavitt and P. Bovie (eds.), *Euripides: Alcestis, Daughters of Troy, The Phoenician Women, Iphigenia at Aulis, Rhesus* (Philadelphia: University of Pennsylvania Press, 1998), pp. 7–59.

Charlesworth, J.H., 'Is it Conceivable that Jesus Married Mary Magdalene?', in A.-J. Levine (ed.), *A Feminist Companion to the Jesus Movement* (forthcoming).

Charlesworth, J.H., (ed.), *The Old Testament Pseudepigrapha* (2 vols.; New York: Doubleday, 1983).

Chavasse, C., *The Bride of Christ: An Enquiry into the Nuptial Element in Early Christianity* (London: Faber and Faber, 1940).

Cheney, E., 'Ten Maidens Awaiting the Bridegroom', paper given at the Society of Biblical Literature annual meeting in Denver, Colorado, November 18, 2001.

Childs, B., *The Book of Exodus* (OTL; Philadelphia: Westminster Press, 1974).

Christian of Stablo, *Expositio in Matthaeum evangelistam*, in J.-P. Migne (ed.), *Patrologiae cursus completus* (Latin series, 106), pp. 1261–1504.

Clarke, J.R., *Looking at Lovemaking: Constructions of Sexuality in Roman Art 100 BC–AD 250* (Berkeley: University of Califorinia Press, 1998).

Clines, D.J.A., *The Dictionary of Classical Hebrew* (4 vols.; Sheffield: Sheffield Academic Press, 1996).

Clines, D.J.A., and T.C. Eskenazi (eds.), *Telling Queen Michal's Story: An Experiment in Comparative Interpretation* (JSOTSup, 119; Sheffield: JSOT Press, 1991).

Coats, G.W., *Exodus 1–18* (2 vols.; Forms of the Old Testament Literature; Grand Rapids: Eerdmans, 1999).

—*Moses: Heroic Man, Man of God* (JSOTSup, 57; Sheffield: Sheffield Academic Press, 1988).

Cohen, J., *The Origins and Evolution of the Moses Nativity Story* (Leiden: Brill, 1993).

Cohen, S.J.D., *The Jewish Family in Antiquity* (BJS, 289; Atlanta: Scholars Press, 1993).

Collard, C. (trans.), *Aeschylus: Oresteia* (Oxford: Oxford University Press, 2002).

Collier, G.D., 'Rethinking Jesus on Divorce', *ResQ* 37 (1995), pp. 80–96.

Collins, A.Y., 'Feminine Symbolism in the Book of Revelation', *BibInt* 1 (1993), pp. 20–33.

Collins, J.J., *The Apocalyptic Imagination: An Introduction to Jewish Apocalyptic Literature* (Grand Rapids: Eerdmans, 2nd edn, 1998).

—'In the Likeness of the Holy Ones: The Creation of Humankind in a Wisdom Text from Qumran', in D.W. Parry and E. Ulrich (eds.), *The Provo International Conference on the Dead Sea Scrolls* (Leiden: Brill, 1999), pp. 609–18.

—'Marriage, Divorce, and Family in Second Temple Judaism', in L.G. Perdue, J. Blenkinsopp, J.J. Collins, and Carol Meyers (eds.), *Families in Ancient Israel* (Family, Religion, and Culture series; Louisville: Westminster/John Knox Press, 1997), pp. 104–62.

Coneybeare, F.C. (trans.), *Philostratus: The Life of Apollonius of Tyana* (LCL, 16; Cambridge, MA: Harvard University Press, 1912, repr. 2000).

Cope, O.L., ' "To the Close of the Age": The Role of Apocalyptic Thought in the Gospel of Matthew', in J. Marcus and M.L. Soards (eds.), *Apocalyptic and the New Testament*, pp. 113–24.

Corbier, M., 'Constructing Kinship in Rome: Marriage, Divorce, Filiation, and Adoption', in D.I. Kertzer and R.P. Saller (eds.), *The Family in Italy from Antiquity to the Present* (New Haven: Yale University Press, 1991), pp. 127–44.

—'Divorce and Adoption as Roman Familial Strategies', in B. Rawson (ed.), *Marriage, Divorce, and Children in Ancient Rome* (Oxford: Clarendon Press, 1996), pp. 47–78.

Corley, K.E., 'Women's Inheritance Rights in Antiquity and Paul's Metaphor of Adoption', in A.-J. Levine (ed.), *A Feminist Companion to Paul*, pp. 98–121.

Cotter, W., 'The Collegia and Roman Law: State Restrictions on Voluntary Associations, 64 BCE–200 CE', in J.S. Kloppenborg and S.G. Wilson (eds.), *Voluntary Associations*, pp. 74–89.

Court, J.M., 'Right and Left: The Implications for Matthew 25.31–46', *NTS* 32 (1985), pp. 223–33.

Cox, A Cleveland (trans.), 'The Acts of Philip', in A. Roberts and J. Donaldson (eds.), *The Ante-Nicene Fathers* (10 vols.; Peabody, MA: Hendrickson Publishers, 1994), VIII.

Craffer, P.F., 'An Exercise in the Critical Use of Models: The "Goodness of Fit" of Wilson's Sect Model', in J.J. Pilch (ed.), *Social Scientific Models*, pp. 21–46.

Cremer, F.G., 'Der Beitrag Augustins zur Auslegung des Fastenstreitgesprächs (Mk 2,18–22 parr) und die mittelalterliche Theologie', *Recherches augustiniennes* 8 (1972), pp. 301–73.

—'Die Söhne des Brautgemachs (Mk 2.19 parr) in der griechischen und lateinischen Schrifterklärung', *BZ* 11 (1967), pp. 246–52.

Cripps, K., 'A Note on Matthew xxii.12', *ExpTim* 69 (1957–58), p. 30.

Crosby, M.H., *House of Disciples: Church, Economics, and Justice in Matthew* (Maryknoll, NY: Orbis, 1988).

Crossan, J.D., *Cliffs of Fall: Paradox and Polyvalence in the Parables of Jesus* (New York: Seabury, 1980).

—*The Historical Jesus: The Life of a Mediterranean Jewish Peasant* (New York: Harper Collins, 1991).

—*In Parables: The Challenge of the Historical Jesus* (New York: Harper and Row, 1973).

—'Parables as Religious and Poetic Experience', *JR* 53 (1973).

Culbertson, P.L., *A Word Fitly Spoken: Context, Transmission, and Adoption of the Parables of Jesus* (SUNY Series in Religious Studies; New York: SUNY Press, 1995).

Cumming, J., *Foreshadows: Lectures on Our Lord's Parables* (Philadelphia: Lindsay and Blakiston, 1854).

Dalman, G.H., *Aramäisch-Neuhebräisches Handwörterbuch zu Targum, Talmud und Midrasch* (Hildesheim: Georg Olms Verlagsbuchhandlung, 1967).

Dan, J., *The Ancient Jewish Mysticism* (Tel Aviv: MOD Books, 1993), pp. 16–22.

D'Angelo, M.R., 'Remarriage and the Divorce Sayings Attributed to Jesus', in W. Roberts (ed.), *Divorce and Remarriage* (Kansas City: Sheed and Ward, 1990), pp. 78–106.

Davidson, D., 'What Metaphors Mean', in S. Sacks (ed.), *On Metaphor*, pp. 29–45.

Davidson, M.J., *Angels at Qumran: A Comparative Study of 1 Enoch 1–36, 72–108 and Sectarian Writings from Qumran* (JSPSup, 11; Sheffield: JSOT Press, 1992).

Davies, S., *The Gospel of Thomas and Christian Wisdom* (New York: Seabury, 1983).

Davies, W.D., and D.C. Allison, *The Gospel According to Saint Matthew* (3 vols.; ICC; Edinburgh: T&T Clark, 1988, 1991, 1997).

Davis, G.F., *Israel in Egypt: Reading Exodus 1–2* (JSOTSup, 135; Sheffield: Sheffield Academic Press, 1992).

Davis, S.T. (ed.), *Encountering Evil: Live Options in Theodicy* (Atlanta: John Knox Press, 1981).

Dawson, W.S., 'The Gate Crasher', *ExpTim* 85 (1974), pp. 304–306.

Day, P.L., 'The Personification of Cities as Female in the Hebrew Bible: The Thesis of Aloysius Fitzberald, F.S.C.', in F.F. Segovia and M.A. Tolbert (eds.), *Reading from This Place.* II. *Social Location and Biblical Interpretation in Global Perspective* (Minneapolis: Fortress Press, 1995), pp. 283–302.

De Conick, A.D. 'The Great Mystery of Marriage: Sex and Conception in Ancient Valentinian Traditions', *VC* 57 (2003), pp. 307–42.

Deferrari, R.J., and M.R.P. McGuire (trans.), *Saint Basil: The Letters* (4 vols.; LCL; Cambridge, MA: Harvard University Press, 1950).

Deissmann, A., *Bible Studies* (trans. A. Grieve; Edinburgh: T&T Clark, 1901; repr. Peabody, MA: Hendrickson, 1988).

Delaney, C., *The Seed and The Soil: Gender and Cosmology in Turkish Village Society* (Berkeley: University of California Press, 1991).

Deller, K., 'The Assyrian Eunuchs and Their Predecessors', in K. Watanabe (ed.), *Priests and Officials in the Ancient Near East* (Heidelberg: Universitätsverlag, 1999), pp. 303–11.

de Man, P., 'The Epistemology of Metaphor', in S. Sacks (ed.), *On Metaphor*, pp. 11-28.

de Selincourt, A. (trans.), *Living: The Early History of Rome* (New York: Penguin Books, 1982).

Deutsch, C.M., 'Jesus as Wisdom: A Feminist Reading of Matthew's Wisdom Christology', in A.-J. Levine (ed.), *A Feminist Companion to Matthew*, pp. 88–113.

—*Lady Wisdom, Jesus, and the Sages: Metaphor and Social Context in Matthew's Gospel* (Valley Forge, PA: Trinity Press, 1996).

Dewey, A.J., 'The Unkindest Cut of All? Matt. 19.11–12', *Foundations and Facets Forum* 8 (1992), pp. 113–22.

Dillon, R.J., 'Towards a Tradition-History of the Parables of the True Israel (Matthew 21.33–22.14)', *Bib* 47 (1966), pp. 1–42.

Dimant, D., 'Men as Angels: The Self-Image of the Qumran Community', in A. Berlin (ed.), *Religion and Politics in the Ancient Near East* (Bethesda, MD: University Press of Maryland, 1996), pp. 93–103.

Dixon, S., *The Roman Family* (Baltimore: The Johns Hopkins University Press, 1992).

Dobrovolny, M.K., 'Who Controls the Resources? Economics and Justice in Mt. 20.15', (Seminar Paper, SBL, San Antonio, TX, November 22, 2004).

Dodd, C.H., *The Bible and the Greeks* (London: Hodder & Stoughton, 1935), pp. 99–103.

—*The Parables of the Kingdom* (New York: Charles Scribner's Sons, rev. edn, 1961).

Donahue, J.R., *The Gospel in Parable: Metaphor, Narrative, and Theology in the Synoptic Gospels* (Minneapolis: Fortress Press, 1988).

Donfried, K.P., 'The Allegory of the Ten Virgins (Matt 25.1–13) as a Summary of Matthean Theology', *JBL* 93 (1974), pp. 415–28.

Doorly, W.J., *Prophet of Love: Understanding the Book of Hosea* (Mahwah, NJ: Paulist Press, 1991).

Drury, J., *The Parables in the Gospels: History and Allegory* (New York: Crossroad, 1985).

Duff, N.J., 'Wise and Foolish Maidens (Matthew 25.1–13)', *USQR* 40 (1985), pp. 55–58.

Duling, D., 'The Jesus Movement and Social Network Analysis: Part II. The Social Network', *BTB* 30 (2000), pp. 3–14.

—'Matthew 18.15–17: Conflict, Confrontation, and Conflict Resolution in a "Fictive Kin" Association', *BTB* 29 (1999), pp. 4–22.

—'Matthew's Plurisignificant "Son of David" in Social Science Perspective: Kinship, Kingship, Magic, and Miracle', *BTB* 22 (1992), pp. 99–116.

Edwards, C.W., 'Bridegroom-Bride Imagery in the New Testament against Its Biblical Background' (Dissertation; Northwestern University, 1964).

Eichholz, G., *Gleichnisse der Evangelien* (Neukirchen-Vluyn: Neukirchener Verlag, 1971).

Eilberg-Schwartz, H., *God's Phallus and Other Problems for Men and Monotheism* (Boston: Beacon Press, 1994).

Elliott, J.H., 'On Wooing Crocodiles for Fun and Profit: Confessions of an Intact Admirer', in J.J. Pilch (ed.), *Social Scientific Models,* pp. 5–20.

—'The Recent Emergence of Social Scientific Criticism', in J.H. Elliott (ed.), *What is Social-scientific Criticism?* (Minneapolis: Fortress Press, 1993), pp. 17–35.

Erickson, R.J., 'Divine Injustice? Matthew's Narrative Strategy and the Slaughter of the Innocents (Matthew 2.13–23)', *JSNT* 64 (1996), pp. 5–27.

Eskenazi, T.C., 'Tobiah', *ABD* 6, pp. 584–85.

Esler, P., *The First Christians in Their Social Worlds: Social-scientific Approaches to New Testament Interpretation* (New York: Routledge, 1994).

Esler, P. (ed.), *Modeling Early Christianity: Social-scientific Studies of the New Testament in Its Context* (New York: Routledge, 1995).

Eslinger, L., 'The Wooing of the Woman at the Well: Jesus, the Reader, and Reader-response Criticism', in M. Stibbe (ed.), *The Gospel of John as Literature: An Anthology of Twentieth-century Perspectives* (Leiden: E.J. Brill, 1993), pp. 165–82.

Etheridge, J.W. (trans.), *The Targums of Onkelos and Jonathan Ben Uzziel on the Pentateuch with the Fragments of the Jerusalem Targum from the Chaldee* (*http://www.tulane.edu/~ntcs/pj/psjon.htm*).

Exum, C., *Fragmented Women: Feminist (Sub)versions of Biblical Narratives* (Valley Forge, PA: Trinity Press International, 1993).

—'Murder They Wrote: Ideology and the Manipulation of Female Presence in Biblical Narrative', in D.J.A. Clines and T.C. Eskenazi (eds.), *Telling Queen Michal's Story*, pp. 176–98.

Farmer, W.R., *The International Bible Commmentary: A Catholic and Ecumenical Commentary for the Twenty-first Century* (Collegeville, MN: Liturgical Press, 1998).

Fatum, L., 'Gender Hermeneutics: The Effective History of Consciousness and the Use of Social Gender in the Gospels', in F.F. Segovia and M.A. Tolbert (eds.), *Reading from This Place*, II, pp. 157–68.

Fehribach, A., 'The Birthing Bridegroom: The Portrayal of Jesus in the Fourth Gospel', in A.-J. Levine (ed.), *A Feminist Companion to John*, II, pp. 104–29.

—*The Women in the Life of the Bridegroom: A Feminist Historical-literary Analysis of the Female Characters in the Fourth Gospel* (Collegeville, MN: The Liturgical Press, 1998).

Fekkes, J., *Isaiah and Prophetic Traditions in the Book of Revelation* (JSNTSup, 93; Sheffield: JSOT Press, 1994).

Fetterley, J., *The Resisting Reader: A Feminist Approach to American Fiction* (Bloomington: Indiana University Press, 1978).

Field, F., *Origenis Hexaplorum quae Supersunt* (2 vols.; Hildesheim: Georg Olms Verlagsbuchhandlung, 1964).

Fishbane, M., 'Accusations of Adultery: A Study of Law and Scribal Practice in Numbers 5.1–31', *HUCA* 45 (1974), pp. 25–45.

Fitzmyer, J.A., *The Gospel According to Luke* (AB, 28A; New York: Doubleday, 1985).

Fohr, S.D., *Adam and Eve: The Spiritual Symbolism of Genesis and Exodus* (New York: University Press of America, 1986).

Follis, E.R., 'Daughter of Zion', *ABD*, 6, p. 1103.

Ford, J.M., 'The Parable of the Foolish Scholars (Matt. 25.1–13)', *NovT* 9 (1967), pp. 107–23.

Foucault, M., *The Use of Pleasure: The History of Sexuality Volume Two* (3 vols.; New York: Vintage Books, 1985).

Fowler. H.N. (trans.), *Plutarch's Moralia* (15 vols.; LCL; Cambridge, MA: Harvard University Press, 1991).

France, R.T., 'Herod and the Children of Bethlehem', *NovT* 21 (1979), pp. 98–120.

—'The Massacre of the Innocents – Fact or Fiction?', in E.A. Livingstone (ed.), *Studia Biblica 1978* (JSNTSup, 2; Sheffield: Sheffield Academic Press, 1980), pp. 83–94.

—'On Being Ready (Matthew 25.1–46)', in R. Longenecker, *The Challenge of Jesus' Parables* (Grand Rapids: Eerdmans, 2000), pp. 177–95.

Friedman, M.A., *Jewish Marriage in Palestine, A Cairo Geniza Study: The Ketuba Traditions of Eretz Israel* (Tel-Aviv/New York: The Jewish Theological Seminary of America, 1980).

Frymer-Kensky, T., 'Deuteronomy', in C.A. Newsom and S.H. Ringe (eds.), *The Women's Bible Commentary*, pp. 52–62.

—*In the Wake of the Goddesses: Women, Culture and the Biblical Transformation of Pagan Myth* (New York: Fawcett Columbine, 1992).

Funk, R. (ed.), *The Five Gospels: The Search for the Authentic Words of Jesus* (San Francisco: HarperSanFrancisco, 1997).

—*Language, Hermeneutic, and the Word of God* (New York: Harper and Row, 1966).

Gaca, K.L., *The Making of Fornication: Eros, Ethics, and Political Reform in Greek Philosophy and Early Christianity* (Berkeley: University of Chicago Press, 2003).

Gager, J.G., *Kingdom and Community: The Social World of Early Christianity* (Englewood Cliffs, NJ: Prentice-Hall, 1975).

—'Shall We Marry Our Enemies? Sociology and the New Testament', *Int* 36 (1982), pp. 256–65.

Galambush, J., *Jerusalem in the Book of Ezekiel* (SBLDS, 130; Atlanta, GA: Scholars Press, 1992).

Galvin, B. (trans.), 'Women of Trachis', in D.R. Slavitt and P. Bovie (eds.), *Sophocles: Ajax, Women of Trachis, Electra, Philoctetes* (Philadelphia: University of Pennsylvania Press, 1998), pp. 77–126.

Gardner, J.F., and T. Wiedemann (eds.), *The Roman Household: A Sourcebook* (London and New York: Routledge, 1991).

Garland, D.E., *Reading Matthew: A Literary and Theological Commentary on the First Gospel* (New York: Crossroad, 1993).

Garrett, S., 'Sociology of Early Christianity', *ABD* VI, pp. 89–98.

Gelb, I.J., T. Jacobsen, B. Landsberger, and A.L. Oppenheim (eds.), *The Assyrian Dictionary* (Chicago: The Oriental Institute, 1956).

Gench, F.T., *Wisdom in the Christology of Matthew* (Lanham, MA: University Press of America, 1997).

George, A.R. (ed.), *The Babylonian Gilgamesh Epic: Introduction, Critical Edition and Cuneiform Texts* (2 vols.; Oxford: Oxford University Press, 2003).

Glombitza, O., 'Das Grosse Abendmahl: Luk. xiv.12–24', *NovT* 5 (1962), pp. 10–16.

Gnilka, J., *Das Matthäusevangelium* (2 vols.; Herders Theologischer Kommentar zum Neuen Testament; Freiburg: Herder, 1988).

Goessler, L., 'Advice to the Bride and Groom: Plutarch Gives a Detailed Account of His Views on Marriage', in S.B. Pomeroy (ed.), *Plutarch's Advice to the Bride and Groom and a Consolation to His Wife* (Oxford: Oxford University Press, 1999), pp. 97–115.

Goold, G.P. (trans.), *Chariton: Callirhoe* (LCL, 481; Cambridge, MA: Harvard University Press, 1995).

Gordon, J.D., *Sister or Wife? 1 Corinthians 7 and Cultural Anthropology* (JSNTSup, 149; Sheffield: Sheffield Academic Press, 1997).

Goulder, M., 'Characteristics of the Parables in the Several Gospels', *JTS* (1968), pp. 51–69.

—'Devotion, Divorce, and Debauchery', in L. Fatum and M. Müller (eds.), *Tro og Historie: Festskrift til Niels Hyldahl i anledning af 65 års fødselsdagen den 30. december 1995* (Copenhagen: Museum Tusculanums Forlag, 1996), pp. 107–17.

Graetz, N., 'The Metaphoric Battering of Hosea's Wife', in A. Brenner (ed.), *A Feminist*

Companion to the Latter Prophets (Sheffield: Sheffield Academic Press, 1995), pp. 126–45.

Granqvist, H., *Marriage Conditions in a Palestinian Village* (Helsingfors: Akademische Buchhandlung, 1935).

Grassi, C., and J. Grassi, 'The Resurrection: The New Age Begins: Mary Madgalene as Mystical Spouse', in C. Grassi and J. Grassi, *Mary Magdalene and the Women in Jesus' Life* (Kansas City: Sheed and Ward, 1986), pp. 104–15.

Green, A., 'The Song of Songs in Early Jewish Mysticism', *Orim* 2 (1987), pp. 49–63.

Grottanelli, C., 'Faithful Bodies: Ancient Greek Sources on Oriental Eunuchs', in A.I. Baumgarten, J. Assmann, and G.G. Stroumsa (eds.), *Self, Soul and Body in Religious Experience* (Studies in the History of Religions, 78; Leiden: Brill, 1998), pp. 404–16.

Guelich, R.A., 'The Matthean Beatitudes: "Entrance-Requirements" or Eschatological Blessing?', *JBL* 95 (1976), pp. 415–34.

Guijarro-Oporto, S., 'The Family in First-century Galilee', in H. Moxnes (ed.), *Constructing Early Christian Families*, pp. 42–65.

—'Kingdom and Family in Conflict: A Contribution to the Study of the Historical Jesus', in J.J. Pilch (ed.), *Social Scientific Models*, pp. 210–38.

Gundry, R., *Matthew: A Commentary on His Handbook for a Mixed Church under Persecution* (Grand Rapids: Eerdmans; 2nd edn, 1994).

Gunkel, H., *Genesis* (trans. M.E. Biddle; Macon, GA: Mercer University Press, repr. 1997).

Haacker, K., 'Das hochzeitliche Kleid von Mt. 22.11–13 und ein palästinisches Märchen', *Zeitschrift des Deutschen Palästina-Vereins* 87 (1971), pp. 95–97.

Haenchen, E., *Die Bibel und Wir: Gesammelte Aufsätze* (Tübingen: J.C.B. Mohr [Paul Siebeck], 1968), pp. 135–41.

Hagner, D.A., 'Apocalyptic Motifs in the Gospel of Matthew: Continuity and Discontinuity', *Horizons in Biblical Theology* 7 (1985), pp. 53–82.

Hahn, F., 'Das Gleichnis von der Einladung zum Festmahl', in Otto Böcher and Klaus Haacker (eds.), *Verborum Veritas: Festschrift für Gustav Stahlin zum 70. Geburtstag* (Wuppertal: Theologischer Verlag Rolf Brockhause, 1970), pp. 51–82.

—'υἱός', *EDNT*, pp. 381–92.

Haimo of Auxerre, *Homilies on the Seasons*, in J.-P. Migne (ed.), *Patrologiae cursus completus*, Latin series, 118 (221 vols.; Paris: Garnier Frères, 1844–64).

Hall, G., 'Origin of the Marriage Metaphor', *Hebrew Studies* 23 (1982), pp. 169–71.

Halpern, B., *David's Secret Demons: Messiah, Murderer, Traitor, King* (Grand Rapids: Eerdmans, 2001).

Hamilton, V.P., *The Book of Genesis: Chapters 1–17* (New International Commentary on the Old Testament; Grand Rapids, MI: Eerdman's, 1990).

Hanson, K.C., 'The Herodians and Mediterranean Kinship Part 1: Genealogy and Descent', *BTB* 19 July, 1989), pp. 75–84.

—'The Herodians and Mediterranean Kinship Part 2: Marriage and Divorce', *BTB* 19 (Oct., 1989), pp. 142-57

—'The Herodians and Mediterranean Kinship Part 3: Economics', *BTB* 20 (Spring, 1990), pp. 10–21.

—'Kinship', in R.L. Rohrbaugh (ed.), *The Social Sciences and New Testament Interpretation* (Peabody, MA: Hendrickson, 1996), pp. 62–79.

Hanson, K.C., and D.E. Oakman, 'Catching the Drift: Introduction to the Social System of

Roman Palestine', in K.C. Hanson and D.E. Oakman, *Palestine in the Time of Jesus*, pp. 3–17.

—*Palestine in the Time of Jesus: Social Structures and Social Conflicts* (Minneapolis: Fortress Press, 1998).

Hare, D.R.A., *Matthew* (Interpretation; Louisville: John Knox Press, 1993).

Harmon, A.M. (trans.), *Lucian* (Cambridge, MA: Harvard University Press, 2000).

Harrington, D., *The Gospel of Matthew* (Sacra Pagina, 1; Collegeville, MN: Liturgical Press, 1991).

—'Polemical Parables in Matthew 24–25', *Union Seminary Quarterly Review*, 44.3–4 (1991), pp. 287–95.

Hasler, V., 'Die königliche Hochzeit, Matth. 22.1–14', *TZ* 18 (1962), pp. 25–35.

Hatch, E., and H.A. Redpath, *A Concordance to the Septuagint and the Other Greek Versions of the Old Testament* (2 vols.; Grand Rapids, MI: Baker Book House, 1987).

Haufe, G., 'παραβολή', *EDNT* 3, p. 16.

Hauptman, *Rereading the Rabbis, A Woman's Voice* (Boulder, CO: Westview Press, 1998).

Hawkins, J.D., 'Eunuchs among the Hittites', in S. Parpola and R.M. Whiting (eds.), *Sex and Gender in the Ancient Near East* (2 vols.; Proceedings of the XLVII *Recontre Assyriologique Internationale*; Helsinki: The Neo-Assyrian Text Corpus Project, 2002), I, pp. 217–33.

Hay, D.M., 'The Veiled Thoughts of the Therapeutae', in R.M. Berchman (ed.), *Mediators of the Divine* (South Florida Studies in the History of Judaism, 163; Atlanta, GA: Scholars Press, 1998), pp. 175–76.

Hays, R. *The Moral Vision of the New Testament: Community, Cross, New Creation: A Comtemporary Introduction to New Testament Ethics* (Edinburgh: T&T Clark, 1997).

Hellerman, J.H., *The Ancient Church as Family* (Minneapolis: Fortress Press, 2001).

Henderson, J. (trans.), *Dionysius of Halicarnassus* (7 vols.; LCL, 319; Cambridge, MA: Harvard University Press, 2001).

Hendrickx, H., *The Parables of Jesus* (San Francisco: Harper and Row, 1986).

Hercher, R. (ed.), *Epistolographi Graeci* (Paris: Institute Franciae Typographo, 1873).

Herion, G.A., 'The Impact of Modern Social Science Assumptions on the Reconstruction of Israelite History', *JSOT* 34 (1986), pp. 3–33.

Herzog II, W.R., *Parables as Subversive Speech: Jesus as Pedagogue of the Oppressed* (Louisville: Westminster/John Knox, 1994).

Hexter, R., and D. Selden (eds.), *Innovations of Antiquity* (New York: Routledge, 1992), pp. 161–96.

Hochschild, R., *Sozialgeschichte Exegese: Entwicklung, Geschichte und Methodik einer neutestamentlichen Forschungsrichtung* (Göttingen: Vandenhoeck & Ruprecht, 1999).

Holmberg, B., *Sociology and the New Testament: An Appraisal* (Minneapolis: Fortress Press, 1990).

Holtz, T., '"Ich aber sage euch": Bemerkungen zum Verhältnis Jesu zur Tora', in I. Broer (ed.), *Jesus und das jüdische Gesetz* (Stuttgart: Verlag W. Kohlhammer, 1992), pp. 135–43.

Hooke, S.H., *The Origins of Early Semitic Ritual* (London: Oxford University Press, 1938).

Horine, S.C., *Interpretive Images in the Song of Songs: From Wedding Chariots to Bridal Chambers* (Studies in the Humanities: Literature–Politics–Society, 55; New York: Peter Lang, 2001).

Horrell, D.G. (ed.), *Social-scientific Approaches to New Testament Interpretation* (Edinburgh: T&T Clark, 1999).

Horsley, R., *Archaeology, History and Society in Galilee: The Social Context of Jesus and the Rabbis* (Harrisburg: Trinity Press International, 1996).

—*Jesus and the Spiral of Violence* (Minneapolis: Fortress Press, 1987, 2nd edn, 1993).

—*Sociology and the Jesus Movement* (New York: Crossroad, 1989).

Houtman, C., *Exodus* (trans. J. Rebel and S. Woudstra; Historical Commentary on the Old Testament; Kampen: Kok Publishing House, 1993).

Hultgren, A.J., *The Parables of Jesus* (Grand Rapids: Eerdmans, 2000).

Humphrey, E.M., *The Ladies and the Cities: Transformation and Apocalyptic Identity in Joseph and Aseneth, 4 Ezra, The Apocalypse, and the Shepherd of Hermas* (JSPSup, 17; Sheffield: Sheffield Academic Press, 1995).

Huntley, W.B., 'Christ the Bridegroom: A Biblical Image' (Dissertation; Duke University, 1964).

Hutchinson, G.O. (ed.), *Aeschylus: Septem Contra Thebas* (Oxford: Clarendon, 1985).

Ilan, T., 'How Women Differed', *BAR* 24 (1998), pp. 38–39, 68.

—*Jewish Women in Greco-Roman Palestine* (Peabody, MA: Hendrickson, 1996).

Jastrow, M., *A Dictonary of the Targumim, the Talmud Babli and Yerushalmi, and the Midrashic Literature* (New York: Pardes Publishing House, Inc., 1950).

Jeremias, J., *Die Gleichnisse Jesu* (*The Parables of Jesus*; Abhandlungen zur Theologie des Alten und Neuen Testaments, 11; Zürich: Zwingli-Verlag, 1947).

—'ΛΑΜΠΑΔΕΣ Mt 25, 1.3f.7f', *ZNW* 56 (1965), pp. 196–201.

—'νύμφη, νυμφίος', *TDNT* 4, pp. 1099–1106.

—'Von der Urkirche zu Jesus Zurück', in W. Harnisch (ed.), *Gleichnisse Jesu* (Darmstadt: Wissenschaftliche Buchgesellschaft, 1982), pp. 180–237.

Jervell, J., *Imago Dei: Gen 1,26 im Spätjudentum, in der Gnosis und in den paulinischen Briefen* (Göttingen: Vandenhoeck & Ruprecht, 1960).

Johnson, L.T., *The Gospel of Luke* (Sacra Pagina, 3; Collegeville, MN: Liturgical Press, 1991).

Johnston, T., *Christ's Watchword: Being The Parable of the Virgins Expanded* (London: printed by W. Jones for John Bartler, 1630).

Jones, I.H., *The Matthean Parables: A Literary and Historical Commentary* (NovTSup, 80; Leiden: Brill, 1995).

Jones, W.H.S., and H.A. Ormerod (trans.), *Pausanias: Description of Greece* (4 vols.; LCL, 93; Cambridge, MA: Harvard University Press, 1992).

Jülicher, A., *Die Gleichnisreden Jesu* (2 vols.; Freiburg: J.C.B. Mohr [Paul Siebeck], 1886, 1899).

Kahl, B., 'Reading Luke against Luke: Non-conformity of Text, Hermeneutics of Conspiracy, and the "Scriptural Principle" in Luke 1', in A.-J. Levine (ed.), *A Feminist Companion to Luke*, pp. 70–88.

Kampen, J., 'The Matthean Divorce Texts Re-examined', in G.J. Brooke (ed.), *New Qumran Texts and Studies: Proceedings of the First Meeting of the International Organization for Qumran Studies, Paris, 1992* (STDJ, 15; Leiden: E.J. Brill, 1994), pp. 149–67.

Keener, C.S., *A Commentary on the Gospel of Matthew* (Grand Rapids: Eerdmans, 1999).

Keller, C., *Apocalypse Now and Then: A Feminist Guide to the End of the World* (Boston: Beacon Press, 1996).

Kingsbury, J.D., *The Parables of Jesus in Matthew 13: A Study in Redaction Criticism* (Richmond, VA: John Knox Press, 1969).

Kirk-Duggan, C.A., *Refiner's Fire: Religious Engagement with Violence* (Minneapolis: Fortress Press, 2001).

Kirsch, J., *Moses: A Life* (New York: Ballantine Books, 1998).

Kitzberger, I.R. (ed.), *The Personal Voice in Biblical Interpretation* (New York: Routledge, 1999).

Klassen-Wiebe, S., 'Matthew 1.18–25', *Int* 46 (1992), pp. 392–95.

Klijn, A.J.F. (trans.), '2 (Syriac Apocalypse of) Baruch', in J.H. Charlesworth (ed.), *The Old Testament Pseudepigrapha* (2 vols.; New York: Doubleday, 1983), I, pp. 615–52.

Kloppenborg, J.S., '*Collegia* and *Thiasoi*: Issues in Function, Taxonomy and Membership', in J.S. Kloppenborg and S.G. Wilson (eds.), *Voluntary Associations*, pp. 16–30.

—'Didache 16.6–8 and Special Matthaean Tradition', *ZNW* 70 (1979), pp. 54–67.

Kloppenborg, J.S., and S.G. Wilson (eds.), *Voluntary Associations in the Graeco-Roman World* (New York: Routledge, 1996).

Kodell, J., 'The Celibacy Logion in Matthew 19.12', *BTB* 8 (1978), pp. 19–23.

Koehler, L., and W. Baumgartner, *The Hebrew and Aramaic Lexicon of the Old Testament* (2 vols.; trans. M.E.J. Richardson; Leiden: Brill, 2001).

Koester, H., 'The Gospel of Thomas', in J.M. Robinson (ed.), *The Nag Hammadi Library* (San Fransisco: Harper San Francisco, 3rd edn, 1990), pp. 124–38.

—'Introduction', in B. Layton (ed.), *Nag Hammadi Codex II, 2–7*, pp. 40–41.

Köstenberger, A., 'Marriage and Family in the New Testament', in K.M. Campbell (ed.), *Marriage and Family in the Biblical World* (Downers Grove, IL: InterVarsity Press, 2003), pp. 240–84.

Kraeling, C.H., *Anthropos and Son of Man: A Study of Religious Syncretism of the Hellenistic Orient* (New York: Columbia University Press, 1927).

Kraemer, R.S., *Her Share of the Blessings: Women's Religions among Pagans, Jews, and Christians in the Greco-Roman World* (New York: Oxford University Press, 1992).

—'Jewish Mothers and Daughters in the Greco-Roman World', in S.J.D. Cohen (ed.), *The Jewish Family in Antiquity*, pp. 89–112.

Kraemer, R.S., and M.R. D'Angelo (eds.), *Women and Christian Origins* (New York and Oxford: Oxford University Press, 1999).

Kraszewski, C.S., *The Gospel of Matthew with Patristic Commentaries* (Studies in Bible and Early Christianity, 40; Lewiston, NY: Edwin Mellen Press, 1999).

Kuefler, M., *The Manly Eunuch: Masculinity, Gender Ambiguity, and Christian Ideology in Late Antiquity* (Chicago: University of Chicago Press, 2001).

Kümmel, W.G., *Promise and Fulfillment: The Eschatological Message of Jesus* (Studies in Biblical Theology, 23; London: SCM, 1957).

Kunin, S., 'The Bridegroom of Blood: A Structural Analysis', *JSOT* 70 (1996), pp. 3–16.

Kurtz, D.C., and Boardman, J., *Greek Burial Customs* (Ithaca: Cornell University Press, 1971).

Kutsch, E., 'חתן', *TDOT* 5, pp. 270–77.

Lakoff, G., and M. Johnson, *Metaphors We Live By* (Chicago: University of Chicago Press, 1980).

—*More Than Cool Reason: A Field Guide to Poetic Metaphor* (Chicago: University of Chicago Press, 1989).

Lambdin, T., *Introduction to Sahidic Coptic* (Macon, GA: Mercer University Press, 1988).

Lambrecht, J., *Out of the Treasure: The Parables in the Gospel of Matthew* (Louvain Theological and Pastoral Monographs, 10; Louvain: Peeters Press, 1991).

Lanham, R.A., *A Handlist of Rhetorical Terms* (Berkeley: University of California Press, 2nd edn, 1991).

Lassen, E.M., 'The Roman Family: Ideal and Metaphor', in H. Moxnes (ed.), *Constructing Early Christian Families*, pp. 103–20.

Layton, B., *Nag Hammadi Codex II, 2–7* (NHS, 20; Coptic Gnostic Library; Leiden: E.J. Brill, 1989).

Lefkowitz, M.R., and M.B. Fant, *Women's Life in Greece and Rome: A Sourcebook in Translation* (Baltimore: Johns Hopkins University Press, 2nd edn, 1992).

Lemcio, E.E., 'The Parables of the Great Supper and the Wedding Feast: History, Redaction, and Canon', *HBT* 8 (1986), pp. 1–26.

León, D.M., 'Jesus y la Apocaliptica Pesimista', *Estudios Bíblicos* 46 (1988), pp. 457–95.

Leske, A., 'Matthew', in W.R. Farmer, *The International Bible Commentary: A Catholic and Ecumenical Commentary for the Twenty-first Century* (Collegeville, MN: Liturgical Press, 1998), pp. 1253–1330.

Levine, A.-J., 'Discharging Responsibility: Matthean Jesus, Biblical Law, and Hemorrhaging Woman', in A.J. Levine, (ed.), *A Feminist Companion to Matthew*, pp. 70–87.

—'Jesus, Divorce, and Sexuality: A Jewish Critique', in L. Greenspoon, D. Hamm, and B. LeBeau (eds.), *The Historical Jesus through Catholic and Jewish Eyes* (Harrisburg, PA: Trinity Press International, 2000), pp. 113–29.

—'Matthew', in C.A. Newsom and S.H. Ringe (eds.), *The Women's Bible Commentary*, pp. 252–62.

—*The Social and Ethnic Dimensions of Matthean Salvation History* (Studies in the Bible and Early Christianity, 14; Lewiston: Edwin Mellen Press, 1988).

—'Women in the Q Communit(ies) and Traditions', in R.S. Kraemer and M.R. D'Angelo (eds.), *Women and Christian Origins*, pp. 150–70.

—'The Word Becomes Flesh: Jesus, Gender, and Sexuality', in J.H. Charlesworth and W.P. Weaver (eds.), *Jesus Two Thousand Years Later* (Harrisburg, PA: Trinity Press International, 2000), pp. 62–83.

—(ed.), *A Feminist Companion to John* (2 vols.; London: Continuum/Sheffield Academic Press, 2003).

—(ed.), *A Feminist Companion to Luke* (Sheffield Sheffield Academic Press, 2002).

—(ed.), *A Feminist Companion to Mark* (Sheffield: Sheffield Academic Press, 2001).

—(ed.), *A Feminist Companion to Matthew* (Sheffield: Sheffield Academic Press, 2001).

—(ed.), *A Feminist Companion to Paul* (London: Continuum/T&T Clark, 2004).

—(ed.), *A Feminist Companion to the Acts of the Apostles* (London: Continuum/T&T Clark, 2004).

—(ed.) *A Feminist Companion to the Deutero-Pauline Epistles* (London: Continuum/T&T Clark, 2003).

—(ed.) *A Feminist Companion to the Jesus Movement* (London: Continuum/T&T Clark, forthcoming).

Levine, M.M., 'The Gendered Grammar of Ancient Mediterranean Hair', in H. Eilberg-Schwartz and W. Doniger (eds.), *Off with Her Head: The Denial of Women's Identity in Myth, Religion, and Culture* (Los Angeles: University of Calif. Press, 1995), pp. 96–102.

Levy, J., *Wörterbuch über die Talmudim und Midraschim* (ed. H.L. Fleischer and L. Goldschmidt; 4 vols.; Berlin: Benjamin Harz Verlag, 2nd edn, 1924).

Liddell, H.G. (ed.), *An Intermediate Greek–English Lexicon Founded on the Seventh Edition of Liddell and Scott's Greek English Lexicon* (Oxford: Clarendon Press, 1889, 1995).

Liebenberg, J., *The Language and the Kingdom of Jesus: Parable, Aphorism, and Metaphor in the Sayings Material Common to the Synoptic Tradition and the Gospel of Thomas* (Berlin: Walter de Gruyter, 2001).

Lincoln, B., 'Thomas-Gospel and Thomas-Community: A New Approach to a Familiar Text', *NovT* 19 (1977), pp. 65–76.

Linnemann, E., *Gleichnisse Jesu Einführung und Auslegung* (Göttingen: Vandenhoeck & Ruprecht, 1966 [English edition: *Parables of Jesus: Introduction and Exposition*, trans. J. Sturdy; London: SPCK, 3rd edn, 1966]).

—'Überlegungen zur Parabel vom grossen Abendmahl', *ZNW* 3–4 (1960), pp. 246–55.

Locke, J., *The Reasonableness of Christianity as Delivered in the Scriptures* (ed. J.C. Higgins-Biddle; Oxford: Clarendon Press, 1999).

Lockyer, H., ' "Michal" and "Michal: The Woman Who Tricked Her Father" ', in D.J.A. Clines (ed.), *Telling Queen Michal's Story*, pp. 227–28.

Lohse, E., 'υἱός', *TDNT* 8, pp. 340–62.

Long, T.G., *Westminster Bible Companion: Matthew* (Louisville: Westminster/John Knox Press, 1997).

Lövestam, E., *Spiritual Wakefulness in the New Testament* (trans. W.F. Salisbury; Gleerup: Lund, 1963).

Lüdemann, G., *Virgin Birth? The Real Story of Mary and Her Son Jesus* (trans. J. Bowden; Harrisburg, PA: Trinity Press International, 1998).

Ludolph of Saxony, *Vita Jesu Christi e quatuor evangeliis* (ed. A.C. Bolard; Paris: V. Palmé, 1865).

Luther, M., *Sermons of Martin Luther: The Church Postils* (trans. J.N. Lenker; 8 vols.; Grand Rapids, MI: Baker Book House, 1995).

—*The Table Talk of Martin Luther* (ed. T.S. Kepler; Grand Rapids, MI: Baker Book House, 1929).

Luttikhuizen, G.P. (ed.), *The Creation of Man and Woman: Interpretations of Biblical Narratives in Jewish and Christian Traditions* (Themes in Biblical Narrative, 3; Leiden: Brill, 2000).

Luz, U., *Das Evangelium nach Matthäus* (EKKNT, 476; Zurich: Benziger Verlag, 1990).

—*Matthew 1–7: A Continental Commentary* (trans. W.C. Linss; Minneapolis: Fortress Press, 1989).

—*Matthew 9–20* (trans. J.E. Crouch; Hermeneia; Minneapolis: Fortress Press, 2001).

McCarter, P.K.', Biblical Detective Work Identifies the Eunuch', *BAR* 28.2 (2002), pp. 46–48, 61.

McCready, W., '*Ekklesia* and Voluntary Associations', in J.S. Kloppenborg and S.G. Wilson (eds.), *Voluntary Associations in the Graeco-Roman World*, pp. 59–73.

MacDonald, D.R., *There Is No Male and Female: The Fate of a Dominical Saying in Paul and Gnosticism* (HDR, 20; Philadelphia: Fortress, 1987).

MacDonald, M.Y., 'Rereading Paul: Early Interpretations of Paul on Women and Gender', in R.S. Kraemer and M.R. D'Angelo (eds.), *Women and Christian Origins*, pp. 236–53.

McKenzie, J.L., 'Matthew', *The Jerome Biblical Commentary* (London: Geoffrey Chapman, 1968), p. 100–101.

McKenzie, S.L., *King David: A Biography* (Oxford: Oxford University Press, 2000).

Maclean, J.K.B, and E.B. Aitken (trans.), *Flavius Philostratus: Heroikos* (Atlanta: Society of Biblical Literature, 1977).

McNeile, A.H., *The Gospel According to St. Matthew* (London: Macmillan, 1949).

Madsen, I.K., 'Zur Erklärung der evangelischen Parabeln', in W. Harisch, *Gleichnisse Jesus* (Darmstadt: Wissenschaftliche Buchgesellschaft, 1982), pp. 113–14.

Malherbe, A.J., *Social Aspects of Early Christianity* (Baton Rouge, LA: Louisiana State University, 1977).

Malina, B.J., *The New Testament World: Insights from Cultural Anthropology* (Louisville: Westminster/John Knox Press, rev. edn, 1993).

—'The Social Sciences and Biblical Interpretation', *Int* 36 (1982), pp. 229–42.

Malina, B.J., and J.H. Neyrey, *Calling Jesus Names: The Social Value of Labels in Matthew* (Sonoma, CA: Polebridge Press, 1988).

Malina, B.J., and R.L. Rohrbaugh, *Social Science Commentary on the Synoptic Gospels* (Minneapolis: Fortress Press, 1992).

Manson, T.W., *The Sayings of Jesus* (London: SCM Press, 1949).

Marcus, J., and M.L. Soards (eds.), *Apocalyptic and the New Testament: Essays in Honor of J. Louis Martyn* (JSNTSup, 24; Sheffield: JSOT Press, 1989).

Martin, C.J., 'Acts of the Apostles', in E. Schüssler Fiorenza (ed.), *Searching the Scriptures*, II, pp. 763–99.

Martin, D.B., *The Corinthian Body* (New Haven: Yale University Press, 1995).

—'Slavery and the Ancient Jewish Family', in S.J.D. Cohen (ed.), *The Jewish Family in Antiquity*, pp. 113–29.

—'Social-scientific Criticism', in S.R. Haynes and S.L. McKenzie (eds.), *To Each Its Own Meaning: An Introduction to Biblical Criticisms and Their Application* (Louisville: Westminster/John Knox Press, 1993), pp. 103–19.

Martínez, F.G. (trans.), *The Dead Sea Scrolls Translated: The Qumran Texts in English* (Leiden: Brill, 2nd edn., 1996).

Martitz, W., 'υἱός', *TDNT* 8, pp. 334–40.

Mason, S., '*Philosophai*: Graeco-Roman, Judean and Christian', in J.S. Kloppenborg and S.G. Wilson (eds.), *Voluntary Associations*, pp. 31–58.

Matter, E.A., *The Voice of My Beloved: The Song of Songs in Western Medieval Christianity* (Philadelphia: University of Pennsylvania Press, 1990).

Matura, T., 'Les Invites à la Noce Royale', *Assemblées du Seigneur* 58 (1974), pp. 16–27.

Meeks, W.A., *The First Urban Christians: The Social World of the Apostle Paul* (New Haven: Yale University Press, 1983).

—'The Image of the Androgyne: Some Uses of a Symbol in Early Christianity', *HR* 13 (1974), pp. 165–208.

—*The Moral World of the First Christians* (Philadelphia: Westminster Press, 1986).

Meier, J.P., *A Marginal Jew: A Sociopolitical and Religious Reading* (3 vols.; New York: Doubleday, 1991–2001).

—*Matthew* (New Testament Message, 3; Dublin: Veritas, 1980).

—'Salvation History in Matthew: In Search of a Starting Point', *CBQ* 37 (1975), pp. 203–15.

Metzger, B., *The Text of the New Testament: Its Transmission, Corruption and Restoration* (Oxford: Oxford University Press, 3rd edn, 1992).

—*A Textual Commentary on the Greek New Testament* 2nd edn, (Stuttgart: Deutsche Bibelgesellschaft, 1994).

Metzger, B., and R. Murphy (eds.), *The New Oxford Annotated Bible* (New York: Oxford University Press, 1991).

Meyer, B.F., 'Many (=All) Are Called, but Few (=Not All) Are Chosen', *NTS* 36 (1990), pp. 89–97.

Meyer, M.W., *The Gospel of Thomas: The Hidden Sayings of Jesus* (San Francisco: HarperSanFrancisco, 1992).

—'Making Mary Male: The Categories of "Male" and "Female" in the Gospel of Thomas', *NTS* 31 (1985), pp. 554–70.

Meyer, M.W. (ed.), *The Ancient Mysteries: A Sourcebook of Sacred Texts* (San Francisco: Harper & Row, 1987).

Michaelis, W., *Das hochzeitliche Kleid* (Berlin: Furche Verlag, 1939).

—*Es ging ein Sämman aus, zu säen: eine Einführung in die Gleichnisse Jesu über das Reich Gottes und die Kirche* (Berlin: Furche Verlag, 1938).

Migne, J.-P. (ed.), *Patrologie cursus completus* (Latin series; 221 vols.; Paris: Garnier Frères, 1844–64).

Miles, G.B., *Livy: Constructing Early Rome* (Ithaca: Cornell University Press, 1995).

Miller, R.J., *Born Divine: The Births of Jesus and Other Sons of God* (New York: Polebridge Press, 2003).

Mitchell, E.C., *The Parables of the New Testament Spiritually Unfolded* (Philadelphia: William H. Alden, 2nd edn, 1900).

Mitchell, T.C., 'The Meaning of the Noun חתן in the Old Testament', *VT* 19 (1969), pp. 93–112.

Mollenkott, V.R., 'Emancipatory Elements in Ephesians 5.21–33: Why Feminist Scholarship Has (Often) Missed Them, and Why They Should Be Emphasized', in A.-J. Levine (ed.), *A Feminist Companion to the Deutero-Pauline Epistles*, pp. 38–59.

Moloney, F., 'Matthew 19.3–12 and Celibacy: A Redactional and Form Critical Study', *JSNT* 2 (1979), pp. 42–60.

Monneyron, F., *L'Androgyne romantique: du mythe au mythe littéraire* (Grenoble: Ellug, 1994).

Moore, C.A., *Tobit* (AB, 40A; New York: Doubleday, 1996).

Moore, S.D., *Mark and Luke in Poststructuralist Perspectives: Jesus Begins to Write* (New Haven: Yale University Press, 1992).

—'Revolting Revelations', in S.D. Moore, *God's Beauty Parlor and Other Queer Spaces in and around the Bible* (Stanford: Stanford University Press, 2001), pp. 173–99.

Morris, L., *The Gospel According to Matthew* (Grand Rapids, MI: Eerdmans, 1992).

Morwood, J. (trans.), *Euripides: Medea and Other Plays* (Oxford World's Classics; Oxford: Oxford University Press, 1998), pp. 1–38.

Mosala, I.J., 'Social Scientific Approaches to the Bible: One Step Forward, Two Steps Backward', *Journal of Theology for Southern Africa* 55 (1986), pp. 15–30.

Moschner, F.M., *The Kingdom of Heaven in Parables* (trans. D. Heimann; London: Herder, 1960).

Moxnes, H. 'Introduction', in H. Moxnes (ed.), *Constructing Early Christian Families*, pp. 1–9.

Moxnes, H. 'What is Family?', in H. Moxnes (ed.), *Constructing Early Christian Families*, pp. 13–41.

Moxnes, H. (ed.), *Constructing Early Christian Families: Family as Social Reality and Metaphor* (New York: Routledge, 1997).

Murphy, R.E., *The Song of Songs* (Hermeneia; Minneapolis: Fortress Press, 1990).

Musurillo, H.A., 'Many Are Called, but Few Are Chosen', *TS* 7 (1946), pp. 583–89.

Nash, K., 'The Language of Motherhood in the *Gospel of Thomas*: Keeping Momma Out of the Kingdom (*Gos. Thom.* 22)', in M.A. Beavis (ed.), *The Lost Coin*, pp. 174–95.

Neufeldt, V., *et al.*, *Webster's New World Dictionary* (New York: MacMillan, 3rd edn, 1994).

Neusner, J., *Israel's Love Affair with God: Song of Songs* (The Bible of Judaism Library; Valley Forge, PA: Trinity Press, International, 1993).

—(trans.), *The Mishnah: A New Translation* (New Haven: Yale University Press, 1988).

—(trans.), *The Talmud of Babylonia: An American Translation. 14A-C: Ketubot* (3 vols.; BJS, 257, 258, 260; Atlanta: Scholars Press, 1992).

Neusner, J. (trans.), *The Talmud of Babylonia: An American Translation. 19A-B: Qiddushin* (2 vols.; BJS, 267, 268; Atlanta: Scholars Press, 1992).

Newsom, C.A., 'A Maker of Metaphors: Ezekiel's Oracles against Tyre', in J.L. Mays and P.J. Achtemeier (eds.), *Interpreting the Prophets* (Philadelphia: Fortress Press, 1987).

Newsom, C.A., and S.H. Ringe (eds.), *The Women's Bible Commentary* (Louisville: Westminster/John Knox Press, 1992).

Neyrey, J.H., *Honor and Shame in the Gospel of Matthew* (Louisville: Westminster/John Knox Press, 1998).

—'Jacob Traditions and the Interpretation of John 4.10–26', *CBQ* 41 (1979), pp. 419–37.

—'Loss of Wealth, Loss of Family and Loss of Honour: The Cultural Context of the Original Makarisms in Q', in P.E. Esler (ed.), *Modeling Early Christianity*, pp. 139–58.

Nicol, G.G., 'The Slaughter of the Innocents', *ExpTim* 97 (1985), pp. 55–56.

Nohrnberg, J., *Like Unto Moses: The Constituting of an Interruption* (Bloomington, IN: Indiana University Press, 1995).

Nolan Fewell, Dana, and David M. Gunn, *Gender, Power, and Promise: The Subject of the Bible's First Story* (Nashville: Abingdon Press, 1993.

Noll, K.L., *The Faces of David* (JSOTSup, 242; Sheffield: Sheffield Academic Press, 1997).

Nolland, J., 'The Gospel Prohibition of Divorce: Tradition History and Meaning', *JSNT* 58 (1995), pp. 19–35.

Noth, M., *Exodus: A Commentary* (OTL; Philadelphia: Westminster Press, 1962).

Nwaoru, E.O., *Imagery in the Prophecy of Hosea* (trans. Manfred Görg; Ägypten und Altes Testament, 41; Wiesbaden: Harrassowitz Verlag, 1999), pp. 58–61.

Oakman, D.E., 'Models and Archaeology in the Social Interpretation of Jesus', in J.J. Pilch (ed.), *Social Scientific Models*, pp. 102–31.

O'Day, G.R., 'Acts', in C.A. Newsom and S.H. Ringe (eds.), *The Women's Bible Commentary*, pp. 305–12.

Oepke, A., 'λάμπω, ἐκλαμπω, περιλάμπω, λαμπάς, λαμπός', *TDNT* 4, pp. 16–28.

Oesterley, W.O.E., *The Gospel Parables in the Light of Their Jewish Background* (New York: Macmillan, 1936).

Okure, T., 'The Significance Today of Jesus' Commission to Mary Magdalene (Jn 20.11–18)', *International Review of Mission* 81 (1992), pp. 177–88.

O'Leary, S.D., *Arguing the Apocalypse: A Theory of Millennial Rhetoric* (Oxford: Oxford University Press, 1994).

O'Neill, J.C., 'The Source of the Parables of the Bridegroom and the Wicked Husbandmen', *JTS* 39 (1988), pp. 485–89.

Origen, *Origenes: Der Kommentar zum Evangelium nach Mattäus* (ed. Hermann J. Vogt; Bibliothek der Griechischen Literatur, 30; Stuttgart: Anton Hiersemann, 1990).

Orton, D.E., *The Understanding Scribe: Matthew and the Apocalyptic Ideal* (JSNTSup, 25; Sheffield: Sheffield Academic Press, 1989).

Osiek, C., 'Jesus and Cultural Values: Family Life as an Example', *Hervormde Teologiese Studies* 53 (1997), pp. 800–11.

Osiek, C., and D.L. Balch, *Families in the New Testament World: Households and House Churches* (Louisville: Westminster/John Knox Press, 1997).

Overman, J.A., *Matthew's Gospel and Formative Judaism: The Social World of the Matthean Community* (Minneapolis: Fortress Press, 1990).

—'Matthew's Parables and Roman Politics: The Imperial Setting of Matthew's Narrative with Special Reference to His Parables', *Society of Biblical Literature Seminar Papers* (SBLSP, 34; Atlanta: Scholars Press, 1995), pp. 425–36.

Palmer, H., 'Just Married, Cannot Come', *NovT* 18 (1976), pp. 241–57.

Pardes, I., 'Zipporah and the Struggle for Deliverance', in I. Pardes, *Contratraditions in the Bible: A Feminist Approach* (Cambridge, MA: Harvard University Press, 1992), pp. 79–97.

Parkin, R., *Kinship: An Introduction to the Basic Concepts* (Oxford: Blackwell, 1997).

Parpola, S., and R.M. Whiting (eds.), *Sex and Gender in the Ancient Near East: Proceedings of the 47th Rencontre Assyriologique Internationale, Helsinki, July 2–6, 2001* (2 vols.; Helsinki: Neo-Assyrian Text Corpus Project, 2002).

Paschasius Radbertus, *Expositio in evangelium Matthaei*, in J.-P. Migne (ed.), *Patrologiae cursus completus*, Latin series, 120.

Patte, D., *The Gospel According to Matthew: A Structural Commentary on Matthew's Faith* (Philadelphia: Fortress Press, 1987).

Patterson, S.J., *The Gospel of Thomas and Jesus* (Sonoma, CA: Polebridge Press, 1993).

Peerbolte, L.J., 'Man, Woman, and the Angels in 1 Cor. 11.2–16', in G. Luttikhuizen (ed.), *The Creation of Man and Woman*, pp. 76–92.

Peristiany, J.G. (ed.), *Mediterranean Family Structures* (Cambridge: Cambridge University Press, 1976).

Perkins, P., 'The Gospel of Thomas', in E. Schüssler Fiorenza (ed.), *Searching the Scriptures: A Feminist Commentary*, II, pp. 534–60.

—*Hearing the Parables of Jesus* (New York: Paulist Press, 1981).

Perrin, N., *Jesus and the Language of the Kingdom: Symbol and Metaphor in New Testament Interpretation* (Philadelphia: Fortress, 1976).

Peskowitz, M., ' "Family/ies" in Antiquity: Evidence from Tannaitic Literature and Roman Galilean Architecture', in S.J.D. Cohen (ed.), *The Jewish Family in Antiquity*, pp. 9–36.

Péter-Contesse, R., 'Was Potiphar a Eunuch?', *BT* 47.1 (1996), pp. 142–46.

Petzke, G., 'εὐνοῦχος', *EDNT* 2, pp. 80–81.

Phipps, W.E., 'The Case for a Married Jesus', *Dialogue* 7 (1972), pp. 44–49.

—*Was Jesus Married? The Distortion of Sexuality in the Christian Tradition* (New York: Harper and Row, 1970).

Pilch, J.J. (ed.), *Social Scientific Models for Interpreting the Bible: Essays in Honor of Bruce J. Malina* (Biblical Interpretation Series, 53; Leiden: Brill, 2001).

Pilchan, L., *The New Jerusalem in the Book of Revelation* (WUNT; Reihe 2, 129; Tübingen: Mohr Siebeck, 2001).

Pippin, T., *Apocalyptic Bodies: The Biblical End of the World in Text and Image* (New York: Routledge, 1999).

—*Death and Desire: The Rhetoric of Gender in the Apocalypse of John* (Louisville: Westminster/John Knox Press, 1992).

Pitre, B., 'Eunuchs for the Sake of the Kingdom? Rethinking Marriage, Children, Sex, and Celibacy in Matthew 19.1–15', (unpublished seminar paper, Vanderbilt University, Fall, 1998).

Platnauer, M. (trans.), *Claudian* (2 vols.; LCL; Cambridge, MA: Harvard University Press, 1922).

Plummer, A. *An Exegetical Commentary on the Gospel According to St. Matthew* (Grand Rapids: Baker Book House, 1982).

Poitiers, H., *Sur Matthieu* (ed. Jean Doignon; Paris: Les Éditions du Cerf, 1929).

Pomeroy, S.B. (ed.), *Plutarch's Advice to the Bride and Groom and A Consolation to His Wife* (New York: Oxford University Press, 1999).

—'Some Greek Families: Production and Reproduction', in S.J.D. Cohen (ed.), *The Jewish Family in Antiquity*, pp. 155–57.

Pope, M., *The Song of Songs* (AB, 7C; New York: Doubleday, 1977).

Powell, M.A., *Chasing the Eastern Star: Adventures in Biblical Reader-response Criticism* (Louisville: Westminster/John Knox Press, 2001).

Prabhu, G.M.S., *The Formula Quotations in the Infancy Narrative of Matthew* (Rome: Biblical Institute Press, 1976), pp. 6–10.

Propp, W. 'That Bloody Bridegroom (Exodus 4.24–6)', *VT* 43 (1993), pp. 495–518.

Rahlfs, A. (ed.), *Septuaginta* (Stuttgart: Deutsche Bibelgesellschaft, 1979).

Rallis, I.K., 'Nuptial Imagery in the Book of Hosea: Israel as the Bride of Yahweh', *St. Vladimir's Theological Quarterly* 34 (1990), pp. 197–219.

Ranke-Heinemann, U., *Eunuchs for the Kingdom of Heaven* (New York: Doubleday, 1990).

Rawson, B. (ed.), *Marriage, Divorce, and Children in Ancient Rome* (Oxford, Clarendon Press, 1991).

Rehm, Rush, *Marriage to Death: The Conflation of Wedding and Funeral Rituals in Greek Tragedy* (Princeton: Princeton University Press, 1994).

Reid, B., *Parables for Preachers: The Gospel of Matthew: Year A* (3 vols.; Collegeville, MN: Liturgical Press, 2001).

—'Violent Endings in Matthew's Parables and Christian Nonviolence', *CBQ* 66 (2004), pp. 237-55.

—'Violent Endings in Matthew's Parables and an End to Violence', unpublished SBL Seminar Paper, Denver, CO, Nov. 17–20, 2001.

Reinhartz, A., 'Parents and Children: A Philonic Perspective', in Shaye J.D. Cohen (ed.), *The Jewish Family in Antiquity*, pp. 61–88.

Reinstorf, D., and A. van Aarde, 'Jesus' Kingdom Parables as Metaphorical Stories: A Challenge to a Conventional Worldview', *Hervormde Teologiese Studies* 54 (1998), pp. 603–22.

Reis, P.T., 'The Bridegroom of Blood: A New Reading', *Judaism* 40 (1991), pp. 324–31.

Reuchlin, J., *On the Art of the Kabbalah* (trans. Martin and Sarah Goodman; Lincoln: University of Nebraska Press, 1983).

Rhoads, D., 'Social Criticism: Crossing Boundaries', in J.C. Anderson and S.D. Moore (eds.), *Mark and Method*, pp. 135–61.

Richards, I.A., *The Philosophy of Rhetoric* (Oxford: Oxford University Press, 1936).

—'The Philosophy of Rhetoric', in M. Johnson (ed.), *Philosophical Perspectives on Metaphor* (Minneapolis: University of Minnesota, 1981), pp. 48–62.

Richardson, P., 'Early Synagogues as Collegia in the Diaspora and Palestine', in J.S. Kloppenborg and S.G. Wilson (eds.), *Voluntary Associations*, pp. 90–109.

Ricoeur, P., 'The Metaphorical Process', in S. Sacks (ed.), *On Metaphor*, pp. 141–57.

—*The Rule of Metaphor: Multi-disciplinary Studies of the Creation of Meaning in Language* (trans. R. Czerny; Toronto: University of Toronto Press, 1977).

Ringe, S.H., 'A Gentile Woman's Story, Revisited: Rereading Mark 7.24–31', in A.-J. Levine (ed.), *A Feminist Companion to Mark*, pp. 78–100.

Robinson, J.A.T., *Re-dating the New Testament* (Philadelphia: Westminster Press, 1976).

Robinson, J.M. (ed.), *The Nag Hammadi Library in English* (San Francisco, CA: HarperSanFrancisco, 3rd edn, 1990).

Rohrbaugh, R.L., 'Introduction', in R.L. Rohrbaugh (ed.), *The Social Sciences and New Testament Interpretation*, pp. 1–14.

Rohrbaugh, R.L. (ed.), *The Social Sciences and New Testament Interpretation* (Peabody, MA: Hendrickson, 1996).

Rose, H.J. (trans.), *The Roman Questions of Plutarch* (Oxford: Clarendon Press, 1924).

Rosenblatt, M.E., 'Got into the Party After All: Women's Issues and the Five Foolish Virgins', in A.-J. Levine (ed.), *A Feminist Companion to Matthew*, pp. 171-95.

Rossing, B.R., *The Choice Between Two Cities: Whore, Bride, and Empire in the Apocalypse* (HTS, 48; Harrisburg: Trinity Press International, 1999).

Roth, J.K., 'A Theodicy of Protest', in S.T. Davis (ed.), *Encountering Evil*, pp. 7–24.

Rothfuchs, W., *Die Erfüllungszitate des Matthäus-Evangeliums* (BWANT, 88; Stuttgart: Kohlhammer, 1969).

Rousselle, A., 'Body Politics', in Pauline Schmitt Panter (ed.), *A History of Women: From Ancient Goddesses to Christian Saints* (Cambridge, MA: Harvard University Press, 1992), pp. 296–337.

—*Porneia: On Desire and the Body in Antiquity* (trans. F. Pheasant; Cambridge, MA: Blackwell, 1988).

Rowland, C., 'Apocalyptic, the Poor, and the Gospel of Matthew', *JTS* 45 (1994), pp. 504–18.

—'In This Place: The Center and the Margins in Theology', in F.F. Segovia and M.A. Tolbert (eds.), *Reading from This Place*, II, pp. 169–98.

Rudall, N. (trans.), *Sophocles: Antigone* (Chicago: Ivan R. Dee, 1998).

Ruether, R.R., *Sexism and God-talk: Toward a Feminist Theology* (Boston: Beacon, 1983).

Rushton, K., 'The (Pro)creative Parables of Labour and Childbirth (Jn 3.1–10 and 16.21–22)', in M.A. Beavis (ed.), *The Lost Coin*, pp. 206–29.

Sabourin, L., 'Apocalyptic Traits in Matthew's Gospel', *Religious Studies Bulletin* 3 (1983), pp. 19–36.

Sacks, S. (ed.), *On Metaphor* (Chicago: University of Chicago Press, 1979).

Saldarini, A.J., 'Babatha's Story: Personal Archive Offers a Glimpse of Ancient Jewish Life', *BAR* 24 (1998), pp. 29–37, 72–74.

—*Matthew's Christian Jewish Community* (Chicago: University of Chicago Press, 1994).

Sampley, J. Paul, *The Second Letter to the Corinthians: Introduction, Commentary, and Reflection* (*NIB*, II, Nashville: Abingdon Press, 2000), pp. 1–180.

Sanders, E.P., *Jesus and Judaism* (Philadelphia: Fortress Press, 1985).

Sanders, J.A., 'The Ethic of Election in Luke's Great Banquet Parable', in J. Crenshaw and J. Willis (eds.), *Essays in Old Testament Ethics* (New York: KTAV, 1974), pp. 245–71.

Satlow, M.L., *Jewish Marriage in Antiquity* (Princeton: Princeton University Press, 2001).

Sawicki, M., *Crossing Galilee: Architectures of Contact in the Occupied Land of Jesus* (Harrisburg, PA: Trinity Press International, 2000).

—'Making Jesus', in A.-J. Levine (ed.), *A Feminist Companion to Mark*, pp. 136–70.

Schaberg, J., *The Illegitimacy of Jesus: A Feminist Theological Interpretation of the Infancy Narratives* (Crossroad: New York: 1990).

Schlier, H., *The Relevance of the New Testament* (New York: Herder and Herder, 1967).

Schmidt, K.L., 'καλέω', *TDNT* 3, pp. 487–536.

Schmidt, K.O., *Die geheimen Herren-Worte des Thomas-Evangeliums: Wegweisungen Christi zur Selbstvollendung* (Pfullingen/Würt: Baum-Verlag, 1966).

Schmitt, J.J., 'Gender Correctness and Biblical Metaphors: The Case of God's Relation to Israel', *BTB* 26 (1996), pp. 96–106.

Schnackenburg, R., *The Gospel of Matthew* (trans. R.R. Barr; Grand Rapids: Eerdmans, 2002 [*Matthäusevangelium* [2 vols.]; Würzburg: Echter Verlag, 1985 and 1987]).

Schneider, J., 'εὐνοῦχος', *TDNT* 2, pp. 765–68.

Schniewind, J., *Das Evangelium nach Matthäus* (Göttingen: Vandenhoeck and Ruprecht, 1954).

Schottroff, L., 'Das Gleichnis vom grossen Gastmahl in der Logienquelle', *EvT* 3 (1987), pp. 192–211.

—*Let the Oppressed Go Free: Feminist Perspectives on the New Testament* (trans. A.S. Kidder; Louisville: Westminster/John Knox Press, 1993).

—*Lydia's Impatient Sisters: A Feminist Social History of Early Christianity* (trans. B. and M. Rumscheidt; Louisville: Westminster/John Knox Press, 1995).

Schüssler Fiorenza, E., *Jesus: Miriam's Child and Sophia's Prophet* (New York: Continuum, 1995).

—'Transforming the Legacy of *The Women's Bible*', in E. Schüssler Fiorenza (ed.), *Searching the Scriptures*, I, pp. 1–24.

Schüssler Fiorenza, E. (ed.), *Searching the Scriptures*: I. *A Feminist Introduction*; II. *A Feminist Commentary* (2 vols.; New York: Crossroad, 1993, 1994).

Schwarz, H., *Eschatology* (Grand Rapids: Eerdmans, 2000).

Schwartz, R.M., *The Curse of Cain: The Violent Legacy of Monotheism* (Chicago: University of Chicago Press, 1997).

Schweizer, E., *The Good News According to Matthew* (trans. David E. Green; Atlanta: John Knox Press, 1975).

—'υἱός', *TDNT* 8, pp. 363–92.

Scott, B.B., 'The Gospel of Matthew: A Sapiential Performance of an Apocalyptic Discourse', in L.G. Perdue, B.B. Scott, and W.J. Wiseman (eds.), *In Search of Wisdom: Essays in Memory of John G. Gammie* (Louisville: Westminster/John Knox Press, 1993), pp. 245–62.

—*Hear Then the Parable: A Commentary on the Parables of Jesus* (Minneapolis: Fortress Press, 1989).

Scroggs, R., 'The Earliest Christian Communities as Sectarian Movement', in J. Neusner (ed.), *Christianity, Judaism and Other Greco-Roman Cults, Studies for Morton Smith at Sixty, Part Two: Early Christianity* (Leiden: Brill, 1975), pp. 1–23; repr. in D.G. Horrell, *Social-scientific Approaches to New Testament Interpretation*, pp. 69–91.

—'Eschatological Existence in Matthew and Paul: Coincidentia Oppositorium', in J. Marcus and M. Soards (eds.), *Apocalyptic and the New Testament*, pp. 125–46.

Segal, A.F., 'Paul's "*Soma Pneumatikon*" and the Worship of Jesus', in C.C. Newman, J.R. Davisa, and G.S. Lewis (eds.), *The Jewish Roots and Christological Monotheism* (Leiden: Brill, 1999).

Segovia, F.F., 'Cultural Studies and Contemporary Biblical Criticism: Ideological Criticism as a Mode of Discourse', in F.F. Segovia and M.A. Tolbert (eds.), *Reading from This Place*, II, pp. 1–17.

Segovia, F.F., and M.A. Tolbert (eds.), *Reading from This Place. II. Social Location and Biblical Interpretation in Global Perspective* (2 vols.; Minneapolis: Fortress Press, 1995).

Senior, D., 'The Death of Jesus and the Resurrection of the Holy Ones (Mt. 27.51-53)', *CBQ* 38 (1976), pp. 312–29.

—*The Gospel of Matthew* (IBT; Nashville: Abingdon Press, 1997).

—*Matthew* (Abingdon New Testament Commentaries; Nashville: Abingdon Press, 1998).

—'Matthew 2.2–12', *Int* 46 (1992), pp. 395–98.

Setel, T.D., 'Feminist Insights and the Question of Method', in A.Y. Collins (ed.), *Feminist Perspectives on Biblical Scholarship* (Atlanta: Scholars Press, 1985), pp. 35–42.

—'Prophets and Pornography: Female Sexual Imagery in Hosea', in L.M. Russell (ed.), *Feminist Interpretation of the Bible* (Philadelphia: Westminster Press, 1985), pp. 86–95.

Sheffield, J., 'The Father in the Gospel of Matthew', in A.-J. Levine (ed.), *A Feminist Companion to Matthew*, pp. 52–69.

Sheriff, J.M., 'Matthew 25.1–13: A Summary of Matthean Eschatology?', in E.A. Livingstone (ed.), *Studia Biblica 1978: Sixth International Congress on Biblical Studies* (JSNTSup, 2; Sheffield: Sheffield Academic Press, 1980), pp. 301–305.

Sim, D.C., 'Angels of Eschatological Punishment in the Jewish and Christian Apocalyptic Traditions in the Gospel of Matthew', *Hervormde Teologiese Studies* 55 (1999), pp. 693–718.

—*Apocalyptic Eschatology in the Gospel of Matthew* (Cambridge: Cambridge University Press, 1996).

—'Matthew 22.13a and 1 Enoch 10.4a: A Case of Literary Dependence?', *JSNT* 47 (1992), pp. 3–19.

Simkins, R.A., and S.L. Cook (eds.), *The Social World of the Hebrew Bible: Twenty-five Years of the Social Sciences in the Academy* (Semeia, 87; Atlanta: Society of Biblical Literature, 1999).

Smith, B.T.D., *The Parables of the Synoptic Gospels* (Cambridge: Cambridge University Press, 1937).

Sokoloff, M., *A Dictionary of Jewish Babylonian Aramaic of the Talmudic and Geonic Periods* (Dictionaries of Talmud, Midrash, and Targum, 3; Ramat-Gan, Israel: Bar Ilan University Press; Baltimore: Johns Hopkins University Press, 2nd edn, 2002).

—*A Dictionary of Jewish Palestinian Aramaic* (Romat-Gan: Bar Ilan University, 1990).

—*A Dictionary of Jewish Palestinian Aramaic of the Byzantine Period* (Dictionaries of Talmud, Midrash, and Targum, 2; Ramat-Gan: Bar Ilan University Press; Baltimore: Johns Hopkins University Press, 2nd edn, 2002).

Solvang, E.K., *A Woman's Place Is in the House: Royal Women of Judah and Their Involvement in the House of David* (JSOTSup, 349; Sheffield: Sheffield Academic Press, 2003).

Sontag, F., 'Anthropodicy and the Return of God', in S.T. Davis, *Encountering Evil*, pp. 137–51.

Spaeth, B.S., *The Roman Goddess Ceres* (Austin, TX: University of Texas Press, 1996).

Spencer, F.S., 'The Ethiopian Eunuch and His Bible: A Social-science Analysis', *BTB* 22 (1992), pp. 155–65.

—'Women of "the Cloth" in Acts: Sewing the Word', in A.-J. Levine (ed.), *A Feminist Companion to Acts*, pp. 134–54.

Stanton, G.N., *A Gospel for a New People: Studies in Matthew* (Louisville: Westminster/John Knox Press, 1992).

—'The Gospel of Matthew and Judaism', *Bulletin of the John Rylands University Library of Manchester* 66 (1984), pp. 264–84.

Stauffer, E., γαμέω, γάμος', *TDNT* 1, pp. 648–57.

Stein, R.H., 'The Genre of Parables', in R.N. Longenecker (ed.), *The Challenge of Jesus' Parables* (Grand Rapids: Eerdmans, 2000), pp. 30–50.

Stendahl, K., 'Matthew', *Peake's Commentary on the Bible* (London: Thomas Nelson and Sons, 1962), pp. 749–98.

—'Quis et Unde? An Analysis of Matthew 1–2', in G.N. Stanton (ed.), *The Interpretation of Matthew* (Edinburgh: T&T Clark, 2nd edn, 1995), pp. 69–80.

Stephen, G.N., *The Roman Family in Late Antiquity: The Endurance of Tradition and the Rise of Christianity* (Ann Arbor, MI: UMI Study Services, 1995).

Steussy, M.J., *David: Biblical Portraits of Power* (Columbia, SC: University of South Carolina Press, 1999).

Stone, L., *Kinship and Gender* (Boulder, CO: Westview Press, 1997).

Streete, G.C., *The Strange Woman: Power and Sex in the Bible* (Louisville: Westminster/John Knox Press, 1997).

Strobel, F.A., *Untersuchungen zum Eschatologischen Vergzögerungsproblem* (Leiden: E.J. Brill, 1961).

—'Zum Verständnis vom Mt XXV 1–13', *NovT* 2 (1958), pp. 199–227.

Stuckenbruck, L.T., *Angel Veneration and Christology: A Study in Early Judaism and in the Christology of the Apocalypse of John* (WUNT, 2.Reihe; Tübingen: J.C.B. Mohr, 1995).

Suggs, M.J., *Wisdom, Christology, and Law in Matthew's Gospel* (Cambridge, MA: Harvard University Press, 1970).

Sviri, S., 'The Song of Songs: Eros and the Mystical Quest', in J. Magonet (ed.), *Jewish Explorations of Sexuality* (Providence: Berghahn Books, 1995).

Swaeles, R., 'L'Orientation ecclésiastique de la parabole du festin nuptial en Mt 22.1-14', *ETL* 36 (1960), pp. 655–84.

Tadmor, H., 'The Role of the Chief Eunuch and the Place of Eunuchs in the Assyrian Empire', in S. Parpola and R.M. Whiting (eds.), *Sex and Gender in the Ancient Near East*, II, pp. 603–611.

—'Was the Biblical *saris* a Eunuch?', in Z. Zevit, S. Gitin, and M. Sokoloff (eds.), *Solving Riddles and Untying Knots: Biblical, Epigraphic, and Semitic Studies in Honor of Jonas C. Greenfield* (Winona Lake, IN: Eisenbrauns, 1995), pp. 317–25.

Tal, I., *Jewish Women in Greco-Roman Palestine* (Peabody, MA: Hendrickson, 1996).

Tàrrech, A.P., *La Parabole des dix vierges: Mt 25, 1–13* (Rome: Biblical Institute Press, 1983).

Taylor, G., 'Contest of Males: The Power of Eunuchs', in G. Taylor, *Castration: An Abbreviated History of Western Manhood* (New York: Routledge, 2000), pp. 33–47.

Teugels, L., 'The Creation of the Human in Rabbinic Interpretations', in G.P. Luttikhuizen (ed.), *The Creation of Man and Woman*, pp. 107–27.

Theissen, G., *The Gospels in Context: Social and Political History in the Synoptic Tradition* (trans. L.M. Moloney; Minneapolis: Fortress Press, 1991).

—'The Wandering Radicals: Light Shed by the Sociology of Literature on the Early Transmission of Jesus Sayings', in D.G. Horrell (ed.), *Social-scientific Approaches to New Testament Interpretation*, pp. 93–121.

—'Wanderradikalismus: Literatursoziologische Aspekte der Überlieferung von Wörten Jesu im Urchristentum', *Zeitschrift für Theologie und Kirche* 70 (1973), pp. 245–71; repr. 'Itinerant Radicalism: The Tradition of Jesus' Sayings from the Perspective of the Sociology of Literature', *Radical Religion* 2 (1975), pp. 84–93.

Theissen, G., and A. Merz, *The Historical Jesus: A Comprehensive Guide* (Minneapolis: Fortress, 1996), pp. 240–80.

Thornley, G. (trans.), *Daphnis and Chloe* (Cambridge, MA: Harvard University Press, 1989).

Tidball, D., *The Social Context of the New Testament: A Sociological Analysis* (Grand Rapids: Zondervan, 1984).

Tobin, T., *The Creation of Man: Philo and the History of Interpretation* (CBQMS; Washington: Catholic Biblical Association of America, 1983).

Tolbert, M.A., 'Social, Sociological, and Anthropological Methods', in E. Schüssler Fiorenza, *Searching the Scriptures*, I, pp. 255–71.

Torjesen, K.J., 'Reconstruction of Women's Early Christian History', in E. Schüssler Fiorenza (ed.), *Searching the Scriptures*, I, pp. 290–310.

—*When Women Were Priests* (San Francisco: Harper San Francisco, 1993).

Torjesen, K.J., and V. Burrus, 'Afterword to Household Management and Women's Authority', in A.-J. Levine (ed.), *A Feminist Companion to Acts of the Apostles*, pp. 171–76.

—'Household Management and Women's Authority', in K.J. Torjesen, *When Women Were Priests* (San Francisco: HarperSanFrancisco, 1993), pp. 53–87.

Traupman, J.C. (ed.), *The New College Latin and English Dictionary* (New York: Bantam Books, 1995).

Treggiari, S., 'Putting the Bride to Bed', *Echos du Monde/Classical Views* 30 (1994), pp. 311–31.

—*Roman Marriage: Iusti Coniuges from the Time of Cicero to the Time of Ulpian* (Oxford: Clarendon Press, 1991).

Trilling, W., *The Gospel According to Matthew* (2 vols.; New York: Herder and Herder, 1969).

Trudinger, P., 'The "Our Father" in Matthew as Apocalyptic Eschatology', *The Downside Review* 107 (1989), pp. 49–54.

Turner, M., *Death is the Mother of Beauty: Mind, Metaphor, Criticism* (Chicago: University of Chicago, 1987).

Turner, V., *Dramas, Fields, and Metaphors: Symbolic Action in Human Society* (Ithaca: Cornell University Press, 1971).

—*Ritual Process: Structure and Anti-Structure* (Chicago/New York: Aldine/Walter de Gruyter, 1969).

Twycross, S., 'Was Jesus Married?', *ExpTim* 107 (1996), pp. 334–35.

Uro, R., *Thomas at the Crossroads: Essays on the Gospel of Thomas* (Edinburgh: T&T Clark, 1998).

Vaage, L.E., and V.L. Wimbush (eds.), *Asceticism in the New Testament* (New York: Routledge, 1999).

Vaccari, A., 'La Parabole du Festin de Noces', *RSR* 39 (1951), pp. 138–45.

Valavanolickal, K.A., *The Use of the Gospel Parables in the Writings of Aphrahat and Ephrem* (Studies in the Religion and History of Early Christianity, 2; Frankfurt am Main: Peter Lang, 1995).

Van den Hoek, A., 'Endowed with Reason or Glued to the Senses: Philo's Thoughts on Adam and Eve', in G.P. Luttikhuizen (ed.), *The Creation of Man and Woman*, pp. 63–75.

Van Gennep, A., *The Rites of Passage* (Chicago: University of Chicago Press, 1960).

Van Seters, J., *The Life of Moses: The Yahwist as Historian in Exodus–Numbers* (Louisville: Westminster/John Knox, 1994).

Veyne, P. (ed.), *A History of the Private Life: From Pagan Rome to Byzantium* (trans. A. Goldhammer; Cambridge, MA: Harvard University Press, 1987).

Via, D.O., 'Narrative World and Ethical Response: The Marvelous and Righteous in Matthew 1–2', *Semeia* 12 (1978), pp. 123–49.

—*The Parables: Their Literary and Existential Dimension* (Philadelphia: Fortress Press, 1967).

—'The Relationship of Form to Content in the Parables: The Wedding Feast', *Int* 25 (1971), pp. 171–84.

Viviano, B.T., 'Matthew', *The New Jerome Biblical Commentary* (Englewood Cliffs, NJ: Prentice Hall, 1990), pp. 630–74.

Vogt, K., ' "Becoming Male": A Gnostic and Early Christian Metaphor', in K.E. Børresen (ed.), *Image of God and Gender Models in Judaeo-Christian Tradition*, pp. 172–187.

Vögtle, A., 'Die matthäische Kindheitsgeschichte', in M. Didier (ed.), *L'Évangile selon Matthieu* (BETL, 29; Gembloux: Duculot, 1972).

Vorster, W.S., 'The Function of Metaphorical and Apocalyptic Language about the Unobservable in the Teaching of Jesus', in T.W. Jennings (ed.), *Text and Logos: The Humanistic Interpretation of the New Testament* (Atlanta: Scholars Press, 1990), pp. 33–51.

Wailes, S.L., *Medieval Allegories of Jesus' Parables* (Berkeley: University of California Press, 1987).

Wainwright, E.M., 'God Wills to Invite All to the Banquet', *International Review of Mission* 77 (1988), pp. 185–93.

—'Matthew', in E. Schüssler Fiorenza (ed.), *Searching the Scriptures*, II, pp. 635–77.

—'A Voice from the Margin: Reading Matthew 15.21–28 in an Australian Feminist Key', in F.F. Segovia and M.A. Tolbert (eds.), *Reading from This Place*, II, pp. 132–53.

Walker-Ramisch, S., 'Graeco-Roman Voluntary Associations and the Damascus Document: A Sociological Analysis', in J.S. Kloppenborg and S.G. Wilson (eds.), *Voluntary Associations*, pp. 128–45.

Wallace-Hadrill, A., 'Houses and Households: Sampling Pompeii and Herculaneum', in Rawson (ed.), *Marriage, Divorce, and Children in Ancient Rome*, pp. 191–227.

Waller, E., 'The Parable of the Ten Virgins', *Proceedings: Eastern Great Lakes Biblical Society* 1 (1981), pp. 85–109.

Wangerin, W., 'A Stranger in Joseph's House', *CToday* 39.14 (Dec. 11, 1995), pp. 16–21.

Warden, D., 'The Words of Jesus on Divorce', *ResQ* 39 (1997), pp. 141–53.

Wasserstrom, S.M., 'Uses of the Androgyne in the History of Religions', *SR* 27/4 (1998), pp. 437–53.

Weder, H., *Die Gleichnisse Jesu als Metaphern* (Göttingen: Vandenhoeck & Ruprecht, 1978).

—'Verstehen durch Metaphern: Überlegungen zur Erkenntnistheorie und Methodik bildhafter religiöser Sprache im Anschluss an Adolf Jülicher', in U. Mell (ed.), *Die Gliechnisreden Jesu 1899–1999: Beiträge zum Dialog mit Adolf Jülicher* (Berlin: Walter de Gruyter, 1999), pp. 97–112.

Weems, R., *Battered Love: Marriage, Sex, and Violence in the Hebrew Prophets* (Minneapolis: Fortress Press, 1995).

—'Gomer: Victim of Violence or Victim of Metaphor?', *Semeia* 47 (1989), pp. 87-104.

—'The Songs of Songs', *NIB* 5, pp. 364–66.

Wegner, J.R., *Chattel or Person? The Status of Women in the Mishnah* (Oxford: Oxford University Press, 1988).

Wellmann, M. (ed.), *Pedanii Dioscoridis anazarbei De Materia Medica* (3 vols.; Berlin: Weidmannsche Verlagsbuchhandlung, 1958).

Wenham, D.O., *The Parables of Jesus* (Downers Grove, IL: InterVarsity Press, 1989).

Wenthe, D.O., 'The Parable of the Ten Bridesmaids', *The Springfielder* 40 (1976), pp. 9–16.

West, G.O., 'Gauging the Grain in a More Nuanced and Literary Manner: A Cautionary Tale Concerning the Contribution of the Social Sciences to Biblical Interpretation', in M.D. Carroll (ed.), *Rethinking Contexts*, pp. 75–105.

Westbrook, R., 'The Character of Ancient Near Eastern Law', in R. Westbrook (ed.), *A History of Ancient Near Eastern Law* (2 vols.; Handbook of Oriental Studies, Section One, The Near and Middle East, 72; Leiden: Brill, 2003), I, pp. 1–90.

Wevers, J.W., *Notes on the Greek Text of Exodus* (Septuagint and Cognate Studies Series, 30; Atlanta: Society of Biblical Literature, 1990).

Wilder, A., *The Language of the Gospel* (New York: Harper & Row, rev. edn, 1971).

Wilson, R.M., *Studies in the Gospel of Thomas* (London: A.R. Mowbray & Co., 1960).

Wilson, S.G., *Related Strangers: Jews and Christians 70–135 CE* (Minneapolis: Fortress Press, 1995).

—'Voluntary Associations: An Overview', in J.S. Kloppenborg and S.G. Wilson (eds.), *Voluntary Associations in the Graeco-Roman World*, pp. 1–15.

Wimbush, V.L. (ed.), *Rhetorics of Resistance: A Colloquy on Early Christianity as Rhetorical Formation* (*Semeia* 79, Atlanta, GA: Scholars Press, 1979).

Winterhalter, R., *The Fifth Gospel* (San Francisco: Harper & Row, 1988).

Winterhalter, R., and G.W. Fisk, *Jesus' Parables: Finding Our God Within* (Mahwah, NJ: Paulist Press, 1993).

Wintermute, O.S. (trans.), 'Jubilees', in J.H. Charlesworth (ed.), *The Old Testament Pseudepigrapha*, I, pp. 35–142.

Witherington, B., *Jesus the Sage: The Pilgrimage of Wisdom* (Minneapolis: Fortress Press, 1994).

—*Jesus the Seer: The Progress of Prophecy* (Peabody, MA: Hendrickson, 1999).

Wright, N.T., *Jesus and the Victory of God* (Christian Origins and the Question of God, 2; Minneapolis: Fortress Press, 1996).

Yamauchi, E.M., 'Was Nehemiah the Cupbearer a Eunuch?', *ZAW* 92.1 (1980), pp. 132–42.

Yarbrough, O.L., 'Parents and Children in the Jewish Family of Antiquity', in S.D. Cohen (ed.), *The Jewish Family in Antiquity*, pp. 39-60.

Yee, G., 'Gomer', in C. Meyers, T. Craven, and R.S. Kraemer (eds.), *Women in Scripture* (Grand Rapids: Eerdmans, 2000), pp. 84–86.

—'Hosea', *NIB* 7, pp. 197–297.

—'Ideological Criticism: Judges 17–21 and the Dismembered Body', in G. Yee (ed.), *Judges and Method: New Approaches to Biblical Studies* (Minneapolis: Fortress Press, 1995), pp. 146–67.

Young, B.H., *The Parables: Jewish Tradition and Christian Interpretation* (Peabody, MA: Hendrickson, 1998).

Zandee, J., 'Der Androgyne Gott in Ägypten: Ein Erscheinungsbild des Weltschöpfers', in M. Görg (ed.), *Religion im Erbe Ägyptens* (Wiesbaden: Otto Harrassowitz, 1988), pp. 240–78.

Zoba, W.M., 'How Shall We Reconcile the Glorious Birth of the Savior with the Bloody Deaths of the Boys of Bethlehem?', *CToday* 41 (Dec. 8, 1997), pp. 24–26.

AB	Anchor Bible
ABD	D.N. Freedman, *et al.* (eds.), *The Anchor Bible Dictionary* (6 vols.; New York: Doubleday, 1992)
BAR	*Biblical Archaeology Review*
BDAG	F.W. Danker (ed.), *A Greek–English Lexicon of the New Testament and Other Early Christian Literature* (Chicago: University of Chicago Press, 3rd edn, 2000)
BDB	F. Brown (ed.), *The New Brown–Driver–Briggs–Gesenius Hebrew and English Lexicon* (Peabody, MA: Hendrickson, 1979)
BTB	*Biblical Theology Bulletin*
BETL	Bibliotheca ephemeridum theologicarum lovaniensium
Bib	*Biblica*
BibInt	*Biblical Interpretation*
BT	*Bible Translator*
BJS	Brown Judaic Studies
BTB	*Biblical Theological Quarterly*
BWANT	Beiträge zur Wissenschaft vom Alten und Neuen Testament
BZ	*Biblische Zeitschrift*
CBQ	*Catholic Biblical Quarterly*
CBQMS	*Catholic Biblical Quarterly*, Monograph Series
CToday	*Christianity Today*
EDNT	H. Balz and G. Schneider (eds.), *Exegetical Dictionary of the New Testament* (3 vols.; Grand Rapids: Eerdmans, 1993)
EKKNT	Evangelisch-Katholischer Kommentar zum Neuen Testament
ETL	*Ephemerides Theologicae Lovanienses*
EvQ	*Evangelical Quarterly*
EvT	*Evangelische Theologie*
ExpTim	*Expository Times*
HBT	*Horizons in Biblical Theology*
HDR	Harvard Dissertations in Religion
Hist. Rech.	*History of the Rechabites*
HR	*History of Religions*

HTKNT	Herders Theologischer Kommentar zum Neuen Testament
HTS	Harvard Theological Studies
HUCA	*Hebrew Union College Annual*
IBT	Interpeting Biblical Texts
ICC	International Critical Commentary
Int	*Interpretation*
JBL	*Journal of Biblical Literature*
JR	*Journal of Religion*
JSNT	*Journal for the Study of the New Testament*
JSNTSup	*Journal for the Study of the New Testament*, Supplement Series
JSOT	*Journal for the Study of the Old Testament*
JSOTSup	*Journal for the Study of the Old Testament*, Supplement Series
JSPSup	*Journal for the Study of the Pseudepigrapha*, Supplement Series
JTS	*Journal of Theological Studies*
KJV	King James Version
LCL	Loeb Classical Library
LXX	Septuagint
NEB	New English Bible
Neot	*Neotestamentica*
NHS	Nag Hammadi Studies
NIB	L.K. Keck, *et al.* (eds.), *The New Interpreter's Bible* (12 vols.; Nashville: Abingdon Press, 1994–2001)
NovT	*Novum Testamentum*
NovTSup	*Novum Testamentum*, Supplement Series
NRSV	New Revised Standard Version
NTS	*New Testament Studies*
OTL	Old Testament Library
ResQ	*Restoration Quarterly*
RSR	*Recherches de science religieuse*
RSV	Revised Standard Version
SBL	Society of Biblical Literature
SBLDS	Society of Biblical Literature, Dissertation Series
SR	*Studies in Religion/Sciences Religieuses*
STDJ	Studies on the Texts of the Desert of Judah
TDNT	G. Kittel and G.W. Bromiley (eds.), *Theological Dictionary of the New Testament* (10 vols.; Grand Rapids, MI: Eerdmans, 1964–1976)
TDOT	B.J. Botterweck and H. Ringgren (eds.), *Theological Dictionary of the Old Testament* ([8] vols.; Grand Rapids, MI: Eerdmans, 1974–)

TS	*Theological Studies*
TZ	*Theologische Zeitschrift*
USQR	*Union Seminary Quarterly Review*
VC	*Vigilae Christianae*
VT	*Vetus Testamentum*
WBC	Word Bible Commentary
WUNT	Wissenschaftliche Untersuchungen zum Neuen Testament
ZAW	*Zeitschrift für die Alttestamentliche Wissenschaft*
ZNW	*Zeitschrift für die Neutestamentliche Wissenschaft*

INDICES

INDEX OF REFERENCES

INDEX OF MODERN AUTHORS